CHAPTER ONE

A friend is brought into the magic,
A mystic pathway is explained,
A perilous journey is begun.

Cover art:
J.H. Williams III
& Jose Villarrubia

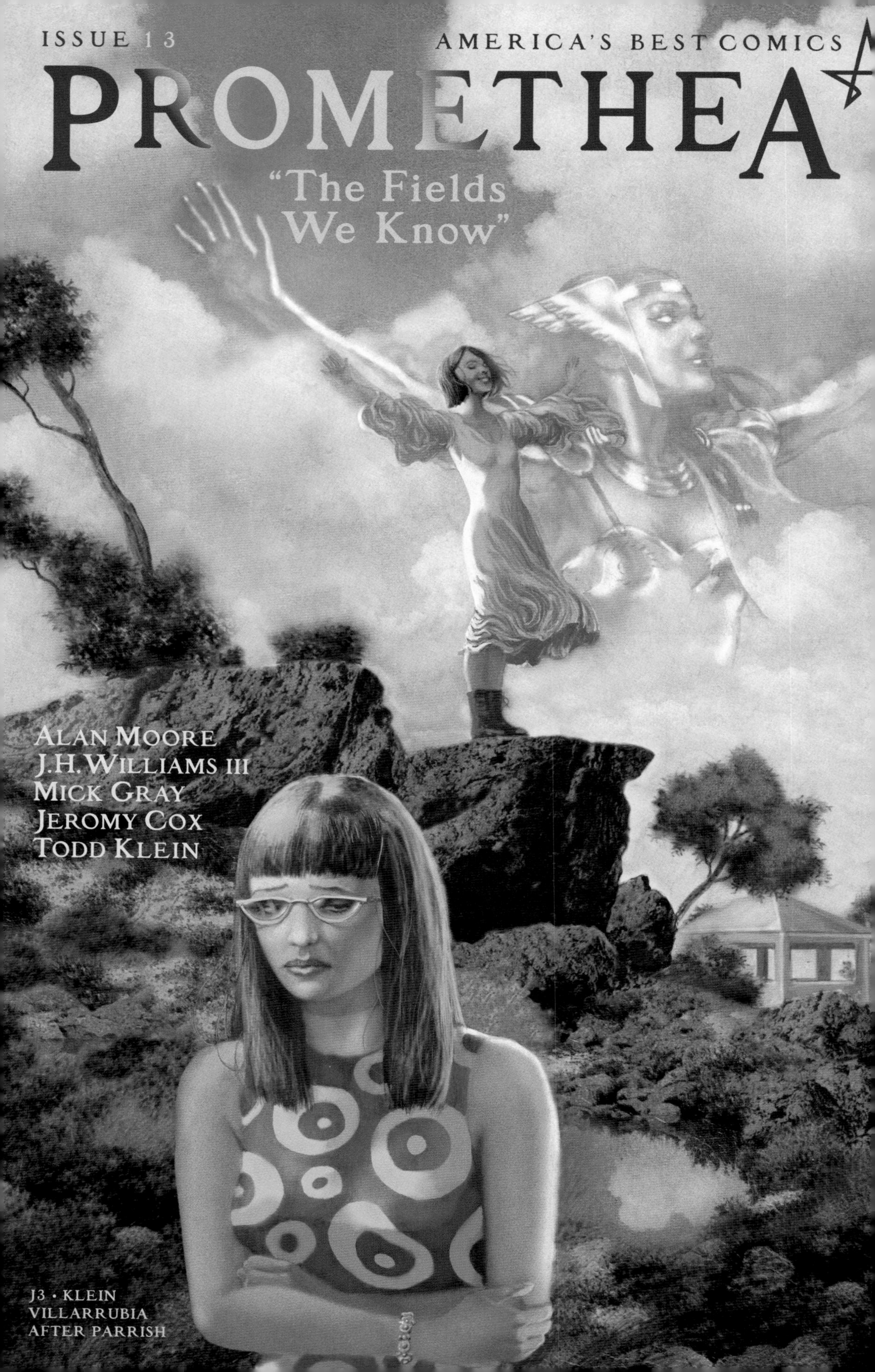
ISSUE 13
AMERICA'S BEST COMICS
PROMETHEA
"The Fields We Know"
ALAN MOORE
J.H. WILLIAMS III
MICK GRAY
JEROMY COX
TODD KLEIN
J3 • KLEIN
VILLARRUBIA
AFTER PARRISH

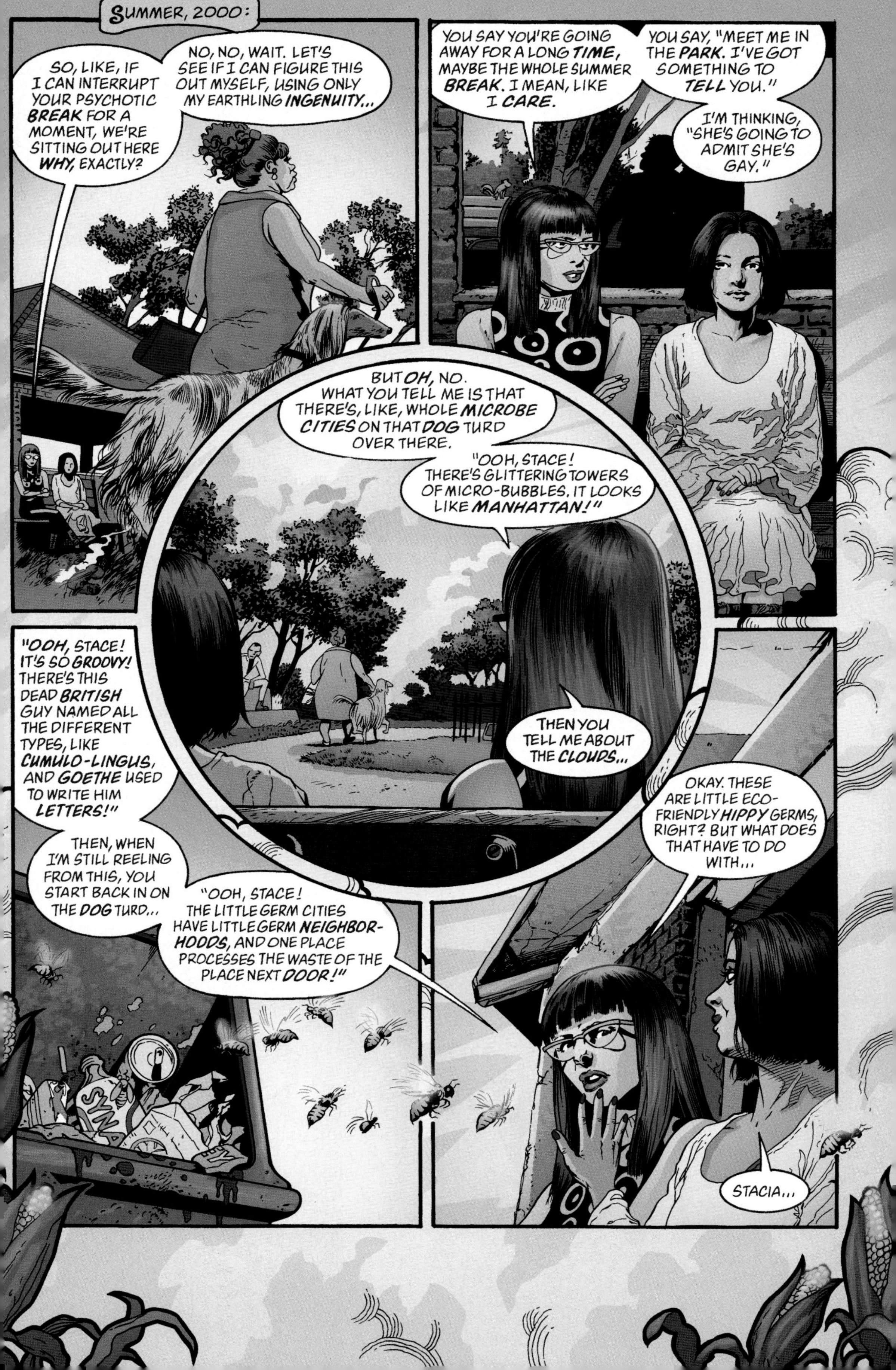
SUMMER, 2000:
SO, LIKE, IF I CAN INTERRUPT YOUR PSYCHOTIC BREAK FOR A MOMENT, WE'RE SITTING OUT HERE WHY, EXACTLY?
NO, NO, WAIT. LET'S SEE IF I CAN FIGURE THIS OUT MYSELF, USING ONLY MY EARTHLING INGENUITY...
YOU SAY YOU'RE GOING AWAY FOR A LONG TIME, MAYBE THE WHOLE SUMMER BREAK. I MEAN, LIKE I CARE.
YOU SAY, "MEET ME IN THE PARK. I'VE GOT SOMETHING TO TELL YOU."
I'M THINKING, "SHE'S GOING TO ADMIT SHE'S GAY."
BUT OH, NO. WHAT YOU TELL ME IS THAT THERE'S, LIKE, WHOLE MICROBE CITIES ON THAT DOG TURD OVER THERE.
"OOH, STACE! THERE'S GLITTERING TOWERS OF MICRO-BUBBLES. IT LOOKS LIKE MANHATTAN!"
THEN YOU TELL ME ABOUT THE CLOUDS...
"OOH, STACE! IT'S SO GROOVY! THERE'S THIS DEAD BRITISH GUY NAMED ALL THE DIFFERENT TYPES, LIKE CUMULO-LINGUS, AND GOETHE USED TO WRITE HIM LETTERS!"
THEN, WHEN I'M STILL REELING FROM THIS, YOU START BACK IN ON THE DOG TURD...
"OOH, STACE! THE LITTLE GERM CITIES HAVE LITTLE GERM NEIGHBORHOODS, AND ONE PLACE PROCESSES THE WASTE OF THE PLACE NEXT DOOR!"
OKAY. THESE ARE LITTLE ECO-FRIENDLY HIPPY GERMS, RIGHT? BUT WHAT DOES THAT HAVE TO DO WITH...
STACIA...

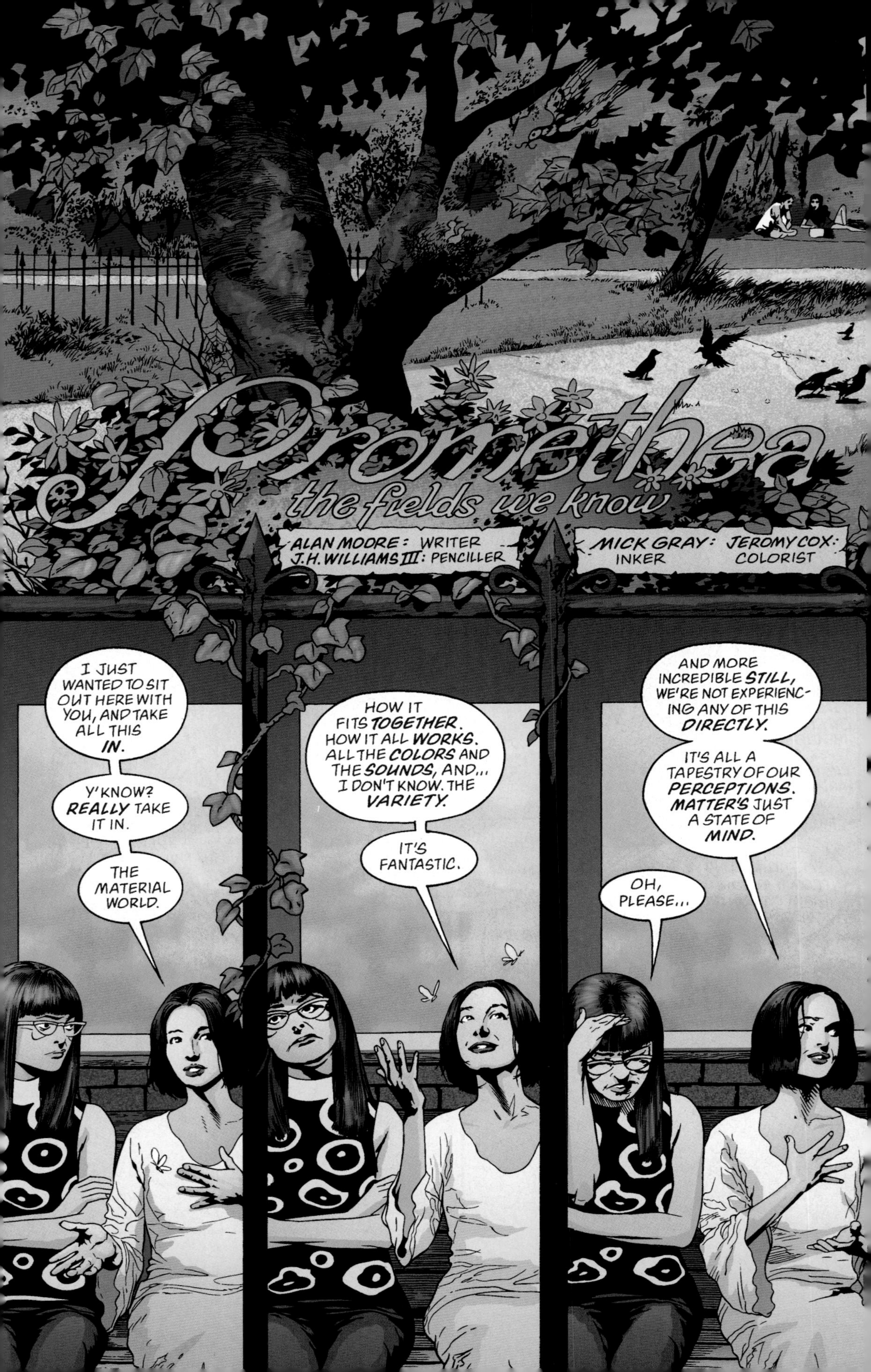
Promethea
the fields we know
ALAN MOORE: WRITER
J.H. WILLIAMS III: PENCILLER
MICK GRAY: INKER
JEROMY COX: COLORIST
I JUST WANTED TO SIT OUT HERE WITH YOU, AND TAKE ALL THIS IN.
Y'KNOW? REALLY TAKE IT IN.
THE MATERIAL WORLD.
HOW IT FITS TOGETHER. HOW IT ALL WORKS. ALL THE COLORS AND THE SOUNDS, AND... I DON'T KNOW. THE VARIETY.
IT'S FANTASTIC.
AND MORE INCREDIBLE STILL, WE'RE NOT EXPERIENCING ANY OF THIS DIRECTLY.
IT'S ALL A TAPESTRY OF OUR PERCEPTIONS. MATTER'S JUST A STATE OF MIND.
OH, PLEASE...

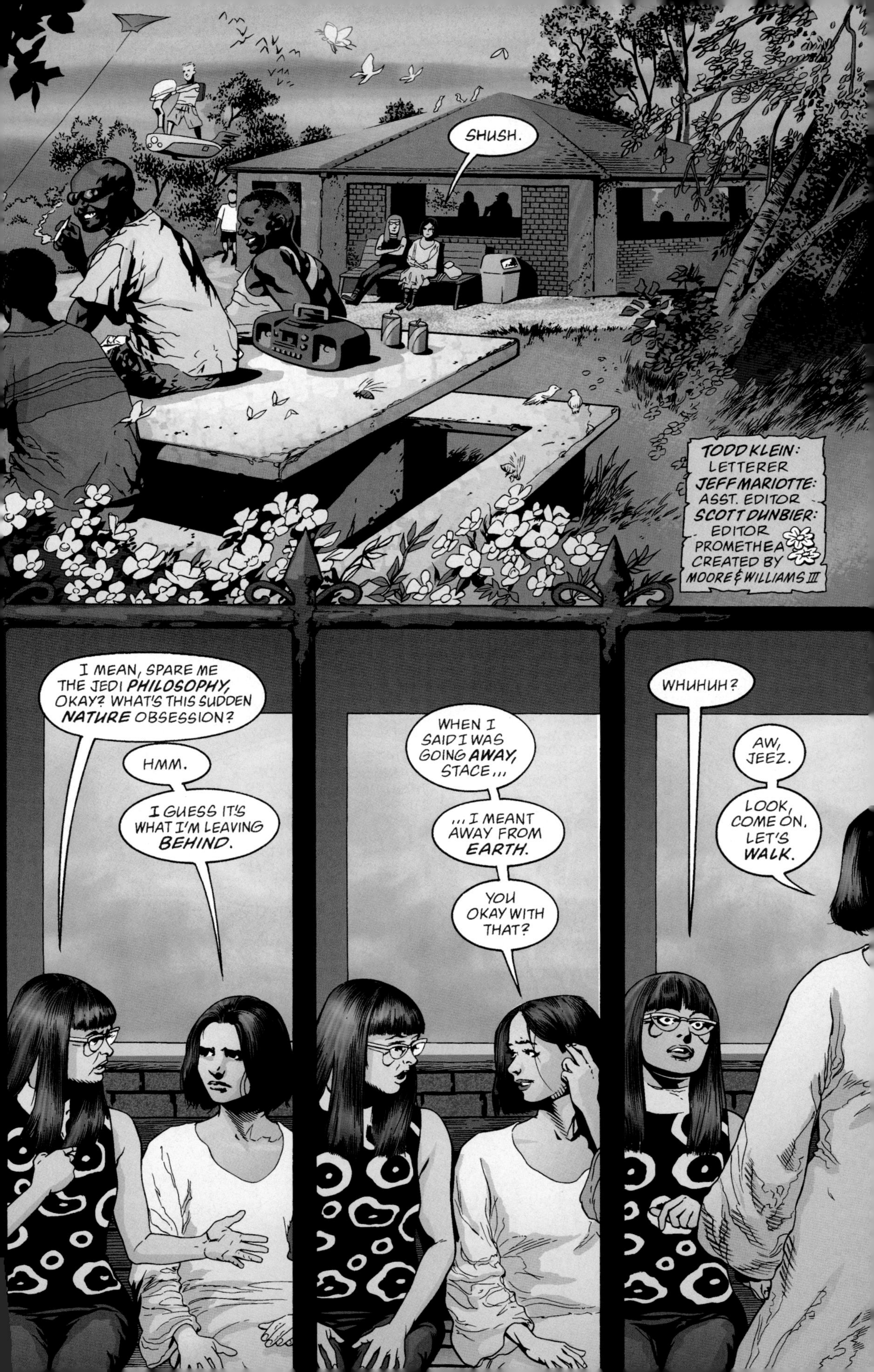
SHUSH.
TODD KLEIN: LETTERER
JEFF MARIOTTE: ASST. EDITOR
SCOTT DUNBIER: EDITOR
PROMETHEA CREATED BY MOORE & WILLIAMS III
I MEAN, SPARE ME THE JEDI PHILOSOPHY, OKAY? WHAT'S THIS SUDDEN NATURE OBSESSION?
HMM.
I GUESS IT'S WHAT I'M LEAVING BEHIND.
WHEN I SAID I WAS GOING AWAY, STACE...
...I MEANT AWAY FROM EARTH.
YOU OKAY WITH THAT?
WHUHUH?
AW, JEEZ.
LOOK, COME ON. LET'S WALK.

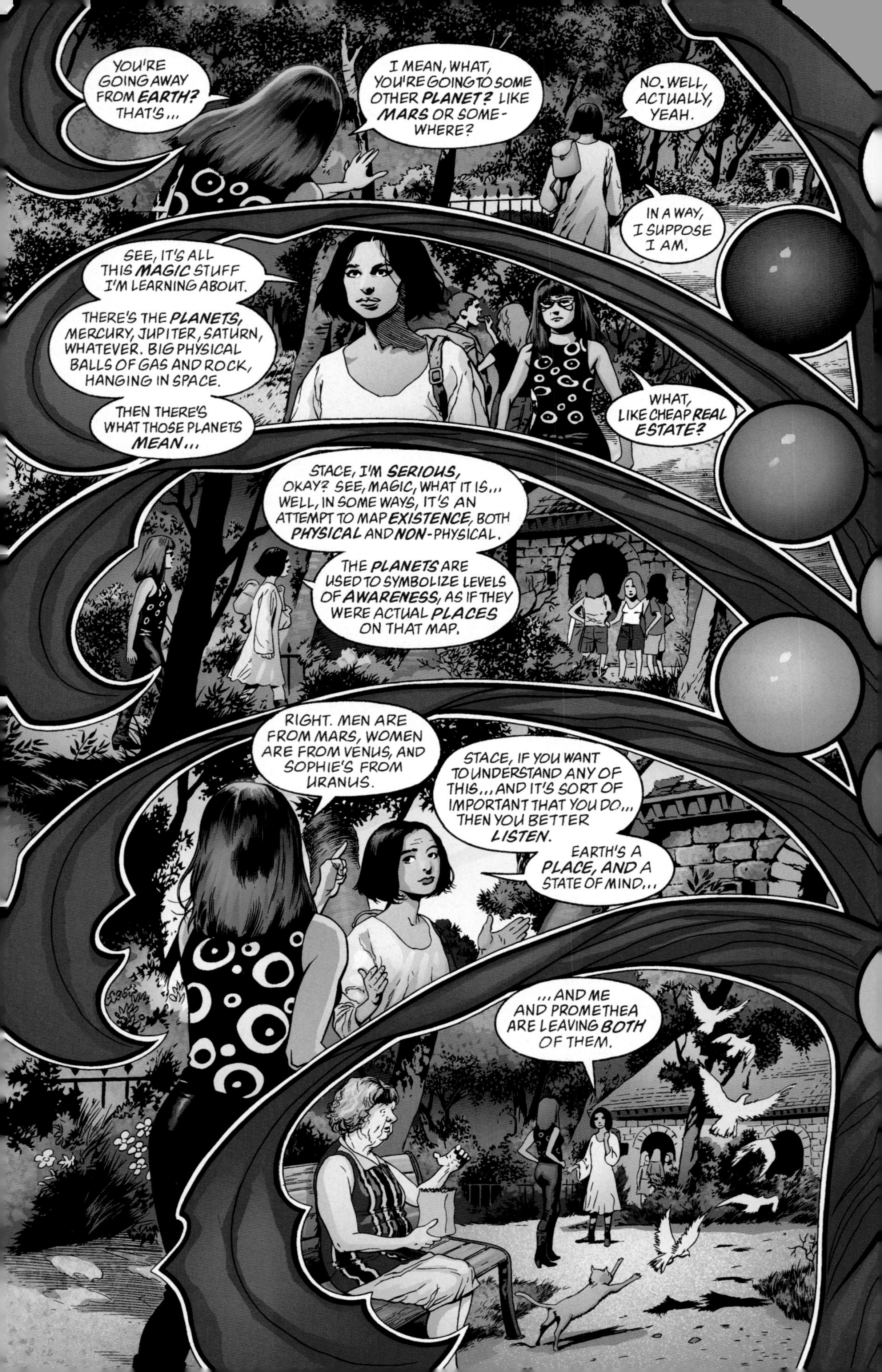
YOU'RE GOING AWAY FROM EARTH? THAT'S...
I MEAN, WHAT, YOU'RE GOING TO SOME OTHER PLANET? LIKE MARS OR SOMEWHERE?
NO. WELL, ACTUALLY, YEAH.
IN A WAY, I SUPPOSE I AM.
SEE, IT'S ALL THIS MAGIC STUFF I'M LEARNING ABOUT.
THERE'S THE PLANETS, MERCURY, JUPITER, SATURN, WHATEVER. BIG PHYSICAL BALLS OF GAS AND ROCK, HANGING IN SPACE.
THEN THERE'S WHAT THOSE PLANETS MEAN...
WHAT, LIKE CHEAP REAL ESTATE?
STACE, I'M SERIOUS, OKAY? SEE, MAGIC, WHAT IT IS... WELL, IN SOME WAYS, IT'S AN ATTEMPT TO MAP EXISTENCE, BOTH PHYSICAL AND NON-PHYSICAL.
THE PLANETS ARE USED TO SYMBOLIZE LEVELS OF AWARENESS, AS IF THEY WERE ACTUAL PLACES ON THAT MAP.
RIGHT. MEN ARE FROM MARS, WOMEN ARE FROM VENUS, AND SOPHIE'S FROM URANUS.
STACE, IF YOU WANT TO UNDERSTAND ANY OF THIS... AND IT'S SORT OF IMPORTANT THAT YOU DO... THEN YOU BETTER LISTEN.
EARTH'S A PLACE, AND A STATE OF MIND...
...AND ME AND PROMETHEA ARE LEAVING BOTH OF THEM.

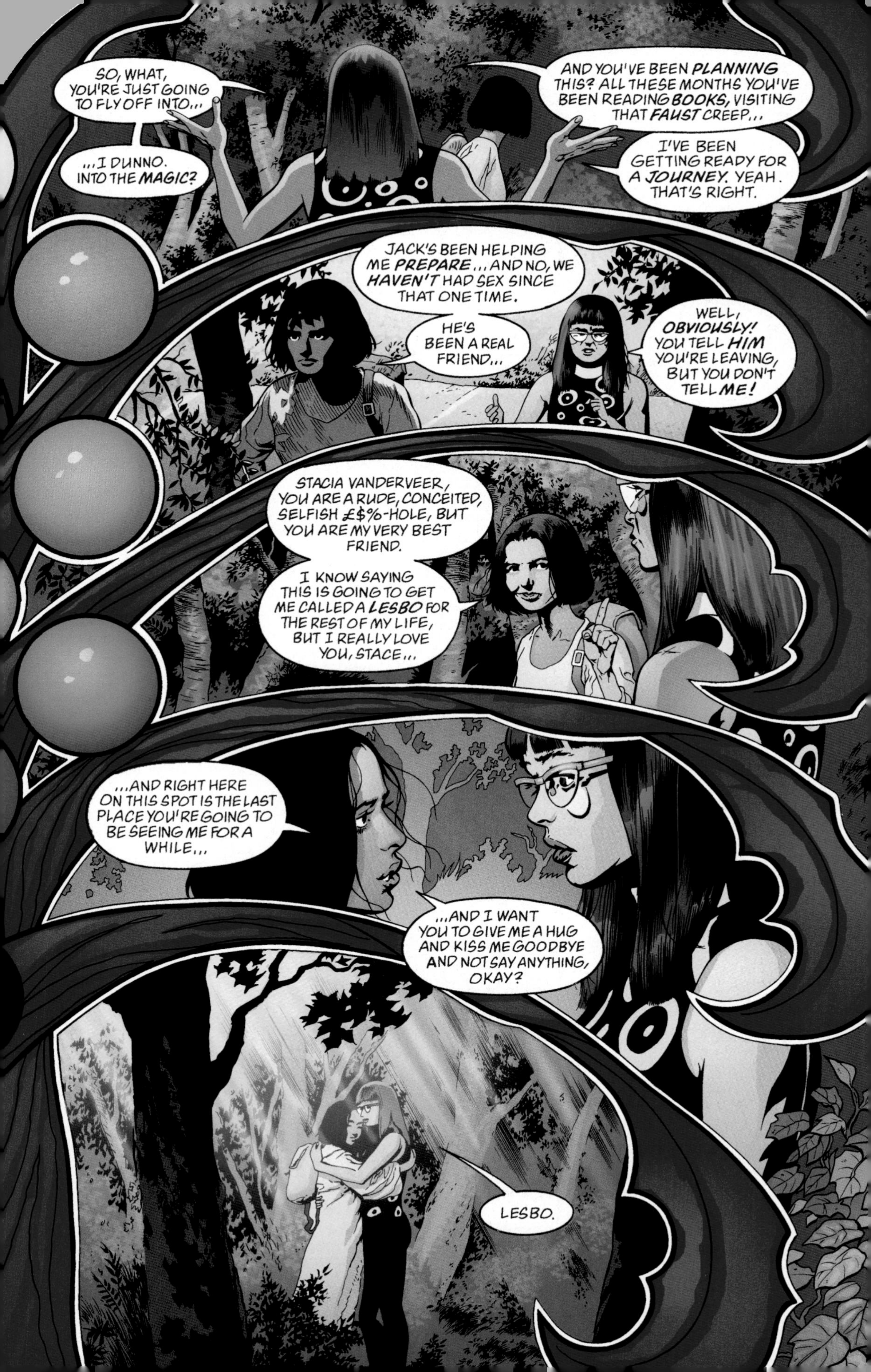
SO, WHAT, YOU'RE JUST GOING TO FLY OFF INTO...
...I DUNNO. INTO THE MAGIC?
AND YOU'VE BEEN PLANNING THIS? ALL THESE MONTHS YOU'VE BEEN READING BOOKS, VISITING THAT FAUST CREEP...
I'VE BEEN GETTING READY FOR A JOURNEY. YEAH. THAT'S RIGHT.
JACK'S BEEN HELPING ME PREPARE... AND NO, WE HAVEN'T HAD SEX SINCE THAT ONE TIME.
HE'S BEEN A REAL FRIEND...
WELL, OBVIOUSLY! YOU TELL HIM YOU'RE LEAVING, BUT YOU DON'T TELL ME!
STACIA VANDERVEER, YOU ARE A RUDE, CONCEITED, SELFISH £$%-HOLE, BUT YOU ARE MY VERY BEST FRIEND.
I KNOW SAYING THIS IS GOING TO GET ME CALLED A LESBO FOR THE REST OF MY LIFE, BUT I REALLY LOVE YOU, STACE...
...AND RIGHT HERE ON THIS SPOT IS THE LAST PLACE YOU'RE GOING TO BE SEEING ME FOR A WHILE...
...AND I WANT YOU TO GIVE ME A HUG AND KISS ME GOODBYE AND NOT SAY ANYTHING, OKAY?
LESBO.

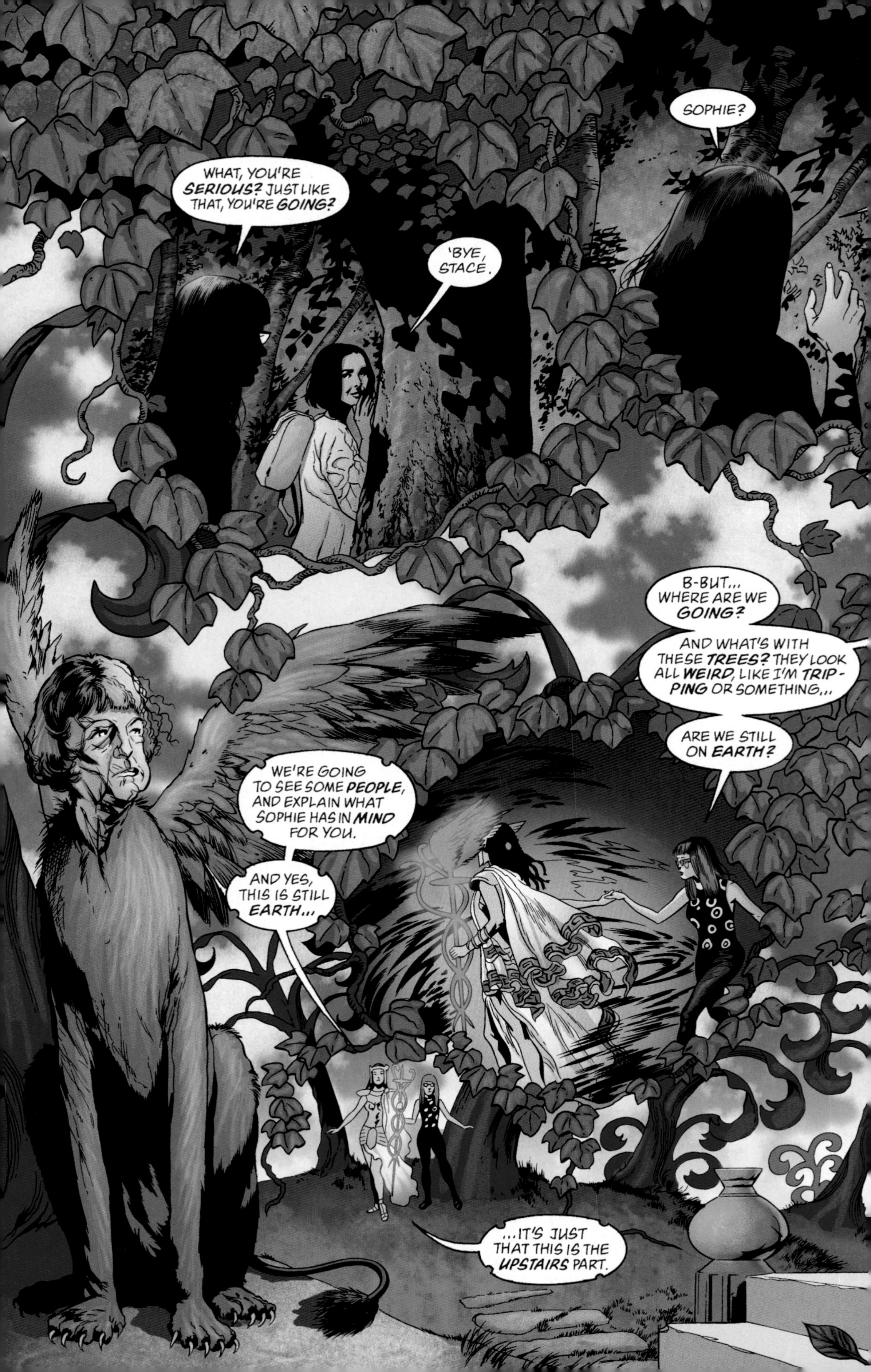
WHAT, YOU'RE SERIOUS? JUST LIKE THAT, YOU'RE GOING?
'BYE, STACE.
SOPHIE?
B-BUT... WHERE ARE WE GOING?
AND WHAT'S WITH THESE TREES? THEY LOOK ALL WEIRD, LIKE I'M TRIP-PING OR SOMETHING...
ARE WE STILL ON EARTH?
WE'RE GOING TO SEE SOME PEOPLE, AND EXPLAIN WHAT SOPHIE HAS IN MIND FOR YOU.
AND YES, THIS IS STILL EARTH...
...IT'S JUST THAT THIS IS THE UPSTAIRS PART.

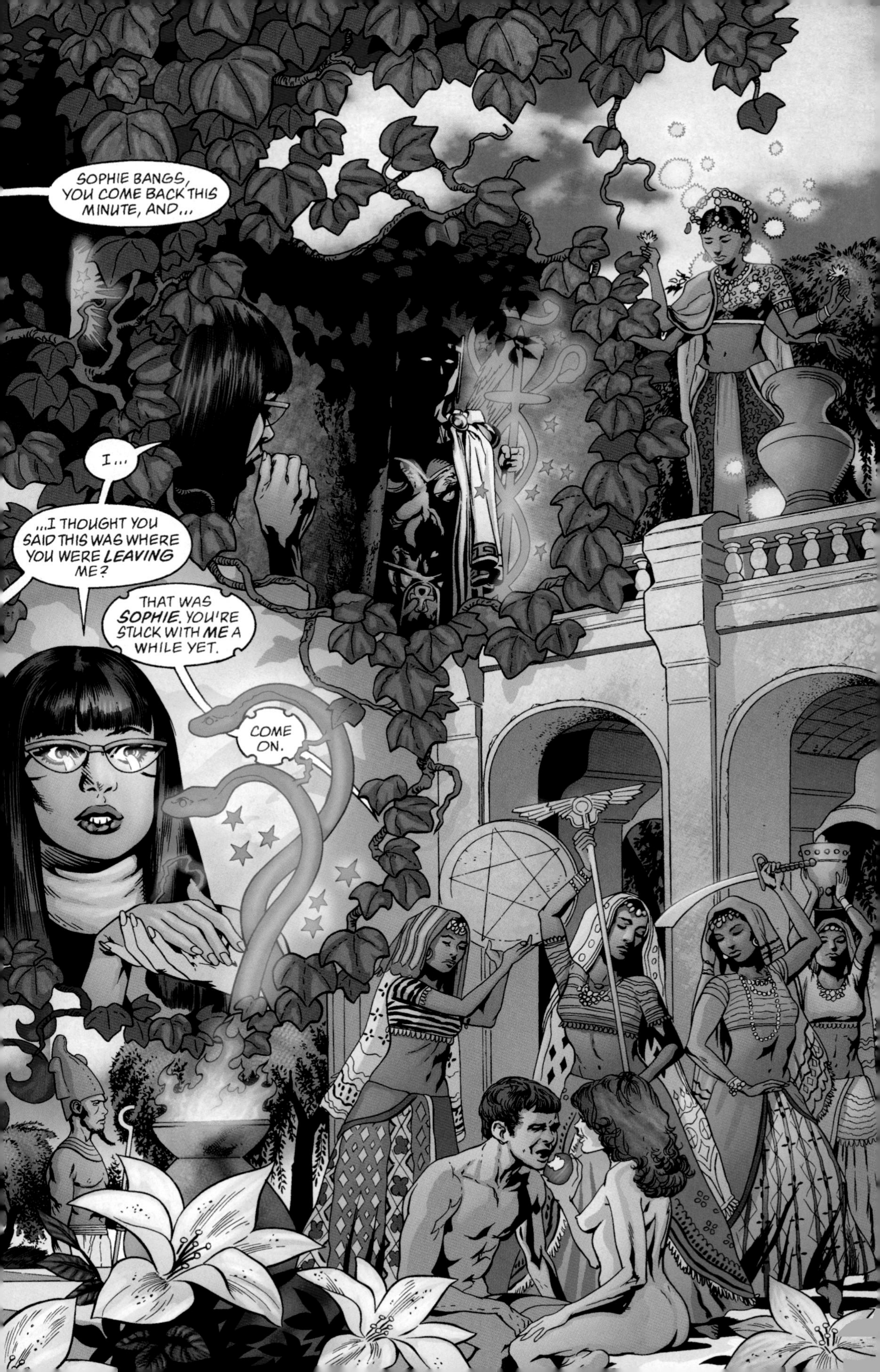
SOPHIE BANGS, YOU COME BACK THIS MINUTE, AND...
I...
...I THOUGHT YOU SAID THIS WAS WHERE YOU WERE LEAVING ME?
THAT WAS SOPHIE. YOU'RE STUCK WITH ME A WHILE YET.
COME ON.

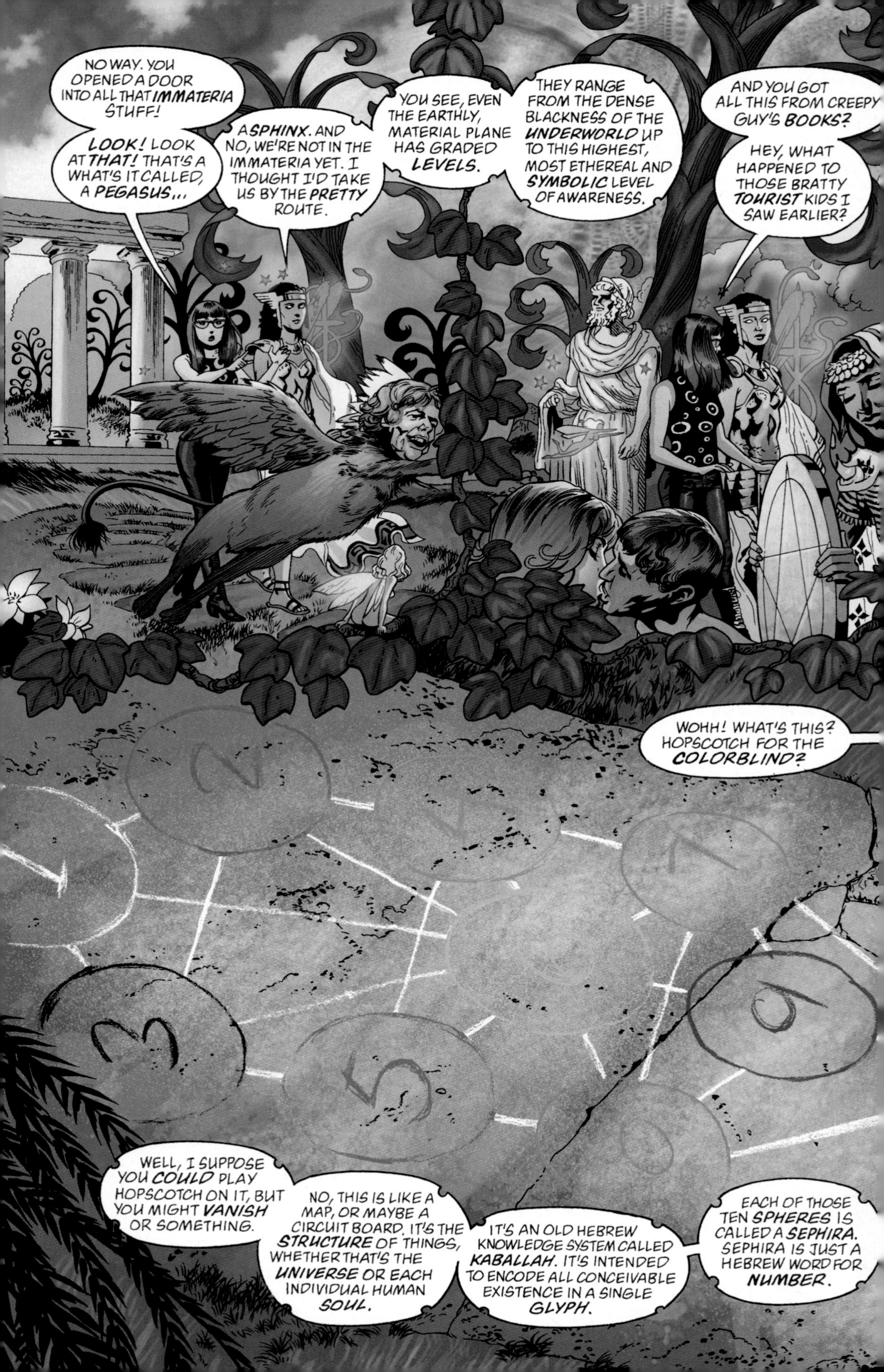

NO WAY. YOU OPENED A DOOR INTO ALL THAT IMMATERIA STUFF!
LOOK! LOOK AT THAT! THAT'S A WHAT'S IT CALLED, A PEGASUS...
A SPHINX. AND NO, WE'RE NOT IN THE IMMATERIA YET. I THOUGHT I'D TAKE US BY THE PRETTY ROUTE.
YOU SEE, EVEN THE EARTHLY, MATERIAL PLANE HAS GRADED LEVELS.
THEY RANGE FROM THE DENSE BLACKNESS OF THE UNDERWORLD UP TO THIS HIGHEST, MOST ETHEREAL AND SYMBOLIC LEVEL OF AWARENESS.
AND YOU GOT ALL THIS FROM CREEPY GUY'S BOOKS?
HEY, WHAT HAPPENED TO THOSE BRATTY TOURIST KIDS I SAW EARLIER?
WOHH! WHAT'S THIS? HOPSCOTCH FOR THE COLORBLIND?
WELL, I SUPPOSE YOU COULD PLAY HOPSCOTCH ON IT, BUT YOU MIGHT VANISH OR SOMETHING.
NO, THIS IS LIKE A MAP, OR MAYBE A CIRCUIT BOARD. IT'S THE STRUCTURE OF THINGS, WHETHER THAT'S THE UNIVERSE OR EACH INDIVIDUAL HUMAN SOUL.
IT'S AN OLD HEBREW KNOWLEDGE SYSTEM CALLED KABALLAH. IT'S INTENDED TO ENCODE ALL CONCEIVABLE EXISTENCE IN A SINGLE GLYPH.
EACH OF THOSE TEN SPHERES IS CALLED A SEPHIRA. SEPHIRA IS JUST A HEBREW WORD FOR NUMBER.

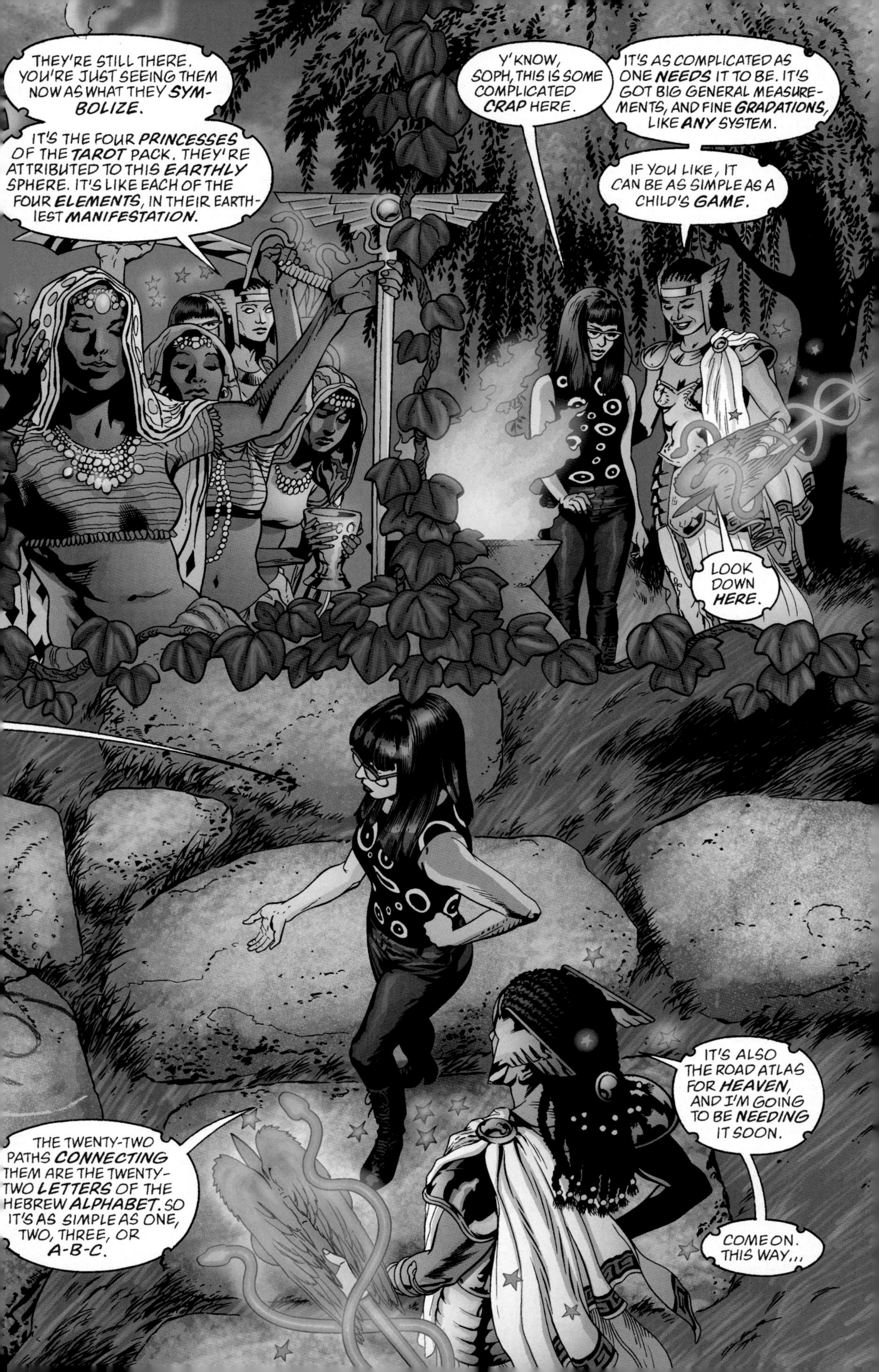

THEY'RE STILL THERE. YOU'RE JUST SEEING THEM NOW AS WHAT THEY SYMBOLIZE.
IT'S THE FOUR PRINCESSES OF THE TAROT PACK. THEY'RE ATTRIBUTED TO THIS EARTHLY SPHERE. IT'S LIKE EACH OF THE FOUR ELEMENTS, IN THEIR EARTHIEST MANIFESTATION.
Y'KNOW, SOPH, THIS IS SOME COMPLICATED CRAP HERE.
IT'S AS COMPLICATED AS ONE NEEDS IT TO BE. IT'S GOT BIG GENERAL MEASUREMENTS, AND FINE GRADATIONS, LIKE ANY SYSTEM.
IF YOU LIKE, IT CAN BE AS SIMPLE AS A CHILD'S GAME.
LOOK DOWN HERE.
THE TWENTY-TWO PATHS CONNECTING THEM ARE THE TWENTY-TWO LETTERS OF THE HEBREW ALPHABET. SO IT'S AS SIMPLE AS ONE, TWO, THREE, OR A-B-C.
IT'S ALSO THE ROAD ATLAS FOR HEAVEN, AND I'M GOING TO BE NEEDING IT SOON.
COME ON. THIS WAY...

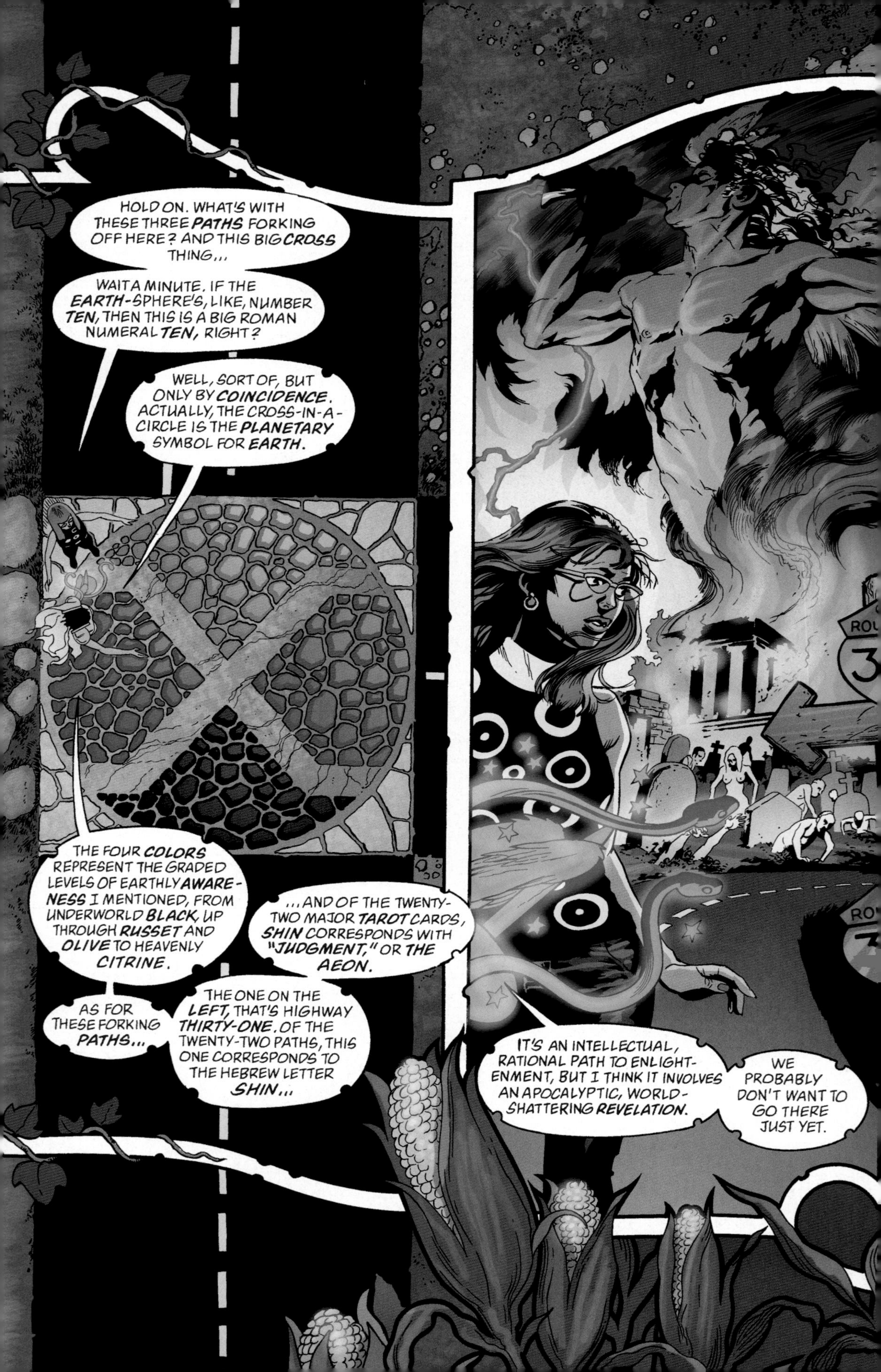
HOLD ON. WHAT'S WITH THESE THREE PATHS FORKING OFF HERE? AND THIS BIG CROSS THING...
WAIT A MINUTE. IF THE EARTH-SPHERE'S, LIKE, NUMBER TEN, THEN THIS IS A BIG ROMAN NUMERAL TEN, RIGHT?
WELL, SORT OF, BUT ONLY BY COINCIDENCE. ACTUALLY, THE CROSS-IN-A-CIRCLE IS THE PLANETARY SYMBOL FOR EARTH.
THE FOUR COLORS REPRESENT THE GRADED LEVELS OF EARTHLY AWARENESS I MENTIONED, FROM UNDERWORLD BLACK, UP THROUGH RUSSET AND OLIVE TO HEAVENLY CITRINE.
AS FOR THESE FORKING PATHS...
THE ONE ON THE LEFT, THAT'S HIGHWAY THIRTY-ONE. OF THE TWENTY-TWO PATHS, THIS ONE CORRESPONDS TO THE HEBREW LETTER SHIN...
...AND OF THE TWENTY-TWO MAJOR TAROT CARDS, SHIN CORRESPONDS WITH "JUDGMENT," OR THE AEON.
IT'S AN INTELLECTUAL, RATIONAL PATH TO ENLIGHTENMENT, BUT I THINK IT INVOLVES AN APOCALYPTIC, WORLD-SHATTERING REVELATION.
WE PROBABLY DON'T WANT TO GO THERE JUST YET.

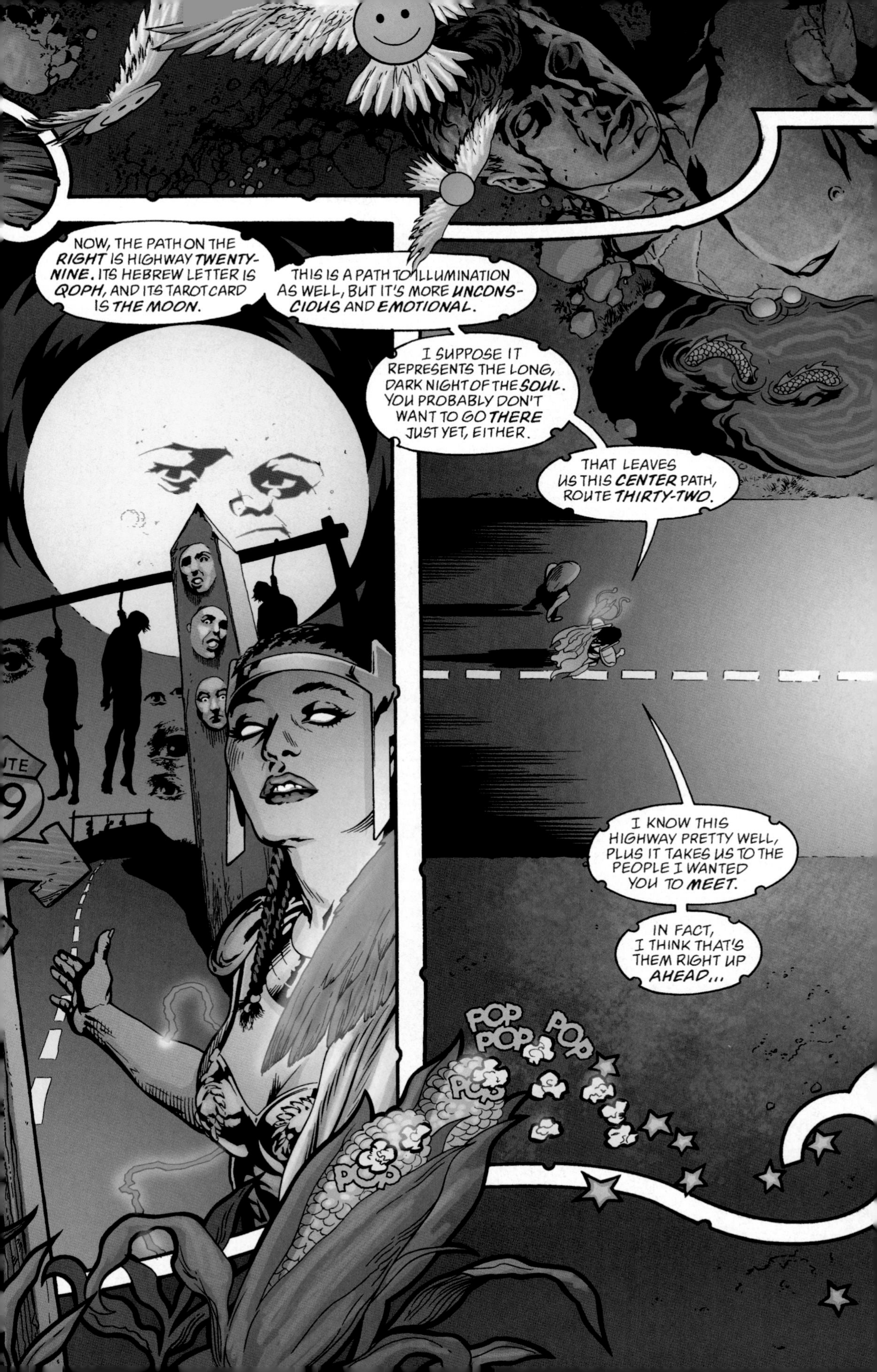

NOW, THE PATH ON THE RIGHT IS HIGHWAY TWENTY-NINE. ITS HEBREW LETTER IS QOPH, AND ITS TAROT CARD IS THE MOON.
THIS IS A PATH TO ILLUMINATION AS WELL, BUT IT'S MORE UNCONSCIOUS AND EMOTIONAL.
I SUPPOSE IT REPRESENTS THE LONG, DARK NIGHT OF THE SOUL. YOU PROBABLY DON'T WANT TO GO THERE JUST YET, EITHER.
THAT LEAVES US THIS CENTER PATH, ROUTE THIRTY-TWO.
I KNOW THIS HIGHWAY PRETTY WELL, PLUS IT TAKES US TO THE PEOPLE I WANTED YOU TO MEET.
IN FACT, I THINK THAT'S THEM RIGHT UP AHEAD...
POP POP POP

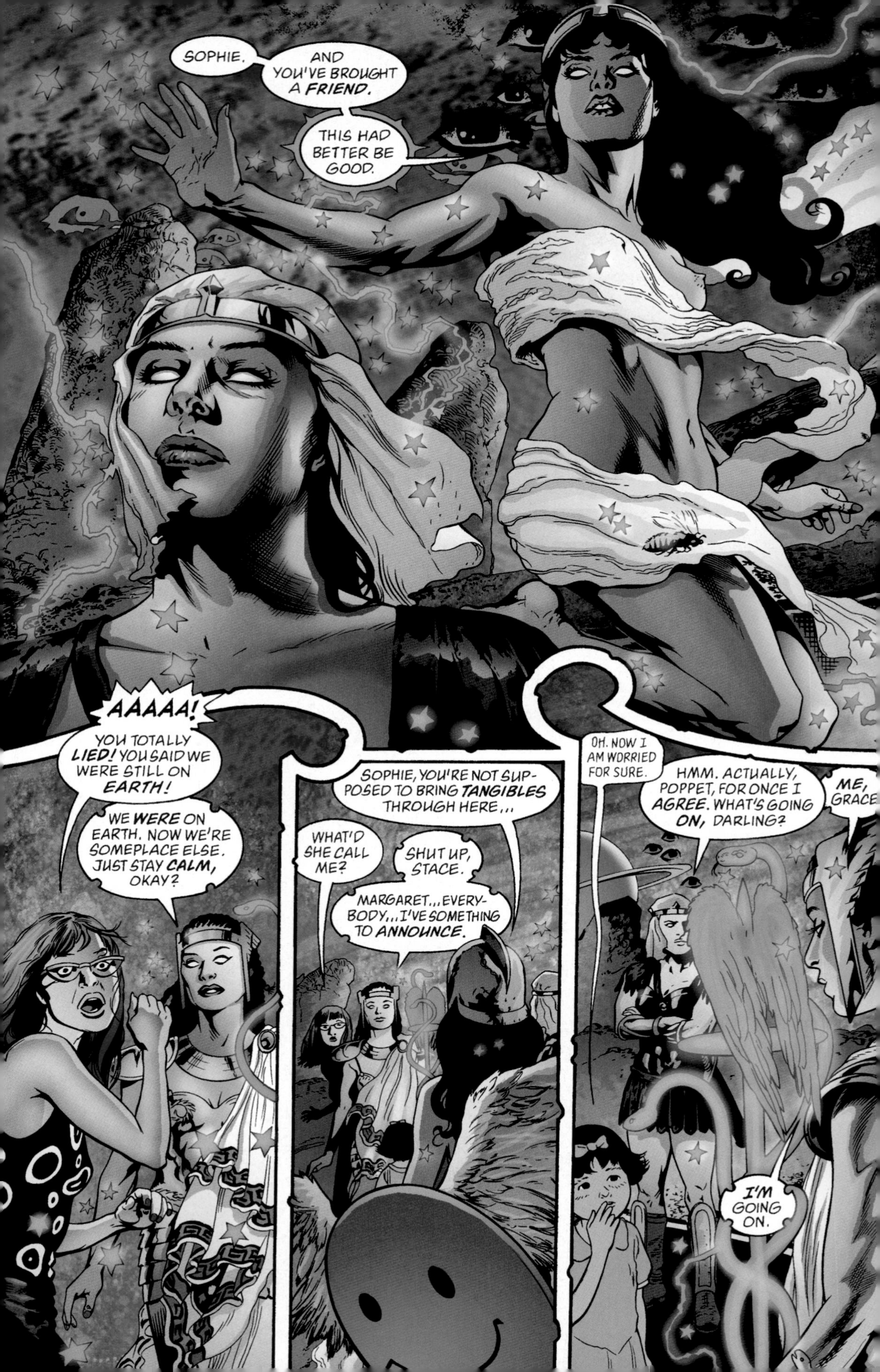
SOPHIE.
AND YOU'VE BROUGHT A FRIEND.
THIS HAD BETTER BE GOOD.
AAAAA!
YOU TOTALLY LIED! YOU SAID WE WERE STILL ON EARTH!
WE WERE ON EARTH. NOW WE'RE SOMEPLACE ELSE. JUST STAY CALM, OKAY?
SOPHIE, YOU'RE NOT SUPPOSED TO BRING TANGIBLES THROUGH HERE...
WHAT'D SHE CALL ME?
SHUT UP, STACE.
MARGARET... EVERYBODY... I'VE SOMETHING TO ANNOUNCE.
OH. NOW I AM WORRIED FOR SURE.
HMM. ACTUALLY, POPPET, FOR ONCE I AGREE. WHAT'S GOING ON, DARLING?
ME, GRACE
I'M GOING ON.

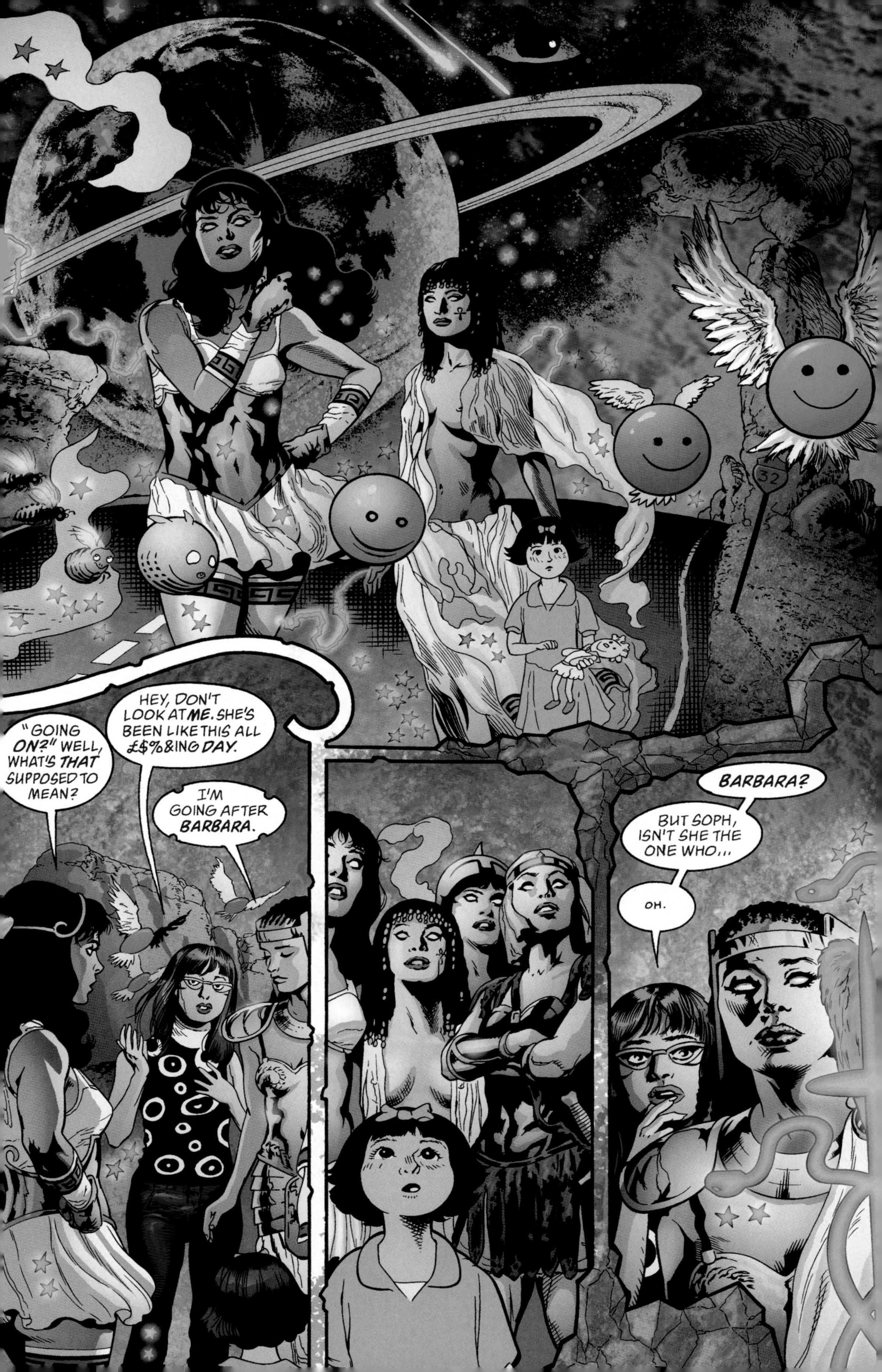
"GOING ON?" WELL, WHAT'S THAT SUPPOSED TO MEAN?
HEY, DON'T LOOK AT ME. SHE'S BEEN LIKE THIS ALL £$%&ING DAY.
I'M GOING AFTER BARBARA.
BARBARA?
BUT SOPH, ISN'T SHE THE ONE WHO...
OH.

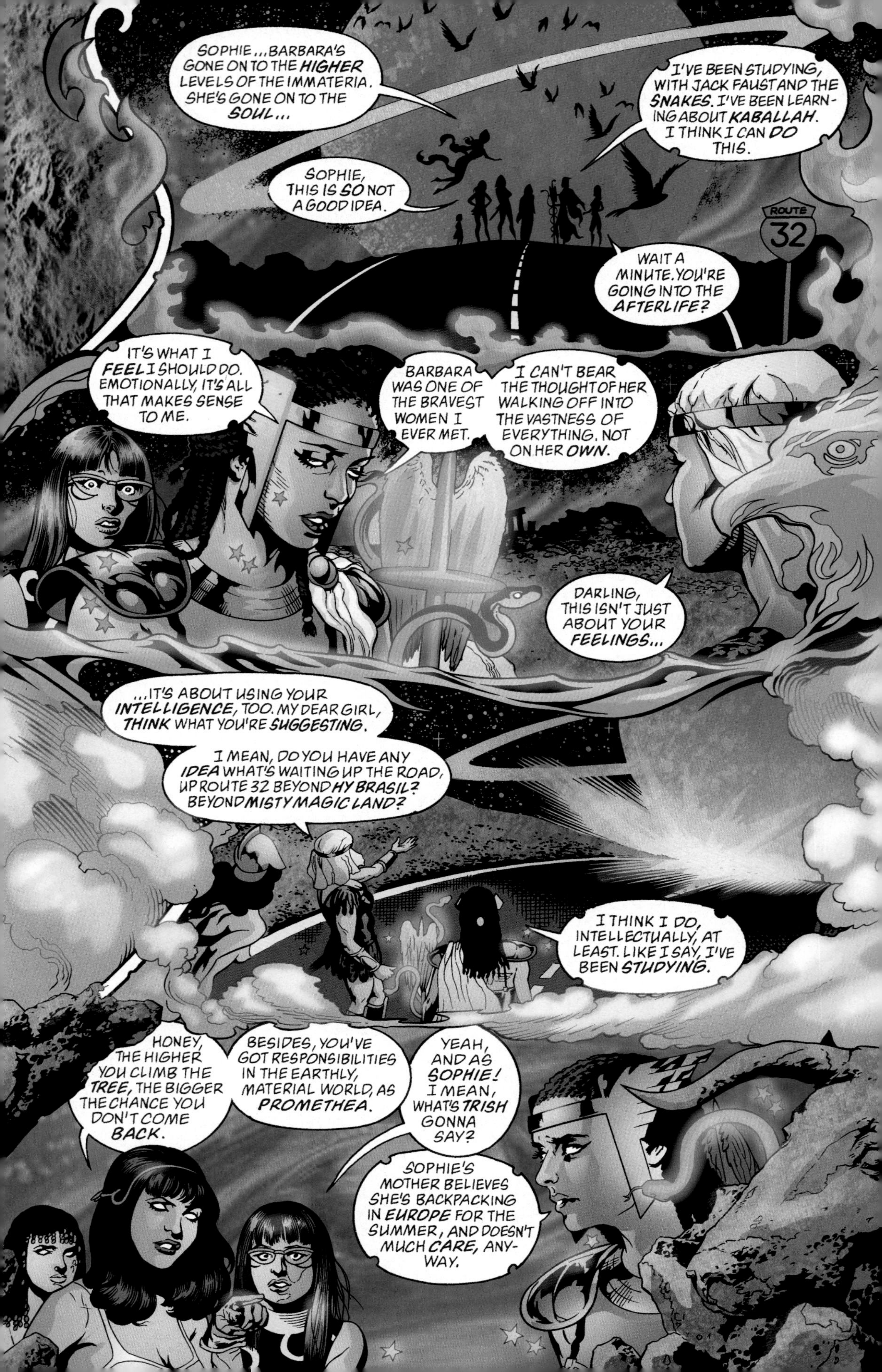
SOPHIE...BARBARA'S GONE ON TO THE HIGHER LEVELS OF THE IMMATERIA. SHE'S GONE ON TO THE SOUL...
I'VE BEEN STUDYING, WITH JACK FAUST AND THE SNAKES. I'VE BEEN LEARNING ABOUT KABALLAH. I THINK I CAN DO THIS.
SOPHIE, THIS IS SO NOT A GOOD IDEA.
ROUTE 32
WAIT A MINUTE. YOU'RE GOING INTO THE AFTERLIFE?
IT'S WHAT I FEEL I SHOULD DO. EMOTIONALLY, IT'S ALL THAT MAKES SENSE TO ME.
BARBARA WAS ONE OF THE BRAVEST WOMEN I EVER MET.
I CAN'T BEAR THE THOUGHT OF HER WALKING OFF INTO THE VASTNESS OF EVERYTHING. NOT ON HER OWN.
DARLING, THIS ISN'T JUST ABOUT YOUR FEELINGS...
...IT'S ABOUT USING YOUR INTELLIGENCE, TOO. MY DEAR GIRL, THINK WHAT YOU'RE SUGGESTING.
I MEAN, DO YOU HAVE ANY IDEA WHAT'S WAITING UP THE ROAD, UP ROUTE 32 BEYOND HY BRASIL? BEYOND MISTY MAGIC LAND?
I THINK I DO, INTELLECTUALLY, AT LEAST. LIKE I SAY, I'VE BEEN STUDYING.
HONEY, THE HIGHER YOU CLIMB THE TREE, THE BIGGER THE CHANCE YOU DON'T COME BACK.
BESIDES, YOU'VE GOT RESPONSIBILITIES IN THE EARTHLY, MATERIAL WORLD, AS PROMETHEA.
YEAH, AND AS SOPHIE! I MEAN, WHAT'S TRISH GONNA SAY?
SOPHIE'S MOTHER BELIEVES SHE'S BACKPACKING IN EUROPE FOR THE SUMMER, AND DOESN'T MUCH CARE, ANYWAY.

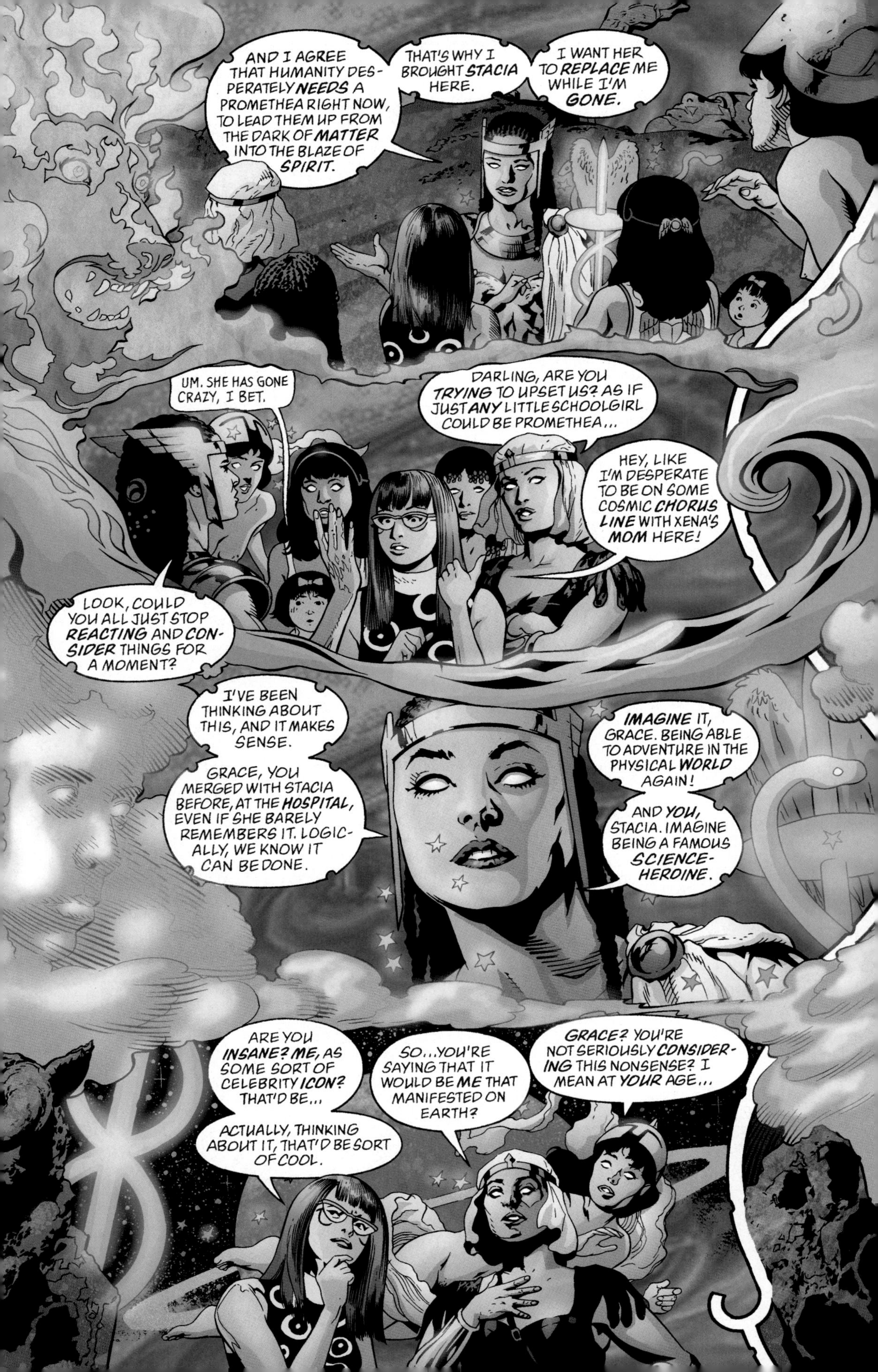

AND I AGREE THAT HUMANITY DESPERATELY NEEDS A PROMETHEA RIGHT NOW, TO LEAD THEM UP FROM THE DARK OF MATTER INTO THE BLAZE OF SPIRIT.
THAT'S WHY I BROUGHT STACIA HERE.
I WANT HER TO REPLACE ME WHILE I'M GONE.
UM. SHE HAS GONE CRAZY, I BET.
DARLING, ARE YOU TRYING TO UPSET US? AS IF JUST ANY LITTLE SCHOOLGIRL COULD BE PROMETHEA...
HEY, LIKE I'M DESPERATE TO BE ON SOME COSMIC CHORUS LINE WITH XENA'S MOM HERE!
LOOK, COULD YOU ALL JUST STOP REACTING AND CONSIDER THINGS FOR A MOMENT?
I'VE BEEN THINKING ABOUT THIS, AND IT MAKES SENSE.
GRACE, YOU MERGED WITH STACIA BEFORE, AT THE HOSPITAL, EVEN IF SHE BARELY REMEMBERS IT. LOGICALLY, WE KNOW IT CAN BE DONE.
IMAGINE IT, GRACE. BEING ABLE TO ADVENTURE IN THE PHYSICAL WORLD AGAIN!
AND YOU, STACIA. IMAGINE BEING A FAMOUS SCIENCE-HEROINE.
ARE YOU INSANE? ME, AS SOME SORT OF CELEBRITY ICON? THAT'D BE...
ACTUALLY, THINKING ABOUT IT, THAT'D BE SORT OF COOL.
SO...YOU'RE SAYING THAT IT WOULD BE ME THAT MANIFESTED ON EARTH?
GRACE? YOU'RE NOT SERIOUSLY CONSIDERING THIS NONSENSE? I MEAN AT YOUR AGE...

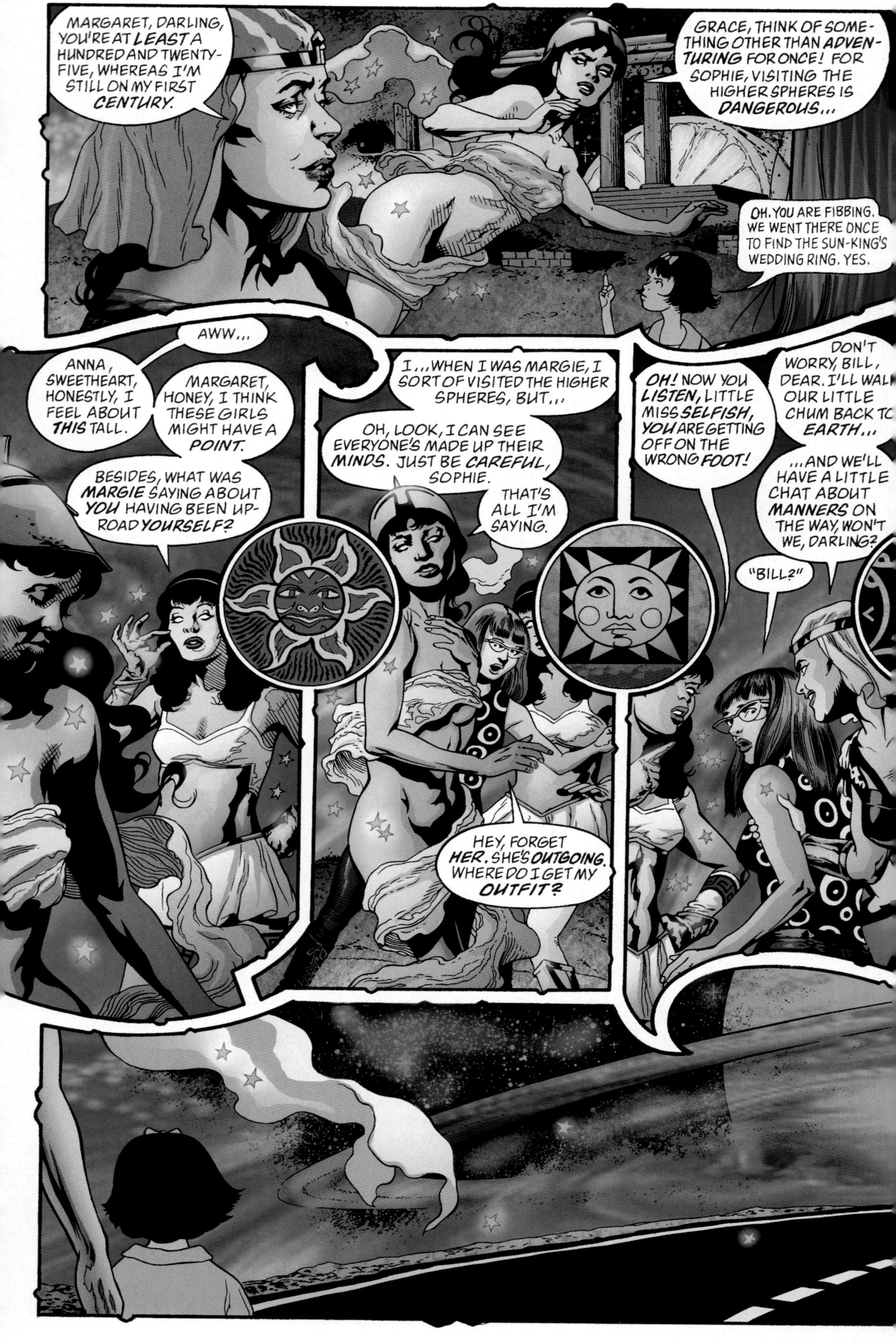
MARGARET, DARLING, YOU'RE AT **LEAST** A HUNDRED AND TWENTY-FIVE, WHEREAS I'M STILL ON MY FIRST **CENTURY**.
GRACE, THINK OF SOMETHING OTHER THAN **ADVENTURING** FOR ONCE! FOR SOPHIE, VISITING THE HIGHER SPHERES IS **DANGEROUS**...
OH. YOU ARE FIBBING. WE WENT THERE ONCE TO FIND THE SUN-KING'S WEDDING RING. YES.
AWW...
ANNA, SWEETHEART, HONESTLY, I FEEL ABOUT **THIS** TALL.
MARGARET, HONEY, I THINK THESE GIRLS MIGHT HAVE A **POINT**.
BESIDES, WHAT WAS **MARGIE** SAYING ABOUT **YOU** HAVING BEEN UP-ROAD **YOURSELF**?
I...WHEN I WAS MARGIE, I SORT OF VISITED THE HIGHER SPHERES, BUT...
OH, LOOK, I CAN SEE EVERYONE'S MADE UP THEIR **MINDS**. JUST BE **CAREFUL**, SOPHIE.
THAT'S ALL I'M SAYING.
HEY, FORGET **HER**. SHE'S **OUTGOING**. WHERE DO I GET MY **OUTFIT**?
OH! NOW YOU **LISTEN**, LITTLE MISS **SELFISH**, **YOU** ARE GETTING OFF ON THE WRONG **FOOT**!
DON'T WORRY, BILL, DEAR. I'LL WALK OUR LITTLE CHUM BACK TO **EARTH**...
...AND WE'LL HAVE A LITTLE CHAT ABOUT **MANNERS** ON THE WAY, WON'T WE, DARLING?
"BILL?"

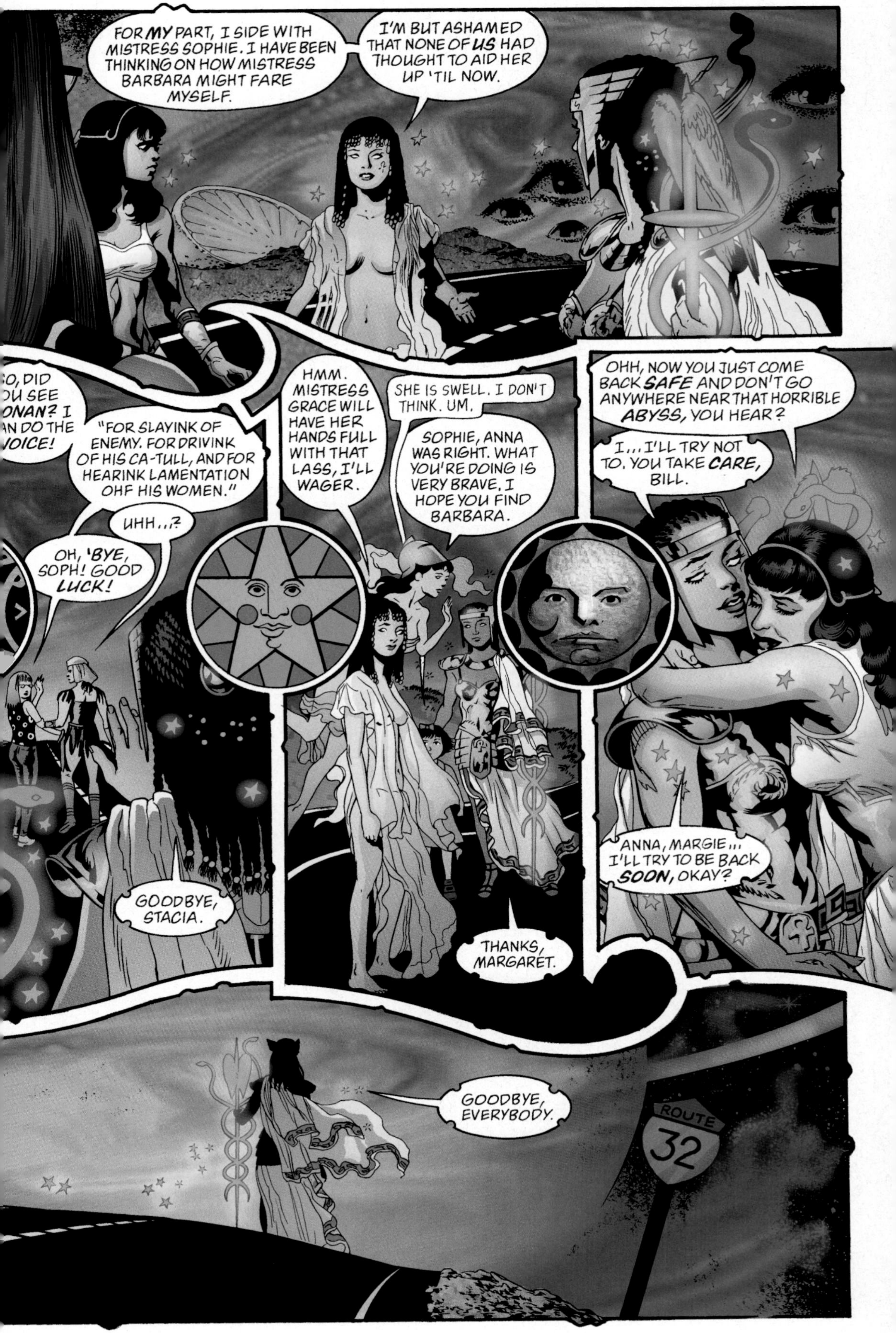
FOR MY PART, I SIDE WITH MISTRESS SOPHIE. I HAVE BEEN THINKING ON HOW MISTRESS BARBARA MIGHT FARE MYSELF.
I'M BUT ASHAMED THAT NONE OF US HAD THOUGHT TO AID HER UP 'TIL NOW.
O, DID OU SEE ONAN? I AN DO THE OICE!
"FOR SLAYINK OF ENEMY. FOR DRIVINK OF HIS CA-TULL, AND FOR HEARINK LAMENTATION OHF HIS WOMEN."
UHH...?
OH, 'BYE, SOPH! GOOD LUCK!
GOODBYE, STACIA.
HMM. MISTRESS GRACE WILL HAVE HER HANDS FULL WITH THAT LASS, I'LL WAGER.
SHE IS SWELL. I DON'T THINK. UM.
SOPHIE, ANNA WAS RIGHT. WHAT YOU'RE DOING IS VERY BRAVE. I HOPE YOU FIND BARBARA.
THANKS, MARGARET.
OHH, NOW YOU JUST COME BACK SAFE AND DON'T GO ANYWHERE NEAR THAT HORRIBLE ABYSS, YOU HEAR?
I... I'LL TRY NOT TO. YOU TAKE CARE, BILL.
ANNA, MARGIE... I'LL TRY TO BE BACK SOON, OKAY?
GOODBYE, EVERYBODY.
ROUTE
32

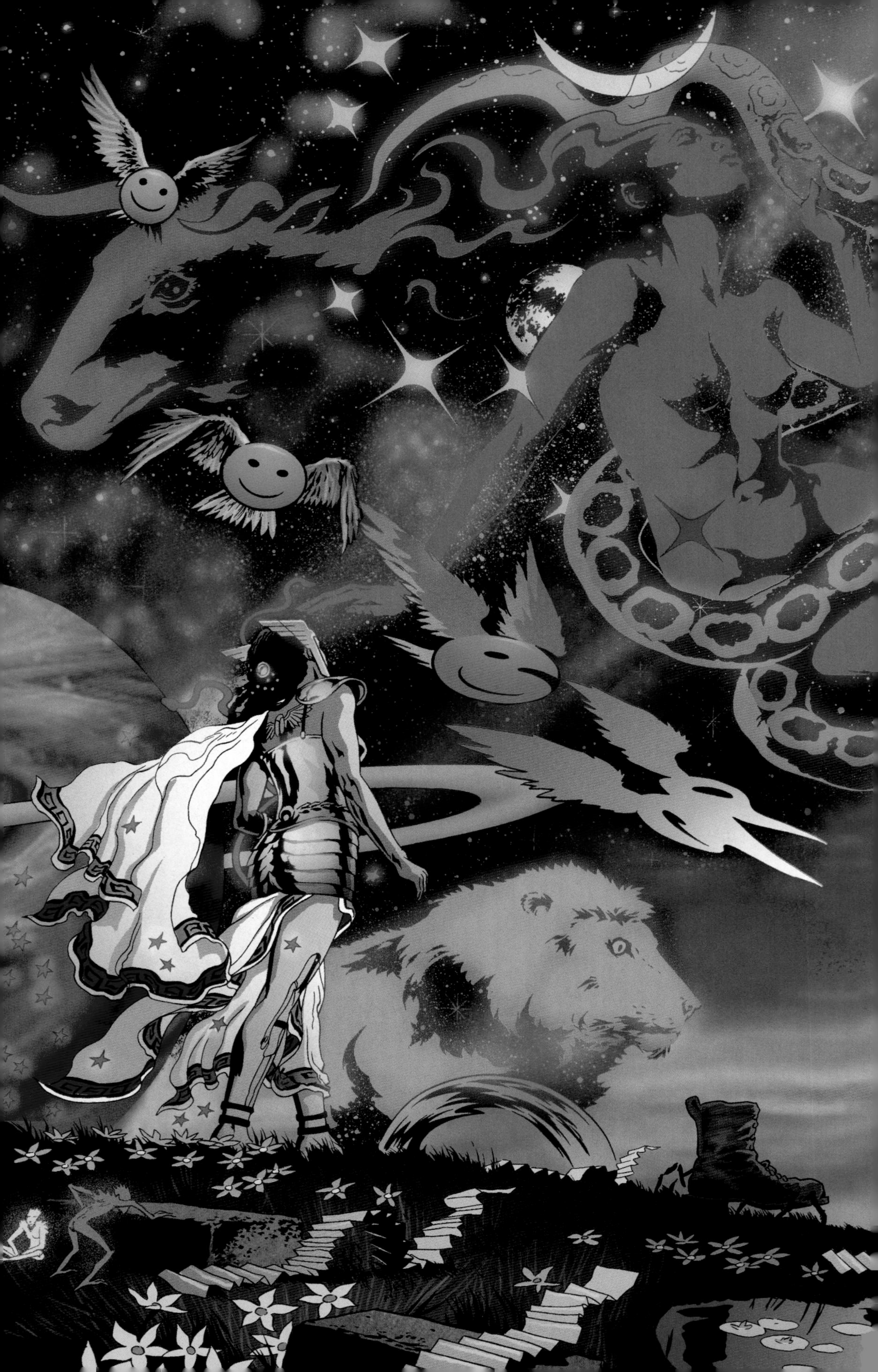

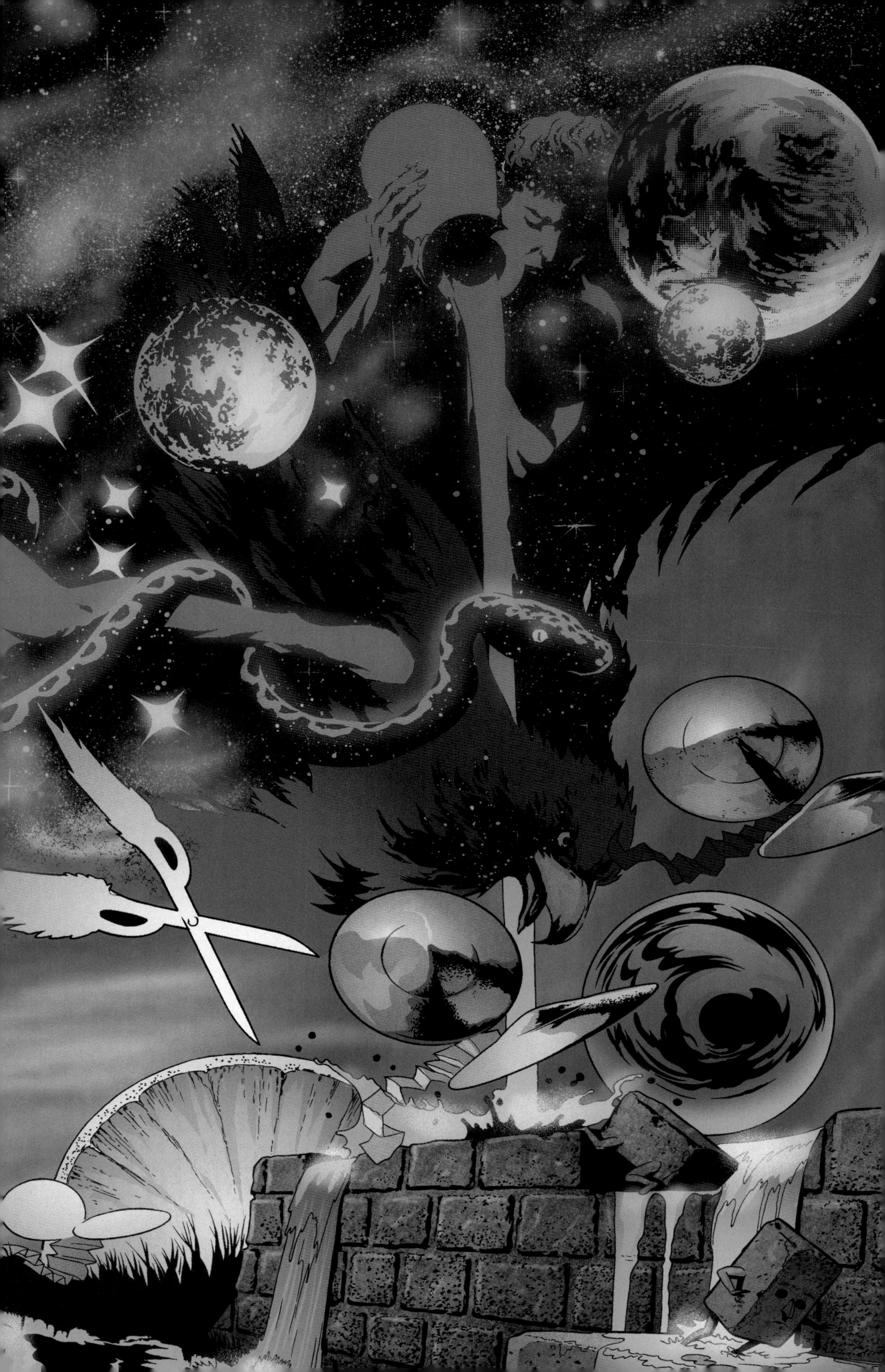

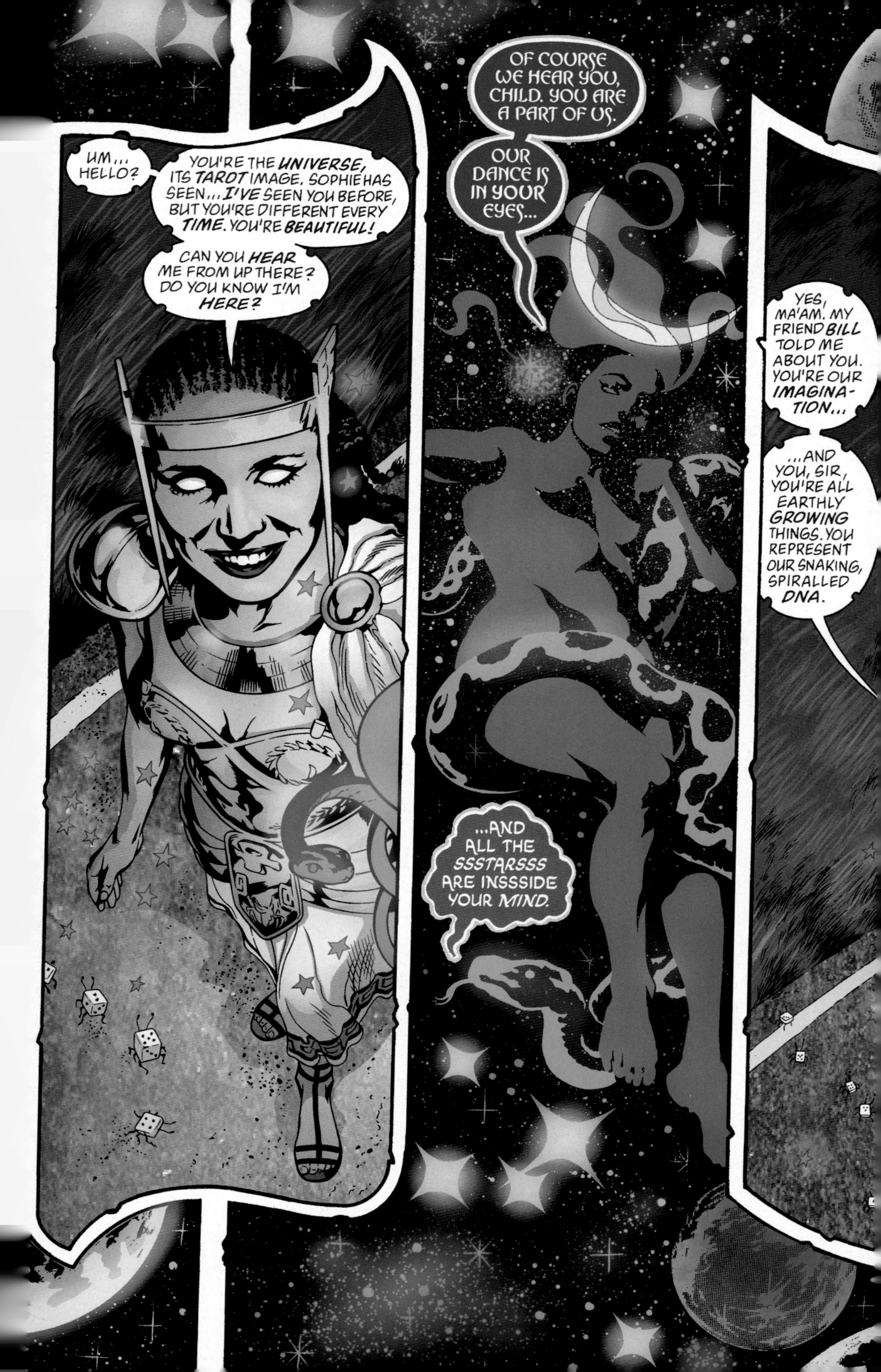
UM... HELLO?
YOU'RE THE UNIVERSE, ITS TAROT IMAGE. SOPHIE HAS SEEN... I'VE SEEN YOU BEFORE, BUT YOU'RE DIFFERENT EVERY TIME. YOU'RE BEAUTIFUL!
CAN YOU HEAR ME FROM UP THERE? DO YOU KNOW I'M HERE?
OF COURSE WE HEAR YOU, CHILD. YOU ARE A PART OF US.
OUR DANCE IS IN YOUR EYES...
...AND ALL THE SSSTARSSS ARE INSSSIDE YOUR MIND.
YES, MA'AM. MY FRIEND BILL TOLD ME ABOUT YOU. YOU'RE OUR IMAGINA-TION...
...AND YOU, SIR, YOU'RE ALL EARTHLY GROWING THINGS. YOU REPRESENT OUR SNAKING, SPIRALLED DNA.

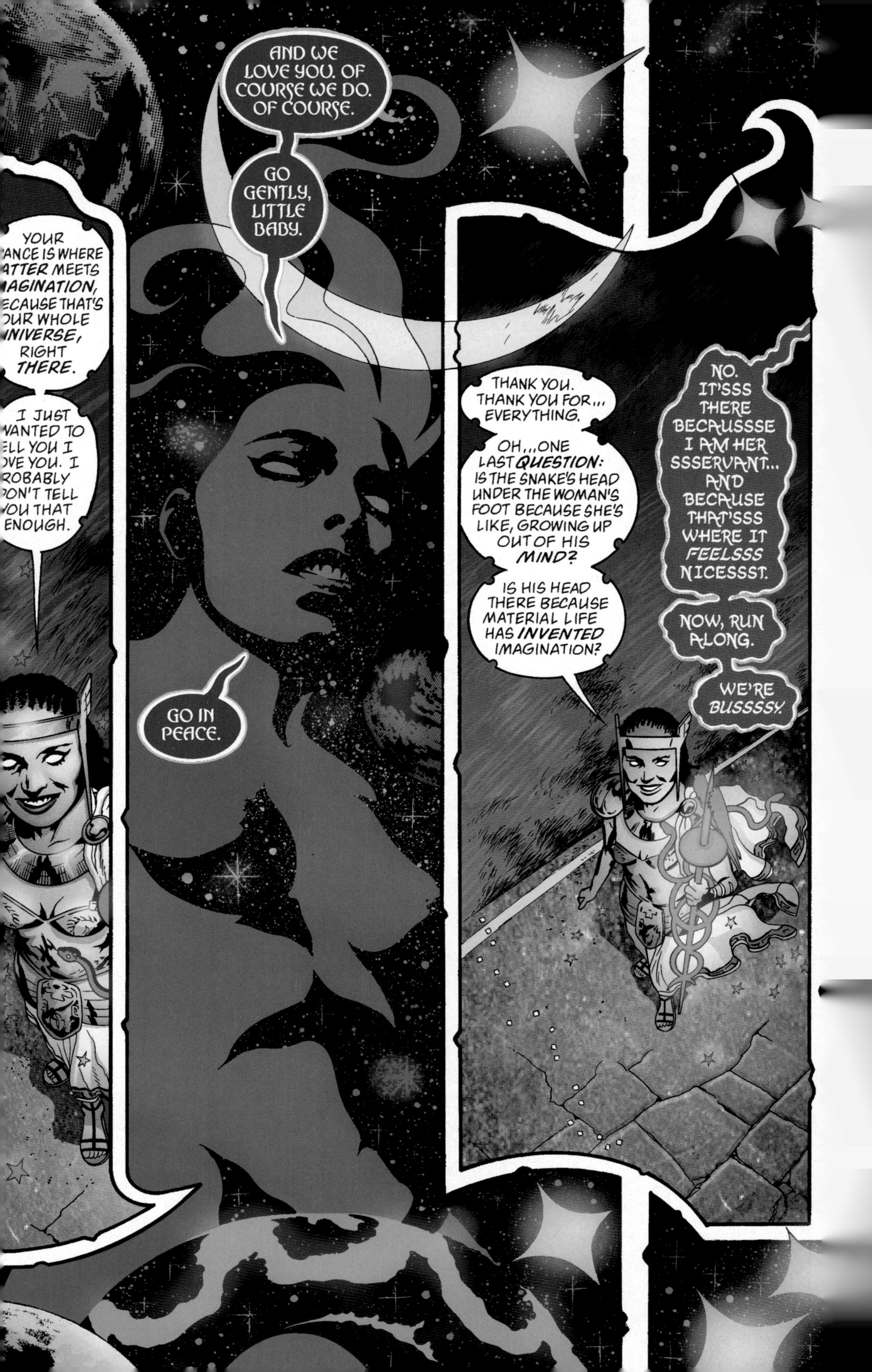
YOUR [S]PANCE IS WHERE [M]ATTER MEETS [I]MAGINATION, [B]ECAUSE THAT'S [Y]OUR WHOLE [U]NIVERSE, RIGHT THERE.
I JUST [W]ANTED TO [T]ELL YOU I [L]OVE YOU. I [P]ROBABLY [D]ON'T TELL YOU THAT ENOUGH.
AND WE LOVE YOU. OF COURSE WE DO. OF COURSE.
GO GENTLY, LITTLE BABY.
GO IN PEACE.
THANK YOU. THANK YOU FOR... EVERYTHING.
OH...ONE LAST QUESTION: IS THE SNAKE'S HEAD UNDER THE WOMAN'S FOOT BECAUSE SHE'S LIKE, GROWING UP OUT OF HIS MIND?
IS HIS HEAD THERE BECAUSE MATERIAL LIFE HAS INVENTED IMAGINATION?
NO. IT'SSS THERE BECAUSSSE I AM HER SSSERVANT... AND BECAUSE THAT'SSS WHERE IT FEELSSS NICESSST.
NOW, RUN ALONG.
WE'RE BUSSSSY.

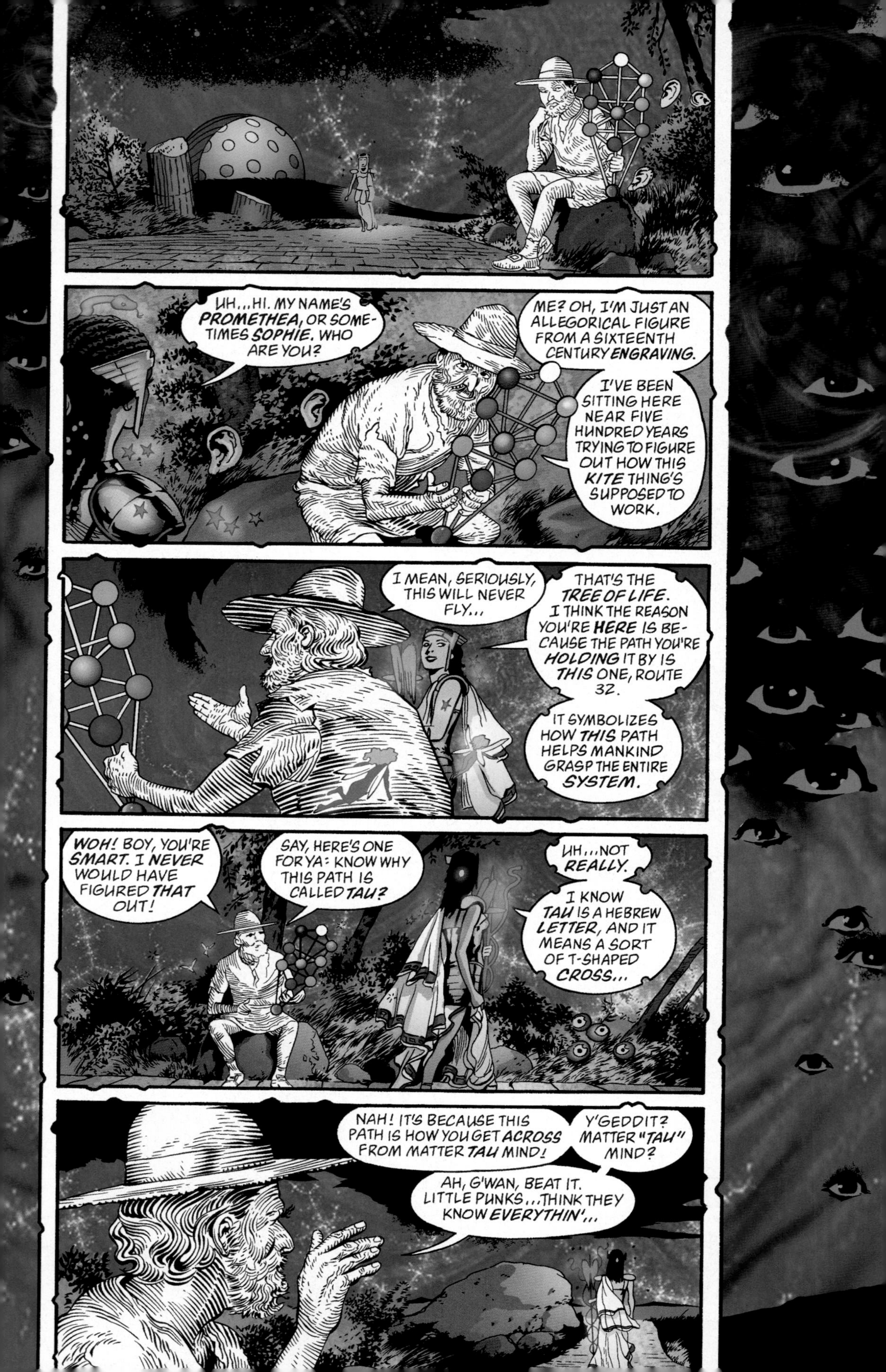
UH...HI. MY NAME'S PROMETHEA, OR SOMETIMES SOPHIE. WHO ARE YOU?
ME? OH, I'M JUST AN ALLEGORICAL FIGURE FROM A SIXTEENTH CENTURY ENGRAVING.
I'VE BEEN SITTING HERE NEAR FIVE HUNDRED YEARS TRYING TO FIGURE OUT HOW THIS KITE THING'S SUPPOSED TO WORK.
I MEAN, SERIOUSLY, THIS WILL NEVER FLY...
THAT'S THE TREE OF LIFE. I THINK THE REASON YOU'RE HERE IS BECAUSE THE PATH YOU'RE HOLDING IT BY IS THIS ONE, ROUTE 32.
IT SYMBOLIZES HOW THIS PATH HELPS MANKIND GRASP THE ENTIRE SYSTEM.
WOH! BOY, YOU'RE SMART. I NEVER WOULD HAVE FIGURED THAT OUT!
SAY, HERE'S ONE FOR YA: KNOW WHY THIS PATH IS CALLED TAU?
UH...NOT REALLY.
I KNOW TAU IS A HEBREW LETTER, AND IT MEANS A SORT OF T-SHAPED CROSS...
NAH! IT'S BECAUSE THIS PATH IS HOW YOU GET ACROSS FROM MATTER TAU MIND!
Y'GEDDIT? MATTER "TAU" MIND?
AH, G'WAN, BEAT IT. LITTLE PUNKS...THINK THEY KNOW EVERYTHIN'...

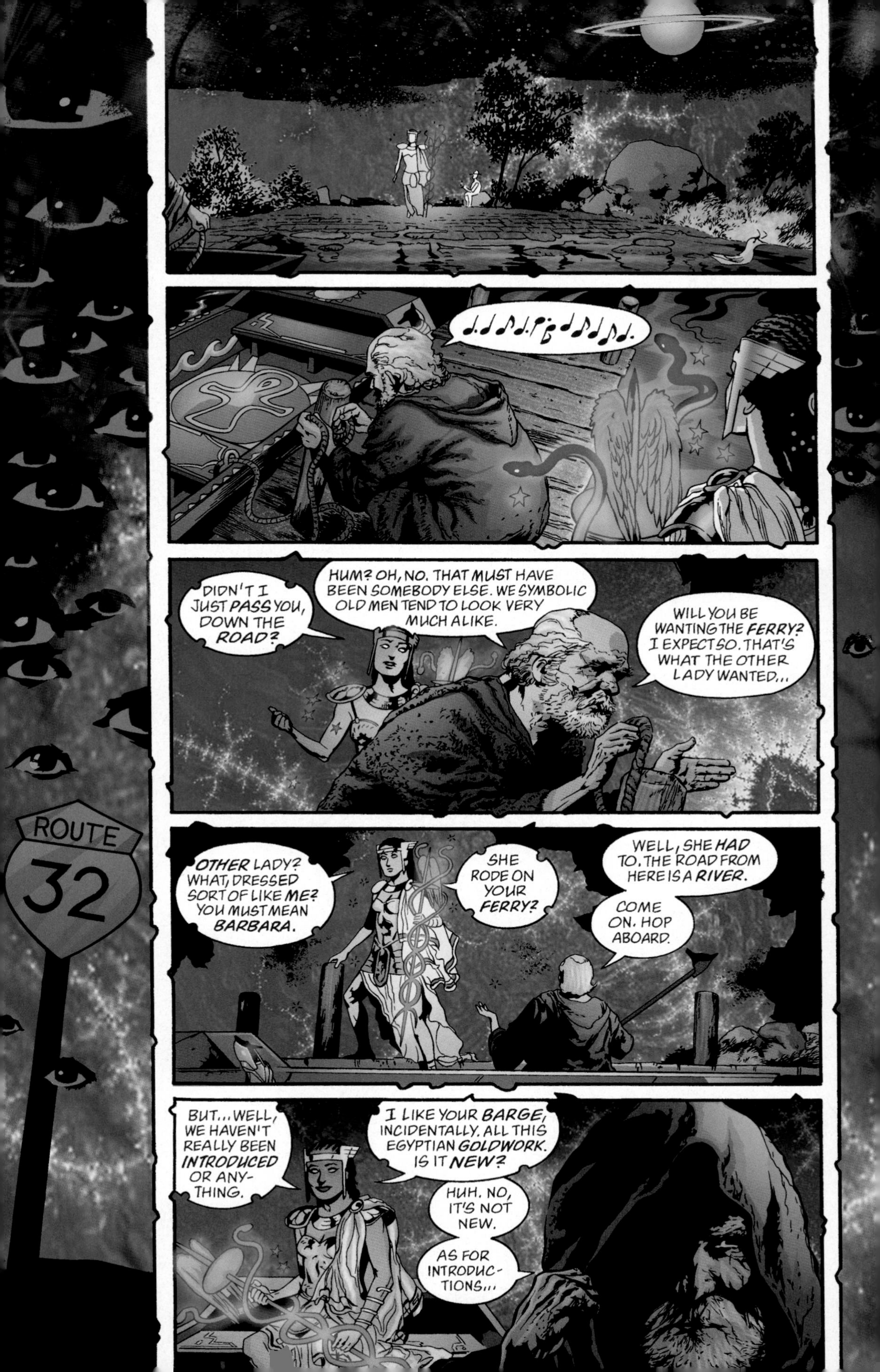
ROUTE 32
DIDN'T I JUST PASS YOU, DOWN THE ROAD?
HUM? OH, NO. THAT MUST HAVE BEEN SOMEBODY ELSE. WE SYMBOLIC OLD MEN TEND TO LOOK VERY MUCH ALIKE.
WILL YOU BE WANTING THE FERRY? I EXPECT SO. THAT'S WHAT THE OTHER LADY WANTED...
OTHER LADY? WHAT, DRESSED SORT OF LIKE ME? YOU MUST MEAN BARBARA.
SHE RODE ON YOUR FERRY?
WELL, SHE HAD TO. THE ROAD FROM HERE IS A RIVER.
COME ON. HOP ABOARD.
BUT... WELL, WE HAVEN'T REALLY BEEN INTRODUCED OR ANY-THING.
I LIKE YOUR BARGE, INCIDENTALLY. ALL THIS EGYPTIAN GOLDWORK. IS IT NEW?
HUH. NO, IT'S NOT NEW.
AS FOR INTRODUC-TIONS...

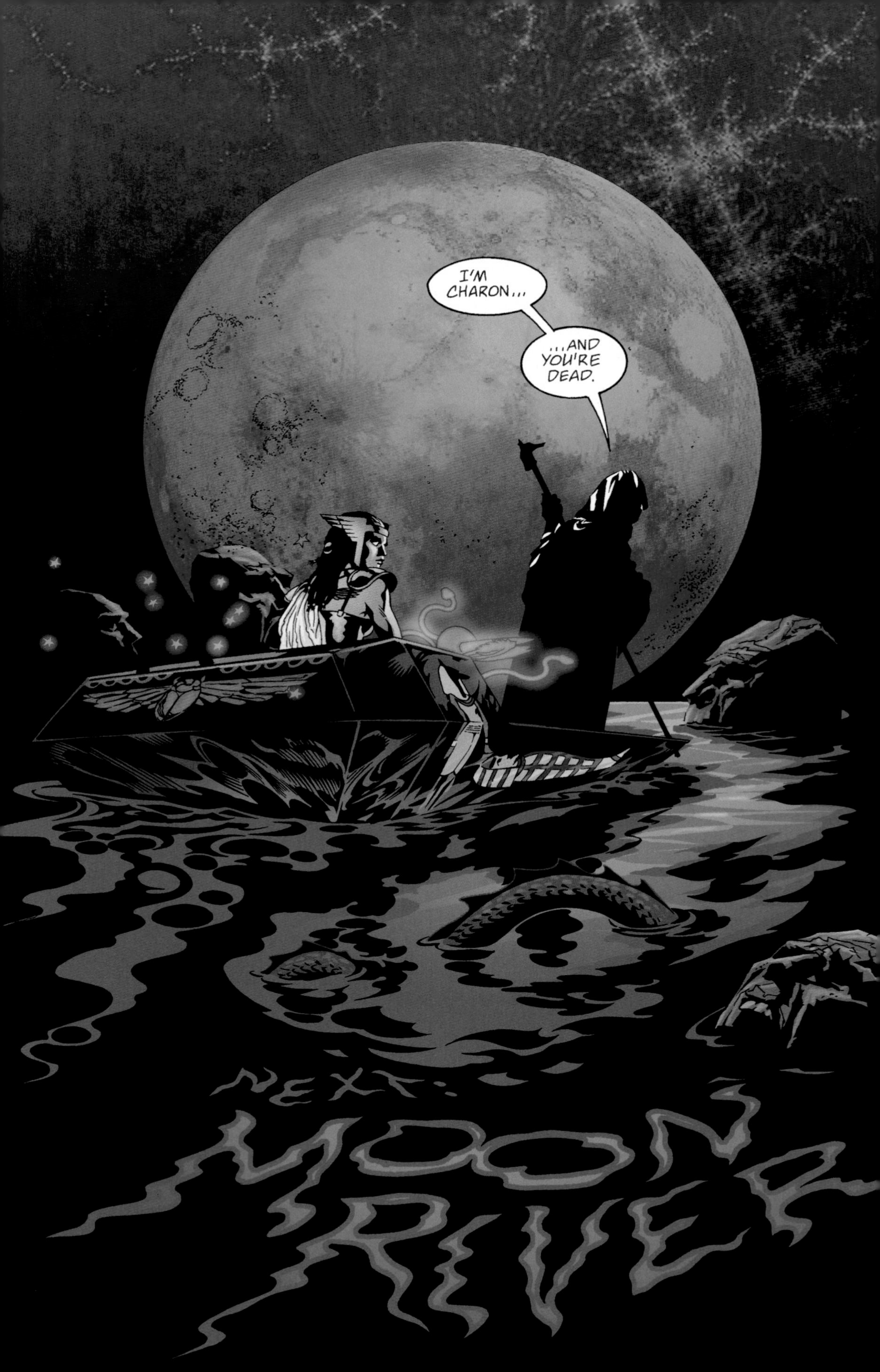
I'M CHARON...
...AND YOU'RE DEAD.
NEXT:
MOON RIVER

CHAPTER TWO

**A moonlit path crosses the water,
A friend is found deep in conversation,
A fabulous company is encountered.**

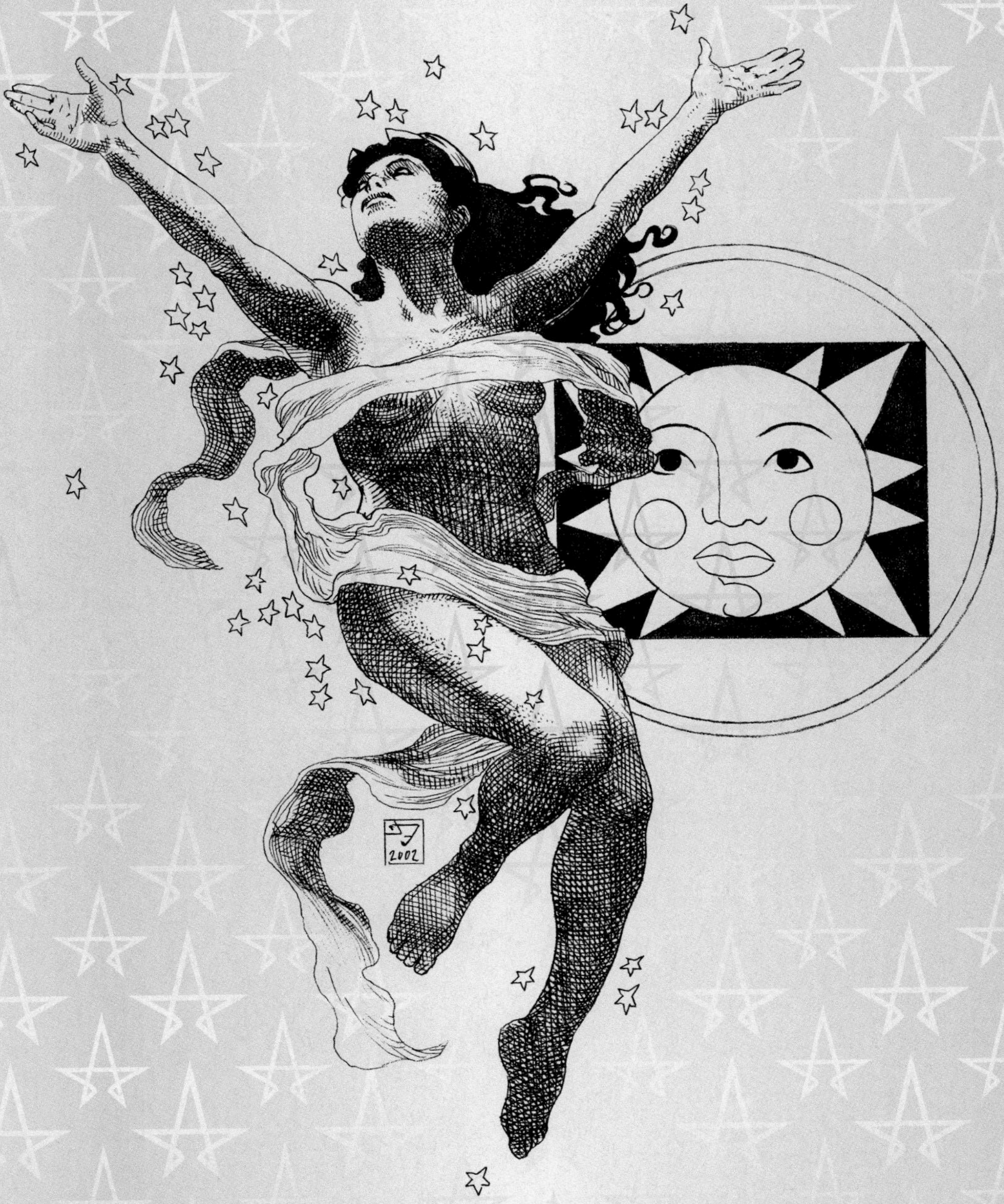
2002

**Cover art:
J.H. Williams III
& Jeromy Cox**

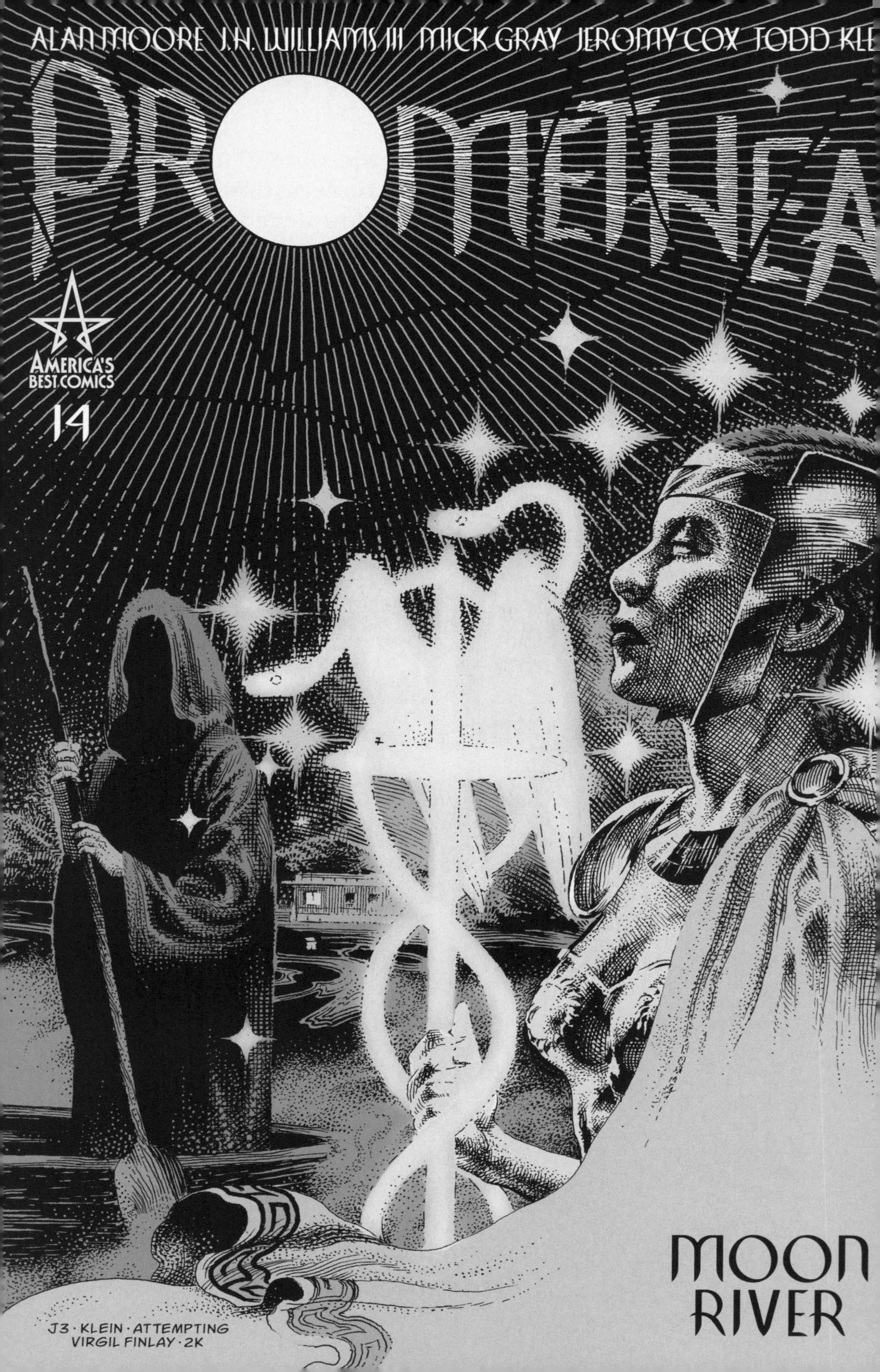

ALAN MOORE J.H. WILLIAMS III MICK GRAY JEROMY COX TODD KLE
PROMETHEA
AMERICA'S BEST COMICS
14
MOON RIVER
J3 · KLEIN · ATTEMPTING VIRGIL FINLAY · 2K

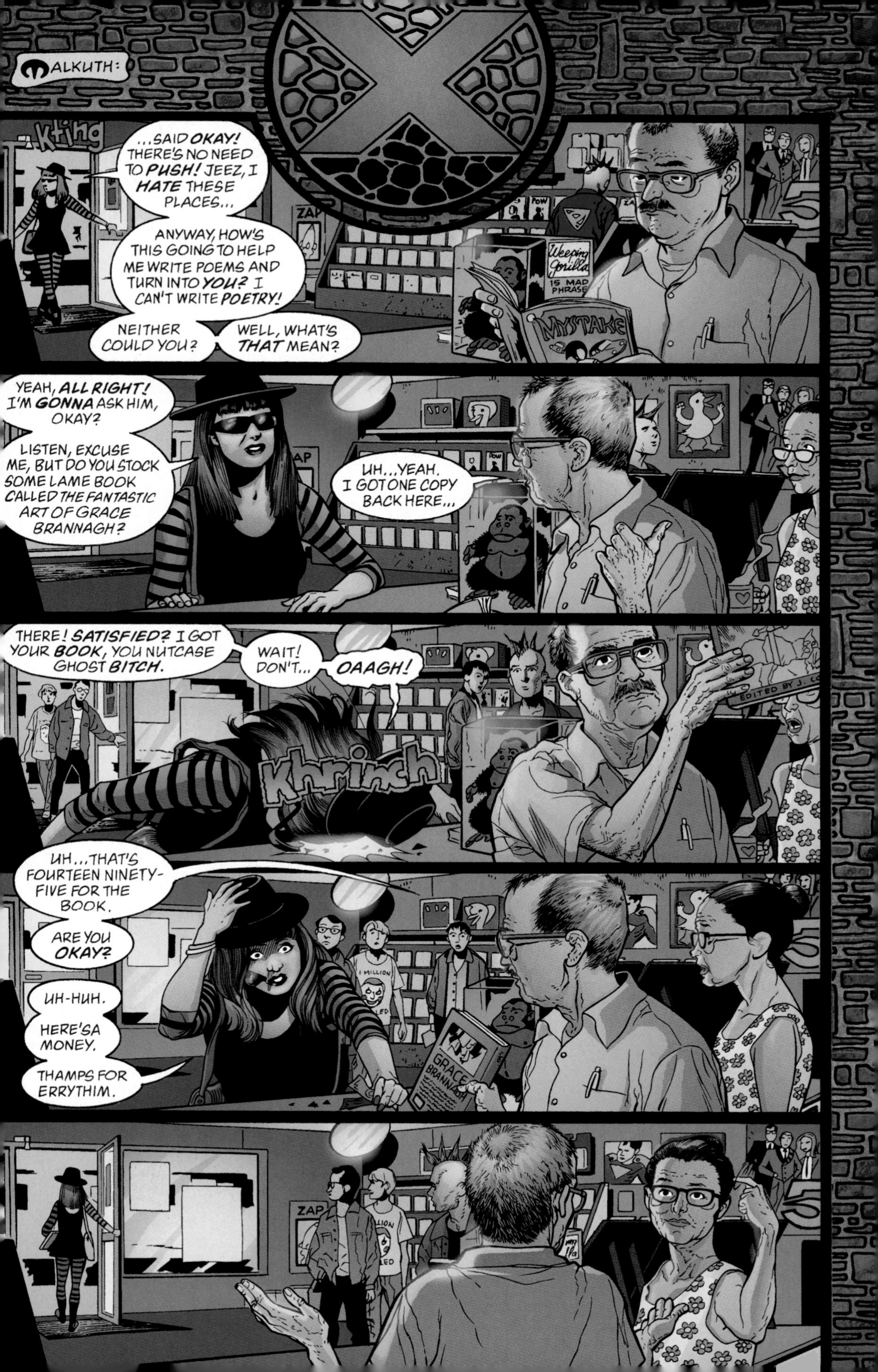
MALKUTH:
...SAID OKAY! THERE'S NO NEED TO PUSH! JEEZ, I HATE THESE PLACES...
ANYWAY, HOW'S THIS GOING TO HELP ME WRITE POEMS AND TURN INTO YOU? I CAN'T WRITE POETRY!
NEITHER COULD YOU?
WELL, WHAT'S THAT MEAN?
Weeping Gorilla
IS MAD PHRASE
MYSTAKE
ZAP
POW
YEAH, ALL RIGHT! I'M GONNA ASK HIM, OKAY?
LISTEN, EXCUSE ME, BUT DO YOU STOCK SOME LAME BOOK CALLED THE FANTASTIC ART OF GRACE BRANNAGH?
UH...YEAH. I GOT ONE COPY BACK HERE...
THERE! SATISFIED? I GOT YOUR BOOK, YOU NUTCASE GHOST BITCH.
WAIT! DON'T...
OAAGH!
Khrinch
EDITED BY J. C
UH...THAT'S FOURTEEN NINETY-FIVE FOR THE BOOK.
ARE YOU OKAY?
UH-HUH.
HERE'SA MONEY.
THAMPS FOR ERRYTHIM.
GRACE BRANNAGH
ZAP

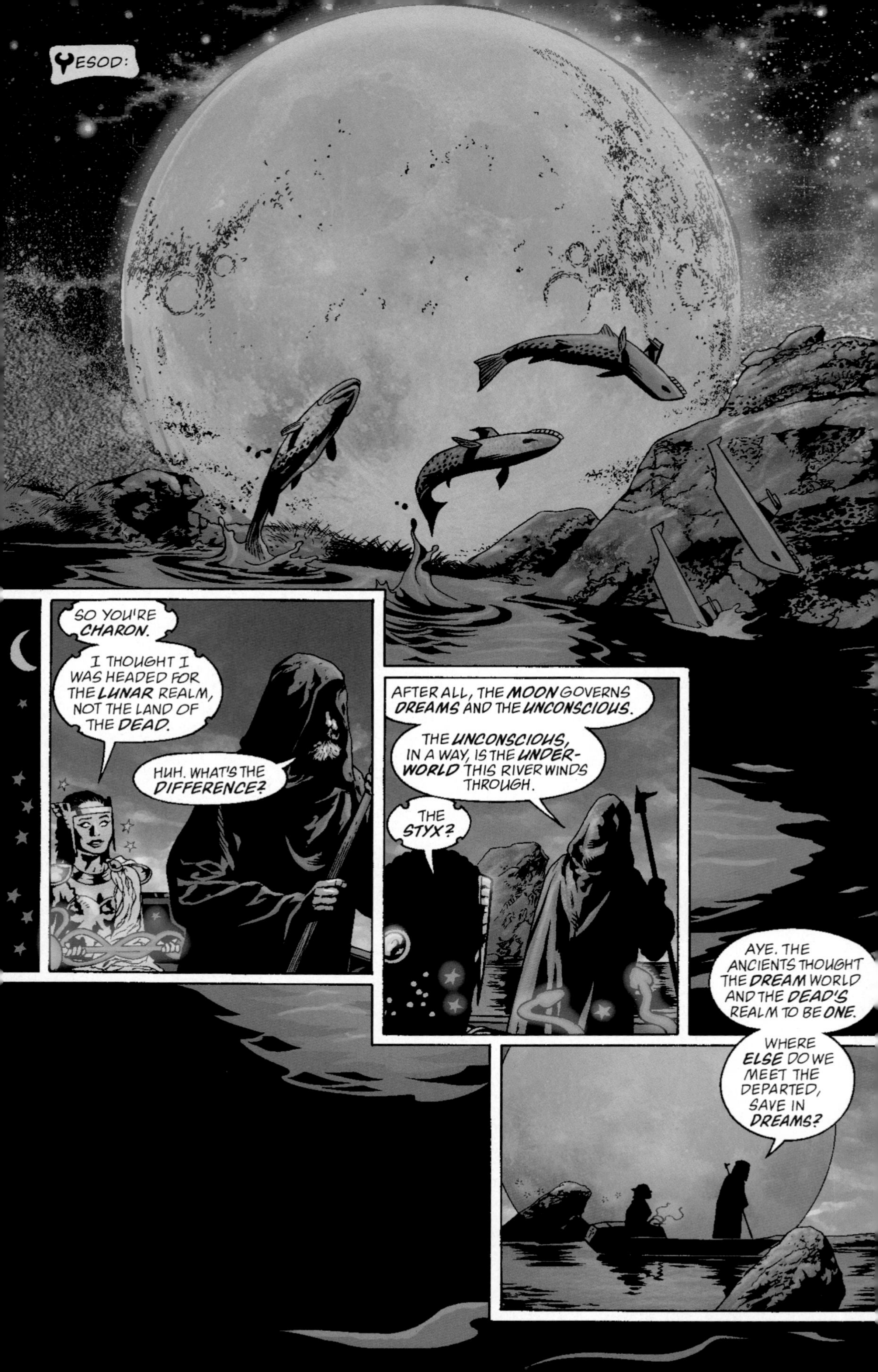
ESOD:
SO YOU'RE CHARON.
I THOUGHT I WAS HEADED FOR THE LUNAR REALM, NOT THE LAND OF THE DEAD.
HUH. WHAT'S THE DIFFERENCE?
AFTER ALL, THE MOON GOVERNS DREAMS AND THE UNCONSCIOUS.
THE UNCONSCIOUS, IN A WAY, IS THE UNDER-WORLD THIS RIVER WINDS THROUGH.
THE STYX?
AYE. THE ANCIENTS THOUGHT THE DREAM WORLD AND THE DEAD'S REALM TO BE ONE.
WHERE ELSE DO WE MEET THE DEPARTED, SAVE IN DREAMS?

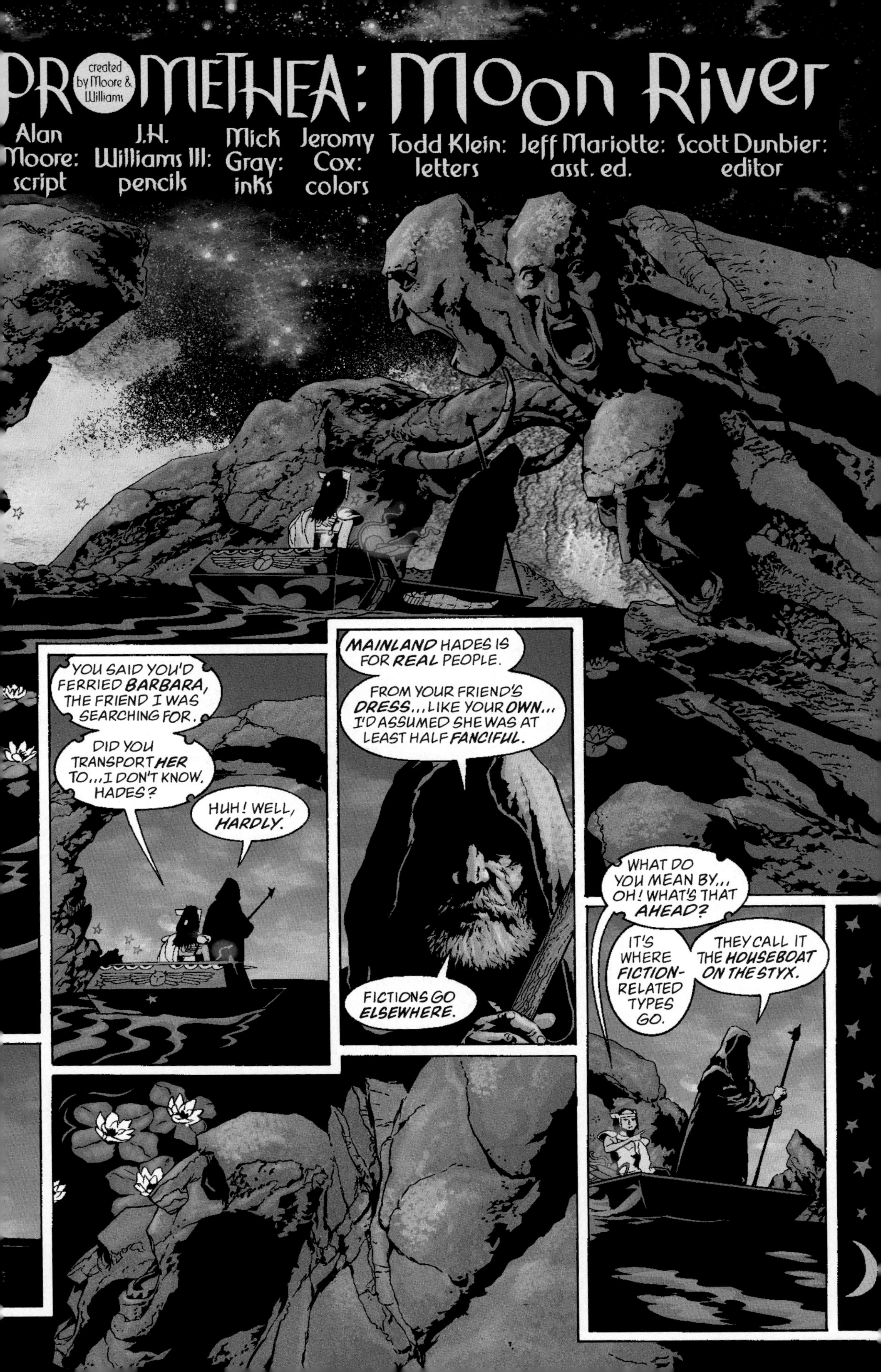
PROMETHEA: Moon River
created by Moore & Williams
Alan Moore: script
J.H. Williams III: pencils
Mick Gray: inks
Jeromy Cox: colors
Todd Klein: letters
Jeff Mariotte: asst. ed.
Scott Dunbier: editor
YOU SAID YOU'D FERRIED BARBARA, THE FRIEND I WAS SEARCHING FOR.
DID YOU TRANSPORT HER TO... I DON'T KNOW. HADES?
HUH! WELL, HARDLY.
MAINLAND HADES IS FOR REAL PEOPLE.
FROM YOUR FRIEND'S DRESS... LIKE YOUR OWN... I'D ASSUMED SHE WAS AT LEAST HALF FANCIFUL.
FICTIONS GO ELSEWHERE.
WHAT DO YOU MEAN BY... OH! WHAT'S THAT AHEAD?
IT'S WHERE FICTION-RELATED TYPES GO.
THEY CALL IT THE HOUSEBOAT ON THE STYX.

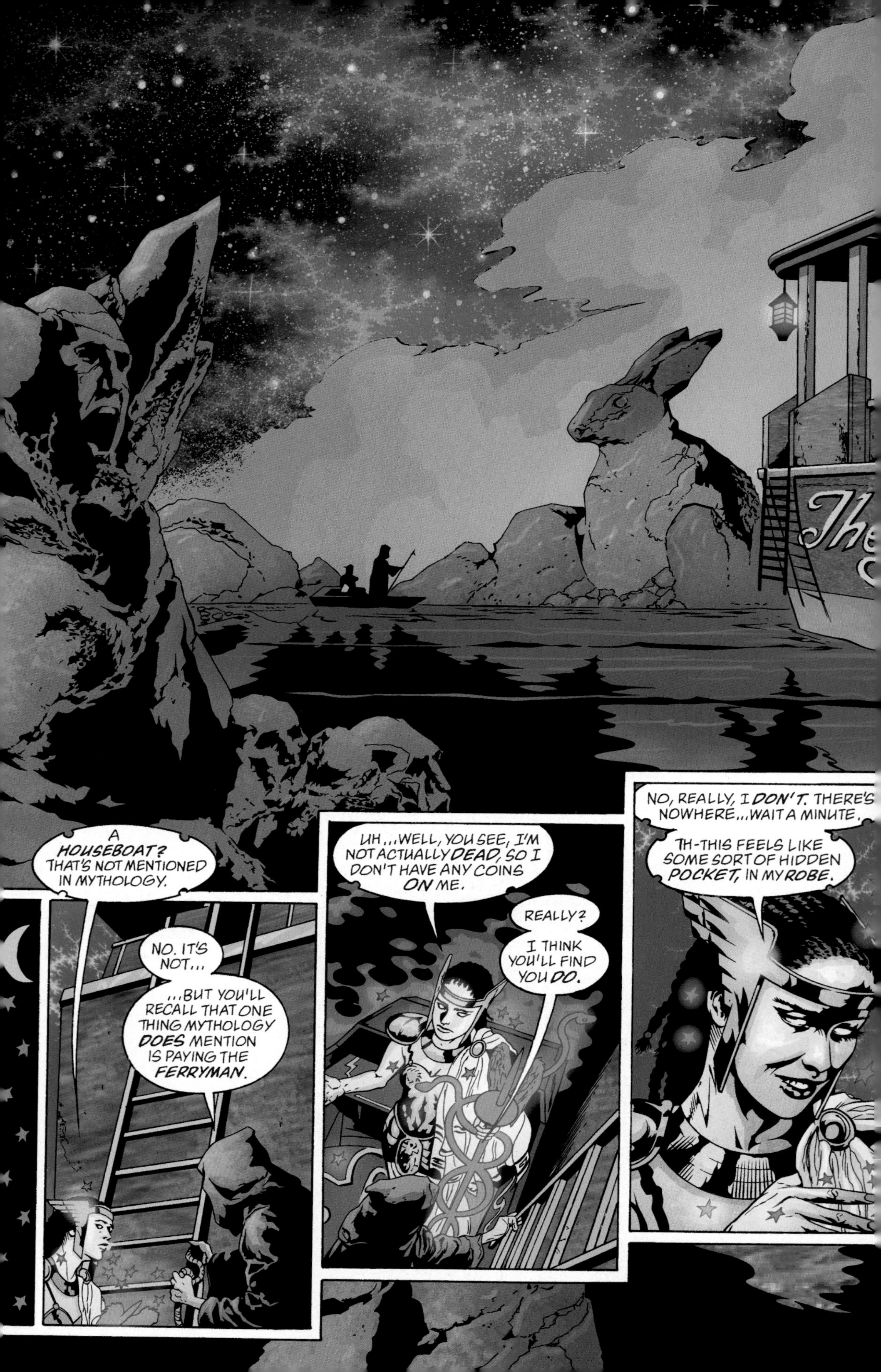

A HOUSEBOAT? THAT'S NOT MENTIONED IN MYTHOLOGY.
NO. IT'S NOT...
...BUT YOU'LL RECALL THAT ONE THING MYTHOLOGY DOES MENTION IS PAYING THE FERRYMAN.
UH...WELL, YOU SEE, I'M NOT ACTUALLY DEAD, SO I DON'T HAVE ANY COINS ON ME.
REALLY?
I THINK YOU'LL FIND YOU DO.
NO, REALLY, I DON'T. THERE'S NOWHERE...WAIT A MINUTE.
TH-THIS FEELS LIKE SOME SORT OF HIDDEN POCKET, IN MY ROBE.

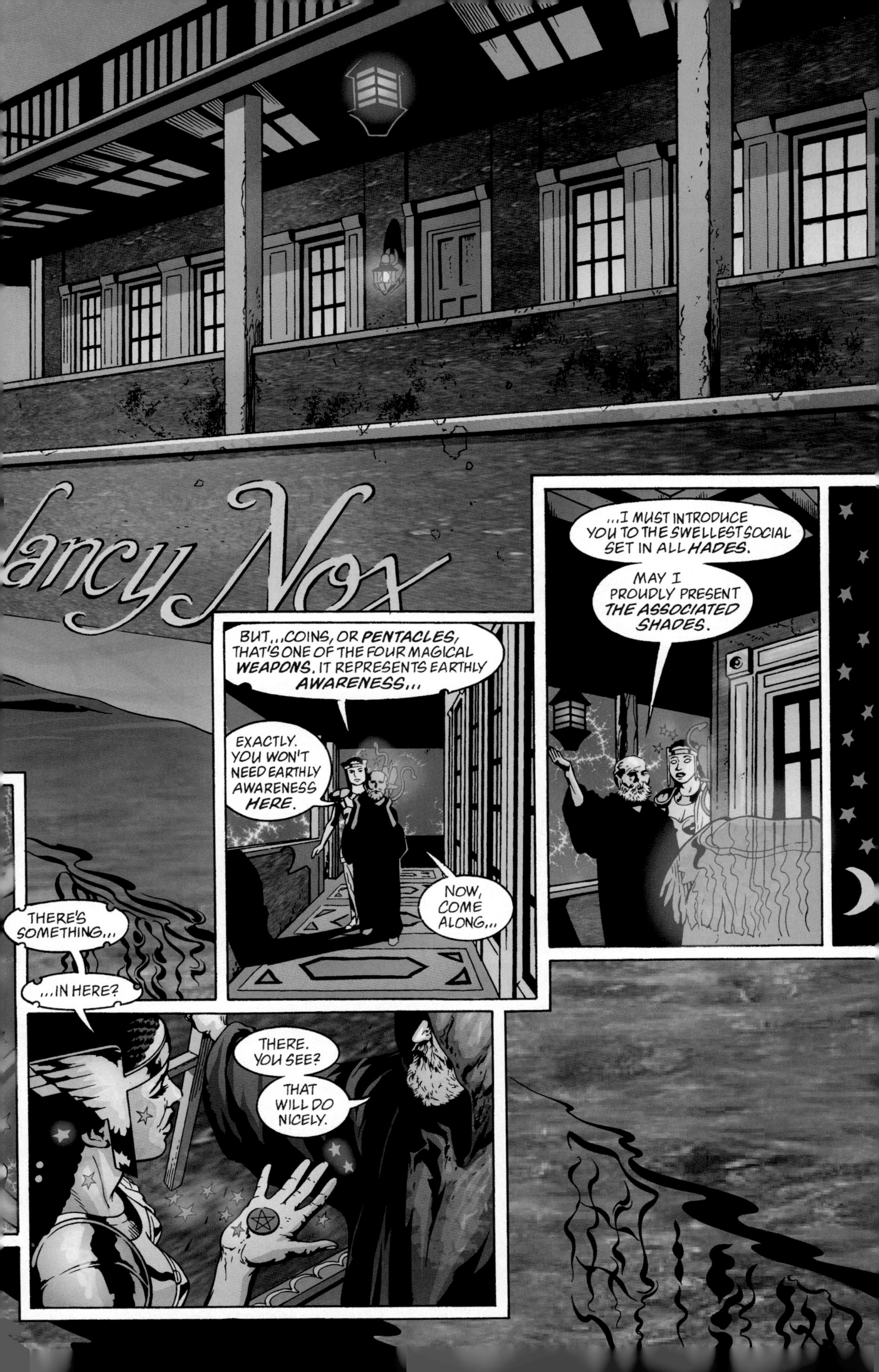
lancy Nox
BUT...COINS, OR PENTACLES, THAT'S ONE OF THE FOUR MAGICAL WEAPONS. IT REPRESENTS EARTHLY AWARENESS...
EXACTLY. YOU WON'T NEED EARTHLY AWARENESS HERE.
NOW, COME ALONG...
...I MUST INTRODUCE YOU TO THE SWELLEST SOCIAL SET IN ALL HADES.
MAY I PROUDLY PRESENT THE ASSOCIATED SHADES.
THERE'S SOMETHING...
...IN HERE?
THERE. YOU SEE?
THAT WILL DO NICELY.

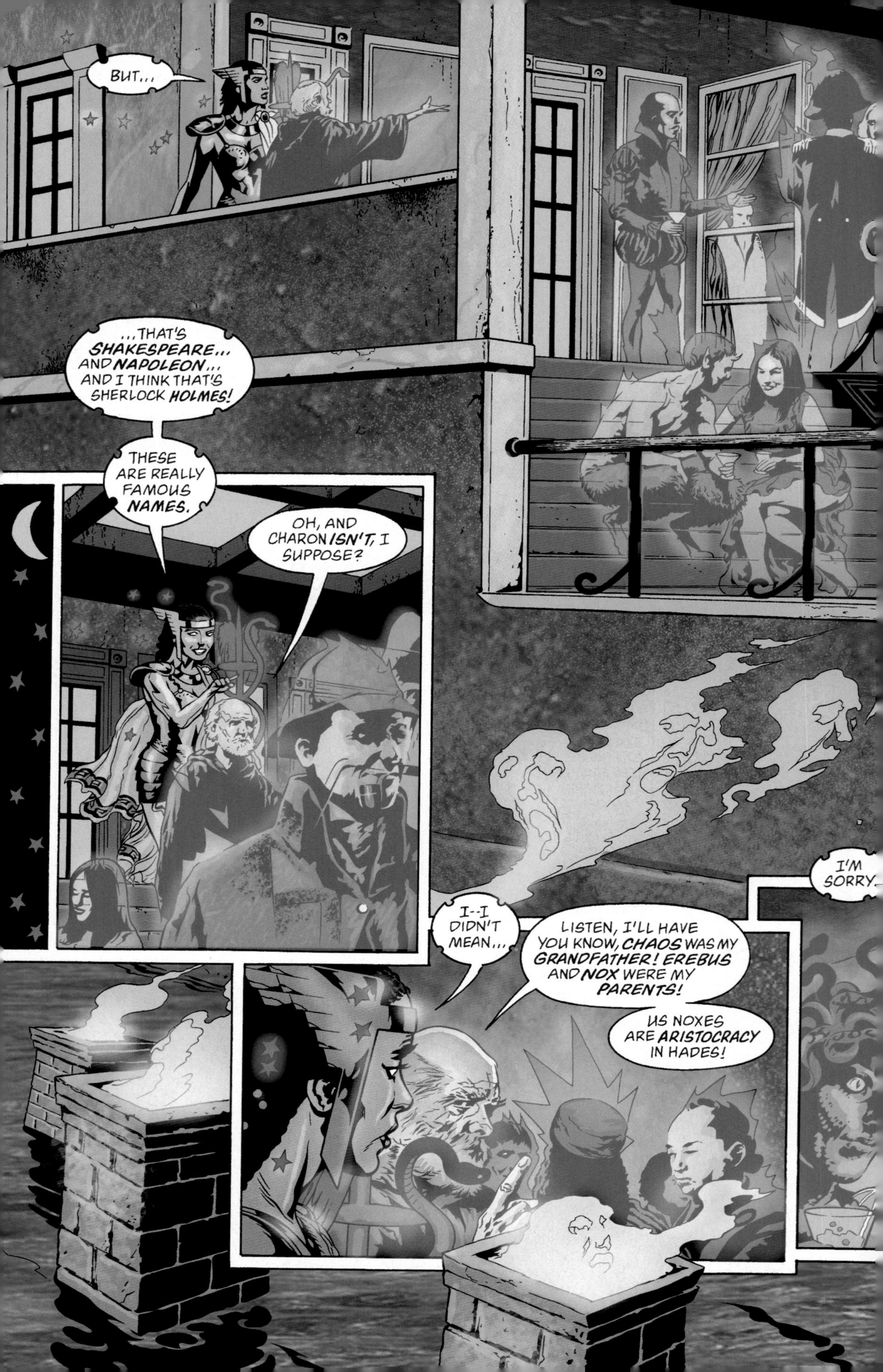
BUT...
...THAT'S SHAKESPEARE... AND NAPOLEON... AND I THINK THAT'S SHERLOCK HOLMES!
THESE ARE REALLY FAMOUS NAMES.
OH, AND CHARON ISN'T, I SUPPOSE?
I'M SORRY.
I--I DIDN'T MEAN...
LISTEN, I'LL HAVE YOU KNOW, CHAOS WAS MY GRANDFATHER! EREBUS AND NOX WERE MY PARENTS!
US NOXES ARE ARISTOCRACY IN HADES!

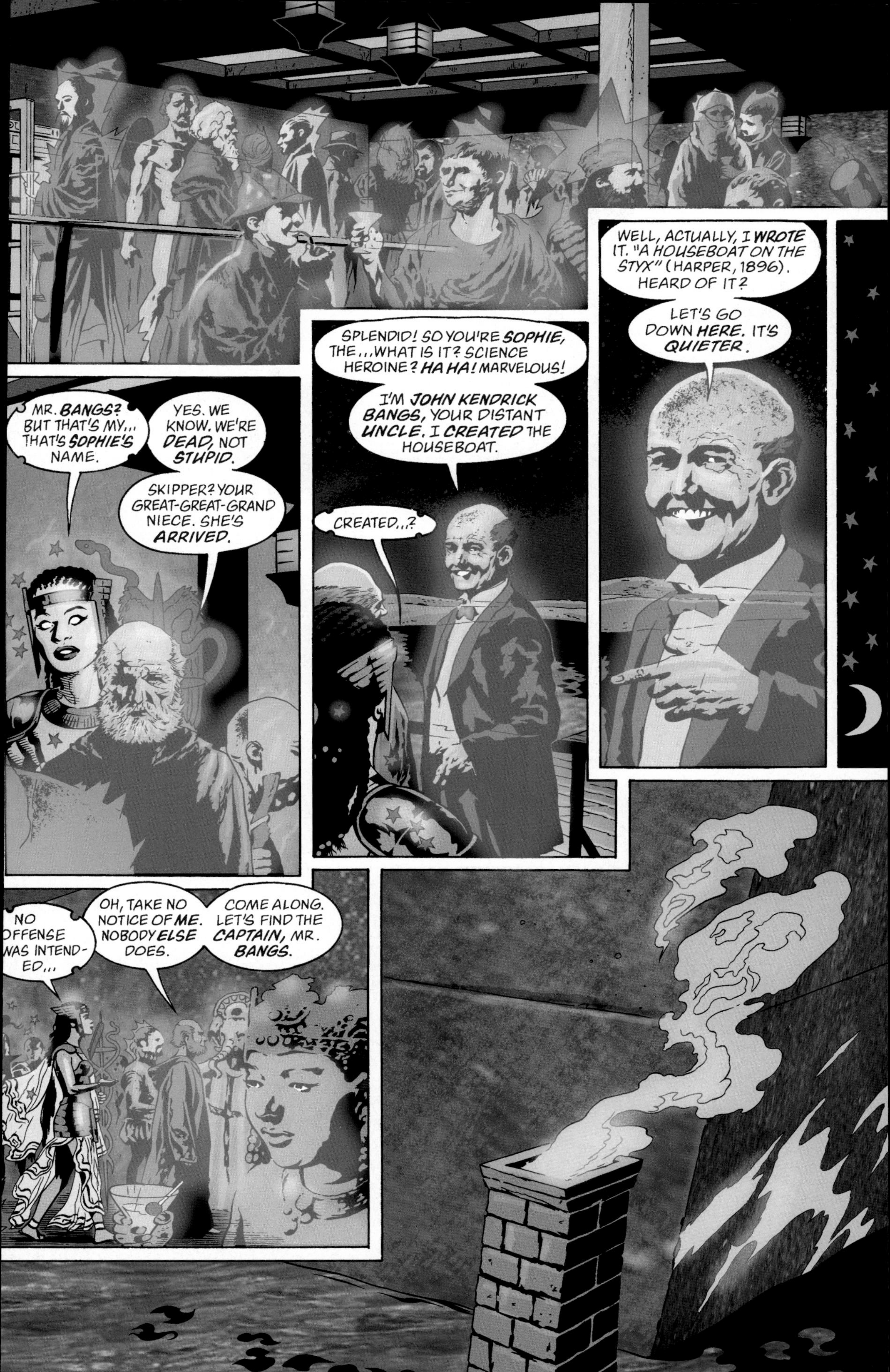
MR. BANGS? BUT THAT'S MY... THAT'S SOPHIE'S NAME.
YES. WE KNOW. WE'RE DEAD, NOT STUPID.
SKIPPER? YOUR GREAT-GREAT-GRAND NIECE. SHE'S ARRIVED.
SPLENDID! SO YOU'RE SOPHIE, THE... WHAT IS IT? SCIENCE HEROINE? HA HA! MARVELOUS!
I'M JOHN KENDRICK BANGS, YOUR DISTANT UNCLE. I CREATED THE HOUSEBOAT.
CREATED...?
WELL, ACTUALLY, I WROTE IT. "A HOUSEBOAT ON THE STYX" (HARPER, 1896). HEARD OF IT?
LET'S GO DOWN HERE. IT'S QUIETER.
NO OFFENSE WAS INTENDED...
OH, TAKE NO NOTICE OF ME. NOBODY ELSE DOES.
COME ALONG. LET'S FIND THE CAPTAIN, MR. BANGS.

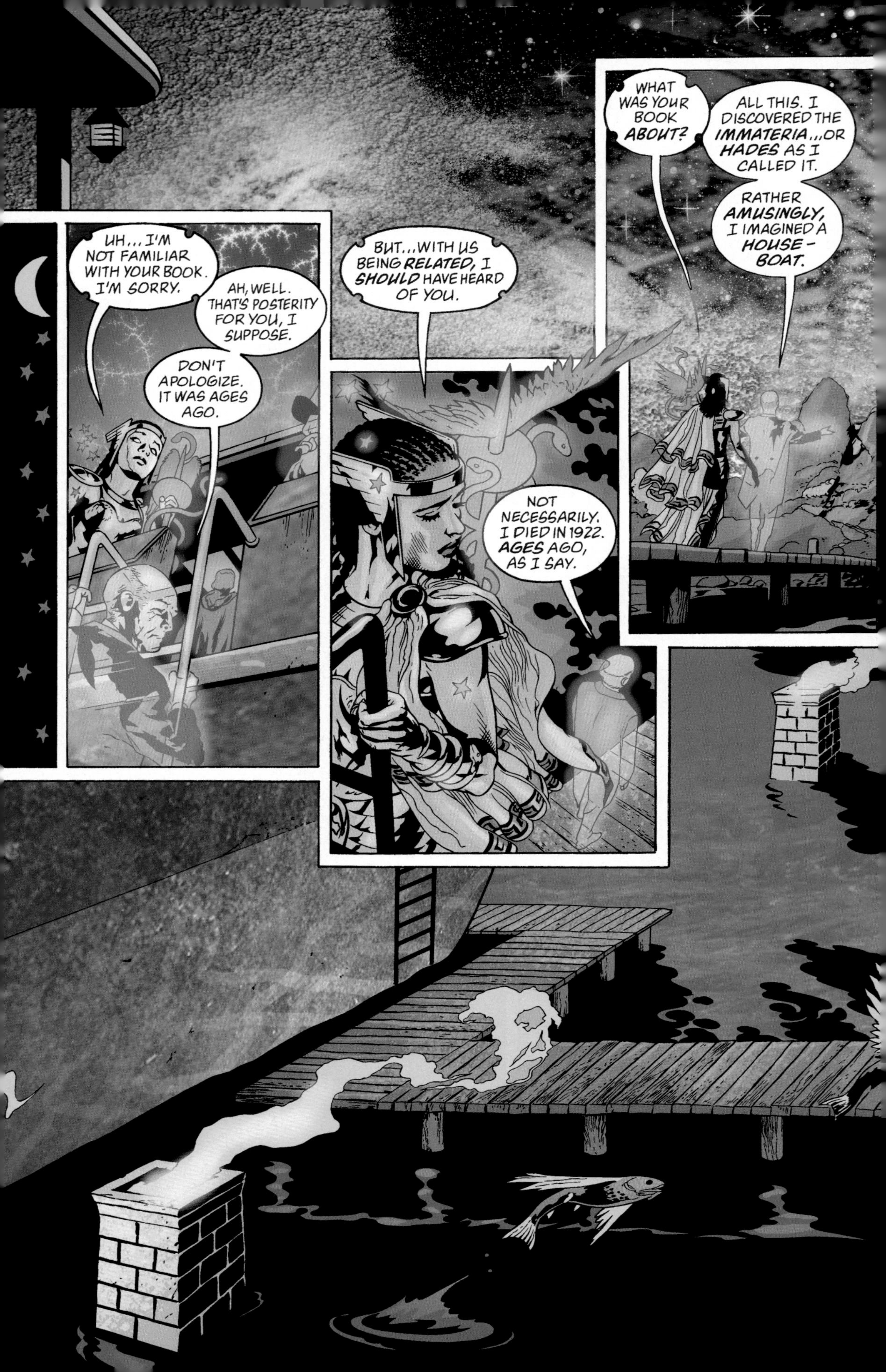
WHAT WAS YOUR BOOK ABOUT?
ALL THIS. I DISCOVERED THE IMMATERIA...OR HADES AS I CALLED IT.
RATHER AMUSINGLY, I IMAGINED A HOUSE-BOAT.
UH... I'M NOT FAMILIAR WITH YOUR BOOK. I'M SORRY.
AH, WELL. THAT'S POSTERITY FOR YOU, I SUPPOSE.
DON'T APOLOGIZE. IT WAS AGES AGO.
BUT...WITH US BEING RELATED, I SHOULD HAVE HEARD OF YOU.
NOT NECESSARILY. I DIED IN 1922. AGES AGO, AS I SAY.

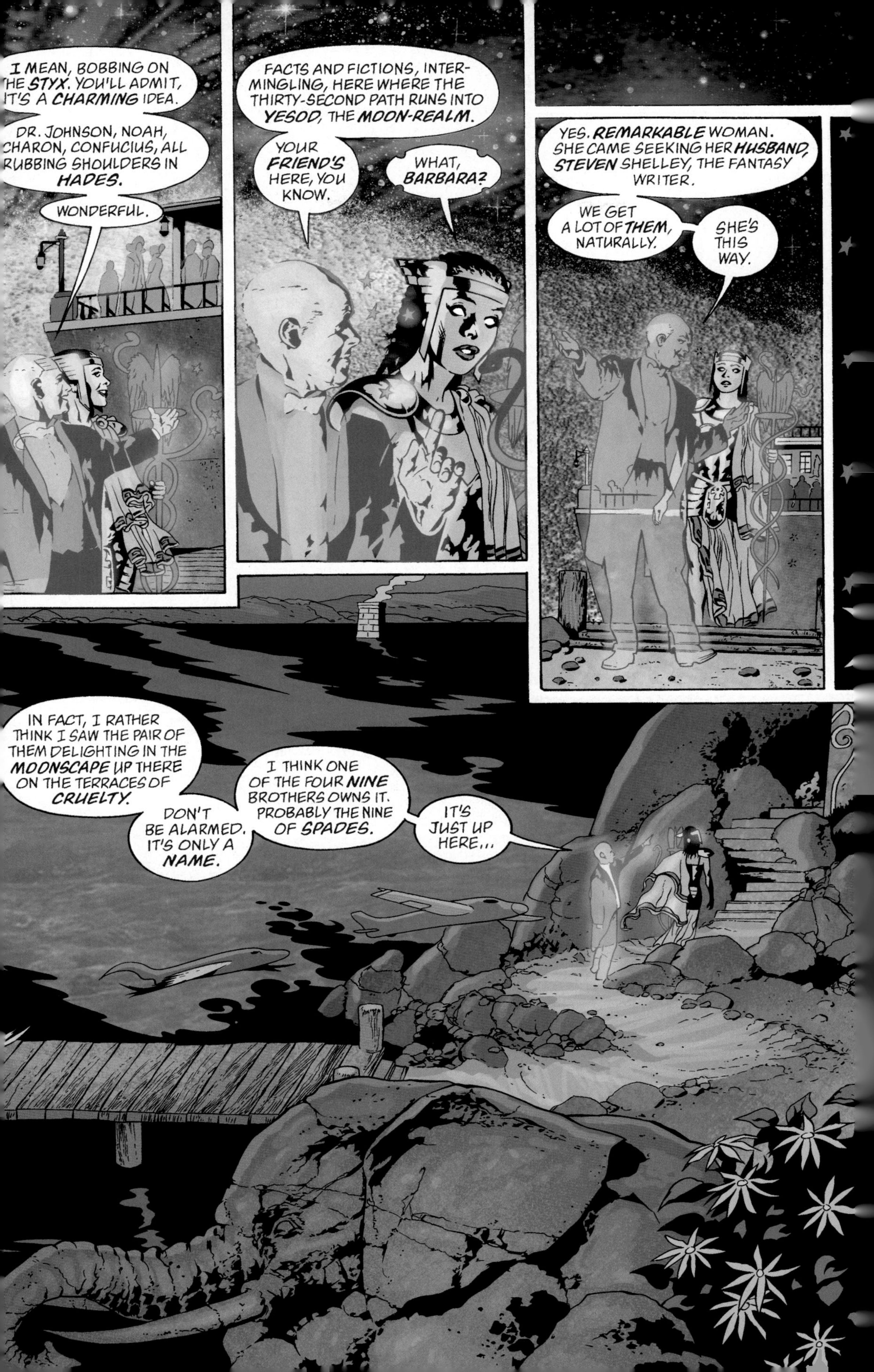
I MEAN, BOBBING ON THE STYX. YOU'LL ADMIT, IT'S A CHARMING IDEA.
DR. JOHNSON, NOAH, CHARON, CONFUCIUS, ALL RUBBING SHOULDERS IN HADES.
WONDERFUL.
FACTS AND FICTIONS, INTER-MINGLING, HERE WHERE THE THIRTY-SECOND PATH RUNS INTO YESOD, THE MOON-REALM.
YOUR FRIEND'S HERE, YOU KNOW.
WHAT, BARBARA?
YES. REMARKABLE WOMAN. SHE CAME SEEKING HER HUSBAND, STEVEN SHELLEY, THE FANTASY WRITER.
WE GET A LOT OF THEM, NATURALLY.
SHE'S THIS WAY.
IN FACT, I RATHER THINK I SAW THE PAIR OF THEM DELIGHTING IN THE MOONSCAPE UP THERE ON THE TERRACES OF CRUELTY.
DON'T BE ALARMED. IT'S ONLY A NAME.
I THINK ONE OF THE FOUR NINE BROTHERS OWNS IT. PROBABLY THE NINE OF SPADES.
IT'S JUST UP HERE...

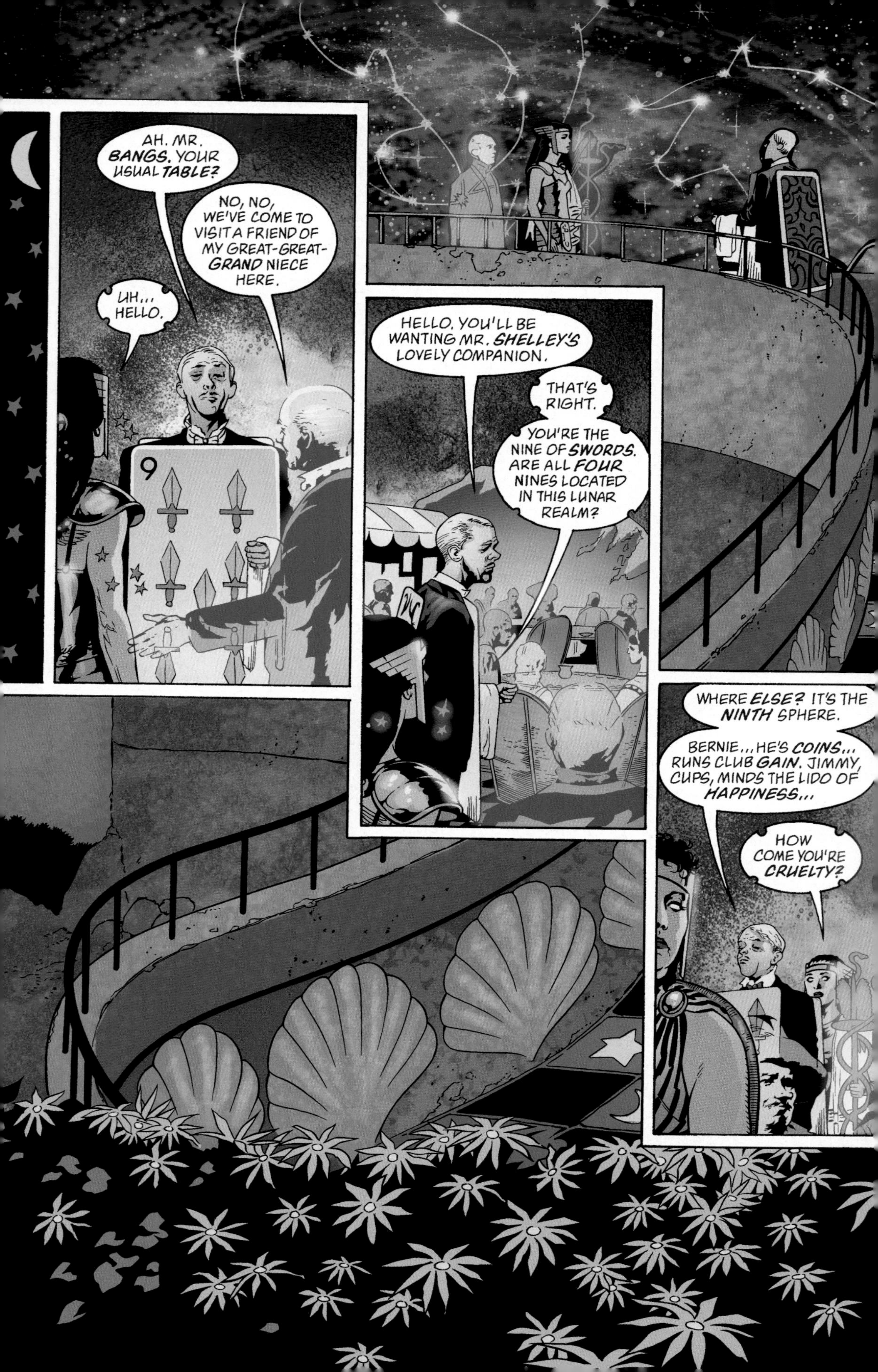

AH. MR. BANGS. YOUR USUAL TABLE?
NO, NO, WE'VE COME TO VISIT A FRIEND OF MY GREAT-GREAT-GRAND NIECE HERE.
UH... HELLO.
9
HELLO. YOU'LL BE WANTING MR. SHELLEY'S LOVELY COMPANION.
THAT'S RIGHT.
YOU'RE THE NINE OF SWORDS. ARE ALL FOUR NINES LOCATED IN THIS LUNAR REALM?
WHERE ELSE? IT'S THE NINTH SPHERE.
BERNIE... HE'S COINS... RUNS CLUB GAIN. JIMMY, CUPS, MINDS THE LIDO OF HAPPINESS...
HOW COME YOU'RE CRUELTY?

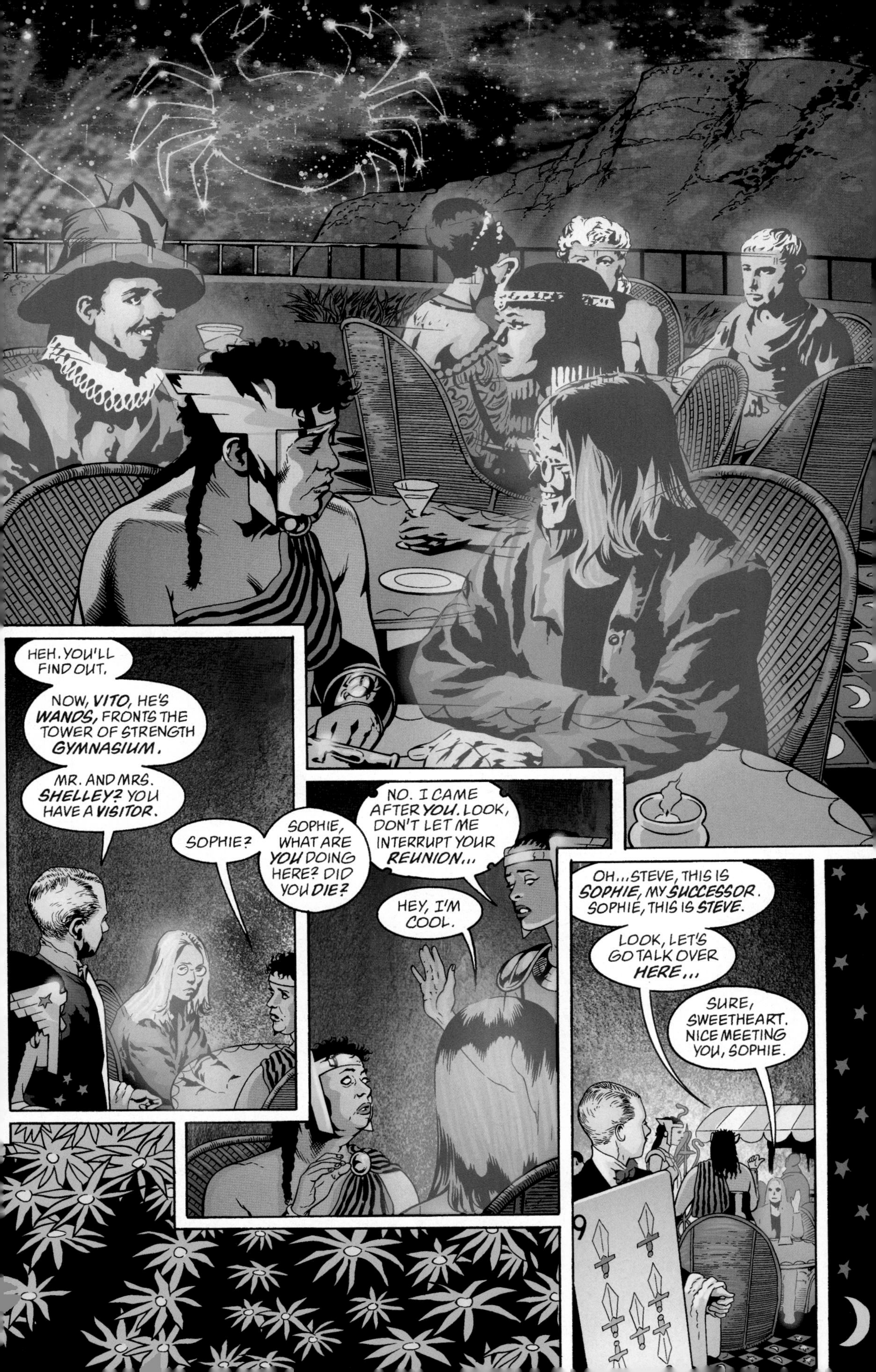

HEH. YOU'LL FIND OUT.
NOW, VITO, HE'S WANDS, FRONTS THE TOWER OF STRENGTH GYMNASIUM.
MR. AND MRS. SHELLEY? YOU HAVE A VISITOR.
SOPHIE?
SOPHIE, WHAT ARE YOU DOING HERE? DID YOU DIE?
NO. I CAME AFTER YOU. LOOK, DON'T LET ME INTERRUPT YOUR REUNION...
HEY, I'M COOL.
OH...STEVE, THIS IS SOPHIE, MY SUCCESSOR. SOPHIE, THIS IS STEVE.
LOOK, LET'S GO TALK OVER HERE...
SURE, SWEETHEART. NICE MEETING YOU, SOPHIE.

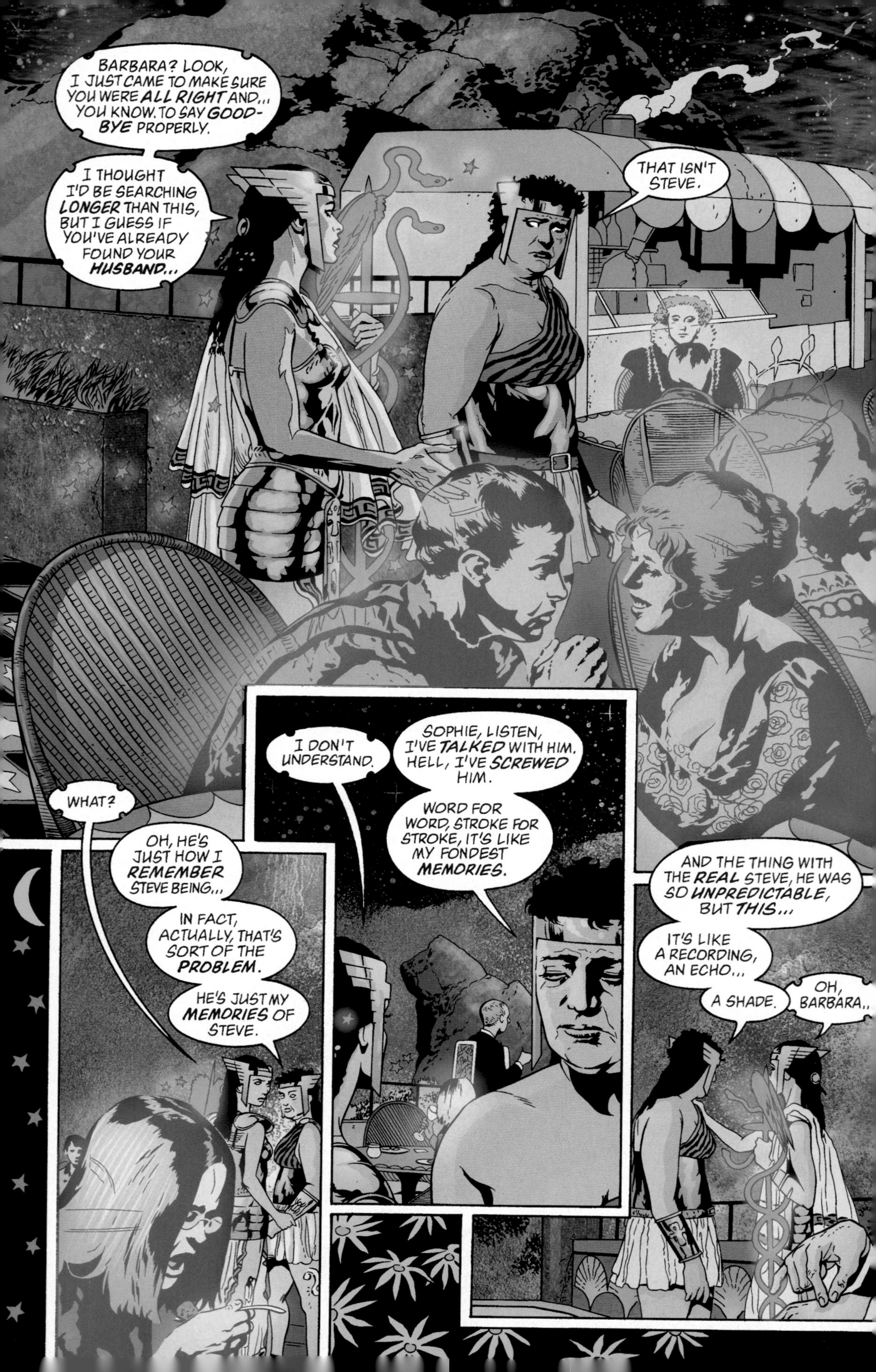
BARBARA? LOOK, I JUST CAME TO MAKE SURE YOU WERE ALL RIGHT AND... YOU KNOW. TO SAY GOOD-BYE PROPERLY.
I THOUGHT I'D BE SEARCHING LONGER THAN THIS, BUT I GUESS IF YOU'VE ALREADY FOUND YOUR HUSBAND...
THAT ISN'T STEVE.
WHAT?
OH, HE'S JUST HOW I REMEMBER STEVE BEING...
IN FACT, ACTUALLY, THAT'S SORT OF THE PROBLEM.
HE'S JUST MY MEMORIES OF STEVE.
I DON'T UNDERSTAND.
SOPHIE, LISTEN, I'VE TALKED WITH HIM. HELL, I'VE SCREWED HIM.
WORD FOR WORD, STROKE FOR STROKE, IT'S LIKE MY FONDEST MEMORIES.
AND THE THING WITH THE REAL STEVE, HE WAS SO UNPREDICTABLE, BUT THIS...
IT'S LIKE A RECORDING, AN ECHO...
A SHADE.
OH, BARBARA...

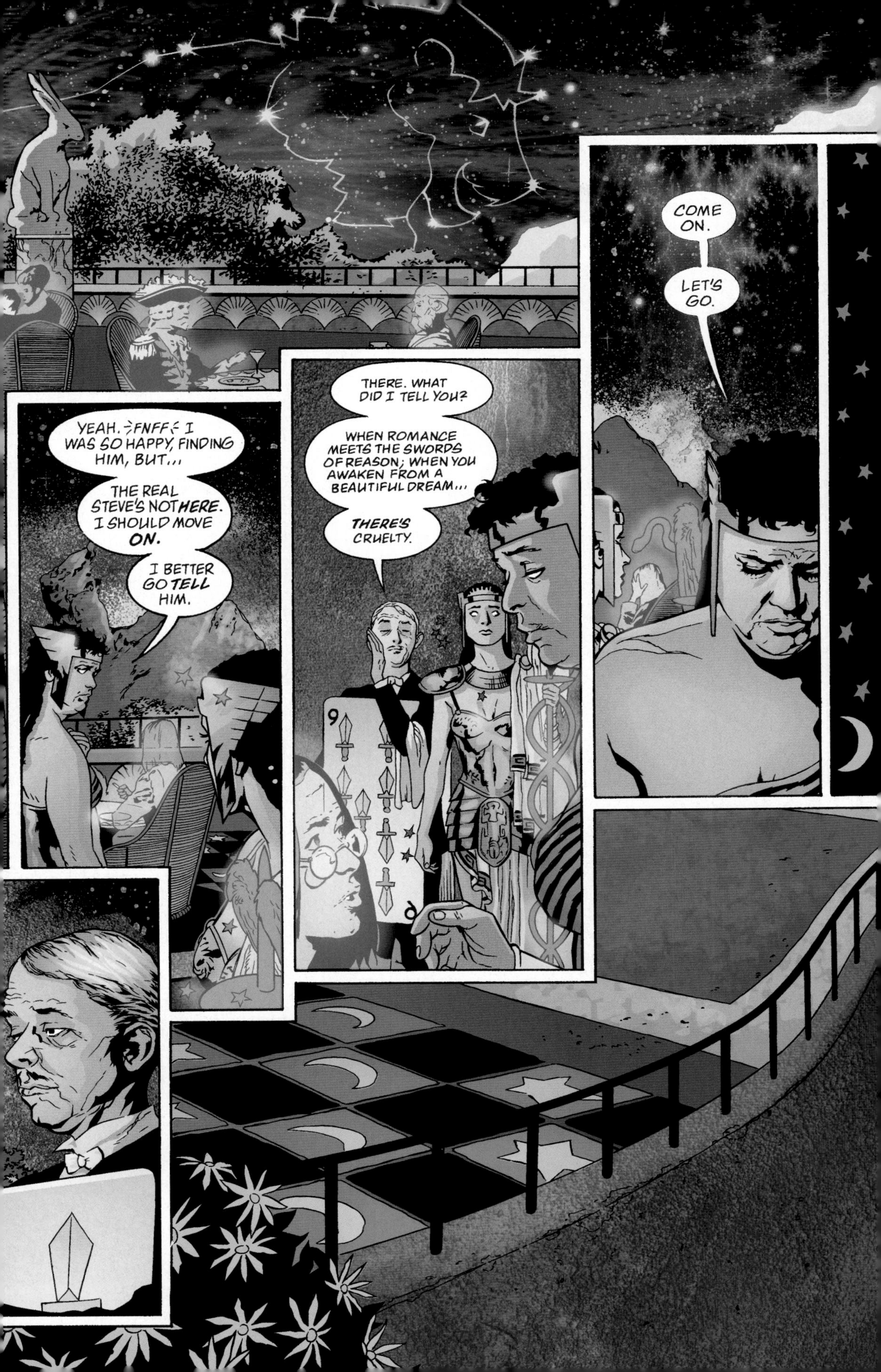
COME ON.
LET'S GO.
YEAH. ≠FNFF≠ I WAS SO HAPPY, FINDING HIM, BUT...
THE REAL STEVE'S NOT **HERE**. I SHOULD MOVE **ON.**
I BETTER GO **TELL** HIM.
THERE. WHAT DID I TELL YOU?
WHEN ROMANCE MEETS THE SWORDS OF REASON; WHEN YOU AWAKEN FROM A BEAUTIFUL DREAM...
THERE'S CRUELTY.

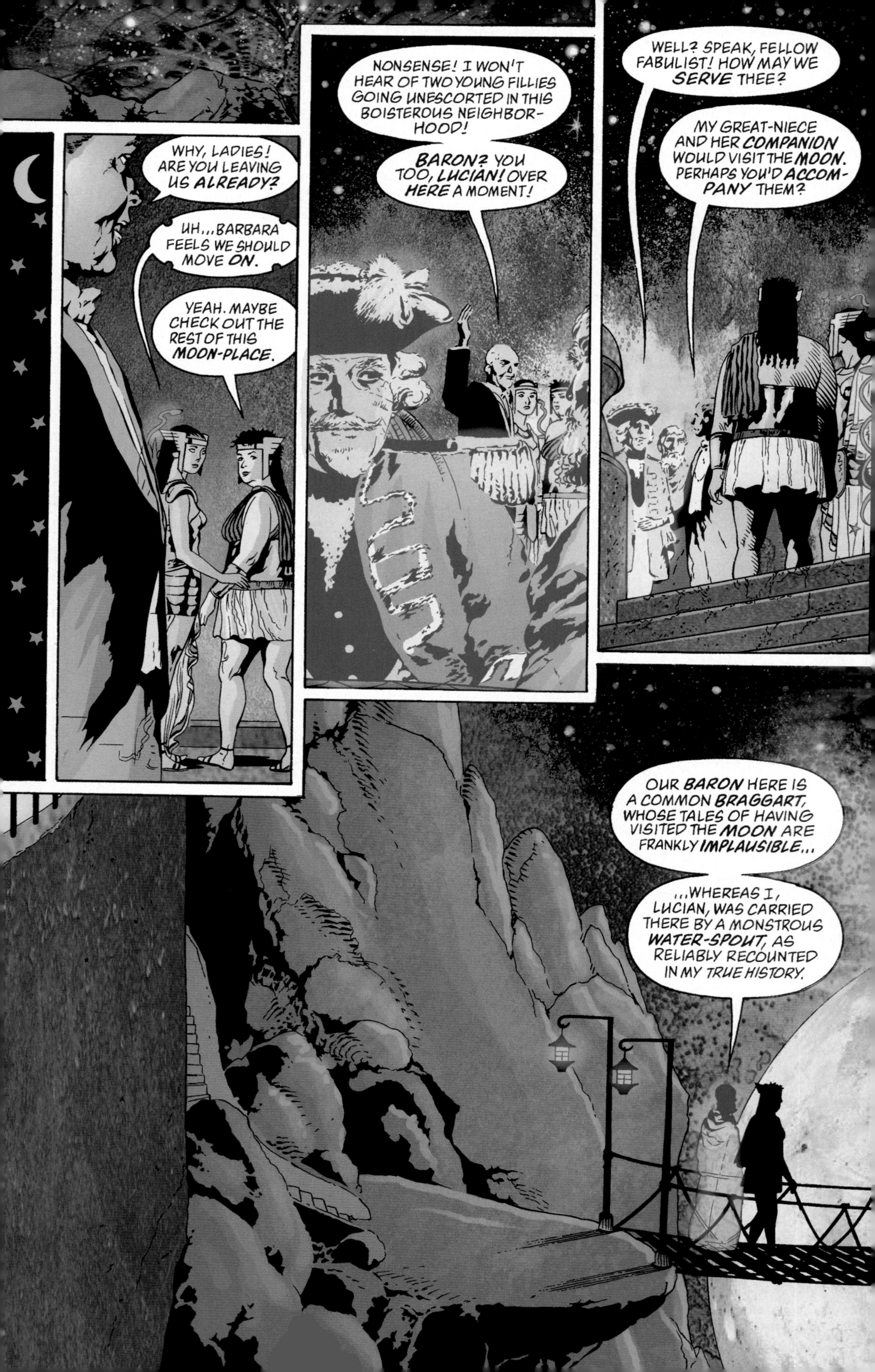
WHY, LADIES! ARE YOU LEAVING US ALREADY?
UH...BARBARA FEELS WE SHOULD MOVE ON.
YEAH. MAYBE CHECK OUT THE REST OF THIS MOON-PLACE.
NONSENSE! I WON'T HEAR OF TWO YOUNG FILLIES GOING UNESCORTED IN THIS BOISTEROUS NEIGHBOR-HOOD!
BARON? YOU TOO, LUCIAN! OVER HERE A MOMENT!
WELL? SPEAK, FELLOW FABULIST! HOW MAY WE SERVE THEE?
MY GREAT-NIECE AND HER COMPANION WOULD VISIT THE MOON. PERHAPS YOU'D ACCOM-PANY THEM?
OUR BARON HERE IS A COMMON BRAGGART, WHOSE TALES OF HAVING VISITED THE MOON ARE FRANKLY IMPLAUSIBLE...
...WHEREAS I, LUCIAN, WAS CARRIED THERE BY A MONSTROUS WATER-SPOUT, AS RELIABLY RECOUNTED IN MY TRUE HISTORY.

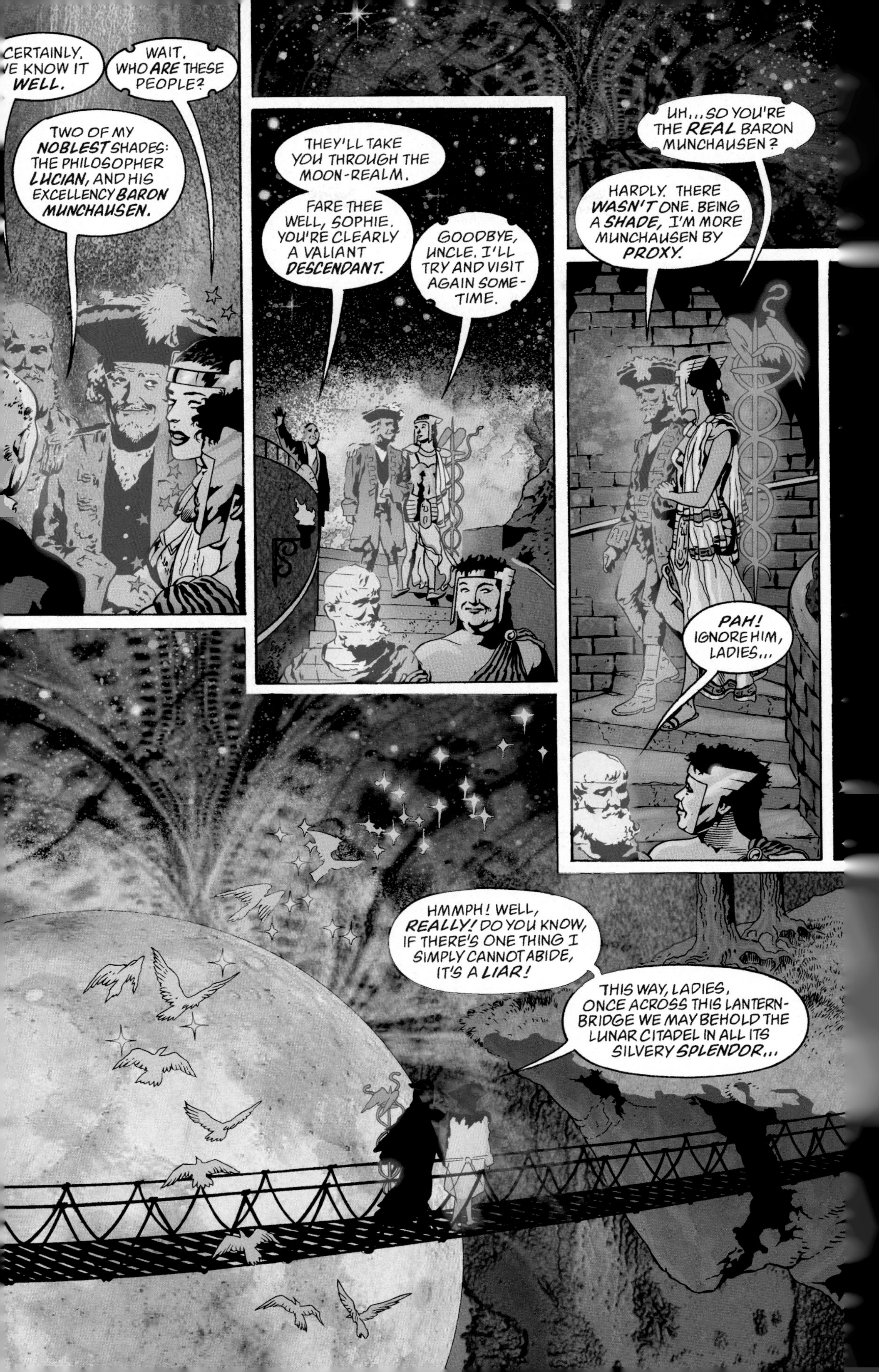
CERTAINLY, WE KNOW IT WELL.
WAIT. WHO ARE THESE PEOPLE?
TWO OF MY NOBLEST SHADES: THE PHILOSOPHER LUCIAN, AND HIS EXCELLENCY BARON MUNCHAUSEN.
THEY'LL TAKE YOU THROUGH THE MOON-REALM.
FARE THEE WELL, SOPHIE. YOU'RE CLEARLY A VALIANT DESCENDANT.
GOODBYE, UNCLE. I'LL TRY AND VISIT AGAIN SOME-TIME.
UH... SO YOU'RE THE REAL BARON MUNCHAUSEN?
HARDLY. THERE WASN'T ONE. BEING A SHADE, I'M MORE MUNCHAUSEN BY PROXY.
PAH! IGNORE HIM, LADIES...
HMMPH! WELL, REALLY! DO YOU KNOW, IF THERE'S ONE THING I SIMPLY CANNOT ABIDE, IT'S A LIAR!
THIS WAY, LADIES, ONCE ACROSS THIS LANTERN-BRIDGE WE MAY BEHOLD THE LUNAR CITADEL IN ALL ITS SILVERY SPLENDOR...

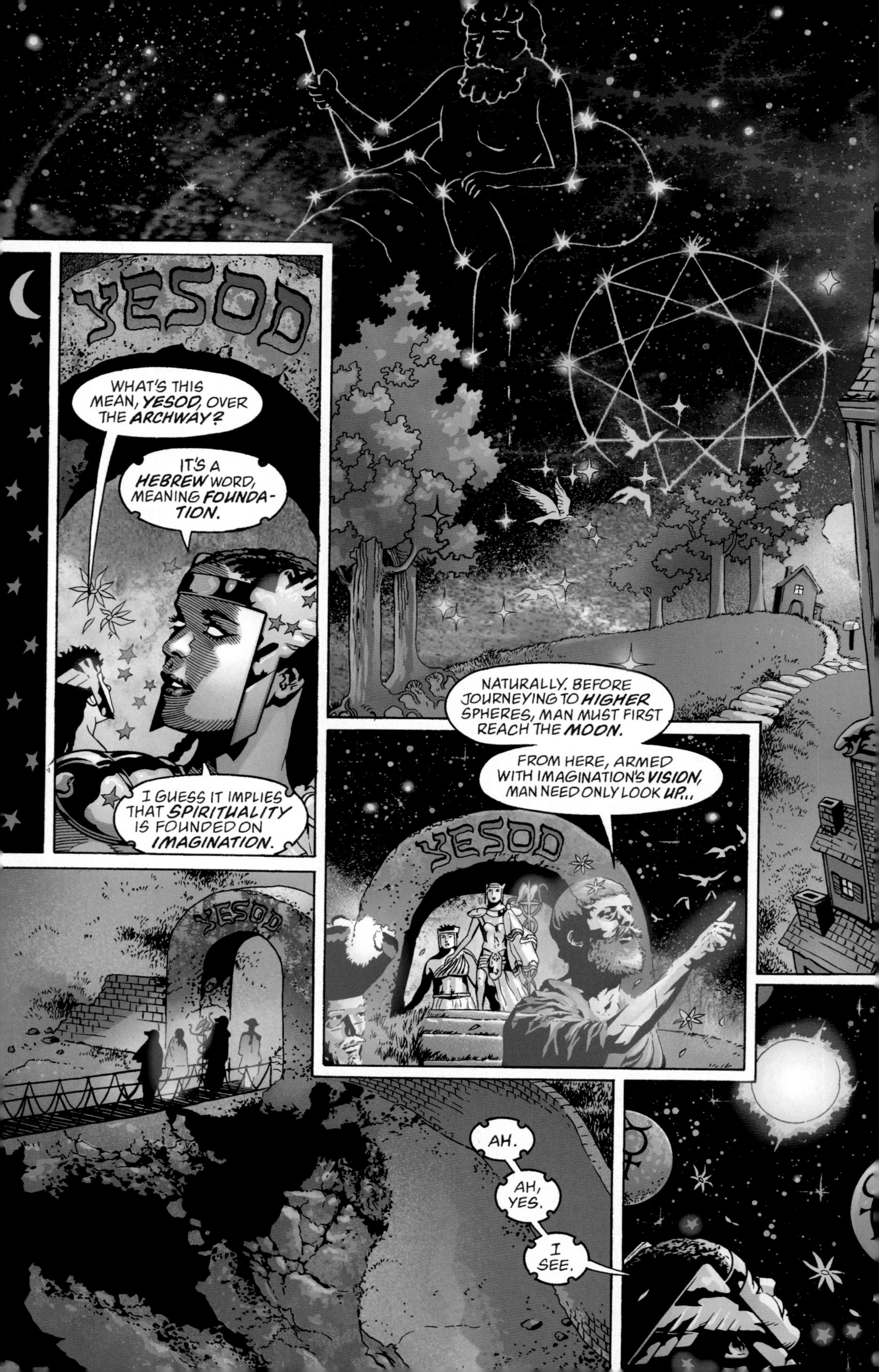
YESOD
WHAT'S THIS MEAN, YESOD, OVER THE ARCHWAY?
IT'S A HEBREW WORD, MEANING FOUNDA-TION.
I GUESS IT IMPLIES THAT SPIRITUALITY IS FOUNDED ON IMAGINATION.
NATURALLY. BEFORE JOURNEYING TO HIGHER SPHERES, MAN MUST FIRST REACH THE MOON.
FROM HERE, ARMED WITH IMAGINATION'S VISION, MAN NEED ONLY LOOK UP...
YESOD
YESOD
AH.
AH, YES.
I SEE.

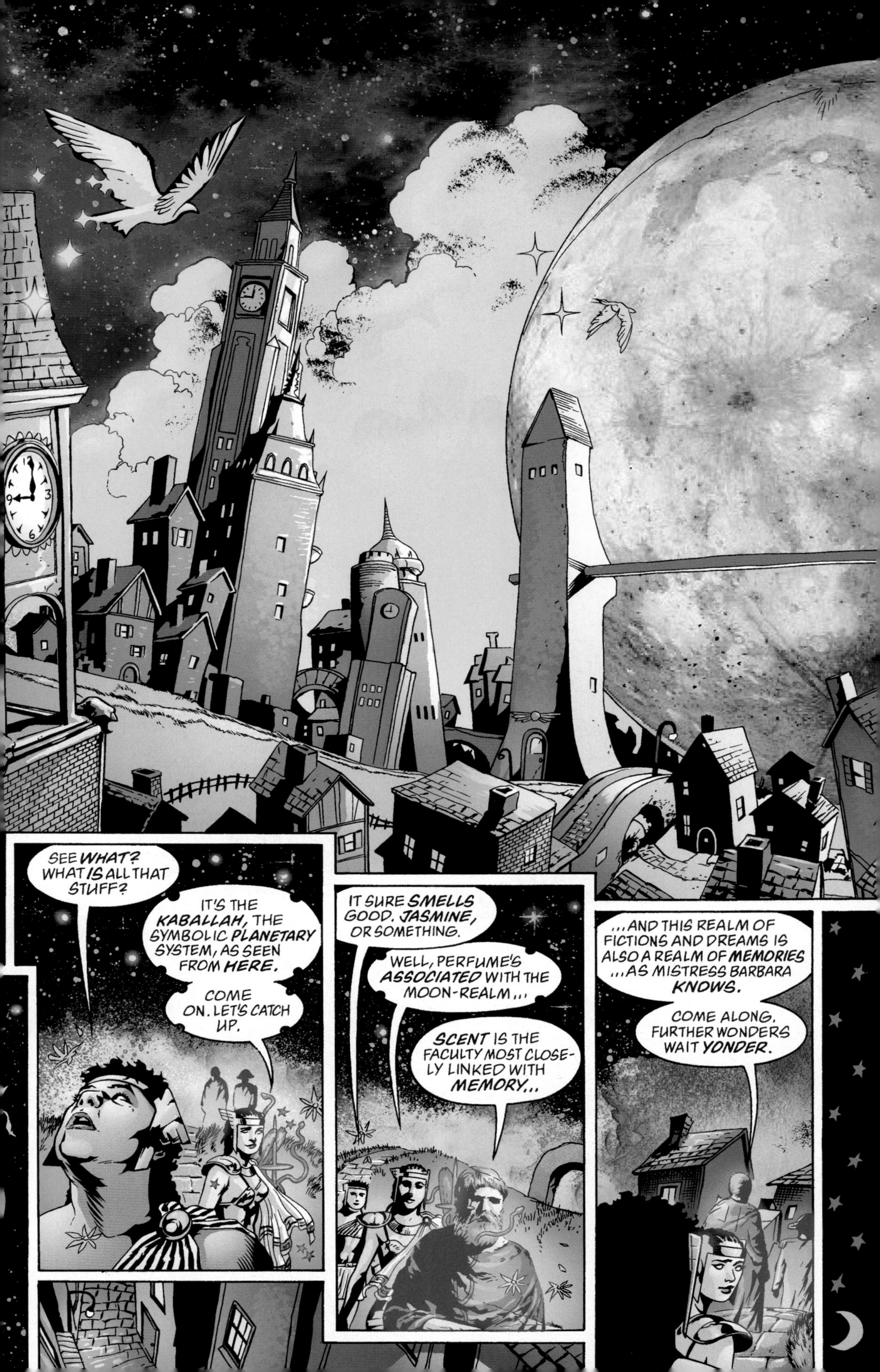
SEE WHAT? WHAT IS ALL THAT STUFF?
IT'S THE KABALLAH, THE SYMBOLIC PLANETARY SYSTEM, AS SEEN FROM HERE.
COME ON. LET'S CATCH UP.
IT SURE SMELLS GOOD. JASMINE, OR SOMETHING.
WELL, PERFUME'S ASSOCIATED WITH THE MOON-REALM...
SCENT IS THE FACULTY MOST CLOSE-LY LINKED WITH MEMORY...
...AND THIS REALM OF FICTIONS AND DREAMS IS ALSO A REALM OF MEMORIES ...AS MISTRESS BARBARA KNOWS.
COME ALONG. FURTHER WONDERS WAIT YONDER.

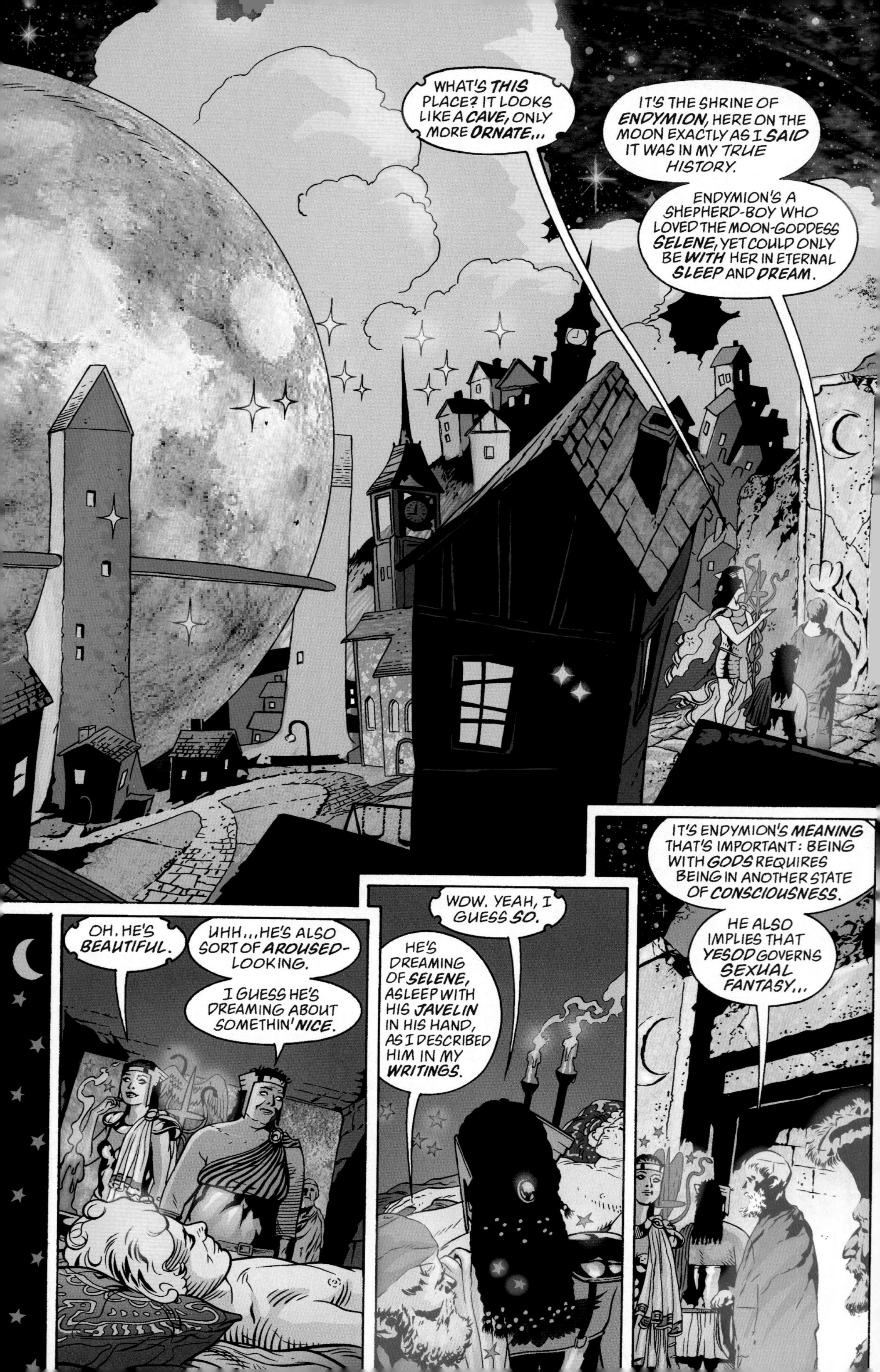
WHAT'S THIS PLACE? IT LOOKS LIKE A CAVE, ONLY MORE ORNATE...
IT'S THE SHRINE OF ENDYMION, HERE ON THE MOON EXACTLY AS I SAID IT WAS IN MY TRUE HISTORY.
ENDYMION'S A SHEPHERD-BOY WHO LOVED THE MOON-GODDESS SELENE, YET COULD ONLY BE WITH HER IN ETERNAL SLEEP AND DREAM.
OH. HE'S BEAUTIFUL.
UHH... HE'S ALSO SORT OF AROUSED-LOOKING.
I GUESS HE'S DREAMING ABOUT SOMETHIN' NICE.
WOW. YEAH, I GUESS SO.
HE'S DREAMING OF SELENE, ASLEEP WITH HIS JAVELIN IN HIS HAND, AS I DESCRIBED HIM IN MY WRITINGS.
IT'S ENDYMION'S MEANING THAT'S IMPORTANT: BEING WITH GODS REQUIRES BEING IN ANOTHER STATE OF CONSCIOUSNESS.
HE ALSO IMPLIES THAT YESOD GOVERNS SEXUAL FANTASY...

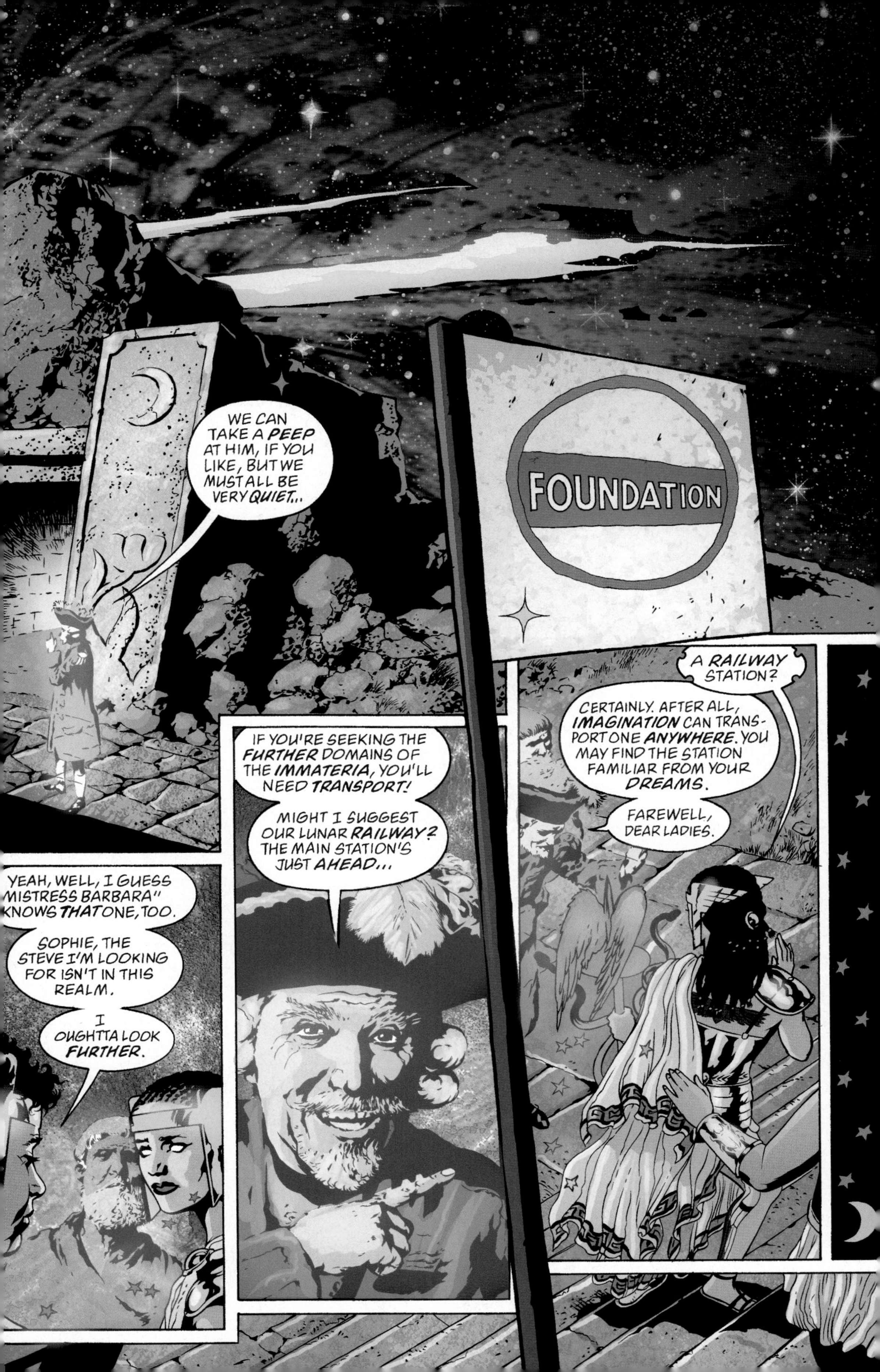
WE CAN TAKE A PEEP AT HIM, IF YOU LIKE, BUT WE MUST ALL BE VERY QUIET...
FOUNDATION
IF YOU'RE SEEKING THE FURTHER DOMAINS OF THE IMMATERIA, YOU'LL NEED TRANSPORT!
MIGHT I SUGGEST OUR LUNAR RAILWAY? THE MAIN STATION'S JUST AHEAD...
A RAILWAY STATION?
CERTAINLY. AFTER ALL, IMAGINATION CAN TRANSPORT ONE ANYWHERE. YOU MAY FIND THE STATION FAMILIAR FROM YOUR DREAMS.
FAREWELL, DEAR LADIES.
YEAH, WELL, I GUESS MISTRESS BARBARA" KNOWS THAT ONE, TOO.
SOPHIE, THE STEVE I'M LOOKING FOR ISN'T IN THIS REALM.
I OUGHTTA LOOK FURTHER.

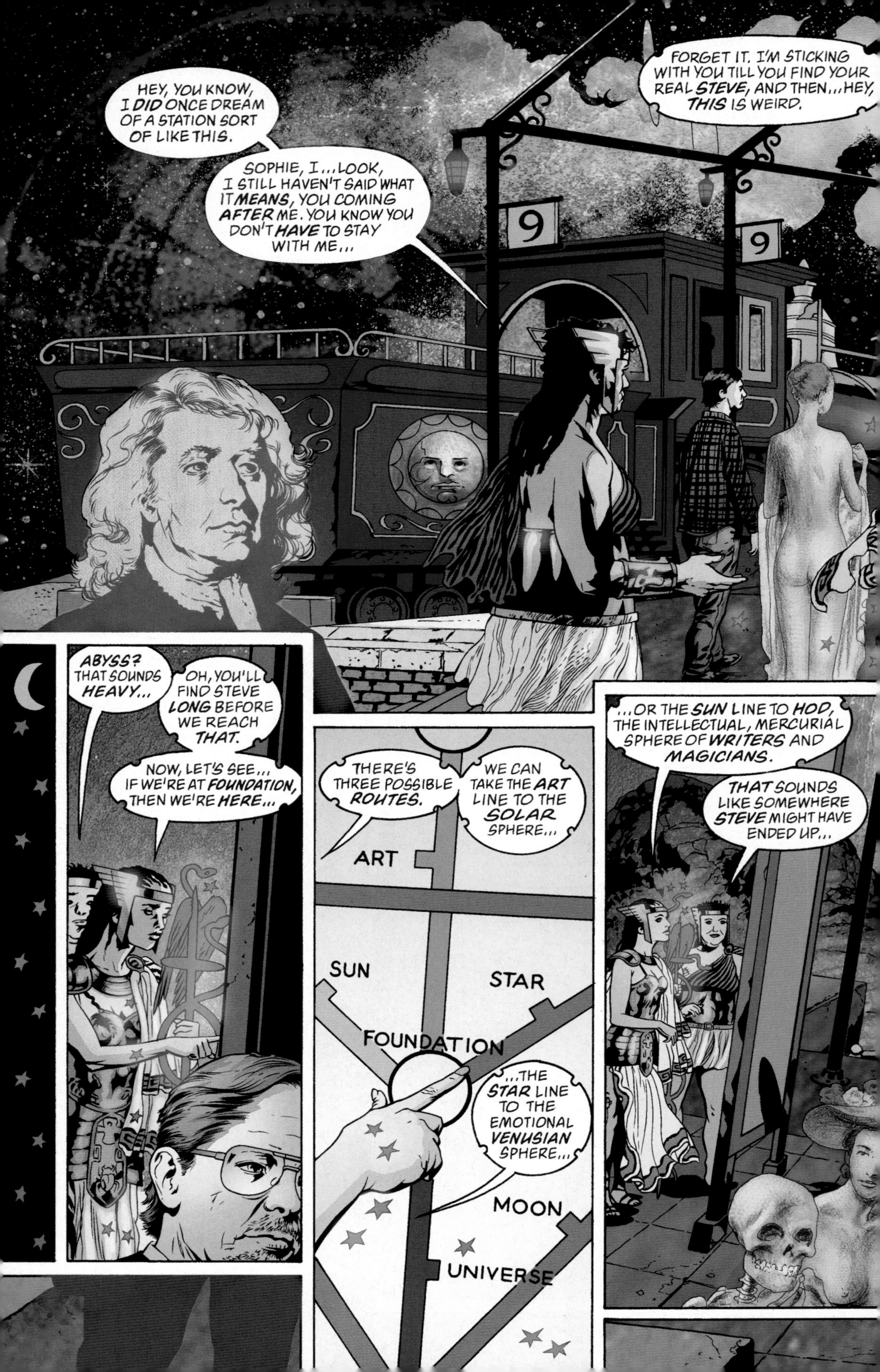
HEY, YOU KNOW, I DID ONCE DREAM OF A STATION SORT OF LIKE THIS.
SOPHIE, I...LOOK, I STILL HAVEN'T SAID WHAT IT MEANS, YOU COMING AFTER ME. YOU KNOW YOU DON'T HAVE TO STAY WITH ME...
FORGET IT. I'M STICKING WITH YOU TILL YOU FIND YOUR REAL STEVE, AND THEN...HEY, THIS IS WEIRD.
9
9
ABYSS? THAT SOUNDS HEAVY...
OH, YOU'LL FIND STEVE LONG BEFORE WE REACH THAT.
NOW, LET'S SEE... IF WE'RE AT FOUNDATION, THEN WE'RE HERE...
THERE'S THREE POSSIBLE ROUTES.
WE CAN TAKE THE ART LINE TO THE SOLAR SPHERE...
ART
SUN
STAR
FOUNDATION
...THE STAR LINE TO THE EMOTIONAL VENUSIAN SPHERE...
MOON
UNIVERSE
...OR THE SUN LINE TO HOD, THE INTELLECTUAL, MERCURIAL SPHERE OF WRITERS AND MAGICIANS.
THAT SOUNDS LIKE SOMEWHERE STEVE MIGHT HAVE ENDED UP...

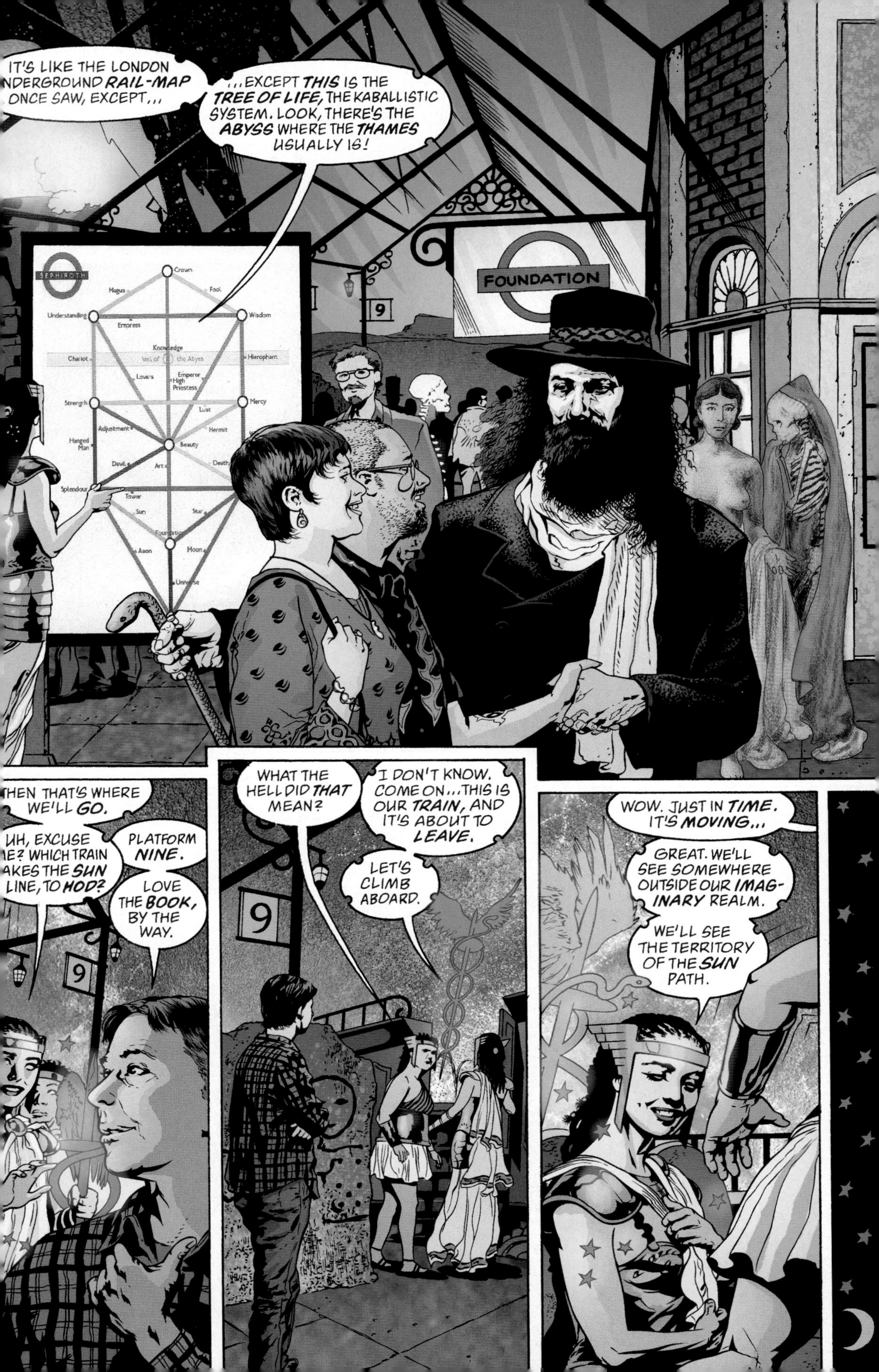
IT'S LIKE THE LONDON NDERGROUND RAIL-MAP ONCE SAW, EXCEPT...
...EXCEPT THIS IS THE TREE OF LIFE, THE KABALLISTIC SYSTEM. LOOK, THERE'S THE ABYSS WHERE THE THAMES USUALLY IS!
SEPHIROTH
Crown
Magus
Fool
Understanding
Wisdom
Empress
Knowledge
Chariot
Veil of the Abyss
Hierophant
Lovers
Emperor
High Priestess
Strength
Mercy
Lust
Adjustment
Hermit
Hanged Man
Beauty
Devil
Art
Death
Splendour
Tower
Sun
Star
Foundation
Aeon
Moon
Universe
FOUNDATION
9
THEN THAT'S WHERE WE'LL GO.
UH, EXCUSE IE? WHICH TRAIN AKES THE SUN LINE, TO HOD?
PLATFORM NINE.
LOVE THE BOOK, BY THE WAY.
9
WHAT THE HELL DID THAT MEAN?
I DON'T KNOW. COME ON... THIS IS OUR TRAIN, AND IT'S ABOUT TO LEAVE.
LET'S CLIMB ABOARD.
9
WOW. JUST IN TIME. IT'S MOVING...
GREAT. WE'LL SEE SOMEWHERE OUTSIDE OUR IMAGINARY REALM.
WE'LL SEE THE TERRITORY OF THE SUN PATH.

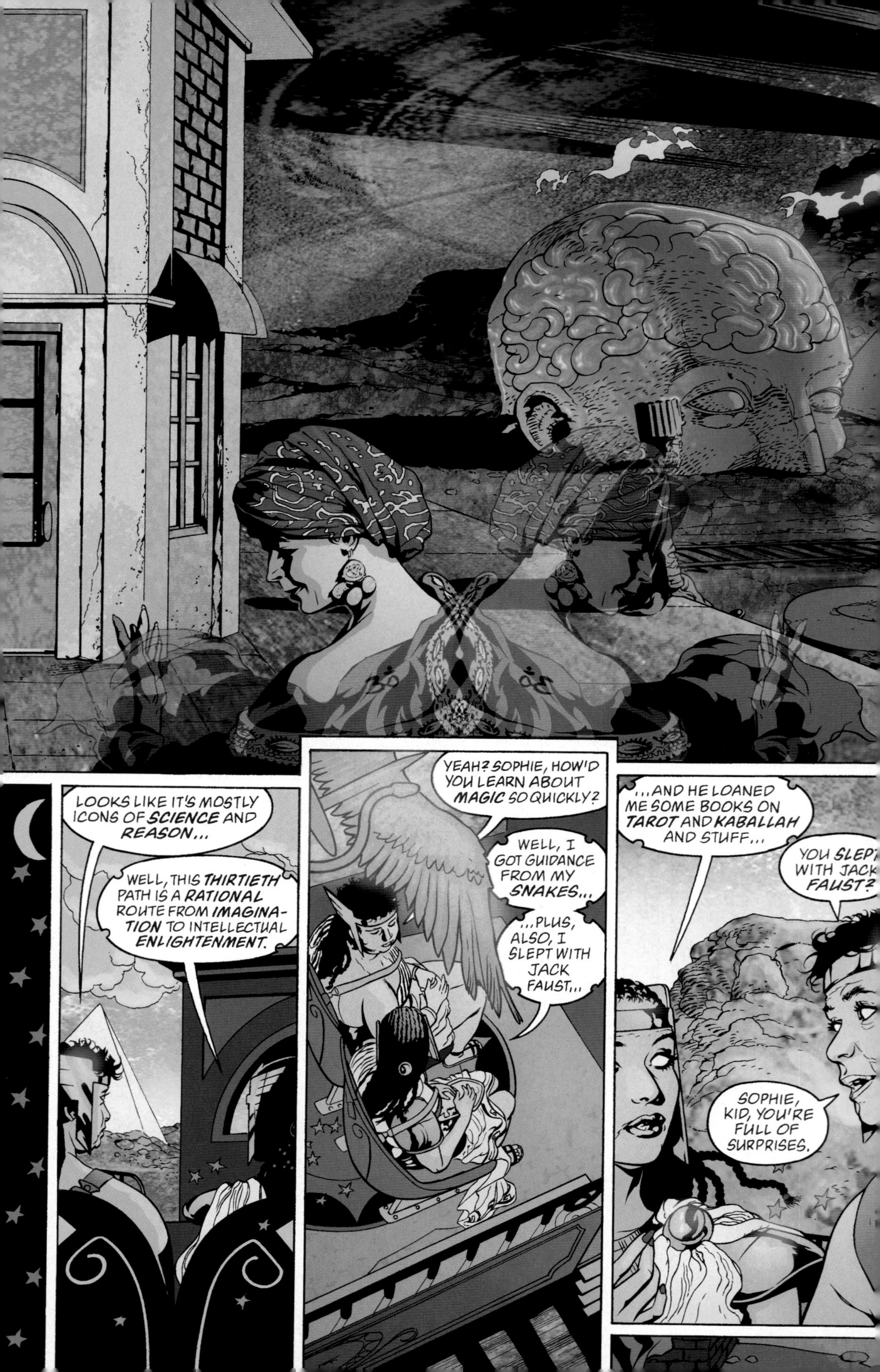
LOOKS LIKE IT'S MOSTLY ICONS OF SCIENCE AND REASON...
WELL, THIS THIRTIETH PATH IS A RATIONAL ROUTE FROM IMAGINATION TO INTELLECTUAL ENLIGHTENMENT.
YEAH? SOPHIE, HOW'D YOU LEARN ABOUT MAGIC SO QUICKLY?
WELL, I GOT GUIDANCE FROM MY SNAKES...
...PLUS, ALSO, I SLEPT WITH JACK FAUST...
...AND HE LOANED ME SOME BOOKS ON TAROT AND KABALLAH AND STUFF...
YOU SLEPT WITH JACK FAUST?
SOPHIE, KID, YOU'RE FULL OF SURPRISES.

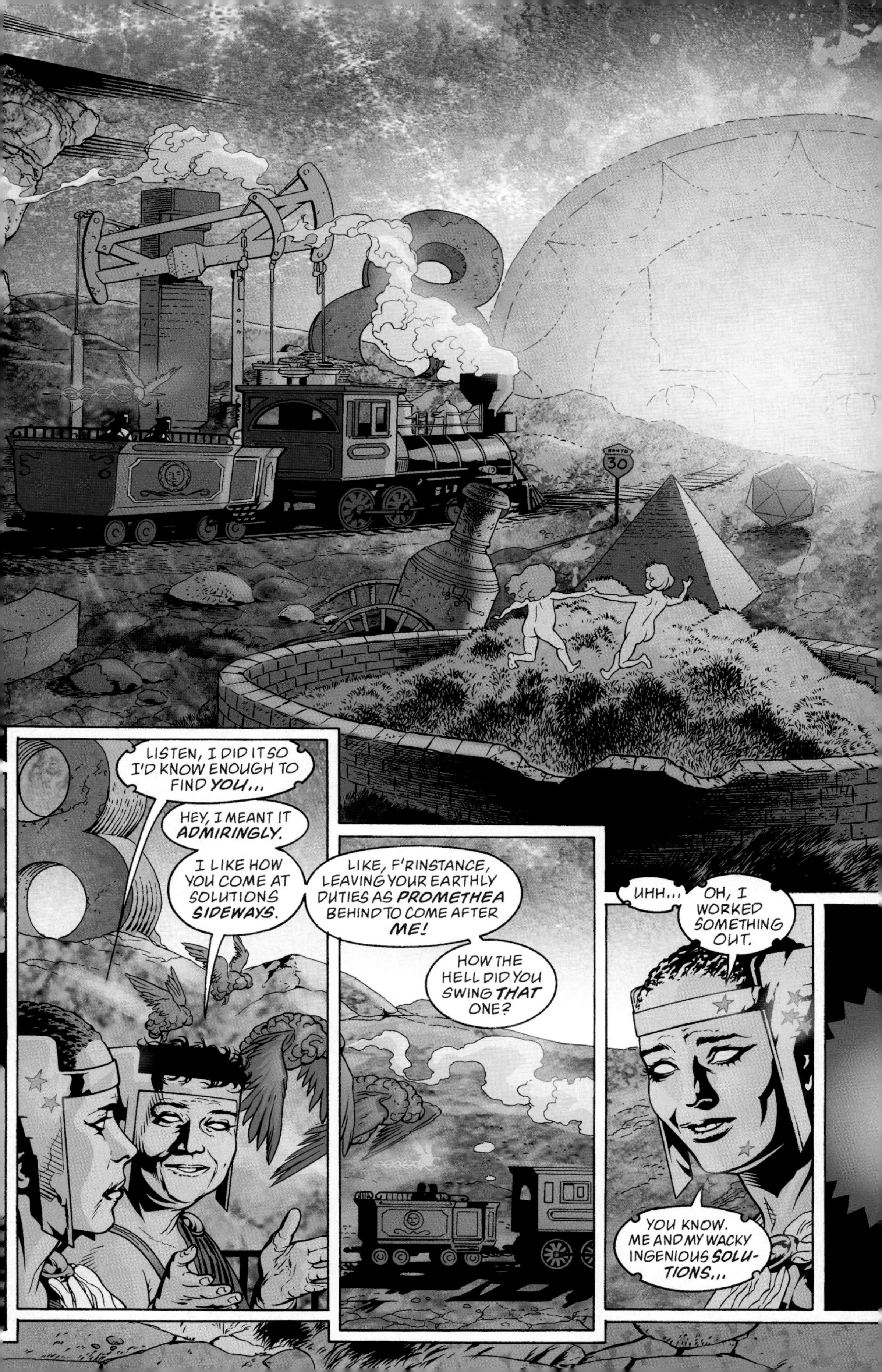

ROUTE
30
LISTEN, I DID IT SO I'D KNOW ENOUGH TO FIND *YOU*...
HEY, I MEANT IT *ADMIRINGLY.*
I LIKE HOW YOU COME AT SOLUTIONS *SIDEWAYS*.
LIKE, F'RINSTANCE, LEAVING YOUR EARTHLY DUTIES AS *PROMETHEA* BEHIND TO COME AFTER *ME!*
HOW THE HELL DID YOU SWING *THAT* ONE?
UHH...
OH, I WORKED SOMETHING OUT.
YOU KNOW. ME AND MY WACKY INGENIOUS *SOLU-TIONS*...

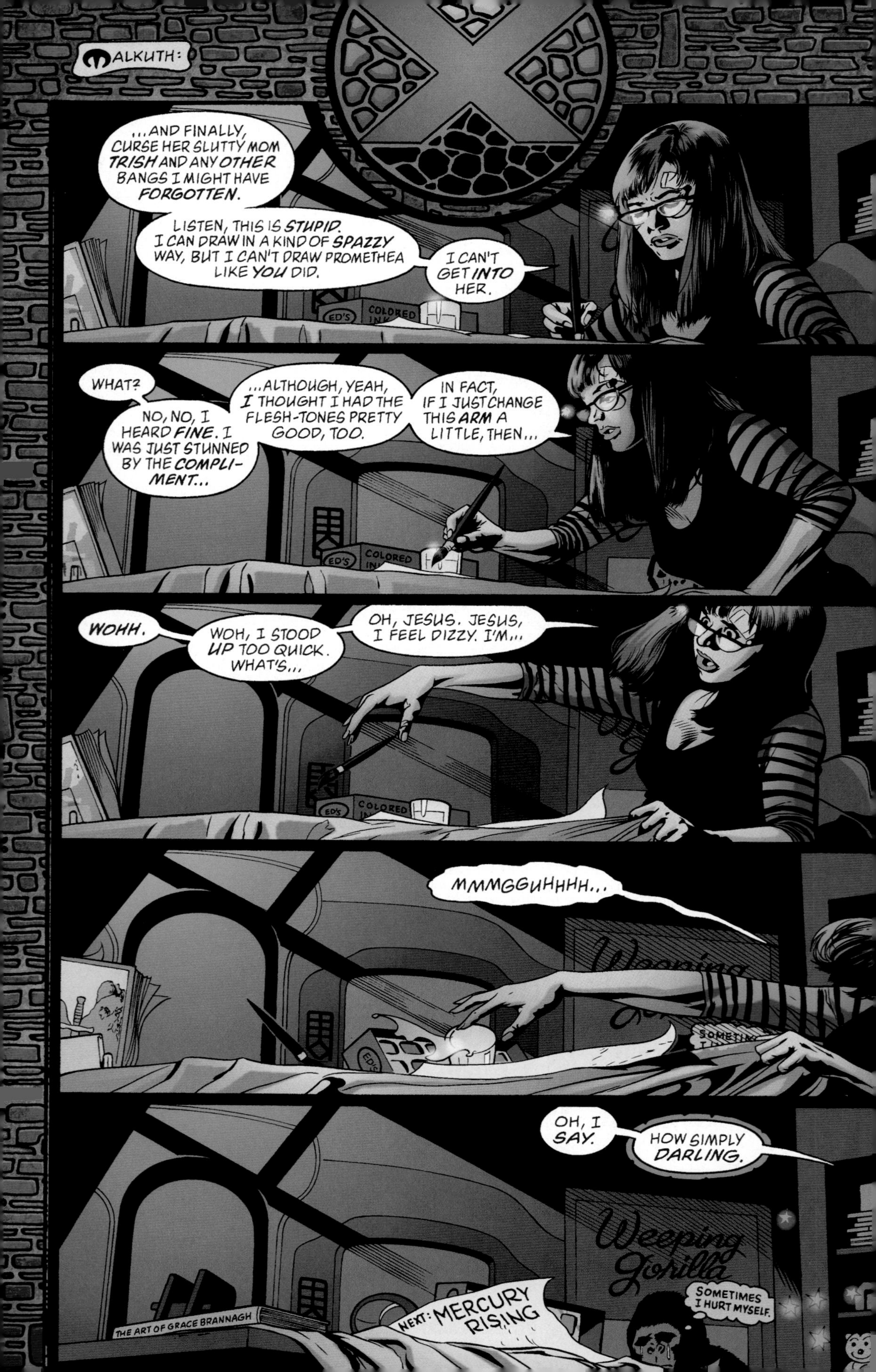
MALKUTH:
...AND FINALLY, CURSE HER SLUTTY MOM TRISH AND ANY OTHER BANGS I MIGHT HAVE FORGOTTEN.
LISTEN, THIS IS STUPID. I CAN DRAW IN A KIND OF SPAZZY WAY, BUT I CAN'T DRAW PROMETHEA LIKE YOU DID.
I CAN'T GET INTO HER.
ED'S COLORED INK
WHAT?
NO, NO, I HEARD FINE. I WAS JUST STUNNED BY THE COMPLIMENT...
...ALTHOUGH, YEAH, I THOUGHT I HAD THE FLESH-TONES PRETTY GOOD, TOO.
IN FACT, IF I JUST CHANGE THIS ARM A LITTLE, THEN...
WOHH.
WOH, I STOOD UP TOO QUICK. WHAT'S...
OH, JESUS. JESUS, I FEEL DIZZY. I'M...
MMMGGUHHHH...
OH, I SAY.
HOW SIMPLY DARLING.
Weeping Gorilla
SOMETIMES I HURT MYSELF.
THE ART OF GRACE BRANNAGH
NEXT: MERCURY RISING

CHAPTER THREE

Another Promethea takes the stage,
A splendourous path turns back on itself,
A mercurial figure explains the game.

Cover art:
J.H. Williams III,
Mick Gray & Jeromy Cox

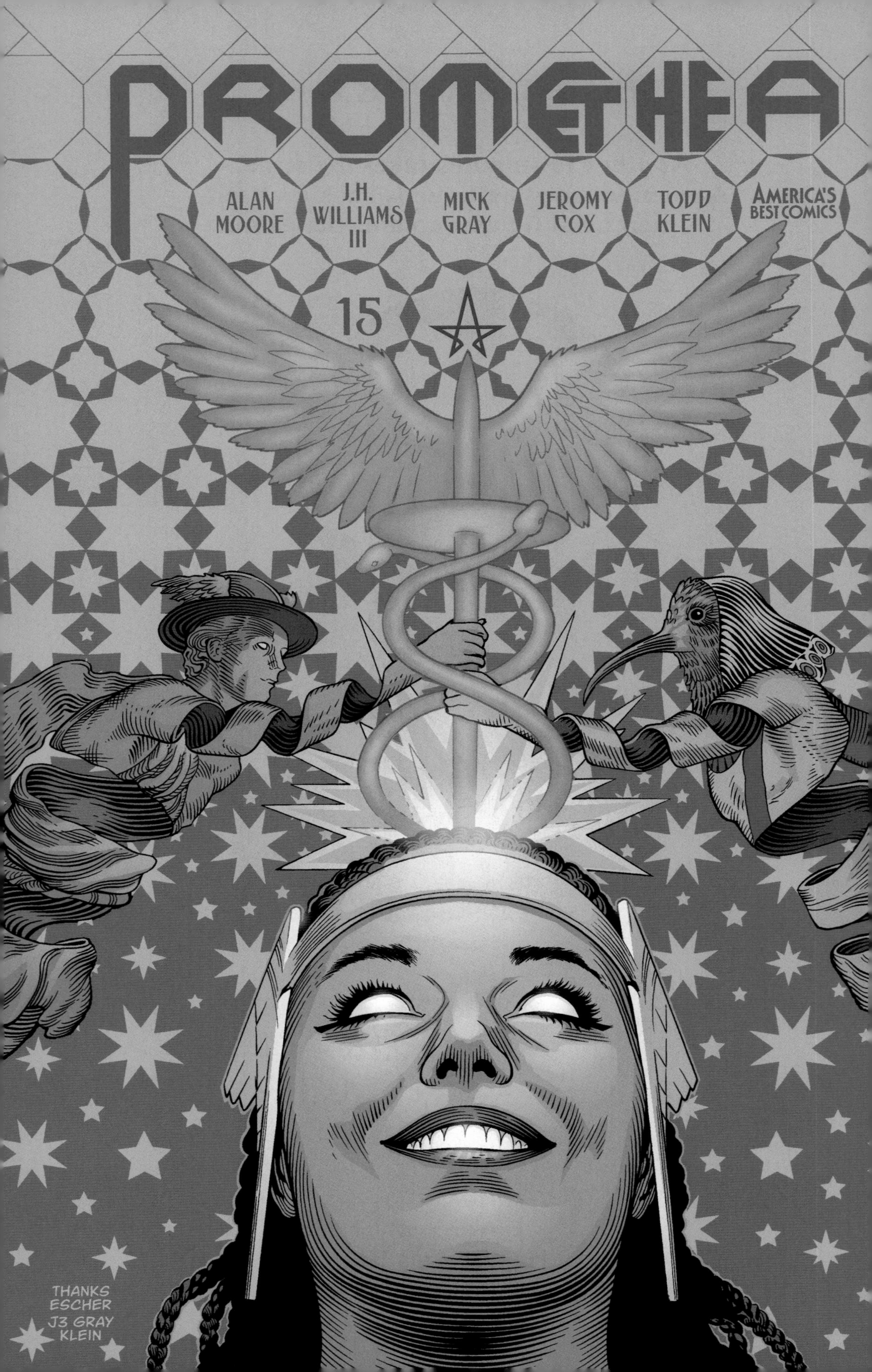
PROMETHEA
ALAN MOORE
J.H. WILLIAMS III
MICK GRAY
JEROMY COX
TODD KLEIN
AMERICA'S BEST COMICS
15
THANKS ESCHER
J3 GRAY KLEIN

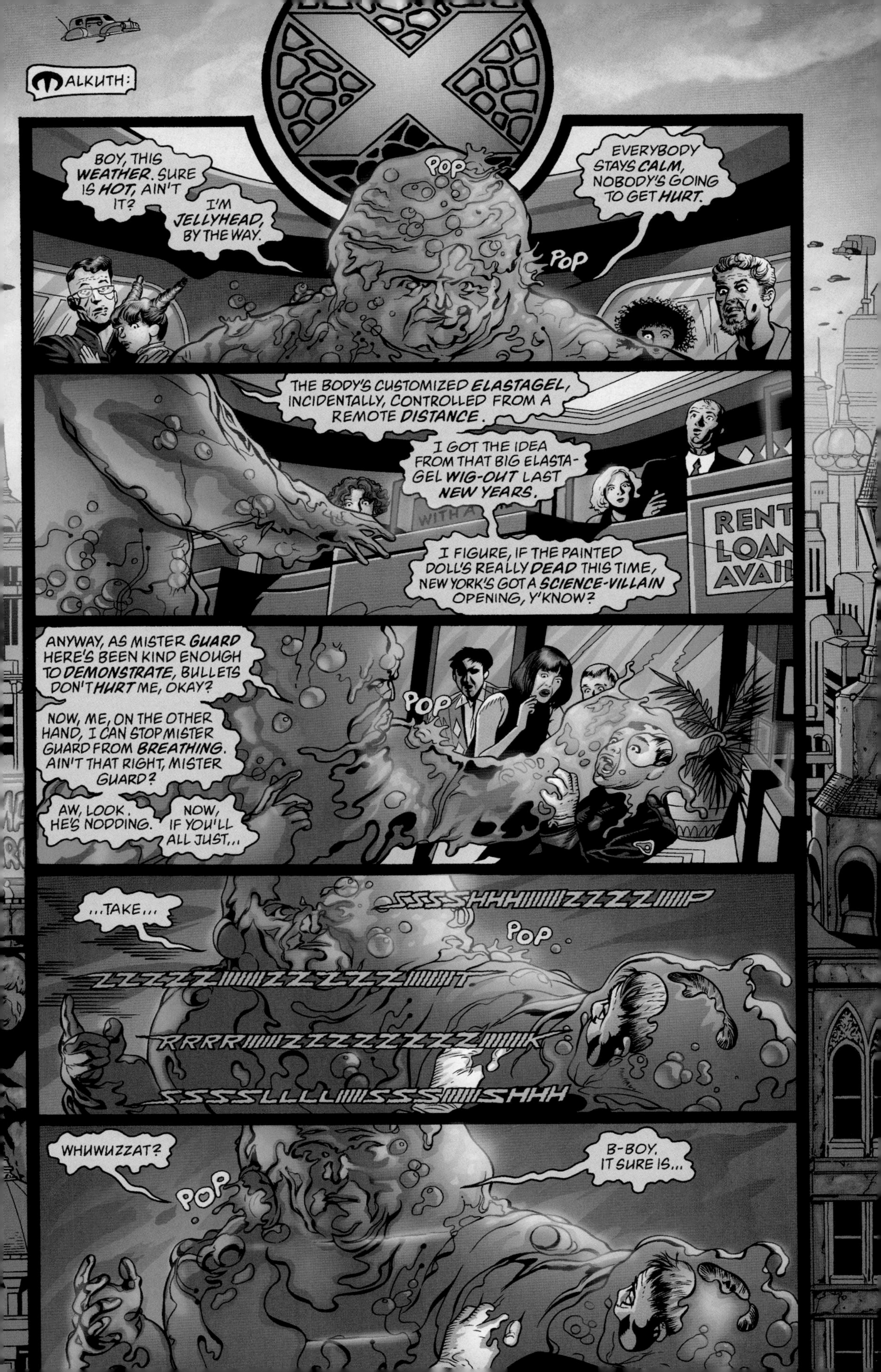
MALKUTH:
BOY, THIS WEATHER. SURE IS HOT, AIN'T IT?
I'M JELLYHEAD, BY THE WAY.
POP
POP
EVERYBODY STAYS CALM, NOBODY'S GOING TO GET HURT.
THE BODY'S CUSTOMIZED ELASTAGEL, INCIDENTALLY, CONTROLLED FROM A REMOTE DISTANCE.
I GOT THE IDEA FROM THAT BIG ELASTA-GEL WIG-OUT LAST NEW YEARS.
I FIGURE, IF THE PAINTED DOLL'S REALLY DEAD THIS TIME, NEW YORK'S GOT A SCIENCE-VILLAIN OPENING, Y'KNOW?
RENT
LOAN
AVAIL
ANYWAY, AS MISTER GUARD HERE'S BEEN KIND ENOUGH TO DEMONSTRATE, BULLETS DON'T HURT ME, OKAY?
NOW, ME, ON THE OTHER HAND, I CAN STOP MISTER GUARD FROM BREATHING. AIN'T THAT RIGHT, MISTER GUARD?
POP
AW, LOOK. HE'S NODDING.
NOW, IF YOU'LL ALL JUST...
...TAKE...
SSSSSHHH////ZZZZ////P
POP
ZZZZZ////ZZZZZZZ////T
RRRR////ZZZZZZZZZ////K
SSSSLLLL////SSS////SHHH
WHUWUZZAT?
POP
B-BOY. IT SURE IS...

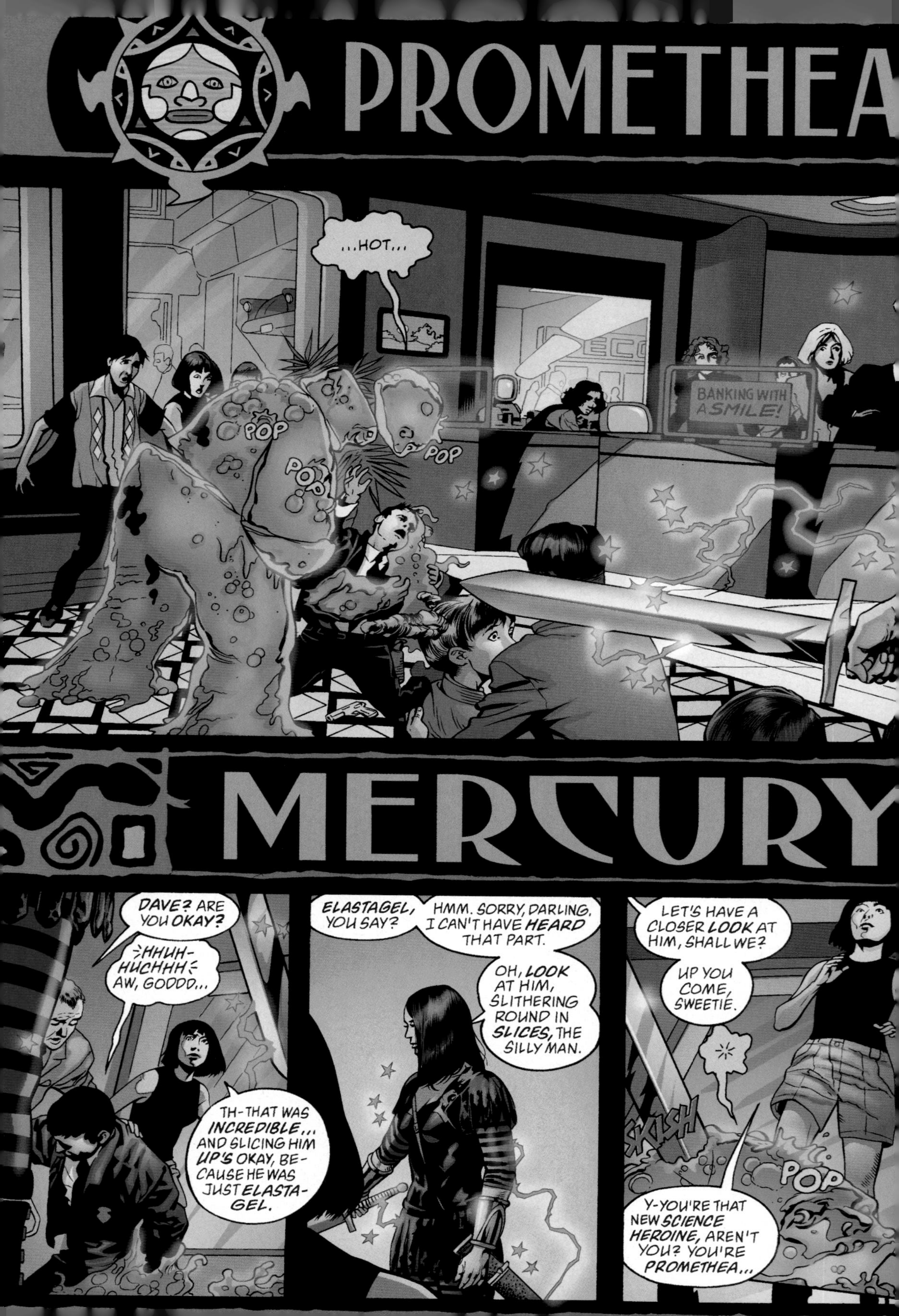
PROMETHEA
...HOT...
BANKING WITH A SMILE!
POP
POP
POP
POP
MERCURY
DAVE? ARE YOU OKAY?
-HHUH-HUCHHH- AW, GODDD...
TH-THAT WAS INCREDIBLE... AND SLICING HIM UP'S OKAY, BECAUSE HE WAS JUST ELASTAGEL.
ELASTAGEL, YOU SAY?
HMM. SORRY, DARLING, I CAN'T HAVE HEARD THAT PART.
OH, LOOK AT HIM, SLITHERING ROUND IN SLICES, THE SILLY MAN.
LET'S HAVE A CLOSER LOOK AT HIM, SHALL WE?
UP YOU COME, SWEETIE.
SKLISH
POP
Y-YOU'RE THAT NEW SCIENCE HEROINE, AREN'T YOU? YOU'RE PROMETHEA...

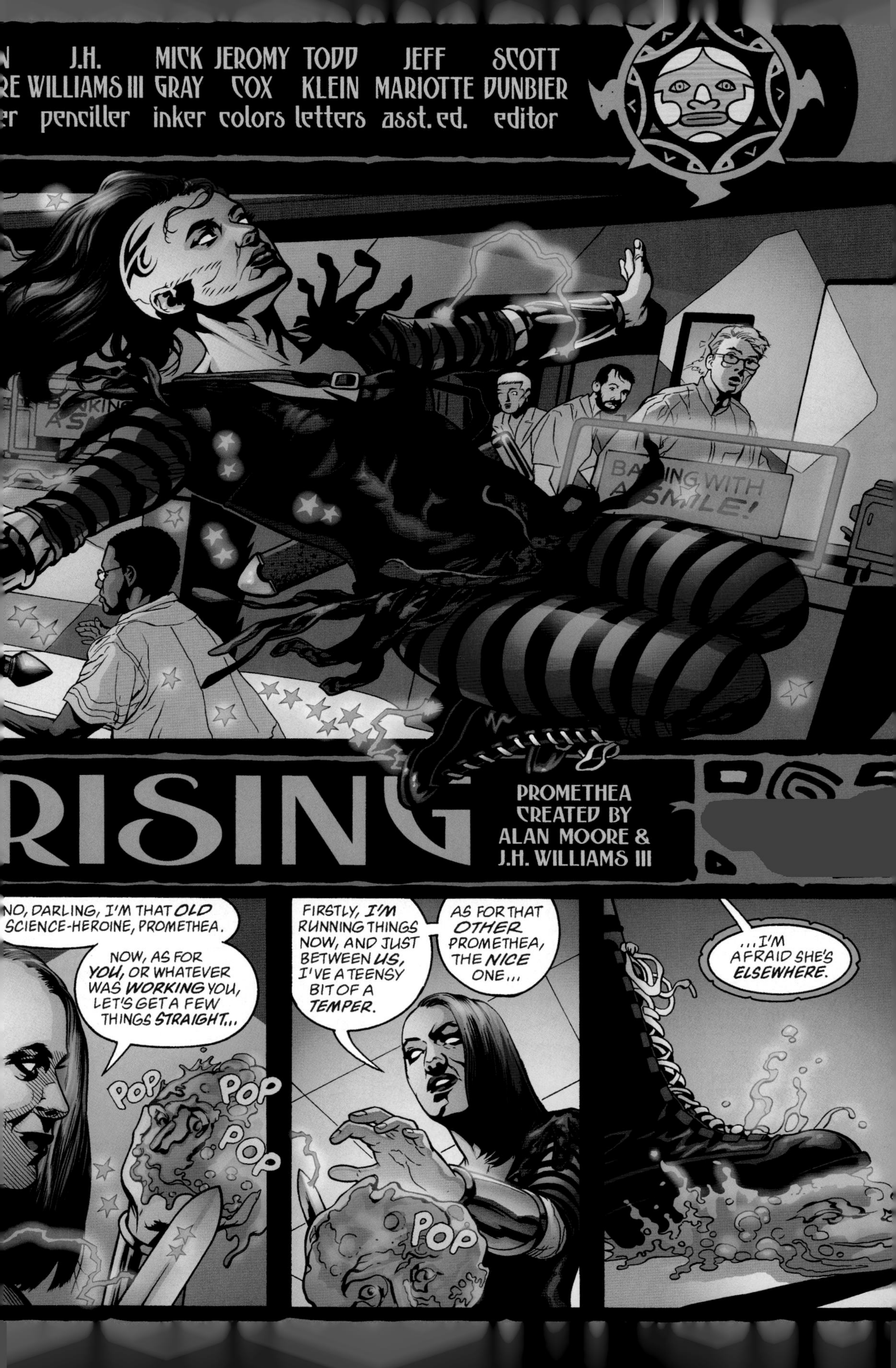
J.H. WILLIAMS III penciller
MICK GRAY inker
JEROMY COX colors
TODD KLEIN letters
JEFF MARIOTTE asst. ed.
SCOTT DUNBIER editor
BANKING WITH A SMILE!
RISING
PROMETHEA CREATED BY ALAN MOORE & J.H. WILLIAMS III
NO, DARLING, I'M THAT OLD SCIENCE-HEROINE, PROMETHEA.
NOW, AS FOR YOU, OR WHATEVER WAS WORKING YOU, LET'S GET A FEW THINGS STRAIGHT...
POP POP POP POP
FIRSTLY, I'M RUNNING THINGS NOW, AND JUST BETWEEN US, I'VE A TEENSY BIT OF A TEMPER.
AS FOR THAT OTHER PROMETHEA, THE NICE ONE...
POP
...I'M AFRAID SHE'S ELSEWHERE.

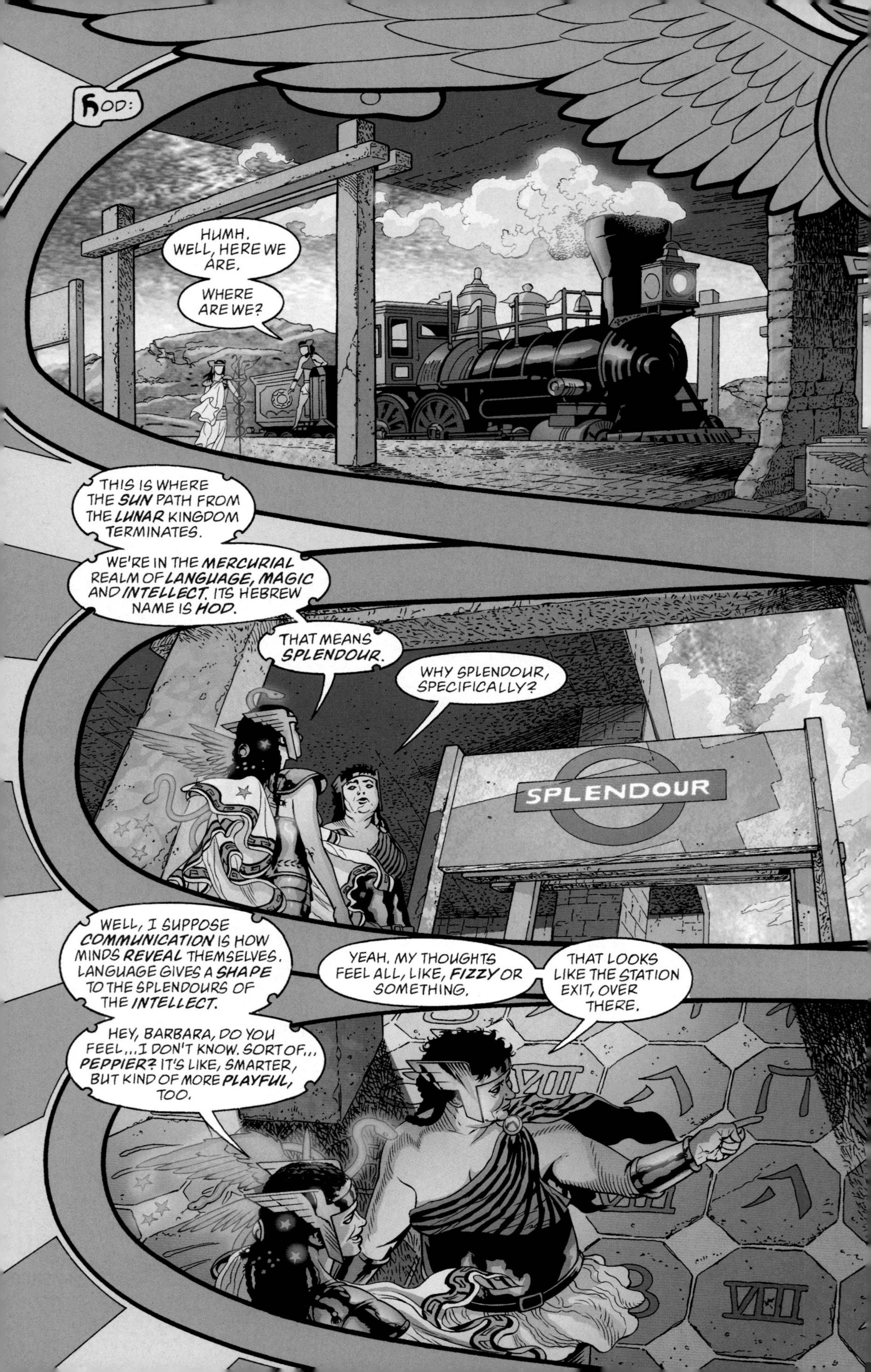
HOD:
HUMH. WELL, HERE WE ARE.
WHERE ARE WE?
THIS IS WHERE THE SUN PATH FROM THE LUNAR KINGDOM TERMINATES.
WE'RE IN THE MERCURIAL REALM OF LANGUAGE, MAGIC AND INTELLECT. ITS HEBREW NAME IS HOD.
THAT MEANS SPLENDOUR.
WHY SPLENDOUR, SPECIFICALLY?
SPLENDOUR
WELL, I SUPPOSE COMMUNICATION IS HOW MINDS REVEAL THEMSELVES. LANGUAGE GIVES A SHAPE TO THE SPLENDOURS OF THE INTELLECT.
HEY, BARBARA, DO YOU FEEL... I DON'T KNOW. SORT OF... PEPPIER? IT'S LIKE, SMARTER, BUT KIND OF MORE PLAYFUL, TOO.
YEAH. MY THOUGHTS FEEL ALL, LIKE, FIZZY OR SOMETHING.
THAT LOOKS LIKE THE STATION EXIT, OVER THERE.

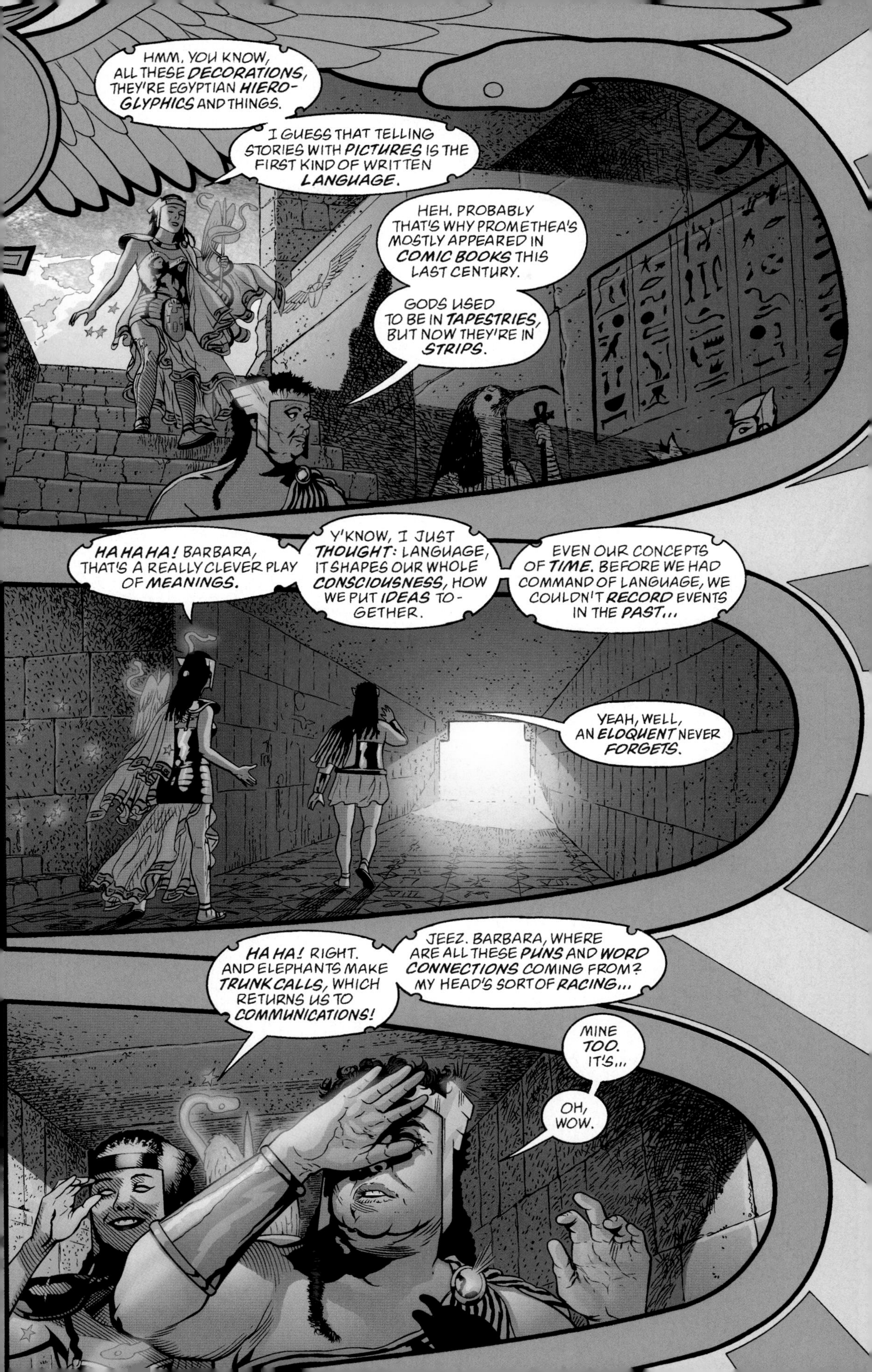
HMM, YOU KNOW, ALL THESE DECORATIONS, THEY'RE EGYPTIAN HIERO-GLYPHICS AND THINGS.
I GUESS THAT TELLING STORIES WITH PICTURES IS THE FIRST KIND OF WRITTEN LANGUAGE.
HEH. PROBABLY THAT'S WHY PROMETHEA'S MOSTLY APPEARED IN COMIC BOOKS THIS LAST CENTURY.
GODS USED TO BE IN TAPESTRIES, BUT NOW THEY'RE IN STRIPS.
HA HA HA! BARBARA, THAT'S A REALLY CLEVER PLAY OF MEANINGS.
Y'KNOW, I JUST THOUGHT: LANGUAGE, IT SHAPES OUR WHOLE CONSCIOUSNESS, HOW WE PUT IDEAS TO-GETHER.
EVEN OUR CONCEPTS OF TIME. BEFORE WE HAD COMMAND OF LANGUAGE, WE COULDN'T RECORD EVENTS IN THE PAST...
YEAH, WELL, AN ELOQUENT NEVER FORGETS.
HA HA! RIGHT. AND ELEPHANTS MAKE TRUNK CALLS, WHICH RETURNS US TO COMMUNICATIONS!
JEEZ. BARBARA, WHERE ARE ALL THESE PUNS AND WORD CONNECTIONS COMING FROM? MY HEAD'S SORT OF RACING...
MINE TOO. IT'S...
OH, WOW.

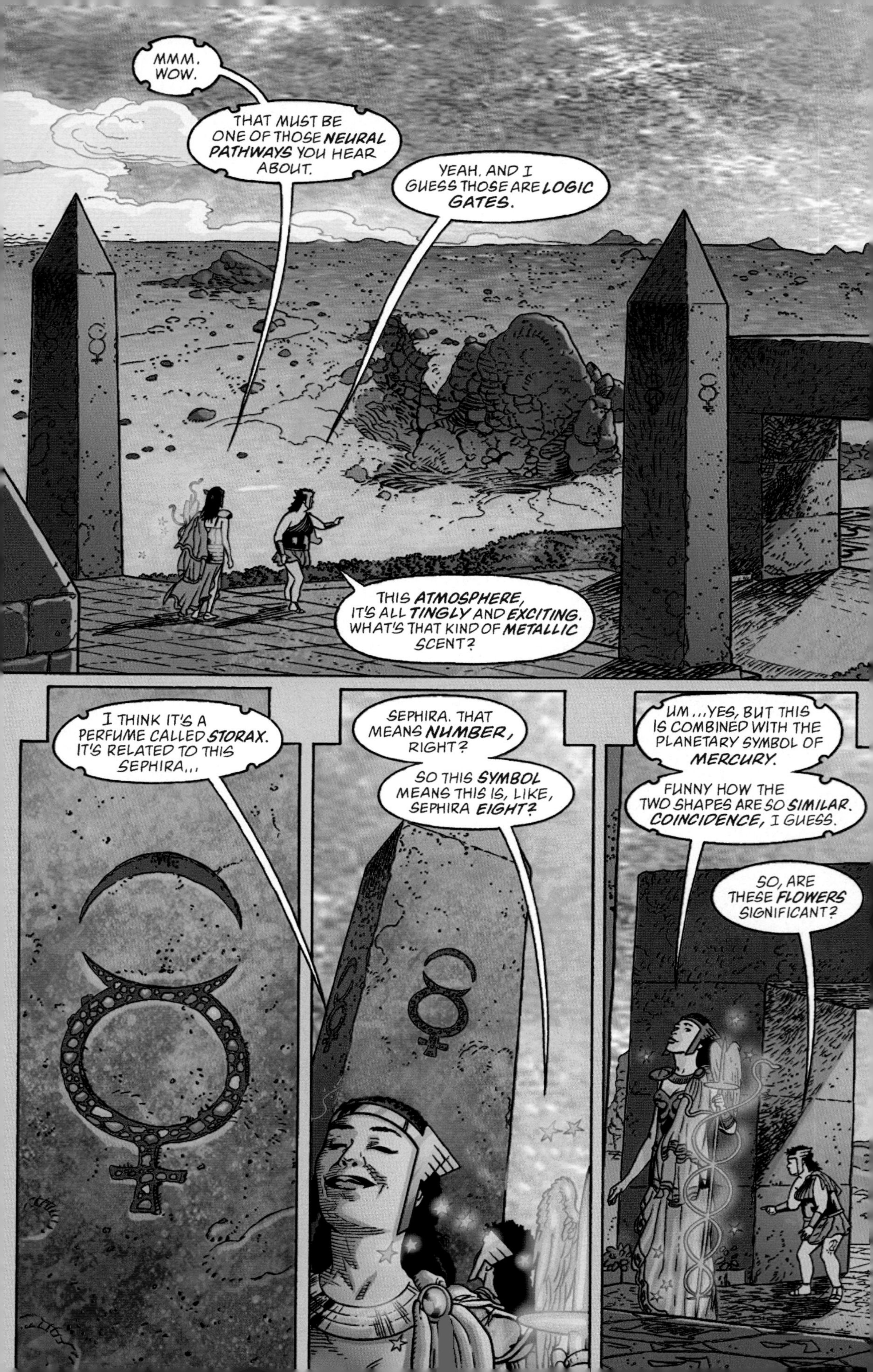
MMM. WOW.
THAT MUST BE ONE OF THOSE NEURAL PATHWAYS YOU HEAR ABOUT.
YEAH. AND I GUESS THOSE ARE LOGIC GATES.
THIS ATMOSPHERE, IT'S ALL TINGLY AND EXCITING. WHAT'S THAT KIND OF METALLIC SCENT?
I THINK IT'S A PERFUME CALLED STORAX. IT'S RELATED TO THIS SEPHIRA...
SEPHIRA. THAT MEANS NUMBER, RIGHT?
SO THIS SYMBOL MEANS THIS IS, LIKE, SEPHIRA EIGHT?
UM...YES, BUT THIS IS COMBINED WITH THE PLANETARY SYMBOL OF MERCURY.
FUNNY HOW THE TWO SHAPES ARE SO SIMILAR. COINCIDENCE, I GUESS.
SO, ARE THESE FLOWERS SIGNIFICANT?

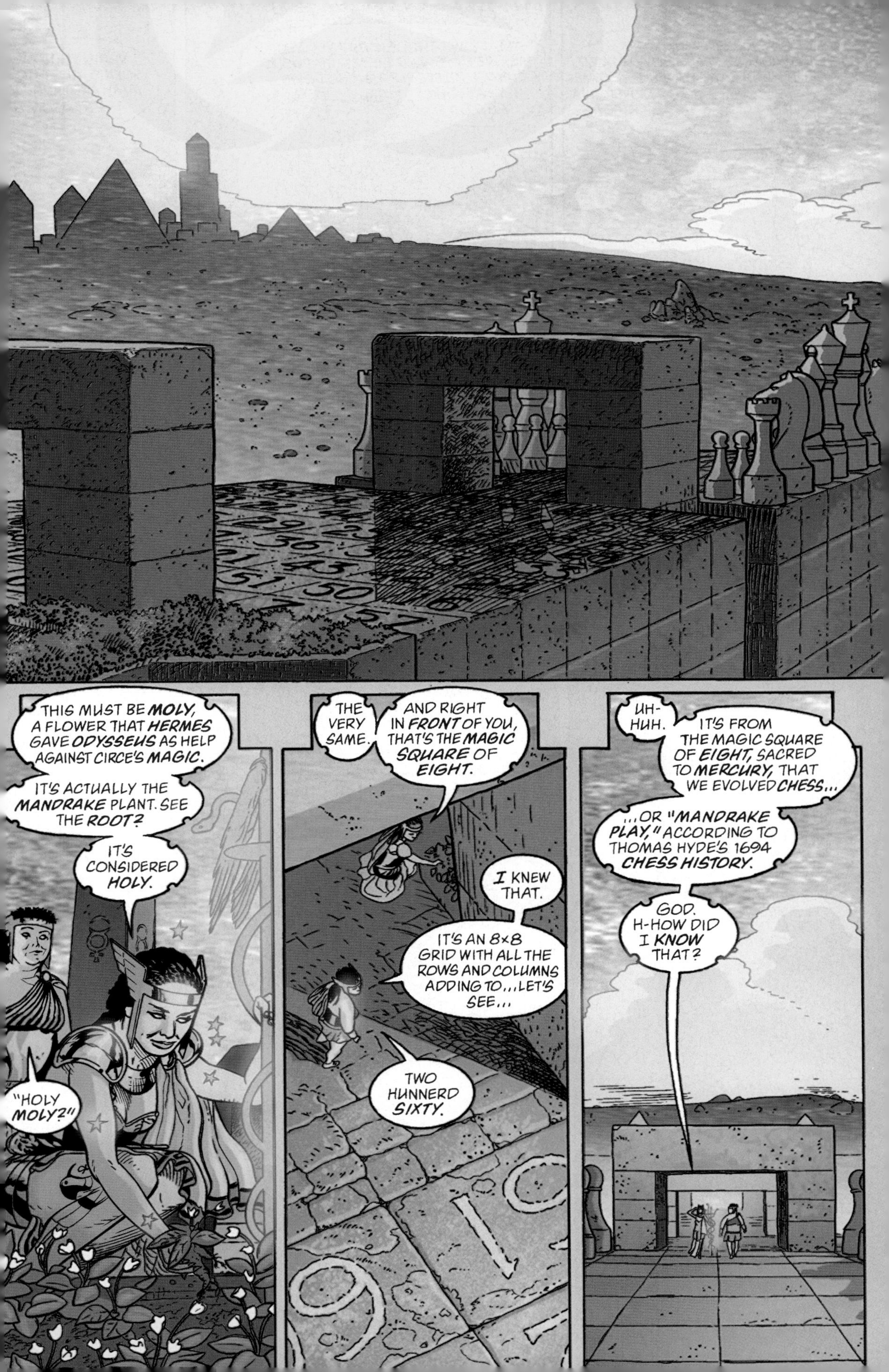
THIS MUST BE MOLY, A FLOWER THAT HERMES GAVE ODYSSEUS AS HELP AGAINST CIRCE'S MAGIC.
IT'S ACTUALLY THE MANDRAKE PLANT. SEE THE ROOT?
IT'S CONSIDERED HOLY.
"HOLY MOLY?"
THE VERY SAME.
AND RIGHT IN FRONT OF YOU, THAT'S THE MAGIC SQUARE OF EIGHT.
I KNEW THAT.
IT'S AN 8×8 GRID WITH ALL THE ROWS AND COLUMNS ADDING TO... LET'S SEE...
TWO HUNNERD SIXTY.
UH-HUH.
IT'S FROM THE MAGIC SQUARE OF EIGHT, SACRED TO MERCURY, THAT WE EVOLVED CHESS...
...OR "MANDRAKE PLAY," ACCORDING TO THOMAS HYDE'S 1694 CHESS HISTORY.
GOD. H-HOW DID I KNOW THAT?

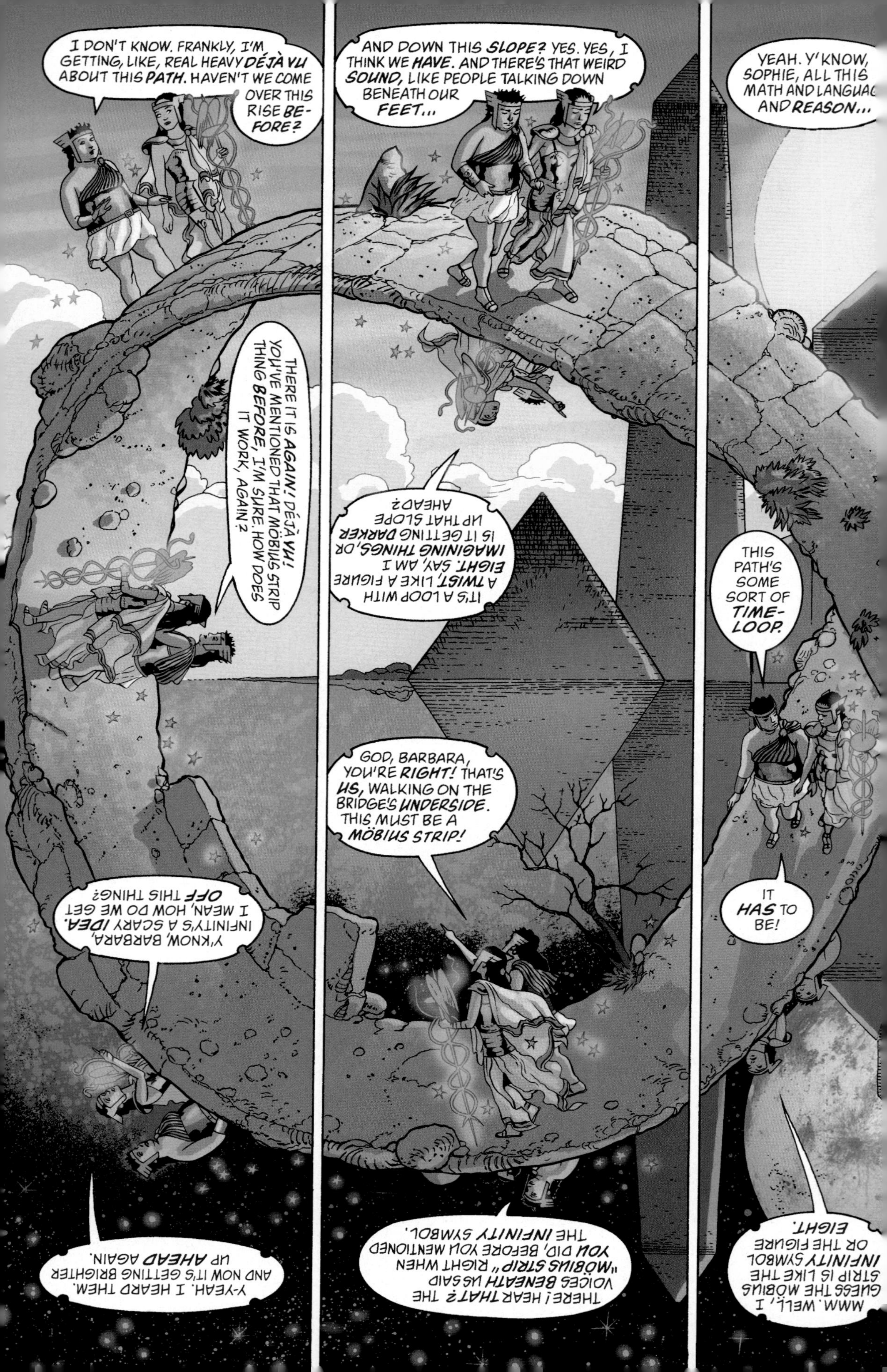
I DON'T KNOW. FRANKLY, I'M GETTING, LIKE, REAL HEAVY DÉJÀ VU ABOUT THIS PATH. HAVEN'T WE COME OVER THIS RISE BEFORE?
THERE IT IS AGAIN! DÉJÀ VU! YOU'VE MENTIONED THAT MÖBIUS STRIP THING BEFORE, I'M SURE. HOW DOES IT WORK, AGAIN?
Y'KNOW, BARBARA, INFINITY'S A SCARY IDEA. I MEAN, HOW DO WE GET OFF THIS THING?
Y-YEAH. I HEARD THEM. AND NOW IT'S GETTING BRIGHTER UP AHEAD AGAIN.
AND DOWN THIS SLOPE? YES. YES, I THINK WE HAVE. AND THERE'S THAT WEIRD SOUND, LIKE PEOPLE TALKING DOWN BENEATH OUR FEET...
IT'S A LOOP WITH A TWIST, LIKE A FIGURE EIGHT. SAY, AM I IMAGINING THINGS, OR IS IT GETTING DARKER UP THAT SLOPE AHEAD?
GOD, BARBARA, YOU'RE RIGHT! THAT'S US, WALKING ON THE BRIDGE'S UNDERSIDE. THIS MUST BE A MÖBIUS STRIP!
THERE! HEAR THAT? THE VOICES BENEATH US SAID "MÖBIUS STRIP" RIGHT WHEN YOU DID, BEFORE YOU MENTIONED THE INFINITY SYMBOL.
YEAH. Y'KNOW, SOPHIE, ALL THIS MATH AND LANGUAG AND REASON...
THIS PATH'S SOME SORT OF TIME-LOOP.
IT HAS TO BE!
MMM. WELL, I GUESS THE MÖBIUS STRIP IS LIKE THE INFINITY SYMBOL OR THE FIGURE EIGHT.

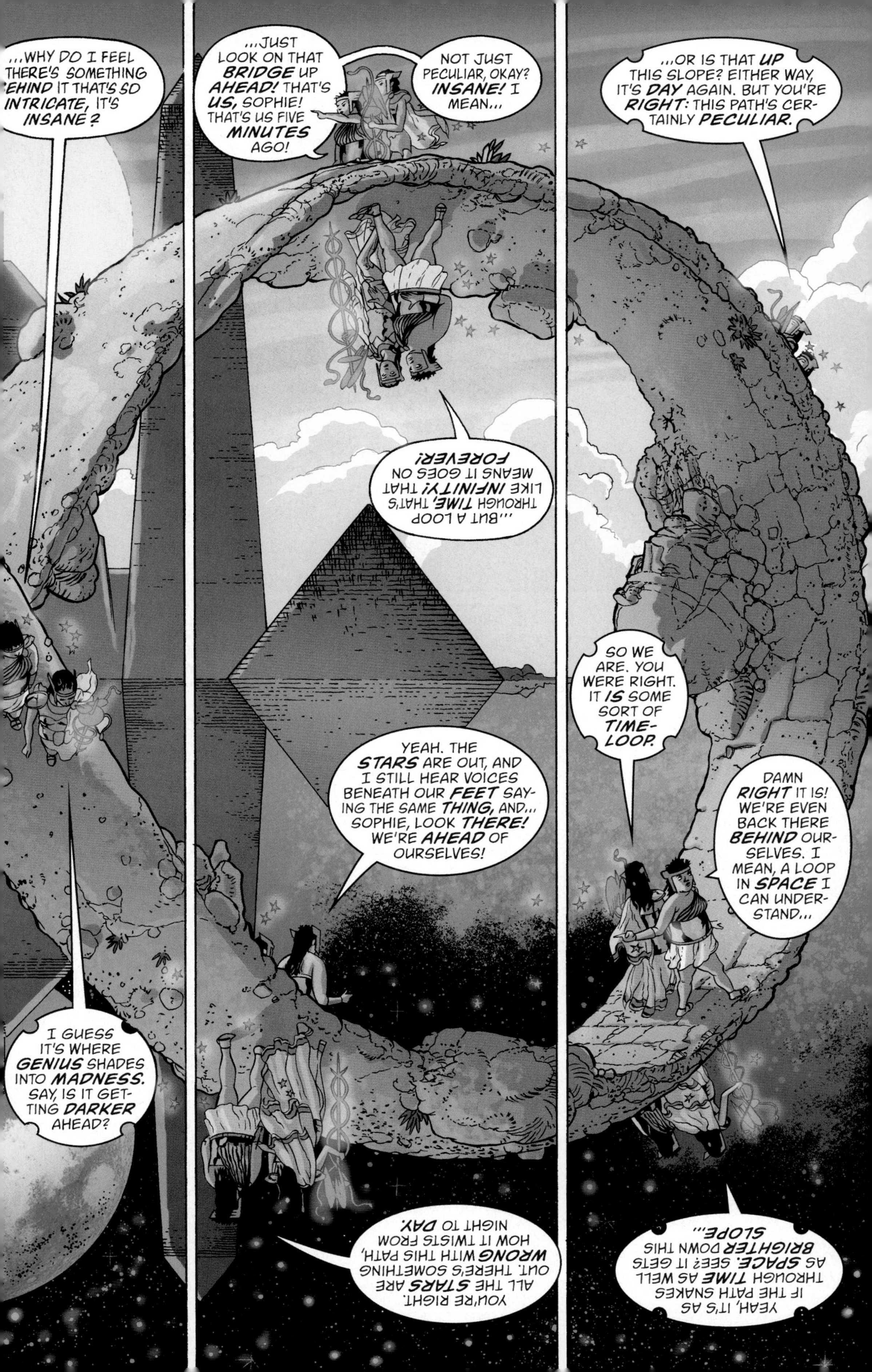

...WHY DO I FEEL THERE'S SOMETHING EHIND IT THAT'S SO INTRICATE, IT'S INSANE?
I GUESS IT'S WHERE GENIUS SHADES INTO MADNESS. SAY, IS IT GETTING DARKER AHEAD?
...JUST LOOK ON THAT BRIDGE UP AHEAD! THAT'S US, SOPHIE! THAT'S US FIVE MINUTES AGO!
NOT JUST PECULIAR, OKAY? INSANE! I MEAN...
...BUT A LOOP THROUGH TIME, THAT'S LIKE INFINITY! THAT MEANS IT GOES ON FOREVER!
YEAH. THE STARS ARE OUT, AND I STILL HEAR VOICES BENEATH OUR FEET SAYING THE SAME THING, AND... SOPHIE, LOOK THERE! WE'RE AHEAD OF OURSELVES!
YOU'RE RIGHT. ALL THE STARS ARE OUT. THERE'S SOMETHING WRONG WITH THIS PATH, HOW IT TWISTS FROM NIGHT TO DAY.
...OR IS THAT UP THIS SLOPE? EITHER WAY, IT'S DAY AGAIN. BUT YOU'RE RIGHT: THIS PATH'S CERTAINLY PECULIAR.
SO WE ARE. YOU WERE RIGHT. IT IS SOME SORT OF TIME-LOOP.
DAMN RIGHT IT IS! WE'RE EVEN BACK THERE BEHIND OURSELVES. I MEAN, A LOOP IN SPACE I CAN UNDERSTAND...
YEAH, IT'S AS IF THE PATH SNAKES THROUGH TIME AS WELL AS SPACE. SEE? IT GETS BRIGHTER DOWN THIS SLOPE...

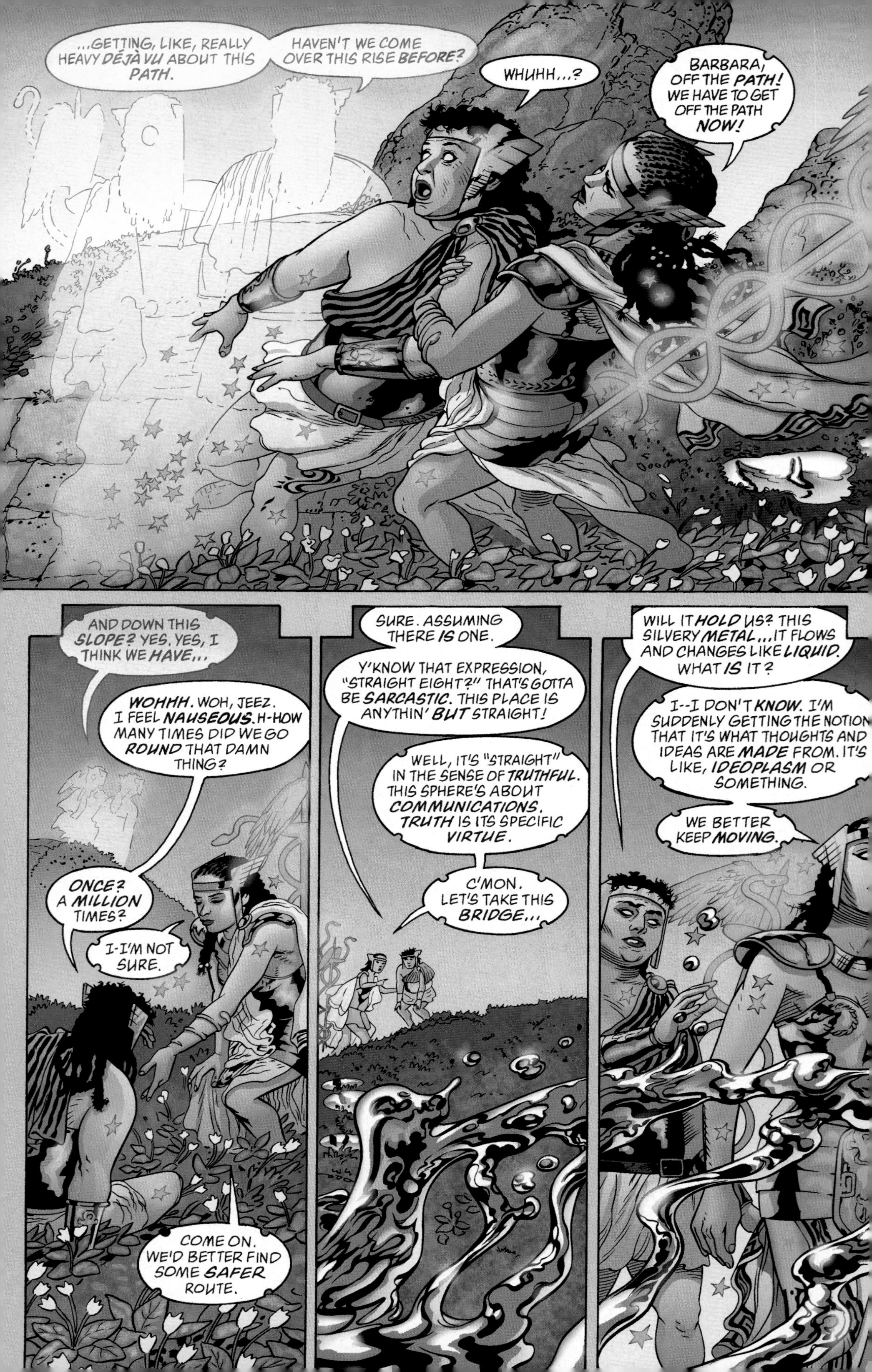
...GETTING, LIKE, REALLY HEAVY *DÉJÀ VU* ABOUT THIS *PATH*.
HAVEN'T WE COME OVER THIS RISE *BEFORE?*
WHUHH...?
BARBARA, OFF THE *PATH!* WE HAVE TO GET OFF THE PATH *NOW!*
AND DOWN THIS *SLOPE?* YES. YES, I THINK WE *HAVE*...
WOHHH. WOH, JEEZ. I FEEL *NAUSEOUS*. H-HOW MANY TIMES DID WE GO *ROUND* THAT DAMN THING?
ONCE? A *MILLION* TIMES?
I-I'M NOT SURE.
COME ON. WE'D BETTER FIND SOME *SAFER* ROUTE.
SURE. ASSUMING THERE *IS* ONE.
Y'KNOW THAT EXPRESSION, "STRAIGHT EIGHT?" THAT'S GOTTA BE *SARCASTIC*. THIS PLACE IS ANYTHIN' *BUT* STRAIGHT!
WELL, IT'S "STRAIGHT" IN THE SENSE OF *TRUTHFUL*. THIS SPHERE'S ABOUT *COMMUNICATIONS*. *TRUTH* IS ITS SPECIFIC *VIRTUE*.
C'MON. LET'S TAKE THIS *BRIDGE*...
WILL IT *HOLD US?* THIS SILVERY *METAL*...IT FLOWS AND CHANGES LIKE *LIQUID*. WHAT *IS* IT?
I--I DON'T *KNOW*. I'M SUDDENLY GETTING THE NOTION THAT IT'S WHAT THOUGHTS AND IDEAS ARE *MADE* FROM. IT'S LIKE, *IDEOPLASM* OR SOMETHING.
WE BETTER KEEP *MOVING*.

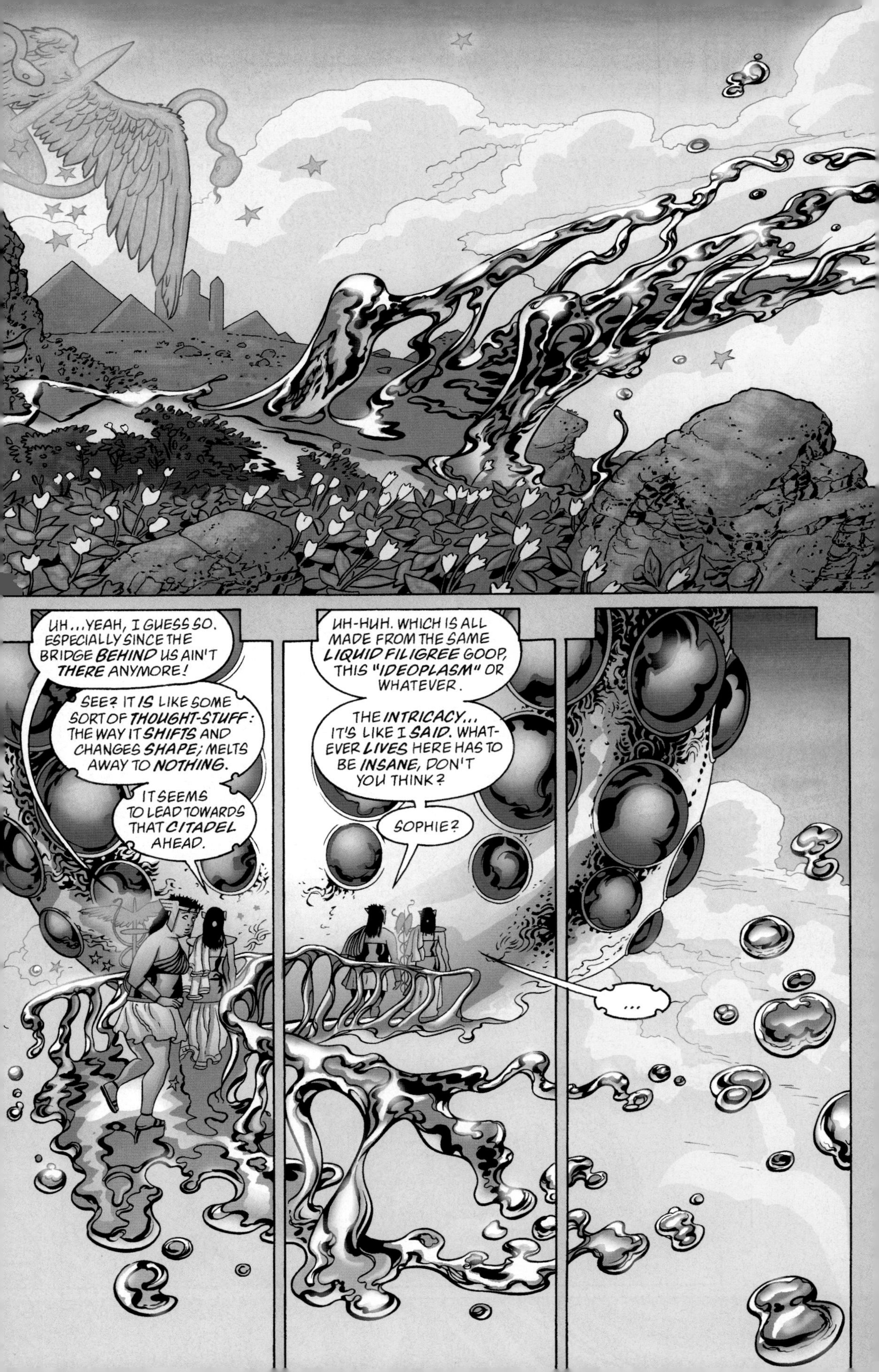
UH...YEAH, I GUESS SO. ESPECIALLY SINCE THE BRIDGE BEHIND US AIN'T THERE ANYMORE!
SEE? IT IS LIKE SOME SORT OF THOUGHT-STUFF: THE WAY IT SHIFTS AND CHANGES SHAPE; MELTS AWAY TO NOTHING.
IT SEEMS TO LEAD TOWARDS THAT CITADEL AHEAD.
UH-HUH. WHICH IS ALL MADE FROM THE SAME LIQUID FILIGREE GOOP, THIS "IDEOPLASM" OR WHATEVER.
THE INTRICACY... IT'S LIKE I SAID. WHATEVER LIVES HERE HAS TO BE INSANE, DON'T YOU THINK?
SOPHIE?
...

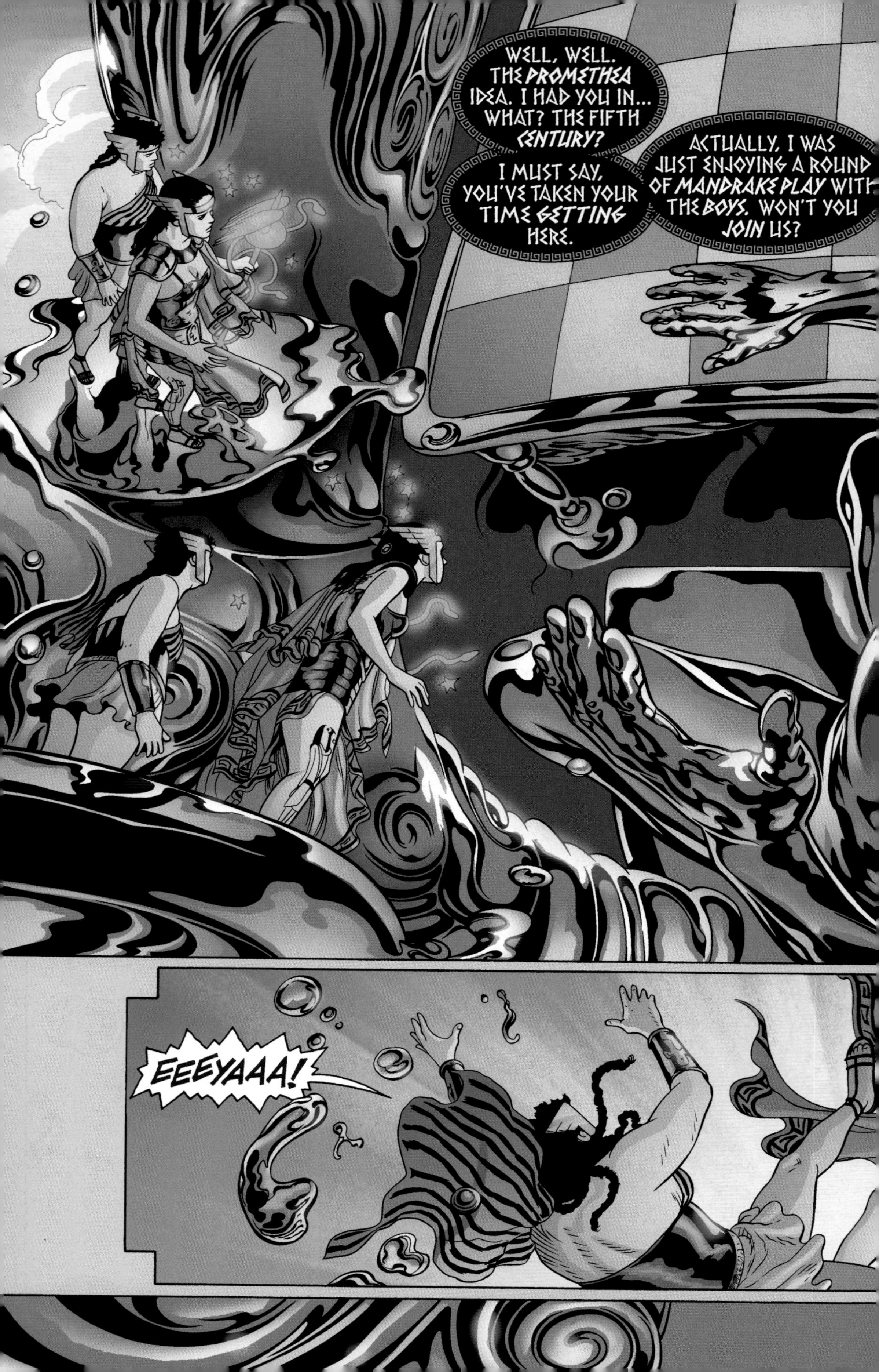
WELL, WELL. THE PROMETHEA IDEA. I HAD YOU IN... WHAT? THE FIFTH CENTURY?
I MUST SAY, YOU'VE TAKEN YOUR TIME GETTING HERE.
ACTUALLY, I WAS JUST ENJOYING A ROUND OF MANDRAKE PLAY WITH THE BOYS. WON'T YOU JOIN US?
EEEYAAA!

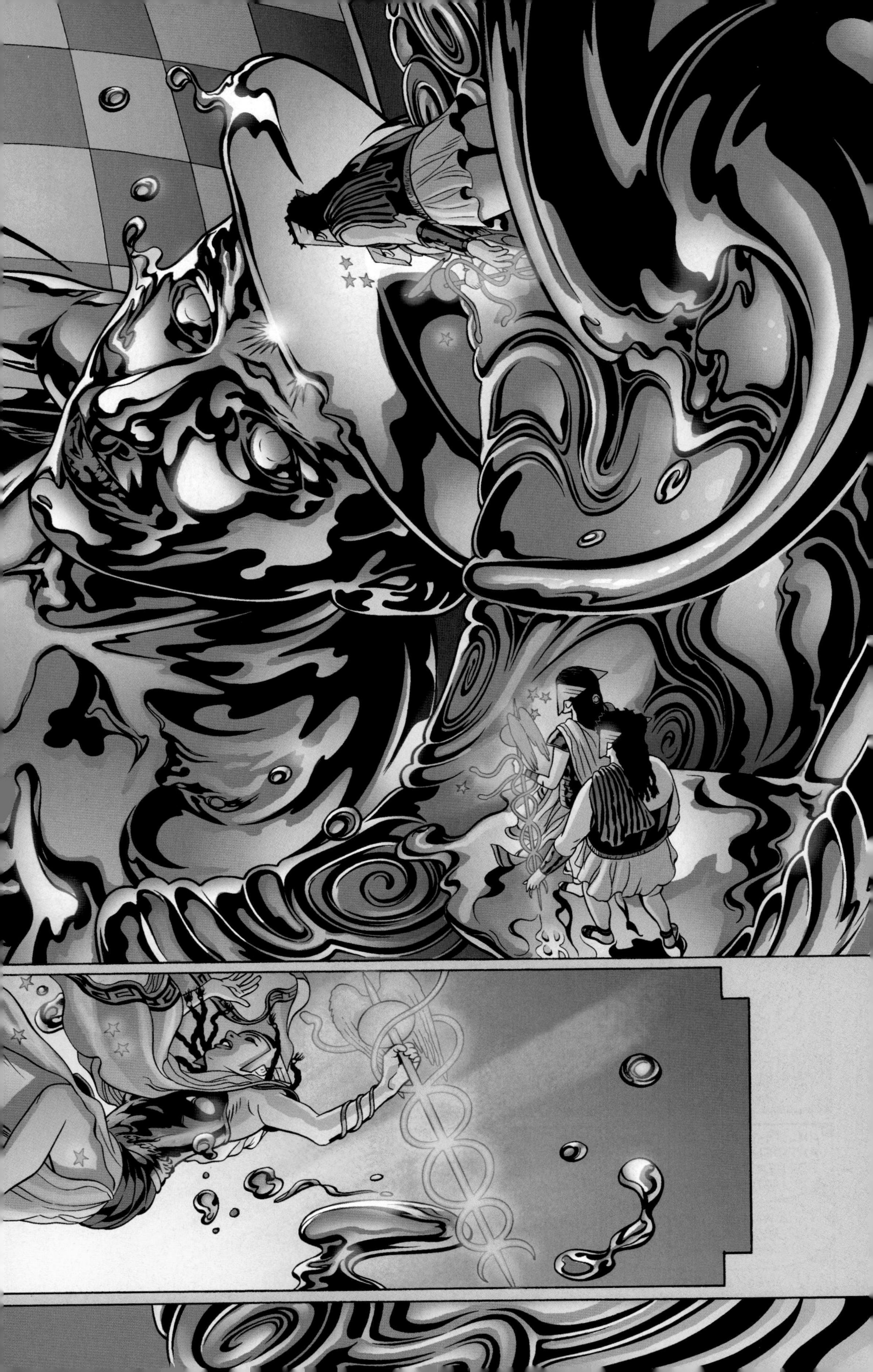

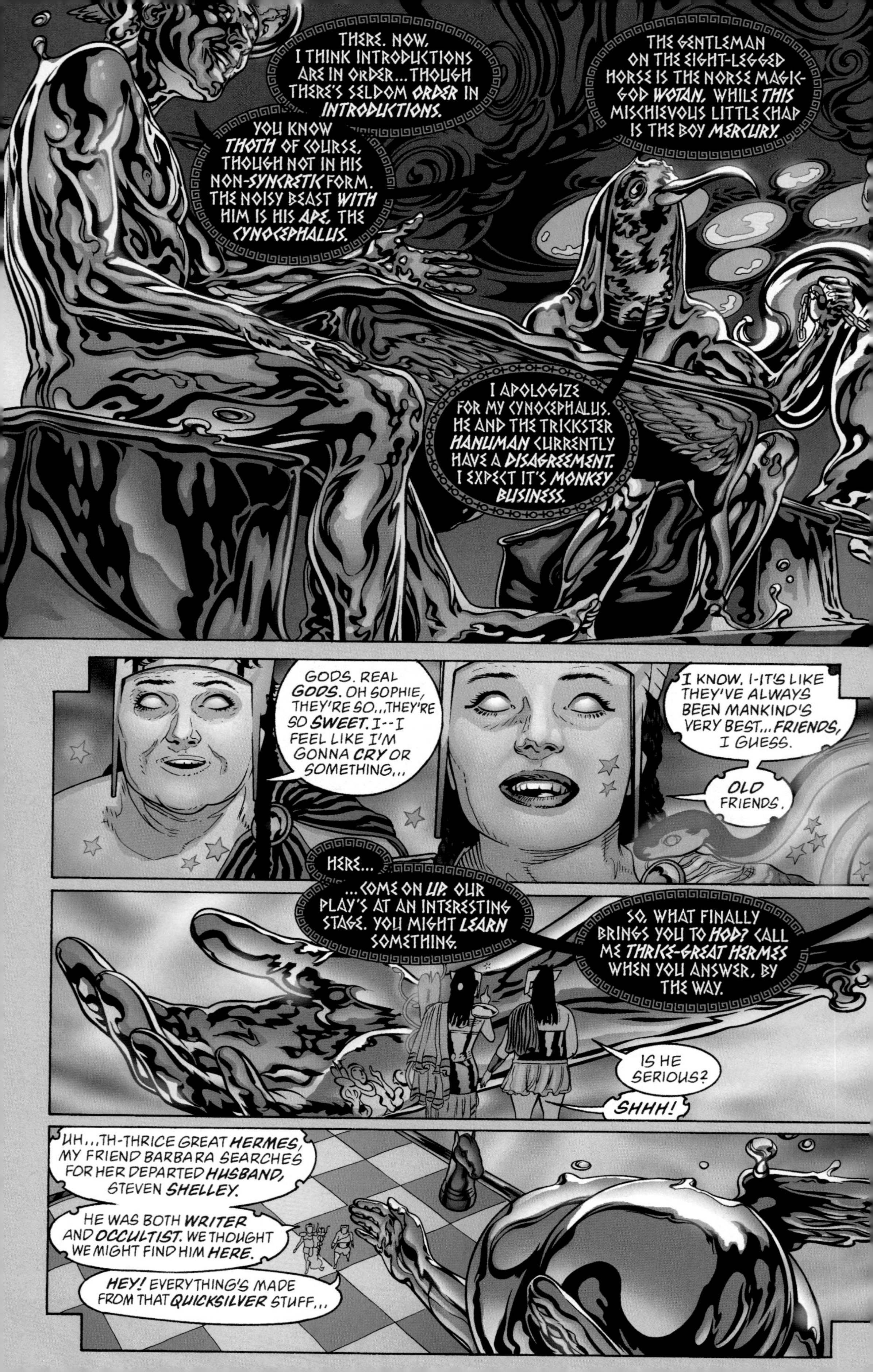
THERE. NOW, I THINK INTRODUCTIONS ARE IN ORDER... THOUGH THERE'S SELDOM ORDER IN INTRODUCTIONS.
YOU KNOW THOTH OF COURSE, THOUGH NOT IN HIS NON-SYNCRETIC FORM. THE NOISY BEAST WITH HIM IS HIS APE, THE CYNOCEPHALUS.
THE GENTLEMAN ON THE EIGHT-LEGGED HORSE IS THE NORSE MAGIC-GOD WOTAN, WHILE THIS MISCHIEVOUS LITTLE CHAP IS THE BOY MERCURY.
I APOLOGIZE FOR MY CYNOCEPHALUS. HE AND THE TRICKSTER HANUMAN CURRENTLY HAVE A DISAGREEMENT. I EXPECT IT'S MONKEY BUSINESS.
GODS. REAL GODS. OH SOPHIE, THEY'RE SO... THEY'RE SO SWEET. I--I FEEL LIKE I'M GONNA CRY OR SOMETHING...
I KNOW. I-IT'S LIKE THEY'VE ALWAYS BEEN MANKIND'S VERY BEST... FRIENDS, I GUESS.
OLD FRIENDS.
HERE...
...COME ON UP. OUR PLAY'S AT AN INTERESTING STAGE. YOU MIGHT LEARN SOMETHING.
SO, WHAT FINALLY BRINGS YOU TO HOD? CALL ME THRICE-GREAT HERMES WHEN YOU ANSWER, BY THE WAY.
IS HE SERIOUS?
SHHH!
UH... TH-THRICE GREAT HERMES, MY FRIEND BARBARA SEARCHES FOR HER DEPARTED HUSBAND, STEVEN SHELLEY.
HE WAS BOTH WRITER AND OCCULTIST. WE THOUGHT WE MIGHT FIND HIM HERE.
HEY! EVERYTHING'S MADE FROM THAT QUICKSILVER STUFF...

NATURALLY. HOD'S WHERE ALL THE *FORM* SEEN IN THE LOWER SPHERES OF *DREAM* AND *MATTER* HAS ITS ORIGINS.

ALL PERCEIVABLE FORM IS MADE FROM THIS *QUICKSILVER STUFF.* WE CALL IT *LANGUAGE.*

HEY, THIS IS *WRONG...*

I MEAN, THERE'S ONLY ONE *KNIGHT* LEFT IN *PLAY.* HOW COME THE GAME'S *CONTINUING?* IT'S *IMPOSSIBLE.*

AH, WELL. THAT'S WHERE BEING *OMNIPOTENT* COMES IN USEFUL.

DEAR ME. JUST *LOOK* AT THAT POOR LITTLE *KNIGHT...*

...HE'S BEEN GOING AROUND THE BOARD ALL *ALONE,* TRYING NOT TO LAND ON THE SAME SQUARE *TWICE.*

YOU CAN SEE THE ORDER OF HIS *MOVES.*

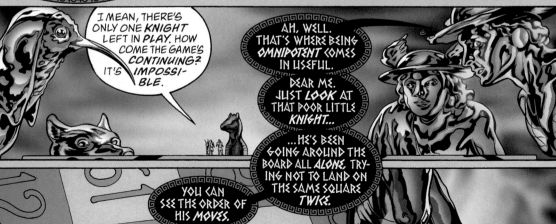

GHAA! SOPHIE, WE'RE BACK ON THAT MAGIC *SQUARE* THING!

Y-YEAH...

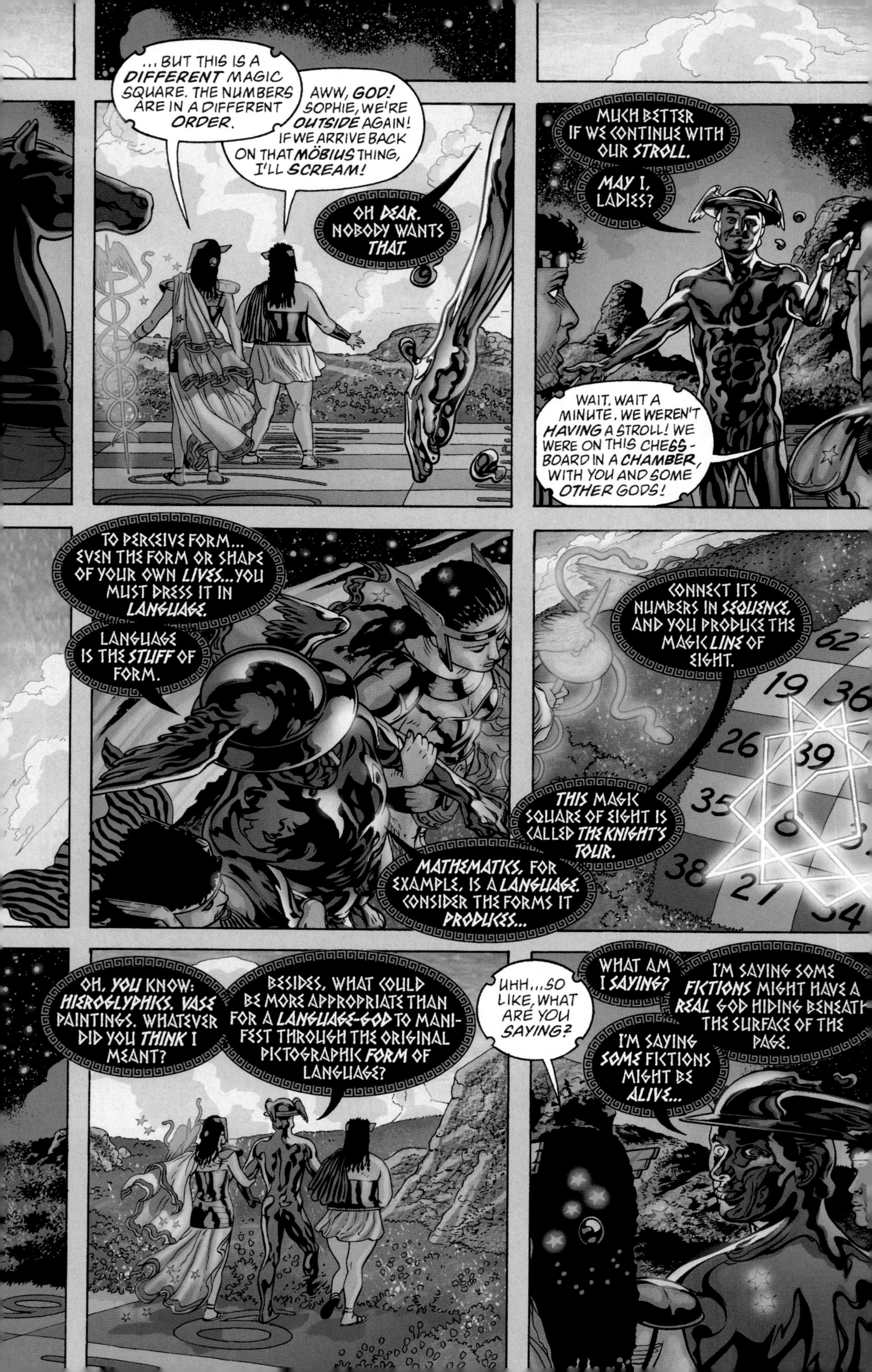

...BUT THIS IS A DIFFERENT MAGIC SQUARE. THE NUMBERS ARE IN A DIFFERENT ORDER.
AWW, GOD! SOPHIE, WE'RE OUTSIDE AGAIN! IF WE ARRIVE BACK ON THAT MÖBIUS THING, I'LL SCREAM!
OH DEAR. NOBODY WANTS THAT.
MUCH BETTER IF WE CONTINUE WITH OUR STROLL.
MAY I, LADIES?
WAIT. WAIT A MINUTE. WE WEREN'T HAVING A STROLL! WE WERE ON THIS CHESS-BOARD IN A CHAMBER, WITH YOU AND SOME OTHER GODS!
TO PERCEIVE FORM... EVEN THE FORM OR SHAPE OF YOUR OWN LIVES... YOU MUST DRESS IT IN LANGUAGE.
LANGUAGE IS THE STUFF OF FORM.
MATHEMATICS, FOR EXAMPLE, IS A LANGUAGE. CONSIDER THE FORMS IT PRODUCES...
THIS MAGIC SQUARE OF EIGHT IS CALLED THE KNIGHT'S TOUR.
CONNECT ITS NUMBERS IN SEQUENCE, AND YOU PRODUCE THE MAGIC LINE OF EIGHT.
62
19
36
26
39
35
8
38
27
54
OH, YOU KNOW: HIEROGLYPHICS. VASE PAINTINGS. WHATEVER DID YOU THINK I MEANT?
BESIDES, WHAT COULD BE MORE APPROPRIATE THAN FOR A LANGUAGE-GOD TO MANIFEST THROUGH THE ORIGINAL PICTOGRAPHIC FORM OF LANGUAGE?
UHH...SO LIKE, WHAT ARE YOU SAYING?
WHAT AM I SAYING?
I'M SAYING SOME FICTIONS MIGHT BE ALIVE...
I'M SAYING SOME FICTIONS MIGHT HAVE A REAL GOD HIDING BENEATH THE SURFACE OF THE PAGE.

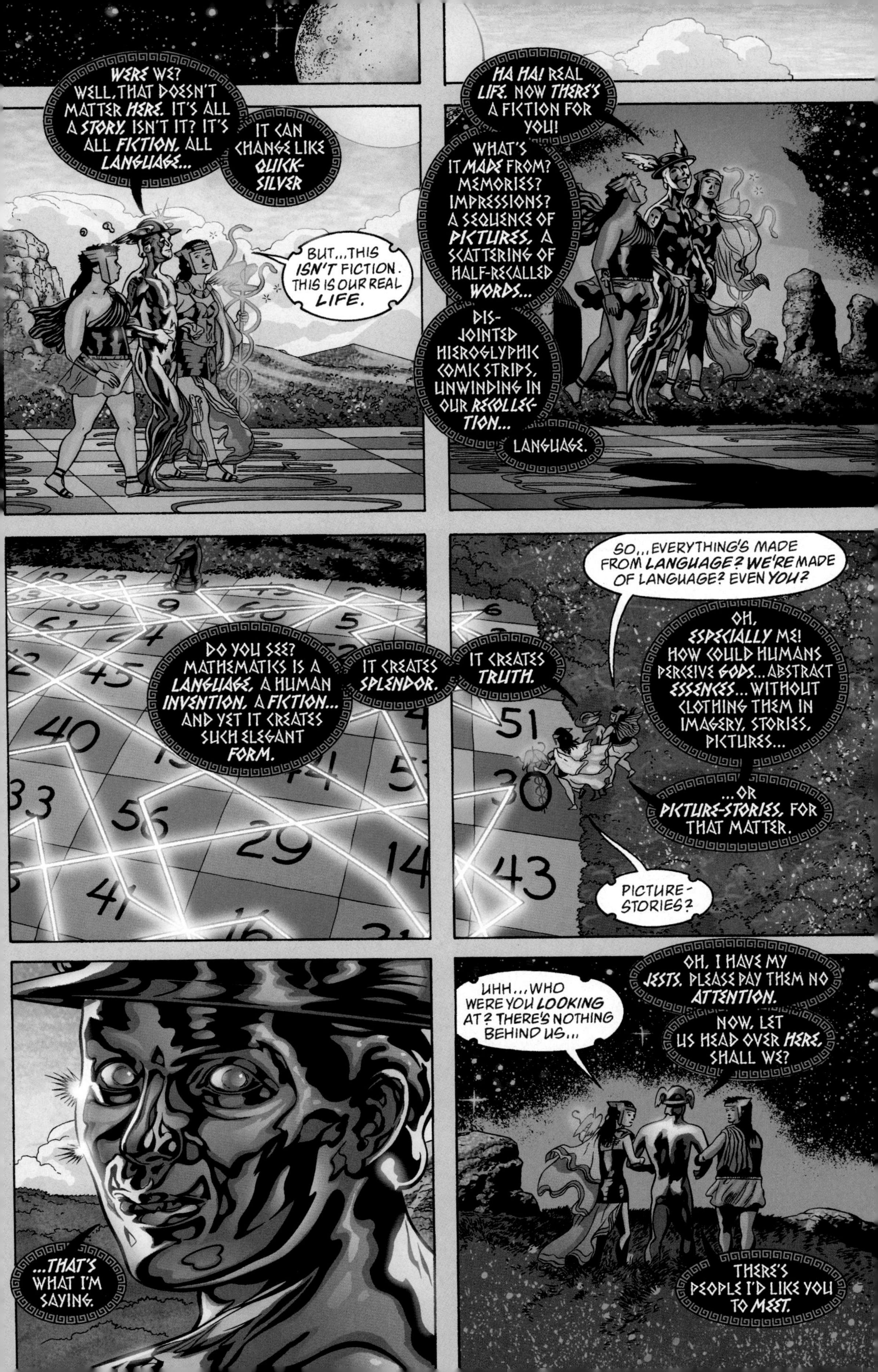
WERE WE? WELL, THAT DOESN'T MATTER HERE. IT'S ALL A STORY, ISN'T IT? IT'S ALL FICTION, ALL LANGUAGE...
IT CAN CHANGE LIKE QUICK-SILVER
BUT...THIS ISN'T FICTION. THIS IS OUR REAL LIFE.
HA HA! REAL LIFE. NOW THERE'S A FICTION FOR YOU!
WHAT'S IT MADE FROM? MEMORIES? IMPRESSIONS? A SEQUENCE OF PICTURES, A SCATTERING OF HALF-RECALLED WORDS...
DIS-JOINTED HIEROGLYPHIC COMIC STRIPS, UNWINDING IN OUR RECOLLEC-TION...
LANGUAGE.
DO YOU SEE? MATHEMATICS IS A LANGUAGE, A HUMAN INVENTION, A FICTION... AND YET IT CREATES SUCH ELEGANT FORM.
IT CREATES SPLENDOR.
IT CREATES TRUTH.
SO...EVERYTHING'S MADE FROM LANGUAGE? WE'RE MADE OF LANGUAGE? EVEN YOU?
OH, ESPECIALLY ME! HOW COULD HUMANS PERCEIVE GODS...ABSTRACT ESSENCES...WITHOUT CLOTHING THEM IN IMAGERY, STORIES, PICTURES...
...OR PICTURE-STORIES, FOR THAT MATTER.
PICTURE-STORIES?
...THAT'S WHAT I'M SAYING.
UHH...WHO WERE YOU LOOKING AT? THERE'S NOTHING BEHIND US...
OH, I HAVE MY JESTS. PLEASE PAY THEM NO ATTENTION.
NOW, LET US HEAD OVER HERE, SHALL WE?
THERE'S PEOPLE I'D LIKE YOU TO MEET.

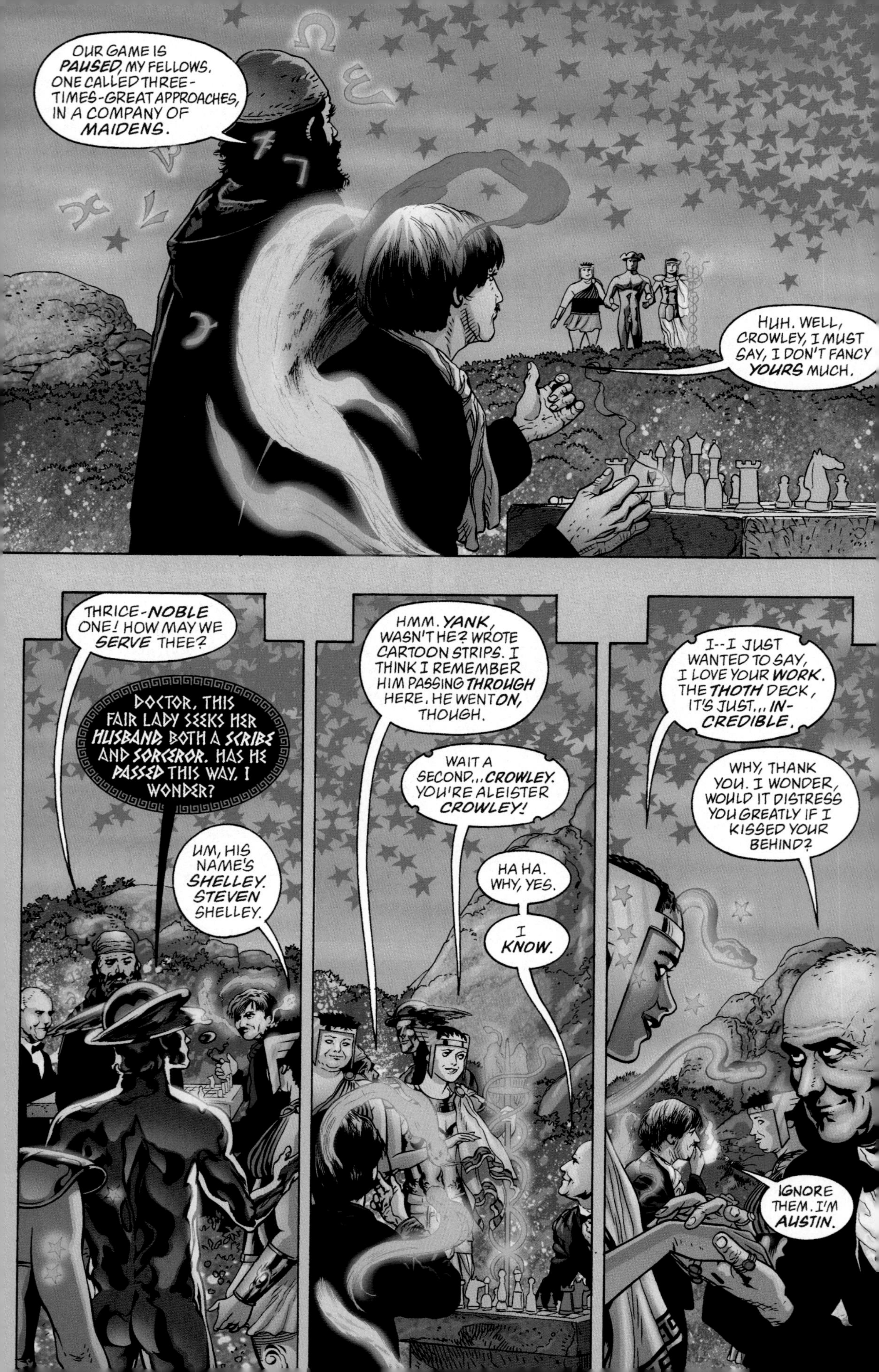
OUR GAME IS PAUSED, MY FELLOWS. ONE CALLED THREE-TIMES-GREAT APPROACHES, IN A COMPANY OF MAIDENS.
HUH. WELL, CROWLEY, I MUST SAY, I DON'T FANCY YOURS MUCH.
THRICE-NOBLE ONE! HOW MAY WE SERVE THEE?
DOCTOR, THIS FAIR LADY SEEKS HER HUSBAND, BOTH A SCRIBE AND SORCEROR. HAS HE PASSED THIS WAY, I WONDER?
UM, HIS NAME'S SHELLEY. STEVEN SHELLEY.
HMM. YANK, WASN'T HE? WROTE CARTOON STRIPS. I THINK I REMEMBER HIM PASSING THROUGH HERE. HE WENT ON, THOUGH.
WAIT A SECOND... CROWLEY. YOU'RE ALEISTER CROWLEY!
HA HA. WHY, YES.
I KNOW.
I--I JUST WANTED TO SAY, I LOVE YOUR WORK. THE THOTH DECK, IT'S JUST... IN-CREDIBLE.
WHY, THANK YOU. I WONDER, WOULD IT DISTRESS YOU GREATLY IF I KISSED YOUR BEHIND?
IGNORE THEM. I'M AUSTIN.

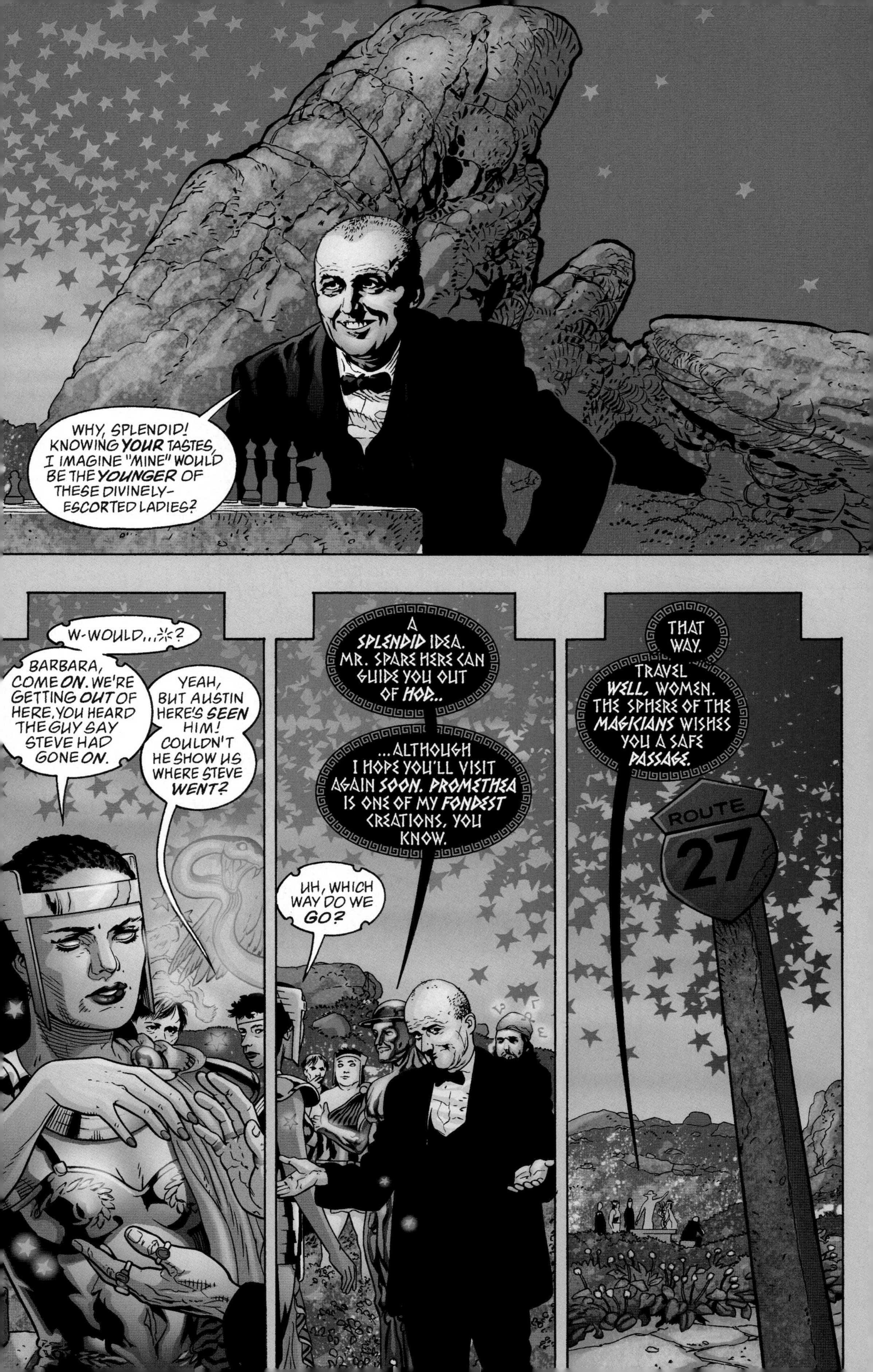
WHY, SPLENDID! KNOWING YOUR TASTES, I IMAGINE "MINE" WOULD BE THE YOUNGER OF THESE DIVINELY-ESCORTED LADIES?
W-WOULD...?
BARBARA, COME ON. WE'RE GETTING OUT OF HERE. YOU HEARD THE GUY SAY STEVE HAD GONE ON.
YEAH, BUT AUSTIN HERE'S SEEN HIM! COULDN'T HE SHOW US WHERE STEVE WENT?
A SPLENDID IDEA. MR. SPARE HERE CAN GUIDE YOU OUT OF HOD...
...ALTHOUGH I HOPE YOU'LL VISIT AGAIN SOON. PROMETHEA IS ONE OF MY FONDEST CREATIONS, YOU KNOW.
UH, WHICH WAY DO WE GO?
THAT WAY.
TRAVEL WELL, WOMEN. THE SPHERE OF THE MAGICIANS WISHES YOU A SAFE PASSAGE.
ROUTE
27

HUH! LIKE **ANYBODY'S** PASSAGE IS SAFE WITH THAT **BALD** CREEP AROUND.

OH, THAT'S JUST **CROWLEY'S WAY.** SOMETIMES EVEN I CAN'T STAND THE CHAP. HE DOES A LOT OF IT TO IRRITATE **DEE,** OF COURSE.

THAT OLD **ENGLISH** GUY! THAT WAS DOCTOR JOHN **DEE,** RIGHT? I'VE SEEN **ENGRAVINGS.**

AND **YOUR** NAME SOUNDED FAMILIAR, MR...?

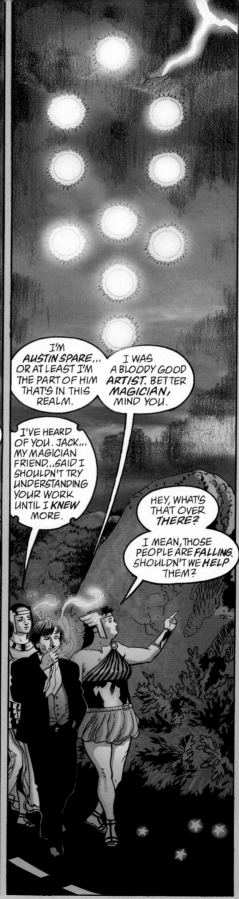

I'M **AUSTIN SPARE...** OR AT LEAST I'M THE PART OF HIM THAT'S IN THIS REALM.

I WAS A BLOODY GOOD **ARTIST.** BETTER **MAGICIAN,** MIND YOU.

I'VE HEARD OF YOU. JACK... MY MAGICIAN FRIEND...SAID I SHOULDN'T TRY UNDERSTANDING YOUR WORK UNTIL I **KNEW** MORE.

HEY, WHAT'S THAT OVER **THERE?**

I MEAN, THOSE PEOPLE ARE **FALLING.** SHOULDN'T WE **HELP** THEM?

THERE'S NO POINT, BARBARA, MY LOVELY. THEY'RE **ALWAYS** FALLING. THAT'S THE LIGHTNING-STRUCK **TOWER.** IT'S THE SYMBOL OF THIS 27TH PATH.

IT'S EVERY TOWER MAN OR WOMAN EVER **BUILT...** A BUILDING, A **MARRIAGE,** A CAREER... THAT WAS MEANT TO REACH **HEAVEN.**

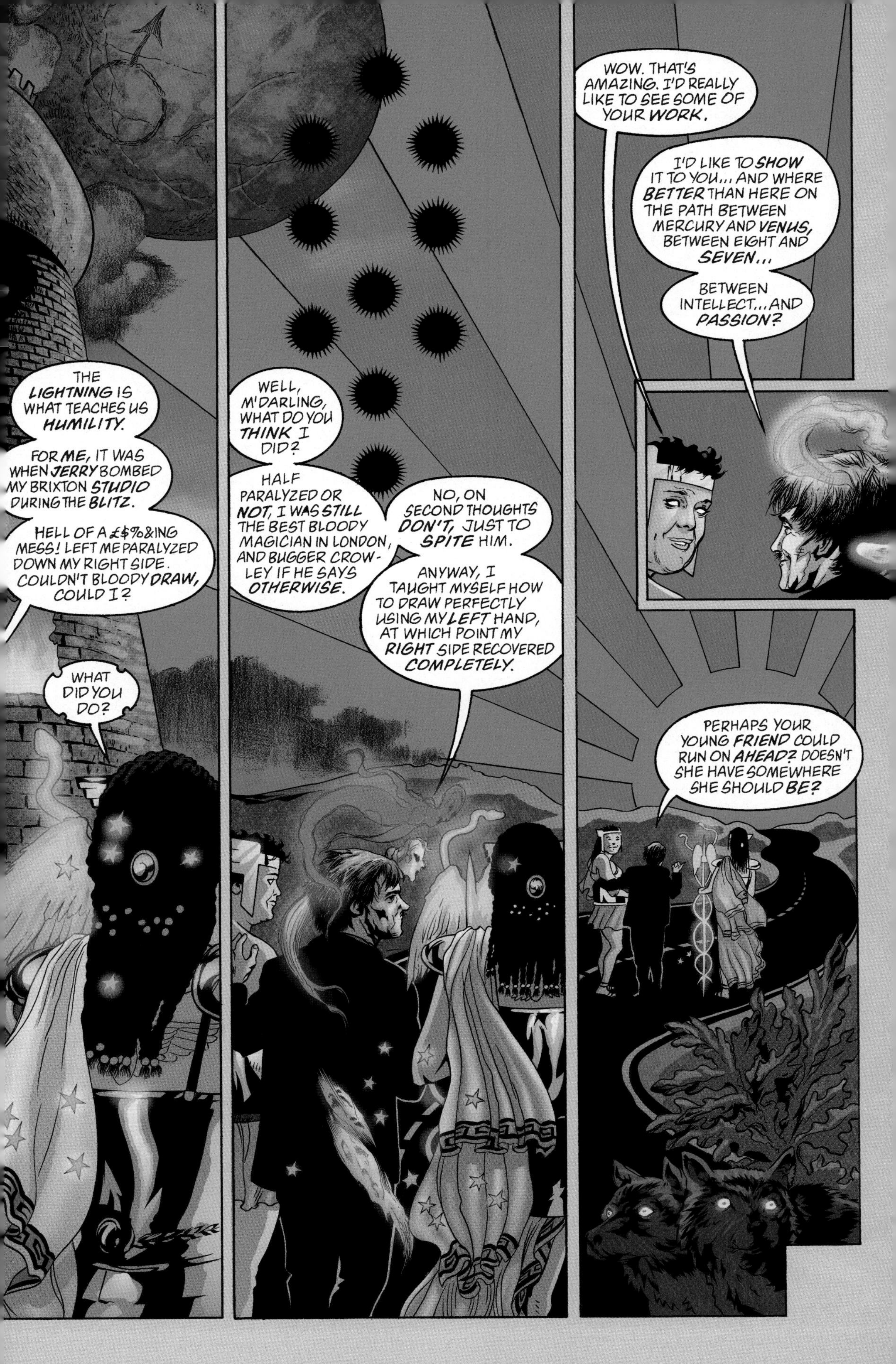
THE LIGHTNING IS WHAT TEACHES US HUMILITY.
FOR ME, IT WAS WHEN JERRY BOMBED MY BRIXTON STUDIO DURING THE BLITZ.
HELL OF A £$%&ING MESS! LEFT ME PARALYZED DOWN MY RIGHT SIDE. COULDN'T BLOODY DRAW, COULD I?
WHAT DID YOU DO?
WELL, M'DARLING, WHAT DO YOU THINK I DID?
HALF PARALYZED OR NOT, I WAS STILL THE BEST BLOODY MAGICIAN IN LONDON, AND BUGGER CROW-LEY IF HE SAYS OTHERWISE.
NO, ON SECOND THOUGHTS DON'T, JUST TO SPITE HIM.
ANYWAY, I TAUGHT MYSELF HOW TO DRAW PERFECTLY USING MY LEFT HAND, AT WHICH POINT MY RIGHT SIDE RECOVERED COMPLETELY.
WOW. THAT'S AMAZING. I'D REALLY LIKE TO SEE SOME OF YOUR WORK.
I'D LIKE TO SHOW IT TO YOU... AND WHERE BETTER THAN HERE ON THE PATH BETWEEN MERCURY AND VENUS, BETWEEN EIGHT AND SEVEN...
BETWEEN INTELLECT... AND PASSION?
PERHAPS YOUR YOUNG FRIEND COULD RUN ON AHEAD? DOESN'T SHE HAVE SOMEWHERE SHE SHOULD BE?

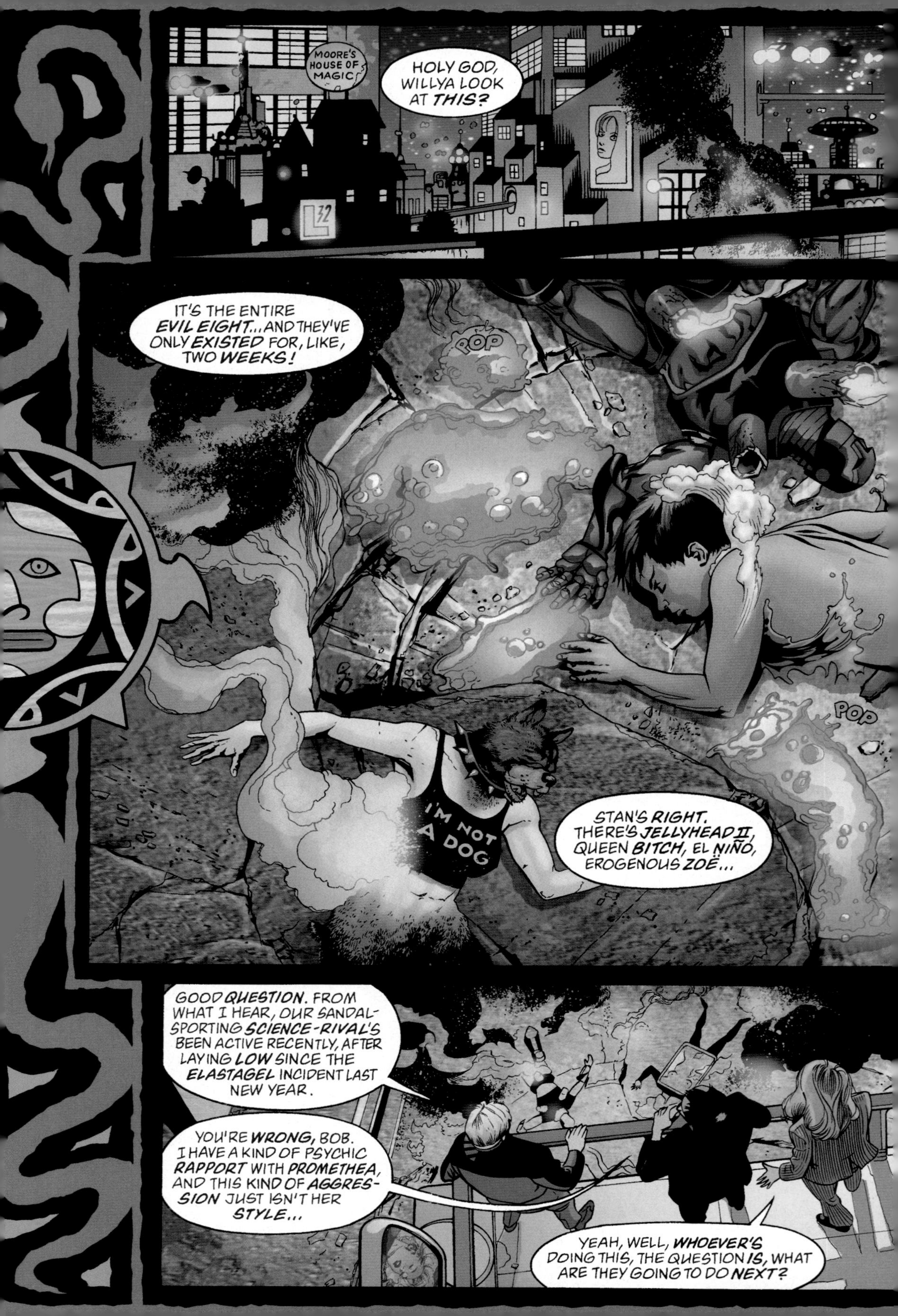
MOORE'S HOUSE OF MAGIC
HOLY GOD, WILLYA LOOK AT THIS?
IT'S THE ENTIRE EVIL EIGHT... AND THEY'VE ONLY EXISTED FOR, LIKE, TWO WEEKS!
POP
POP
I'M NOT A DOG
STAN'S RIGHT. THERE'S JELLYHEAD II, QUEEN BITCH, EL NIÑO, EROGENOUS ZOË...
GOOD QUESTION. FROM WHAT I HEAR, OUR SANDAL-SPORTING SCIENCE-RIVAL'S BEEN ACTIVE RECENTLY, AFTER LAYING LOW SINCE THE ELASTAGEL INCIDENT LAST NEW YEAR.
YOU'RE WRONG, BOB. I HAVE A KIND OF PSYCHIC RAPPORT WITH PROMETHEA, AND THIS KIND OF AGGRESSION JUST ISN'T HER STYLE...
YEAH, WELL, WHOEVER'S DOING THIS, THE QUESTION IS, WHAT ARE THEY GOING TO DO NEXT?

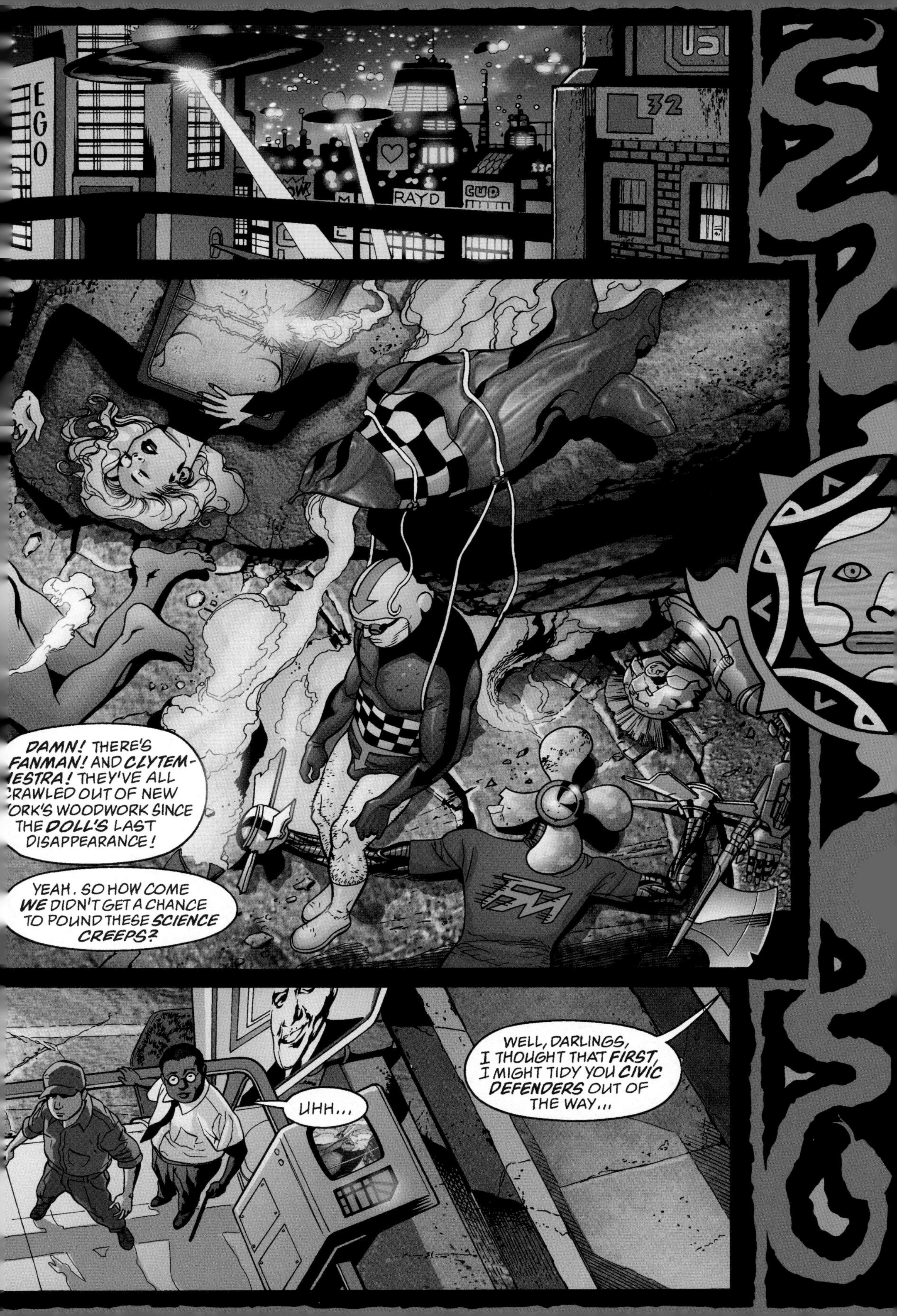
EGO
32
RAYD
GUD
DAMN! THERE'S FANMAN! AND CLYTEM- ESTRA! THEY'VE ALL RAWLED OUT OF NEW ORK'S WOODWORK SINCE THE DOLL'S LAST DISAPPEARANCE!
YEAH. SO HOW COME WE DIDN'T GET A CHANCE TO POUND THESE SCIENCE CREEPS?
UHH...
WELL, DARLINGS, I THOUGHT THAT FIRST, I MIGHT TIDY YOU CIVIC DEFENDERS OUT OF THE WAY...

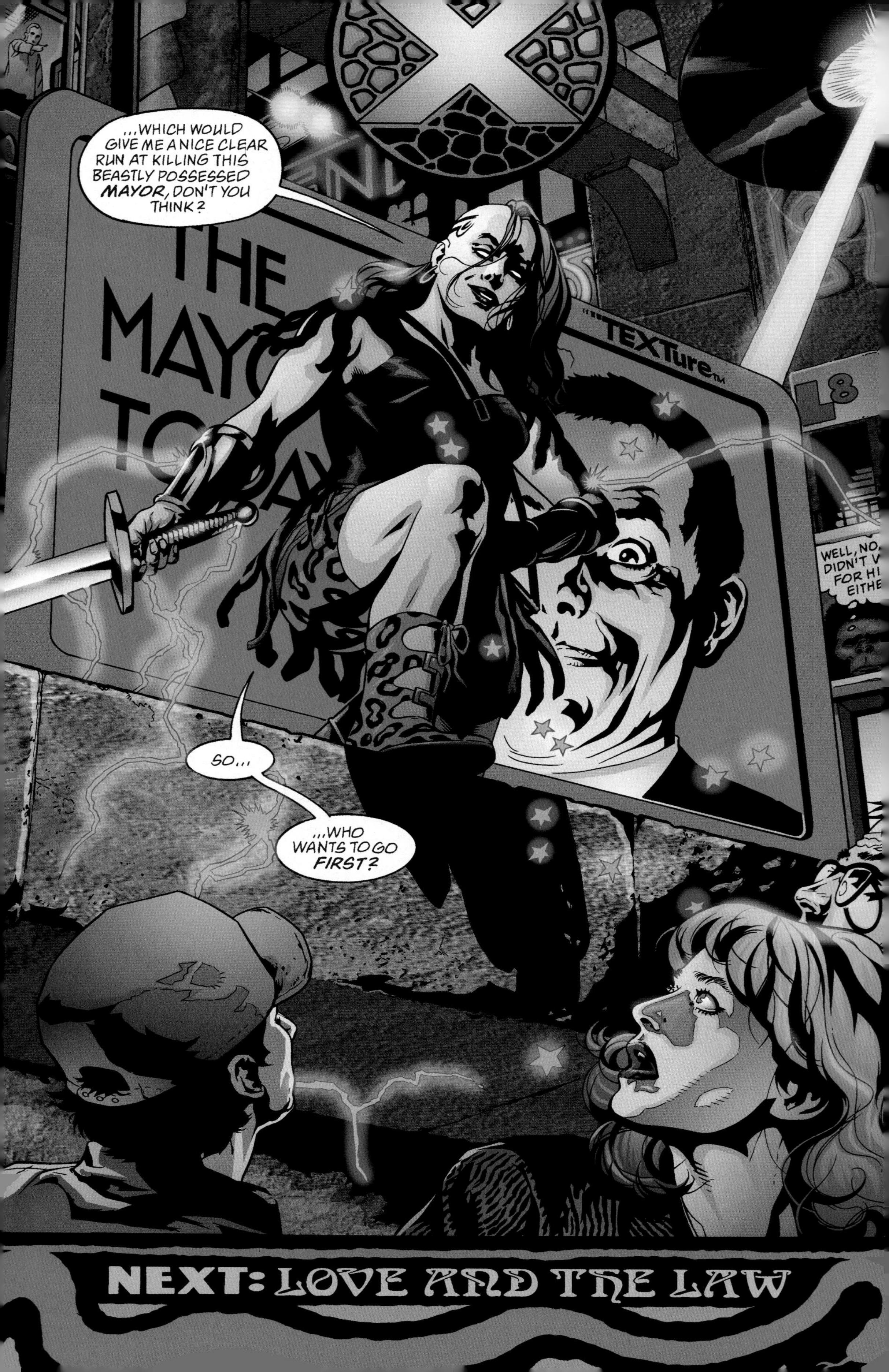
...WHICH WOULD GIVE ME A NICE CLEAR RUN AT KILLING THIS BEASTLY POSSESSED MAYOR, DON'T YOU THINK?
TEXTure™
SO...
...WHO WANTS TO GO FIRST?
NEXT: LOVE AND THE LAW

CHAPTER FOUR

**An ocean of emotion is plunged into,
A memory of motherhood is explored,
And new realizations flow forth.**

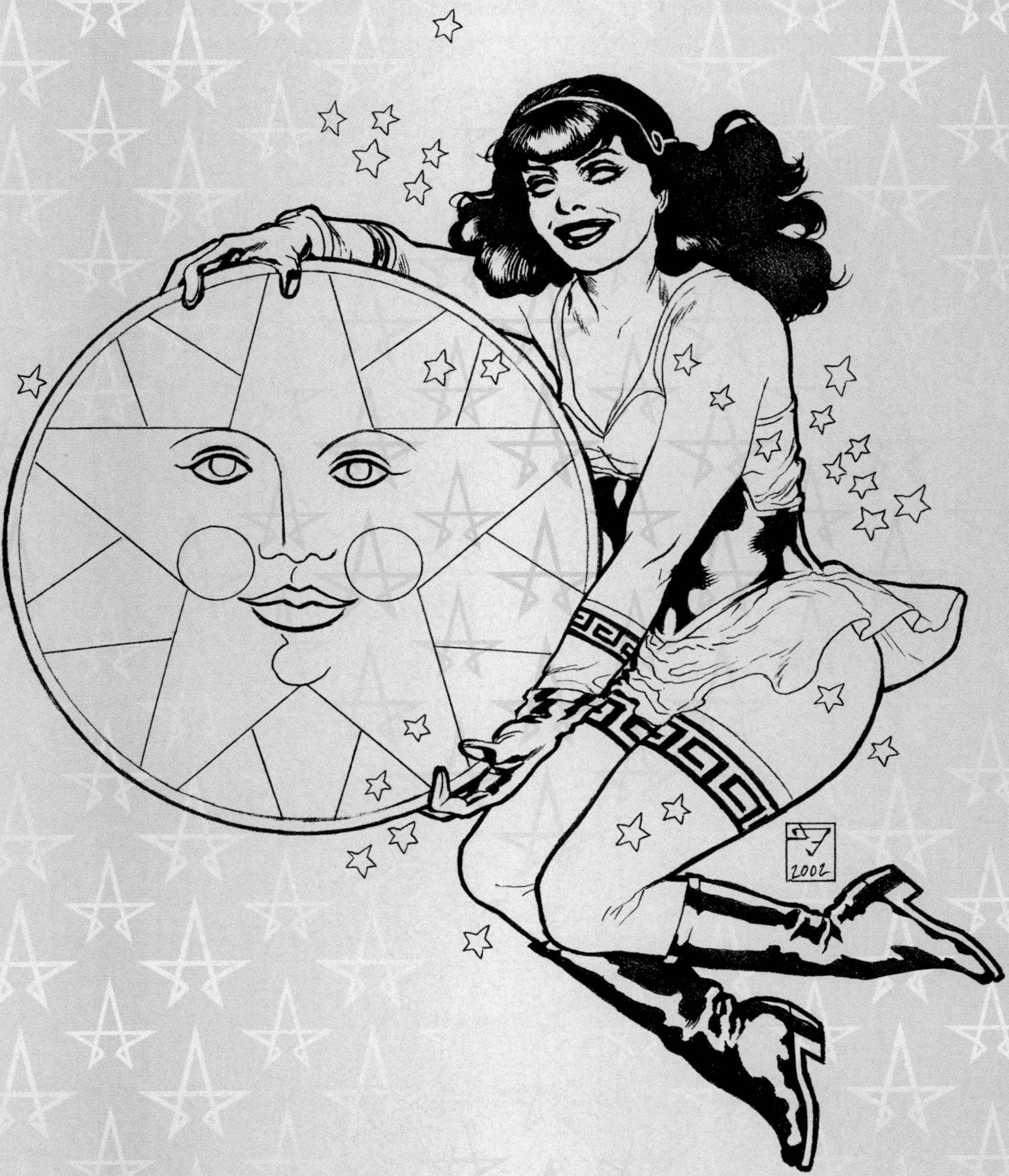
2002

**Cover art:
J.H. Williams III,
Mick Gray & Jeromy Cox**

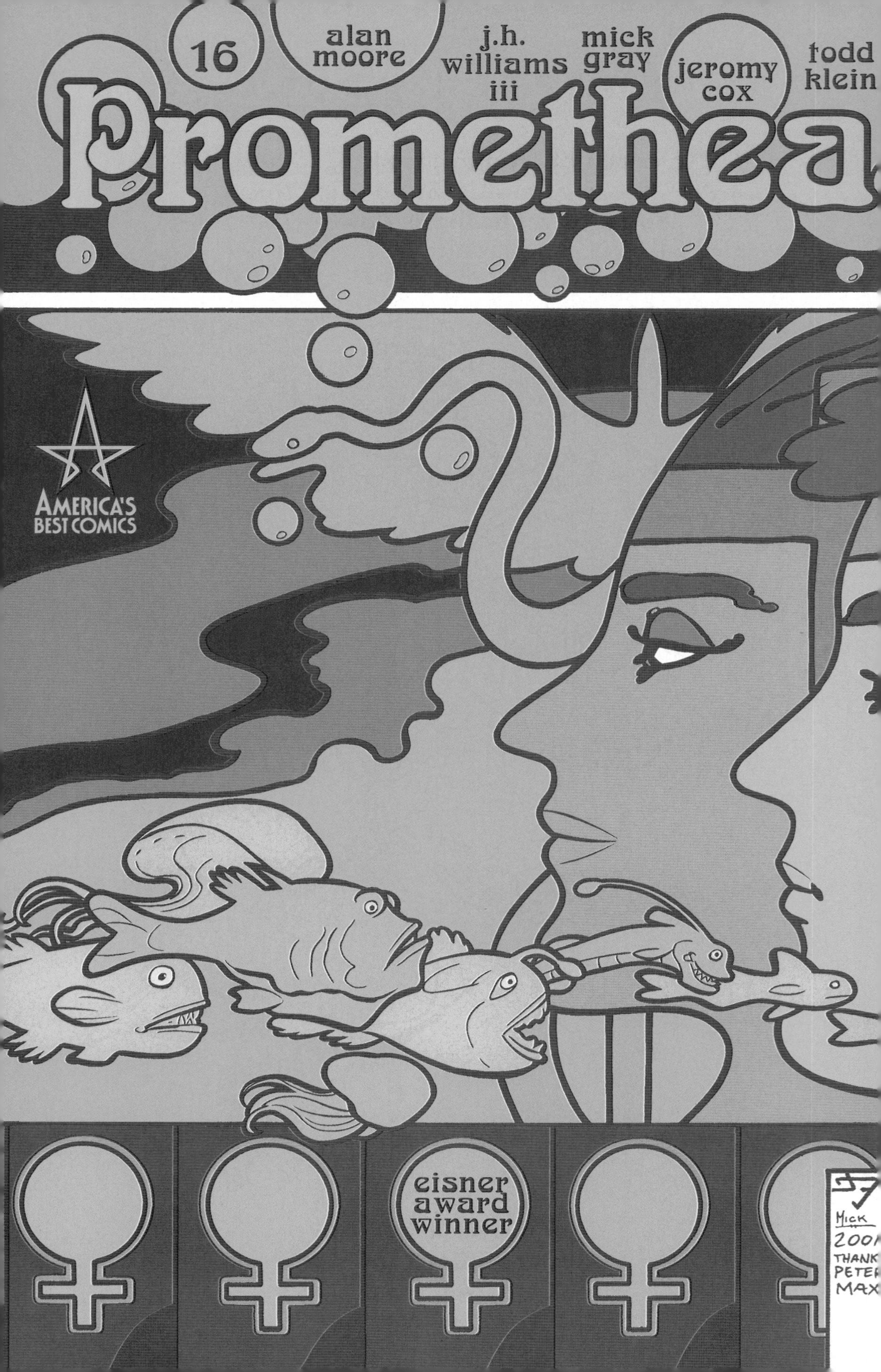
16
alan moore
j.h. williams iii
mick gray
jeromy cox
todd klein
Promethea
AMERICA'S BEST COMICS
eisner award winner
MICK

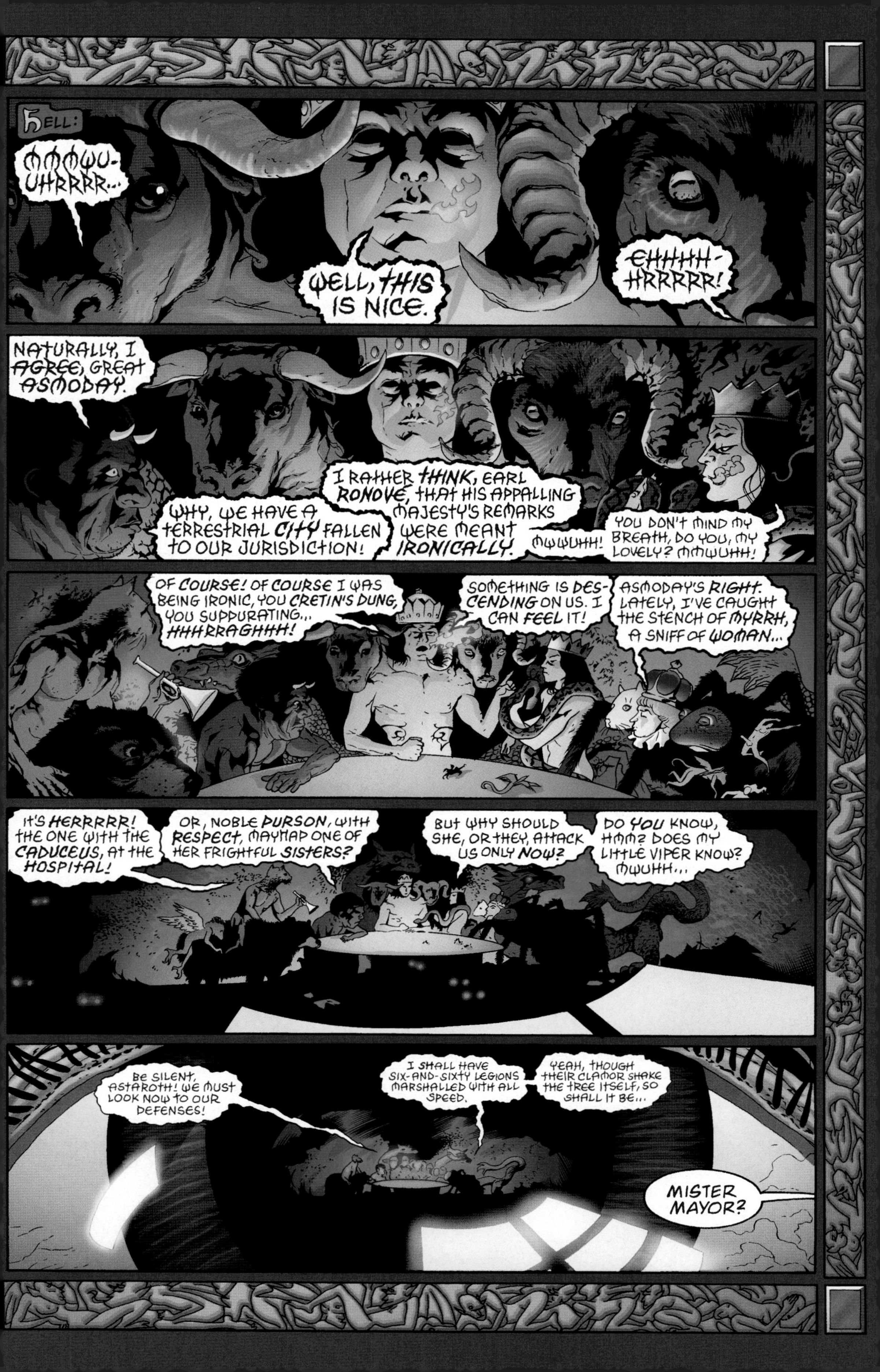
HELL:
MMMWU-UHRRRR...
WELL, THIS IS NICE.
EHHHH-HRRRRR!
NATURALLY, I AGREE, GREAT ASMODAY.
WHY, WE HAVE A TERRESTRIAL CITY FALLEN TO OUR JURISDICTION!
I RATHER THINK, EARL RONOVE, THAT HIS APPALLING MAJESTY'S REMARKS WERE MEANT IRONICALLY.
MWWUHH!
YOU DON'T MIND MY BREATH, DO YOU, MY LOVELY? MMWUHH!
OF COURSE! OF COURSE I WAS BEING IRONIC, YOU CRETIN'S DUNG, YOU SUPPURATING... HHHRRAGHHH!
SOMETHING IS DESCENDING ON US. I CAN FEEL IT!
ASMODAY'S RIGHT. LATELY, I'VE CAUGHT THE STENCH OF MYRRH, A SNIFF OF WOMAN...
IT'S HERRRRR! THE ONE WITH THE CADUCEUS, AT THE HOSPITAL!
OR, NOBLE PURSON, WITH RESPECT, MAYHAP ONE OF HER FRIGHTFUL SISTERS?
BUT WHY SHOULD SHE, OR THEY, ATTACK US ONLY NOW?
DO YOU KNOW, HMM? DOES MY LITTLE VIPER KNOW? MWUHH...
BE SILENT, ASTAROTH! WE MUST LOOK NOW TO OUR DEFENSES!
I SHALL HAVE SIX-AND-SIXTY LEGIONS MARSHALLED WITH ALL SPEED.
YEAH, THOUGH THEIR CLAMOR SHAKE THE TREE ITSELF, SO SHALL IT BE...
MISTER MAYOR?

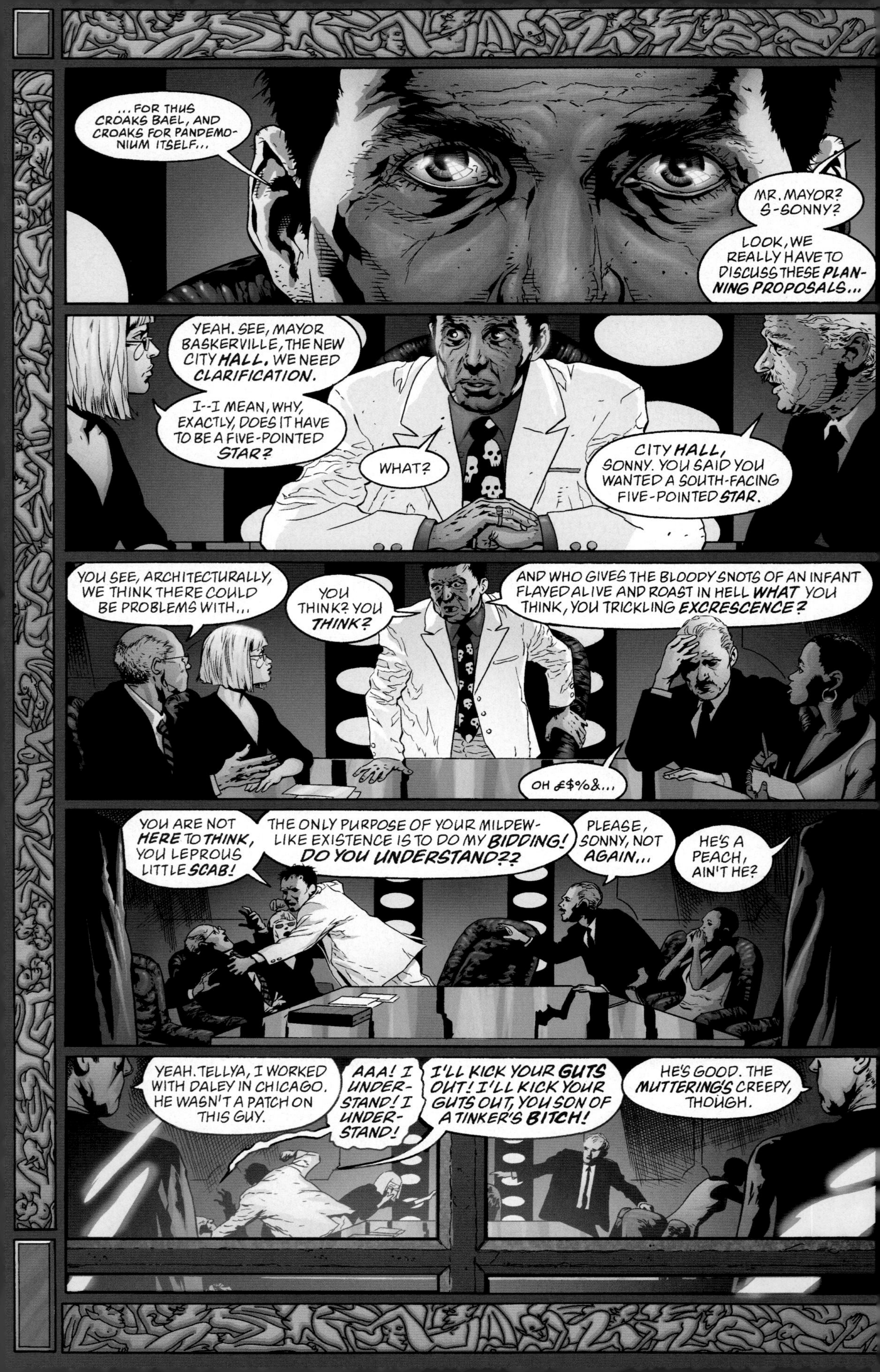
...FOR THUS CROAKS BAEL, AND CROAKS FOR PANDEMONIUM ITSELF...
MR. MAYOR? S-SONNY?
LOOK, WE REALLY HAVE TO DISCUSS THESE PLANNING PROPOSALS...
YEAH. SEE, MAYOR BASKERVILLE, THE NEW CITY HALL. WE NEED CLARIFICATION.
I--I MEAN, WHY, EXACTLY, DOES IT HAVE TO BE A FIVE-POINTED STAR?
WHAT?
CITY HALL, SONNY. YOU SAID YOU WANTED A SOUTH-FACING FIVE-POINTED STAR.
YOU SEE, ARCHITECTURALLY, WE THINK THERE COULD BE PROBLEMS WITH...
YOU THINK? YOU THINK?
AND WHO GIVES THE BLOODY SNOTS OF AN INFANT FLAYED ALIVE AND ROAST IN HELL WHAT YOU THINK, YOU TRICKLING EXCRESCENCE?
OH £$%&...
YOU ARE NOT HERE TO THINK, YOU LEPROUS LITTLE SCAB!
THE ONLY PURPOSE OF YOUR MILDEW-LIKE EXISTENCE IS TO DO MY BIDDING! DO YOU UNDERSTAND??
PLEASE, SONNY, NOT AGAIN...
HE'S A PEACH, AIN'T HE?
YEAH. TELLYA, I WORKED WITH DALEY IN CHICAGO. HE WASN'T A PATCH ON THIS GUY.
AAA! I UNDERSTAND! I UNDERSTAND!
I'LL KICK YOUR GUTS OUT! I'LL KICK YOUR GUTS OUT, YOU SON OF A TINKER'S BITCH!
HE'S GOOD. THE MUTTERING'S CREEPY, THOUGH.

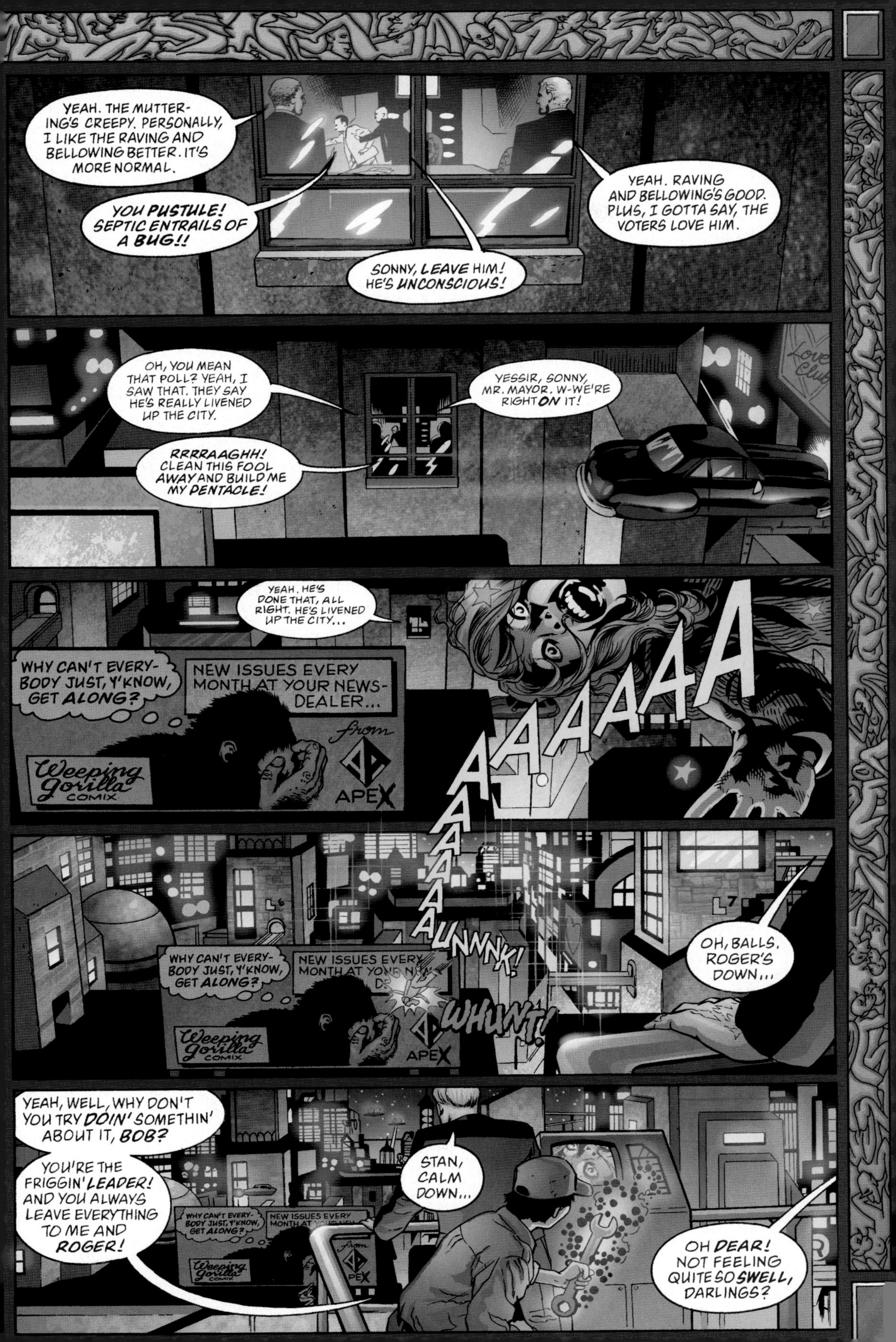
YEAH. THE MUTTERING'S CREEPY. PERSONALLY, I LIKE THE RAVING AND BELLOWING BETTER. IT'S MORE NORMAL.
YOU PUSTULE! SEPTIC ENTRAILS OF A BUG!!
SONNY, LEAVE HIM! HE'S UNCONSCIOUS!
YEAH. RAVING AND BELLOWING'S GOOD. PLUS, I GOTTA SAY, THE VOTERS LOVE HIM.
OH, YOU MEAN THAT POLL? YEAH, I SAW THAT. THEY SAY HE'S REALLY LIVENED UP THE CITY.
RRRRAAGHH! CLEAN THIS FOOL AWAY AND BUILD ME MY PENTACLE!
YESSIR, SONNY, MR. MAYOR. W-WE'RE RIGHT ON IT!
YEAH. HE'S DONE THAT, ALL RIGHT. HE'S LIVENED UP THE CITY...
WHY CAN'T EVERYBODY JUST, Y'KNOW, GET ALONG?
NEW ISSUES EVERY MONTH AT YOUR NEWSDEALER...
Weeping Gorilla COMIX
from APEX
AAAAAAAAAAAAAAUNNNK!
WHUNT!
OH, BALLS. ROGER'S DOWN...
YEAH, WELL, WHY DON'T YOU TRY DOIN' SOMETHIN' ABOUT IT, BOB?
YOU'RE THE FRIGGIN' LEADER! AND YOU ALWAYS LEAVE EVERYTHING TO ME AND ROGER!
STAN, CALM DOWN...
OH DEAR! NOT FEELING QUITE SO SWELL, DARLINGS?

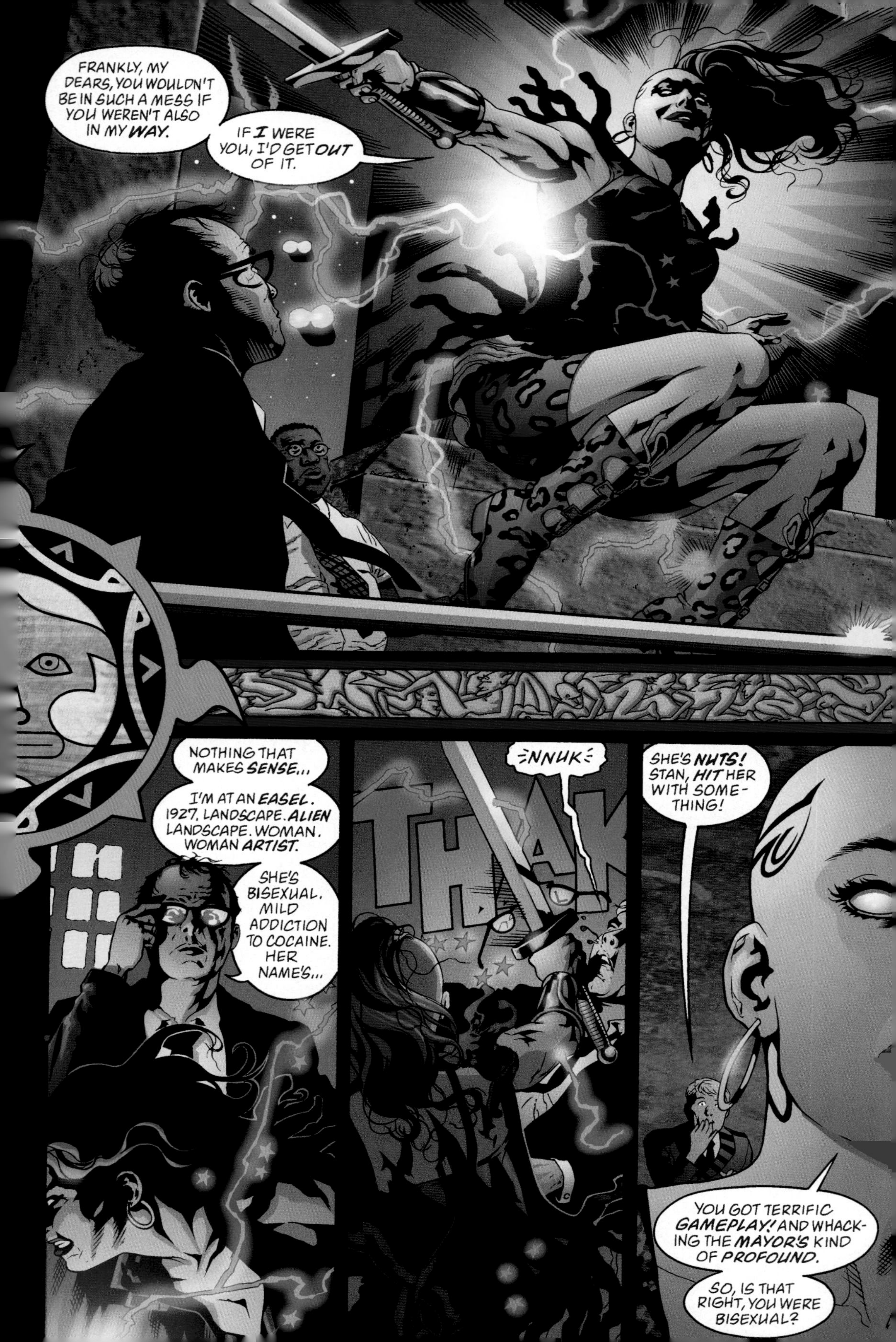
FRANKLY, MY DEARS, YOU WOULDN'T BE IN SUCH A MESS IF YOU WEREN'T ALSO IN MY WAY.
IF I WERE YOU, I'D GET OUT OF IT.
NOTHING THAT MAKES SENSE...
I'M AT AN EASEL. 1927. LANDSCAPE. ALIEN LANDSCAPE. WOMAN. WOMAN ARTIST.
SHE'S BISEXUAL. MILD ADDICTION TO COCAINE. HER NAME'S...
THAK
=NNUK=
SHE'S NUTS! STAN, HIT HER WITH SOME-THING!
YOU GOT TERRIFIC GAMEPLAY! AND WHACK-ING THE MAYOR'S KIND OF PROFOUND.
SO, IS THAT RIGHT, YOU WERE BISEXUAL?

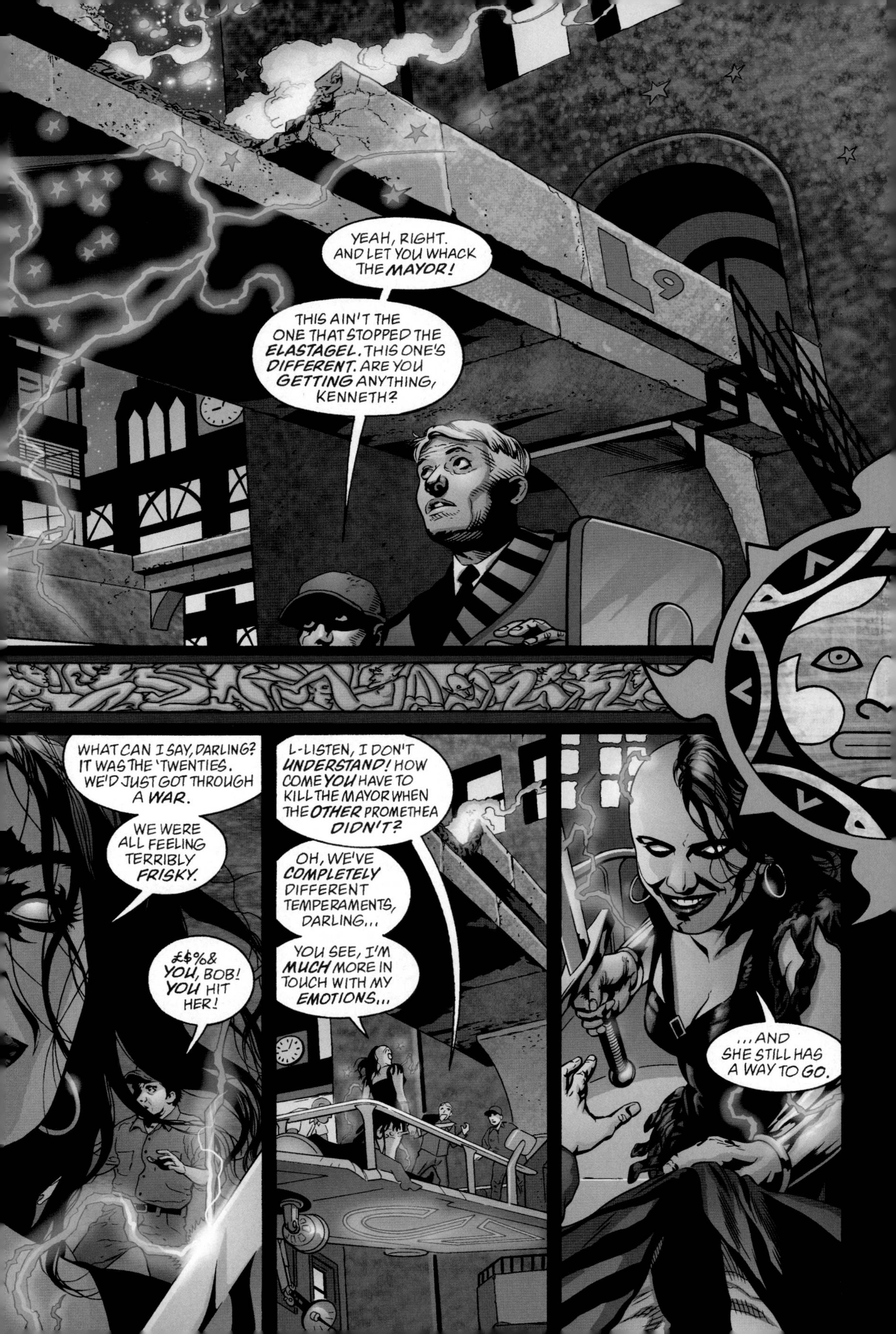
YEAH, RIGHT. AND LET YOU WHACK THE MAYOR!
THIS AIN'T THE ONE THAT STOPPED THE ELASTAGEL. THIS ONE'S DIFFERENT. ARE YOU GETTING ANYTHING, KENNETH?
L9
WHAT CAN I SAY, DARLING? IT WAS THE 'TWENTIES. WE'D JUST GOT THROUGH A WAR.
WE WERE ALL FEELING TERRIBLY FRISKY.
£$%& YOU, BOB! YOU HIT HER!
L-LISTEN, I DON'T UNDERSTAND! HOW COME YOU HAVE TO KILL THE MAYOR WHEN THE OTHER PROMETHEA DIDN'T?
OH, WE'VE COMPLETELY DIFFERENT TEMPERAMENTS, DARLING...
YOU SEE, I'M MUCH MORE IN TOUCH WITH MY EMOTIONS...
...AND SHE STILL HAS A WAY TO GO.

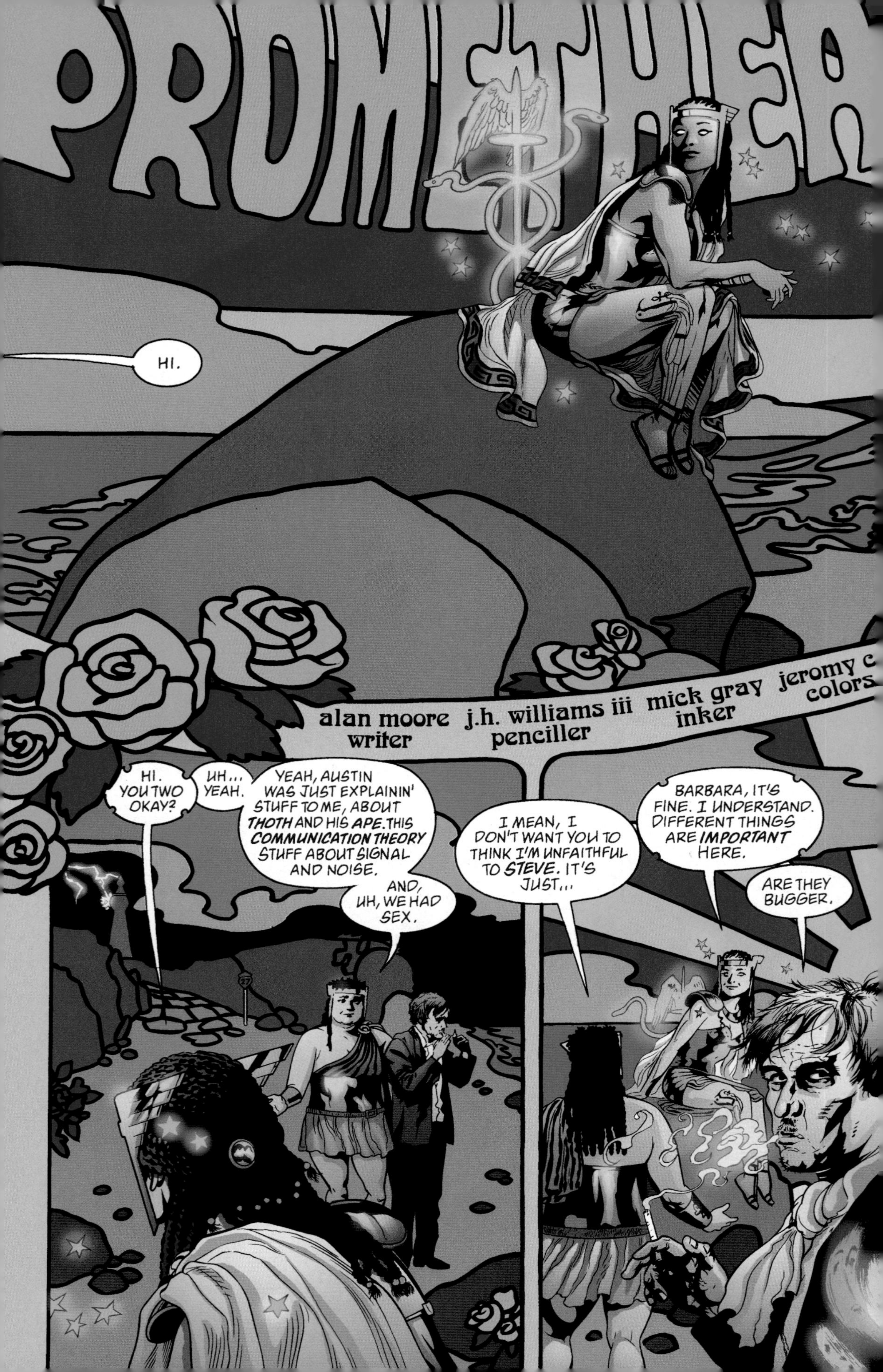
PROMETHEA
HI.
alan moore writer
j.h. williams iii penciller
mick gray inker
jeromy c
colors
HI. YOU TWO OKAY?
UH... YEAH.
YEAH, AUSTIN WAS JUST EXPLAININ' STUFF TO ME, ABOUT THOTH AND HIS APE. THIS COMMUNICATION THEORY STUFF ABOUT SIGNAL AND NOISE.
AND, UH, WE HAD SEX.
I MEAN, I DON'T WANT YOU TO THINK I'M UNFAITHFUL TO STEVE. IT'S JUST...
BARBARA, IT'S FINE. I UNDERSTAND. DIFFERENT THINGS ARE IMPORTANT HERE.
ARE THEY BUGGER.

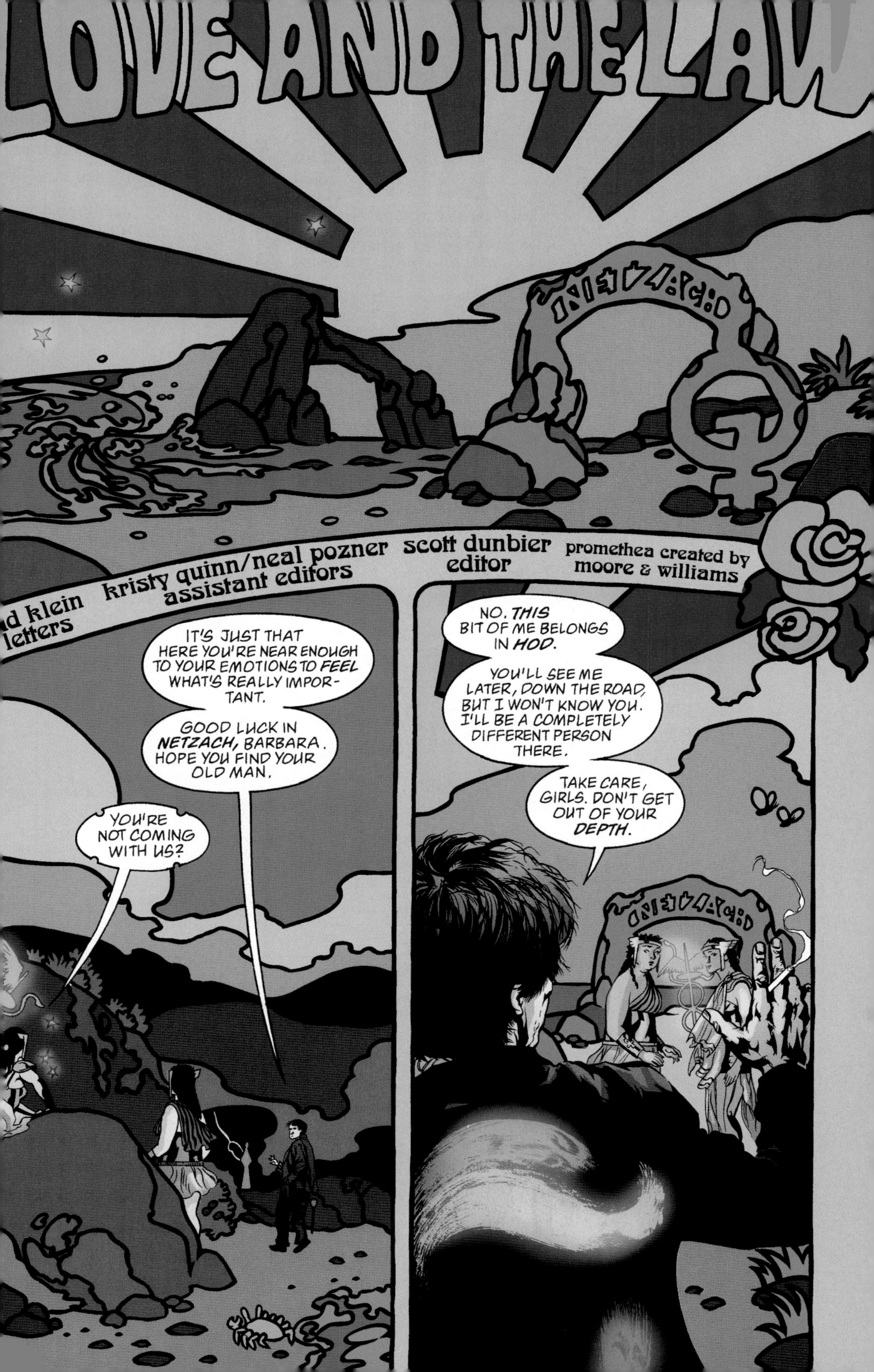

LOVE AND THE LAW
d klein
letters
kristy quinn/neal pozner
assistant editors
scott dunbier
editor
promethea created by
moore & williams
IT'S JUST THAT HERE YOU'RE NEAR ENOUGH TO YOUR EMOTIONS TO FEEL WHAT'S REALLY IMPORTANT.
GOOD LUCK IN NETZACH, BARBARA. HOPE YOU FIND YOUR OLD MAN.
YOU'RE NOT COMING WITH US?
NO. THIS BIT OF ME BELONGS IN HOD.
YOU'LL SEE ME LATER, DOWN THE ROAD, BUT I WON'T KNOW YOU. I'LL BE A COMPLETELY DIFFERENT PERSON THERE.
TAKE CARE, GIRLS. DON'T GET OUT OF YOUR DEPTH.

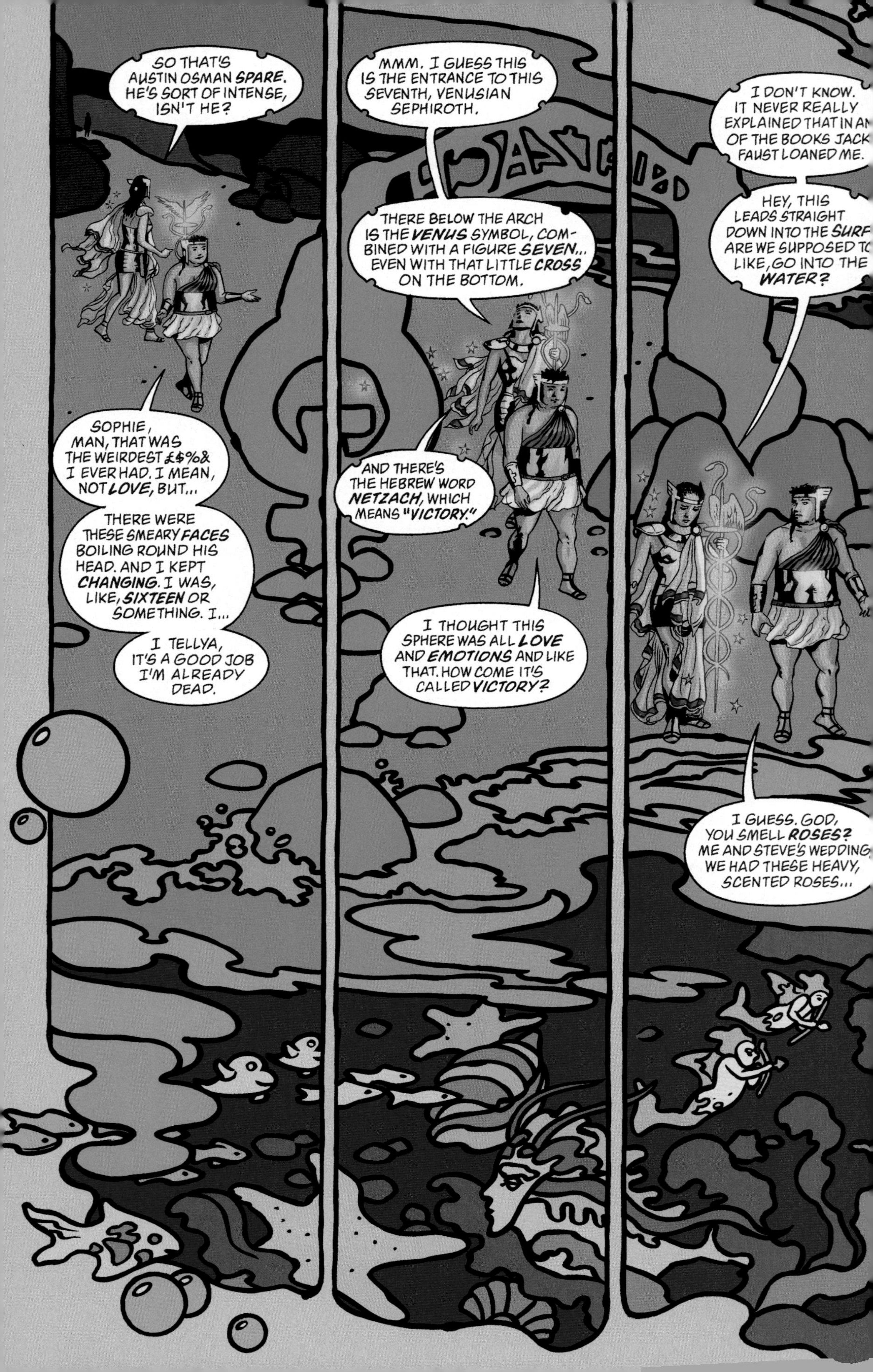
SO THAT'S AUSTIN OSMAN SPARE. HE'S SORT OF INTENSE, ISN'T HE?
SOPHIE, MAN, THAT WAS THE WEIRDEST £$%& I EVER HAD. I MEAN, NOT LOVE, BUT...
THERE WERE THESE SMEARY FACES BOILING ROUND HIS HEAD. AND I KEPT CHANGING. I WAS, LIKE, SIXTEEN OR SOMETHING. I...
I TELLYA, IT'S A GOOD JOB I'M ALREADY DEAD.
MMM. I GUESS THIS IS THE ENTRANCE TO THIS SEVENTH, VENUSIAN SEPHIROTH.
THERE BELOW THE ARCH IS THE VENUS SYMBOL, COMBINED WITH A FIGURE SEVEN... EVEN WITH THAT LITTLE CROSS ON THE BOTTOM.
AND THERE'S THE HEBREW WORD NETZACH, WHICH MEANS "VICTORY."
I THOUGHT THIS SPHERE WAS ALL LOVE AND EMOTIONS AND LIKE THAT. HOW COME IT'S CALLED VICTORY?
I DON'T KNOW. IT NEVER REALLY EXPLAINED THAT IN AN OF THE BOOKS JACK FAUST LOANED ME.
HEY, THIS LEADS STRAIGHT DOWN INTO THE SURF ARE WE SUPPOSED TO LIKE, GO INTO THE WATER?
I GUESS. GOD, YOU SMELL ROSES? ME AND STEVE'S WEDDING WE HAD THESE HEAVY, SCENTED ROSES...

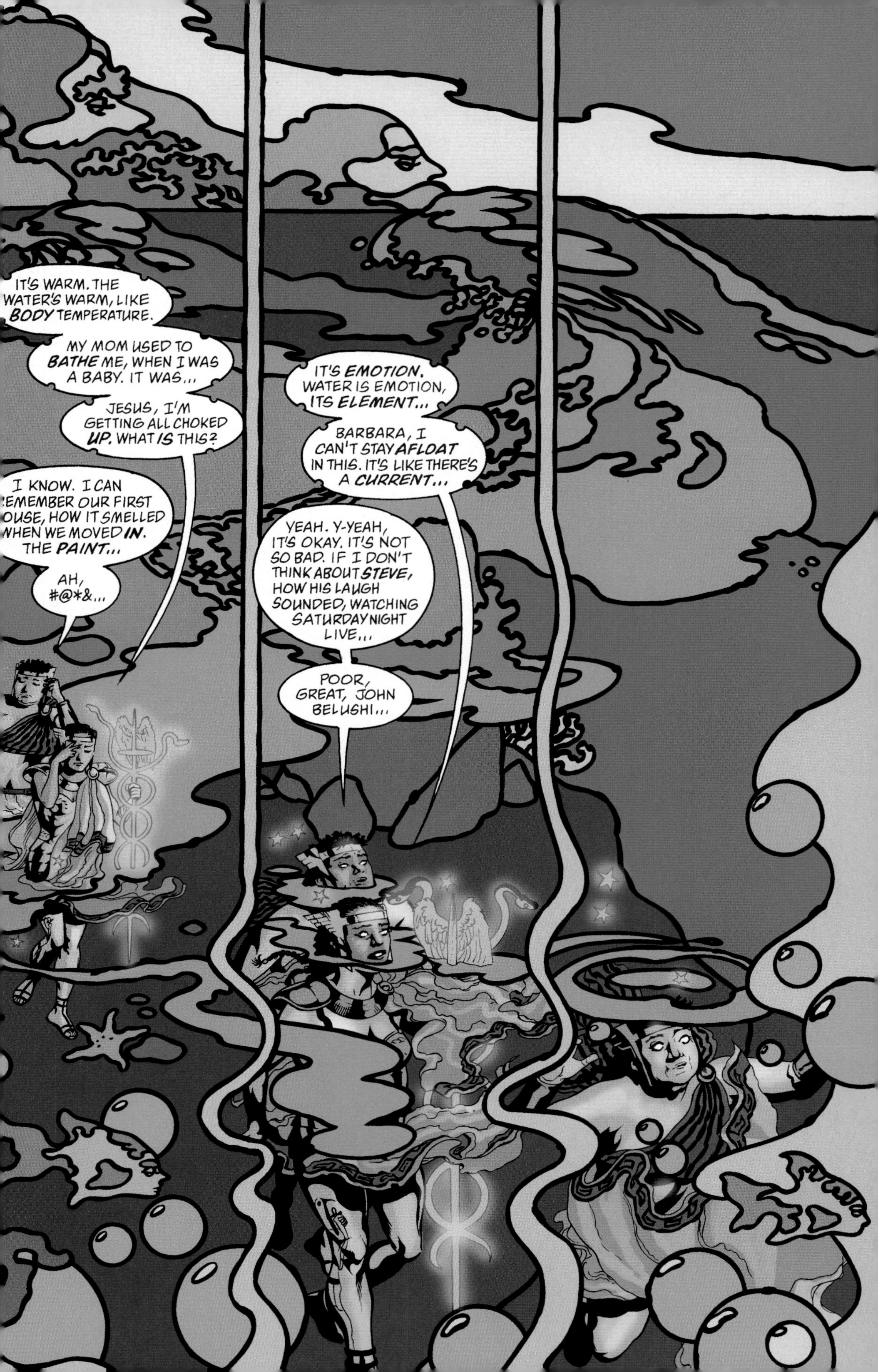
IT'S WARM. THE WATER'S WARM, LIKE BODY TEMPERATURE.
MY MOM USED TO BATHE ME, WHEN I WAS A BABY. IT WAS...
JESUS, I'M GETTING ALL CHOKED UP. WHAT IS THIS?
I KNOW. I CAN REMEMBER OUR FIRST HOUSE, HOW IT SMELLED WHEN WE MOVED IN. THE PAINT...
AH, #@*&...
IT'S EMOTION. WATER IS EMOTION, ITS ELEMENT...
BARBARA, I CAN'T STAY AFLOAT IN THIS. IT'S LIKE THERE'S A CURRENT...
YEAH. Y-YEAH, IT'S OKAY. IT'S NOT SO BAD. IF I DON'T THINK ABOUT STEVE, HOW HIS LAUGH SOUNDED, WATCHING SATURDAY NIGHT LIVE...
POOR, GREAT, JOHN BELUSHI...

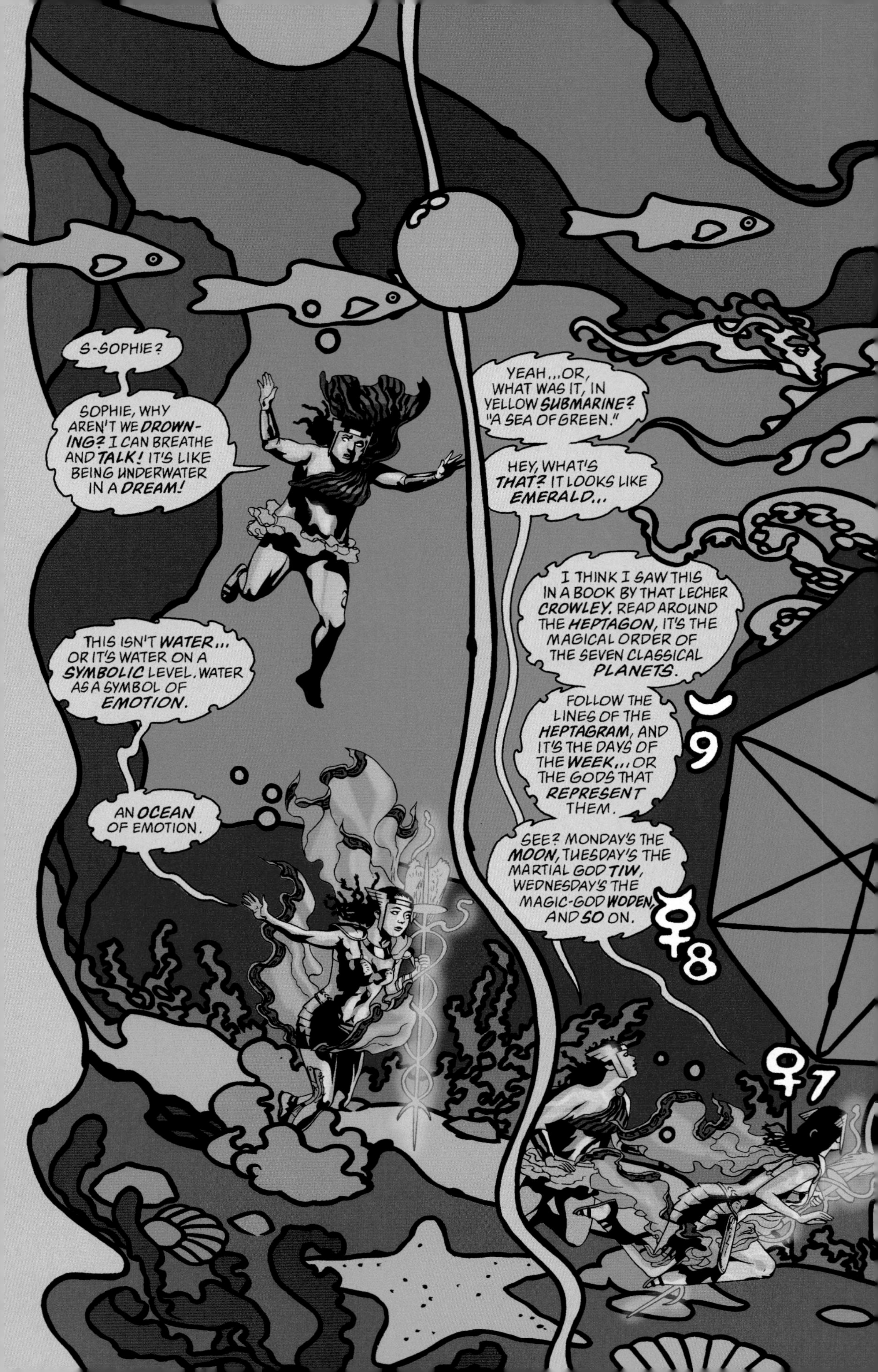
S-SOPHIE?
SOPHIE, WHY AREN'T WE DROWNING? I CAN BREATHE AND TALK! IT'S LIKE BEING UNDERWATER IN A DREAM!
THIS ISN'T WATER... OR IT'S WATER ON A SYMBOLIC LEVEL. WATER AS A SYMBOL OF EMOTION.
AN OCEAN OF EMOTION.
YEAH... OR, WHAT WAS IT, IN YELLOW SUBMARINE? "A SEA OF GREEN."
HEY, WHAT'S THAT? IT LOOKS LIKE EMERALD...
I THINK I SAW THIS IN A BOOK BY THAT LECHER CROWLEY. READ AROUND THE HEPTAGON, IT'S THE MAGICAL ORDER OF THE SEVEN CLASSICAL PLANETS.
FOLLOW THE LINES OF THE HEPTAGRAM, AND IT'S THE DAYS OF THE WEEK... OR THE GODS THAT REPRESENT THEM.
SEE? MONDAY'S THE MOON, TUESDAY'S THE MARTIAL GOD TIW, WEDNESDAY'S THE MAGIC-GOD WODEN, AND SO ON.
9
8
7

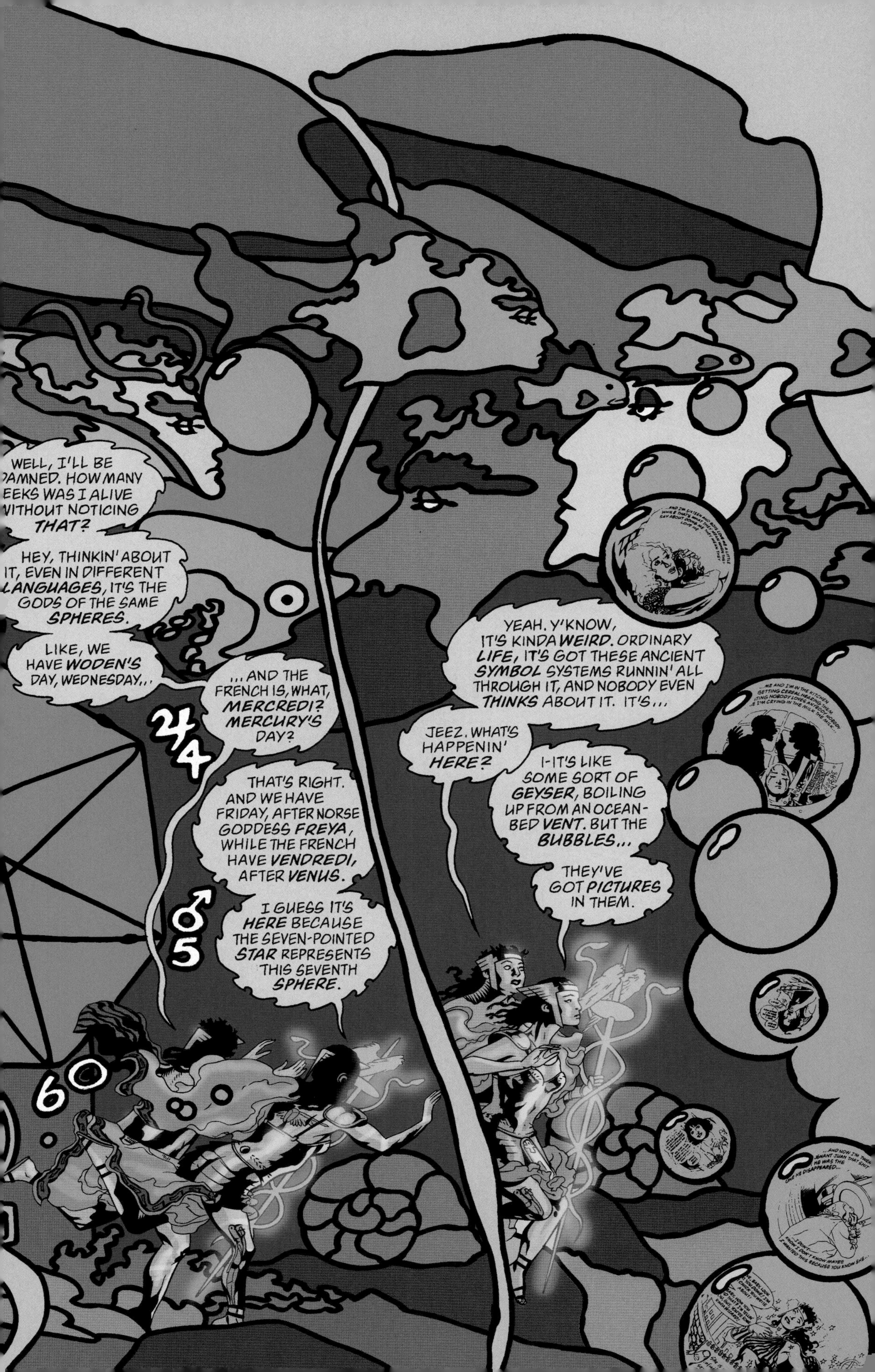

WELL, I'LL BE DAMNED. HOW MANY EEKS WAS I ALIVE WITHOUT NOTICING THAT?
HEY, THINKIN' ABOUT IT, EVEN IN DIFFERENT LANGUAGES, IT'S THE GODS OF THE SAME SPHERES.
LIKE, WE HAVE WODEN'S DAY, WEDNESDAY...
...AND THE FRENCH IS, WHAT, MERCREDI? MERCURY'S DAY?
THAT'S RIGHT. AND WE HAVE FRIDAY, AFTER NORSE GODDESS FREYA, WHILE THE FRENCH HAVE VENDREDI, AFTER VENUS.
I GUESS IT'S HERE BECAUSE THE SEVEN-POINTED STAR REPRESENTS THIS SEVENTH SPHERE.
YEAH. Y'KNOW, IT'S KINDA WEIRD. ORDINARY LIFE, IT'S GOT THESE ANCIENT SYMBOL SYSTEMS RUNNIN' ALL THROUGH IT, AND NOBODY EVEN THINKS ABOUT IT. IT'S...
JEEZ. WHAT'S HAPPENIN' HERE?
I-IT'S LIKE SOME SORT OF GEYSER, BOILING UP FROM AN OCEAN-BED VENT. BUT THE BUBBLES...
THEY'VE GOT PICTURES IN THEM.
4
5
6

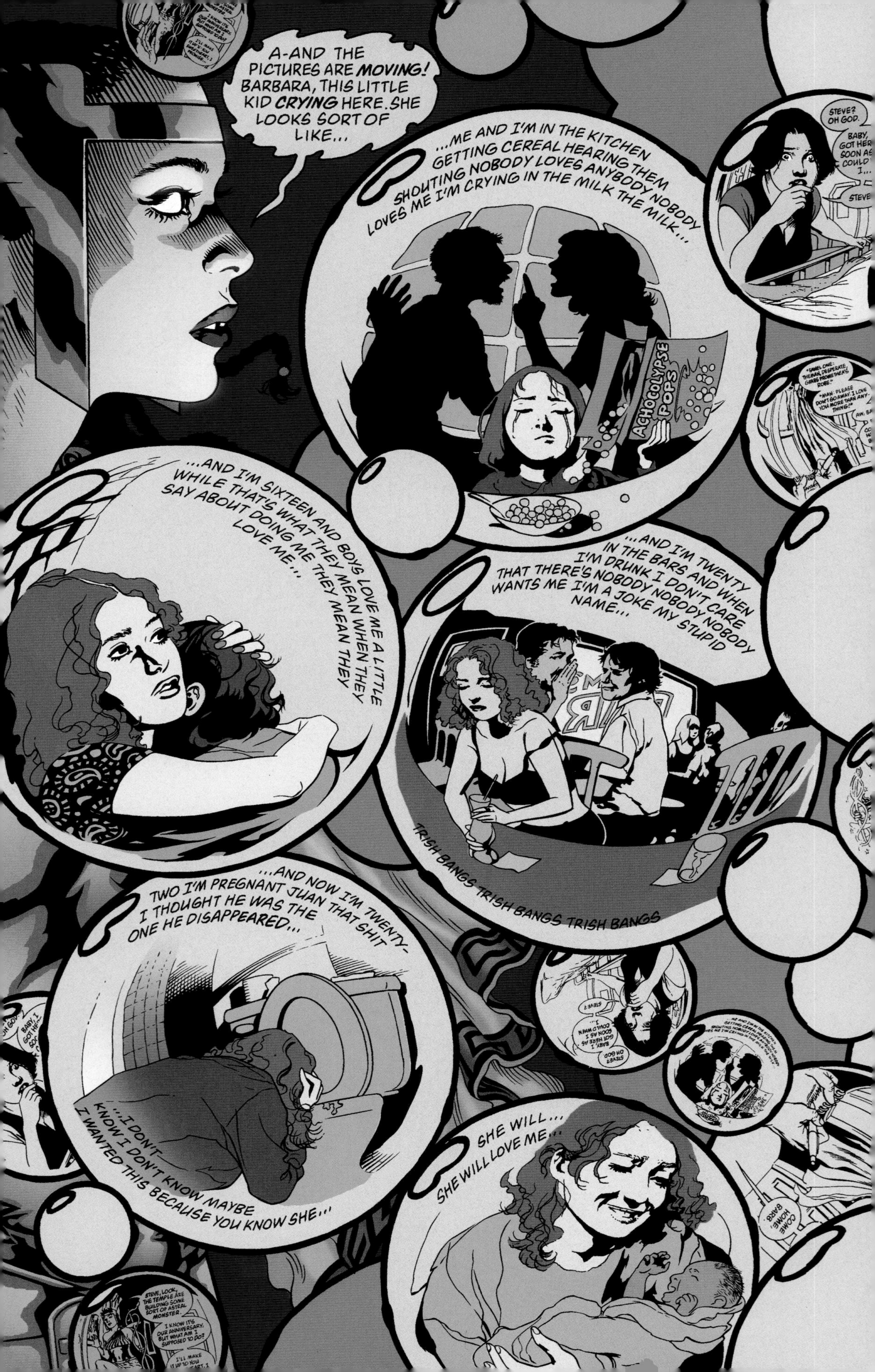

A-AND THE PICTURES ARE MOVING! BARBARA, THIS LITTLE KID CRYING HERE. SHE LOOKS SORT OF LIKE...
...ME AND I'M IN THE KITCHEN GETTING CEREAL HEARING THEM SHOUTING NOBODY LOVES ANYBODY NOBODY LOVES ME I'M CRYING IN THE MILK THE MILK...
ACHOCOLYPSE POPS
STEVE? OH GOD.
BABY, I GOT HERE AS SOON AS I COULD WHEN I...
...AND I'M SIXTEEN AND BOYS LOVE ME A LITTLE WHILE THAT'S WHAT THEY SAY ABOUT DOING ME THEY MEAN WHEN THEY MEAN THEY LOVE ME...
...AND I'M TWENTY IN THE BARS AND WHEN I'M DRUNK I DON'T CARE THAT THERE'S NOBODY NOBODY NOBODY WANTS ME I'M A JOKE MY STUPID NAME...
TRISH BANGS TRISH BANGS TRISH BANGS
...AND NOW I'M TWENTY-TWO I'M PREGNANT JUAN THAT SHIT I THOUGHT HE WAS THE ONE HE DISAPPEARED...
...I DON'T KNOW I DON'T KNOW MAYBE I WANTED THIS BECAUSE YOU KNOW SHE...
SHE WILL... SHE WILL LOVE ME...
COME HOME, BARB.
STEVE, LOOK, THE TEMPLE ARE BUILDING SOME SORT OF ASTRAL MONSTER.
I KNOW IT'S OUR ANNIVERSARY, BUT WHAT AM I SUPPOSED TO DO?

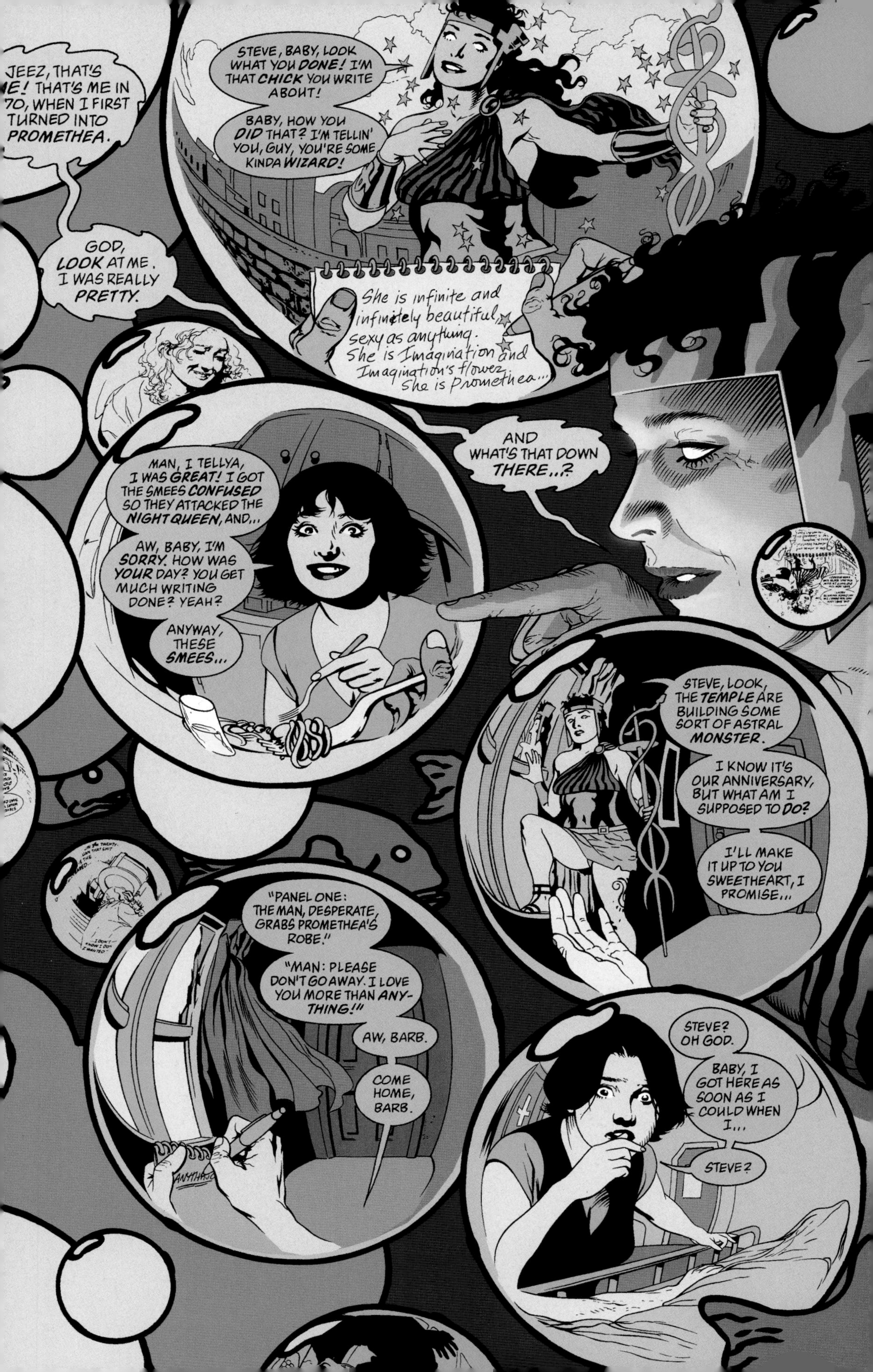

JEEZ, THAT'S E! THAT'S ME IN 70, WHEN I FIRST TURNED INTO PROMETHEA.
STEVE, BABY, LOOK WHAT YOU DONE! I'M THAT CHICK YOU WRITE ABOUT!
BABY, HOW YOU DID THAT? I'M TELLIN' YOU, GUY, YOU'RE SOME KINDA WIZARD!
GOD, LOOK AT ME. I WAS REALLY PRETTY.
She is infinite and infinitely beautiful, sexy as anything. She is Imagination and Imagination's flower She is Promethea...
AND WHAT'S THAT DOWN THERE...?
MAN, I TELLYA, I WAS GREAT! I GOT THE SMEES CONFUSED SO THEY ATTACKED THE NIGHT QUEEN, AND...
AW, BABY, I'M SORRY. HOW WAS YOUR DAY? YOU GET MUCH WRITING DONE? YEAH?
ANYWAY, THESE SMEES...
STEVE, LOOK, THE TEMPLE ARE BUILDING SOME SORT OF ASTRAL MONSTER.
I KNOW IT'S OUR ANNIVERSARY, BUT WHAT AM I SUPPOSED TO DO?
I'LL MAKE IT UP TO YOU SWEETHEART, I PROMISE...
"PANEL ONE: THE MAN, DESPERATE, GRABS PROMETHEA'S ROBE."
"MAN: PLEASE DON'T GO AWAY. I LOVE YOU MORE THAN ANYTHING!"
AW, BARB.
COME HOME, BARB.
STEVE? OH GOD.
BABY, I GOT HERE AS SOON AS I COULD WHEN I...
STEVE?

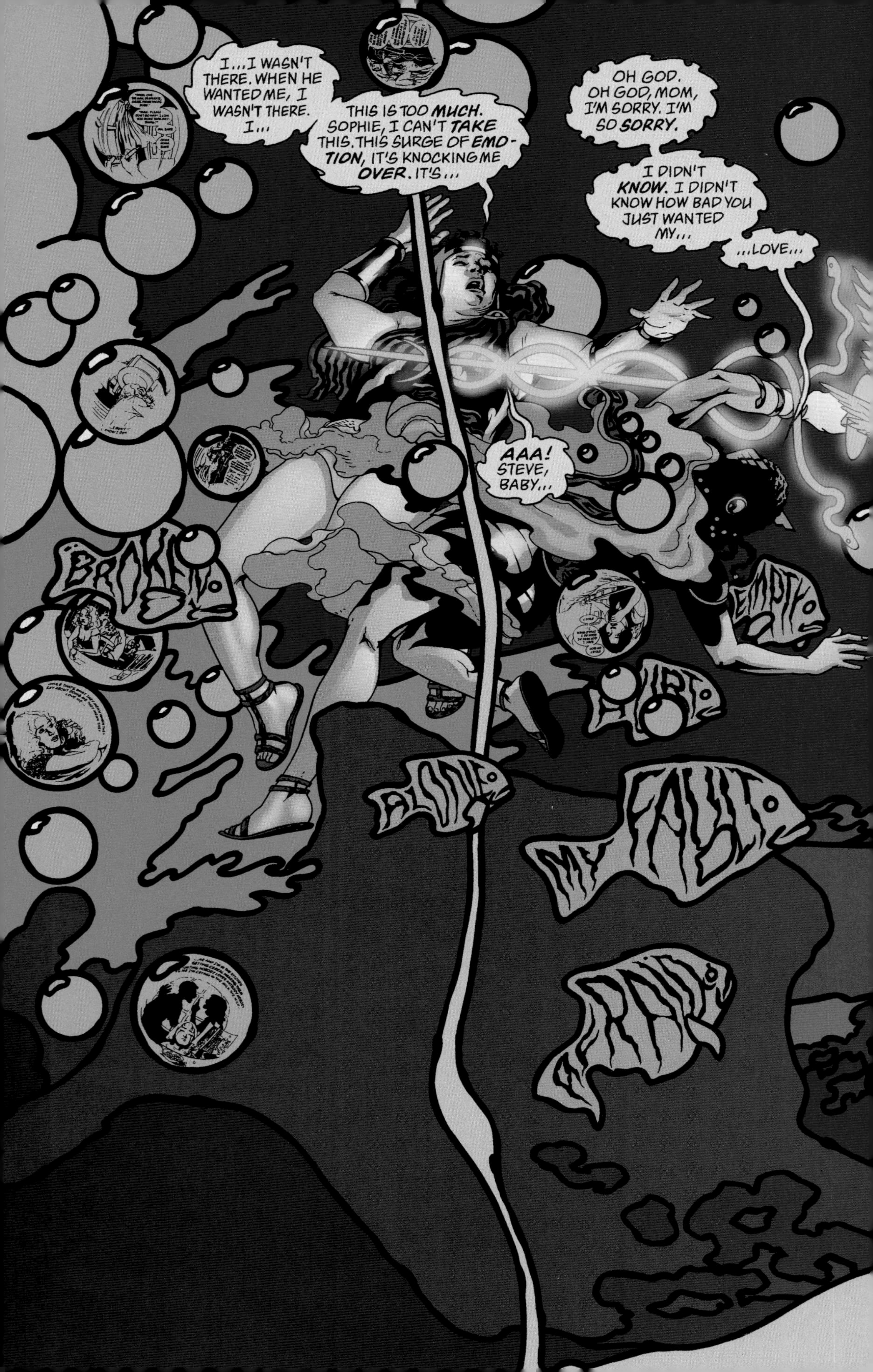

I...I WASN'T THERE. WHEN HE WANTED ME, I WASN'T THERE. I...
THIS IS TOO MUCH. SOPHIE, I CAN'T TAKE THIS. THIS SURGE OF EMOTION, IT'S KNOCKING ME OVER. IT'S...
OH GOD. OH GOD, MOM, I'M SORRY. I'M SO SORRY.
I DIDN'T KNOW. I DIDN'T KNOW HOW BAD YOU JUST WANTED MY...
...LOVE...
AAA! STEVE, BABY...
BROKEN
EMPTY
HURT
ALONE
MY FAULT
AFRAID

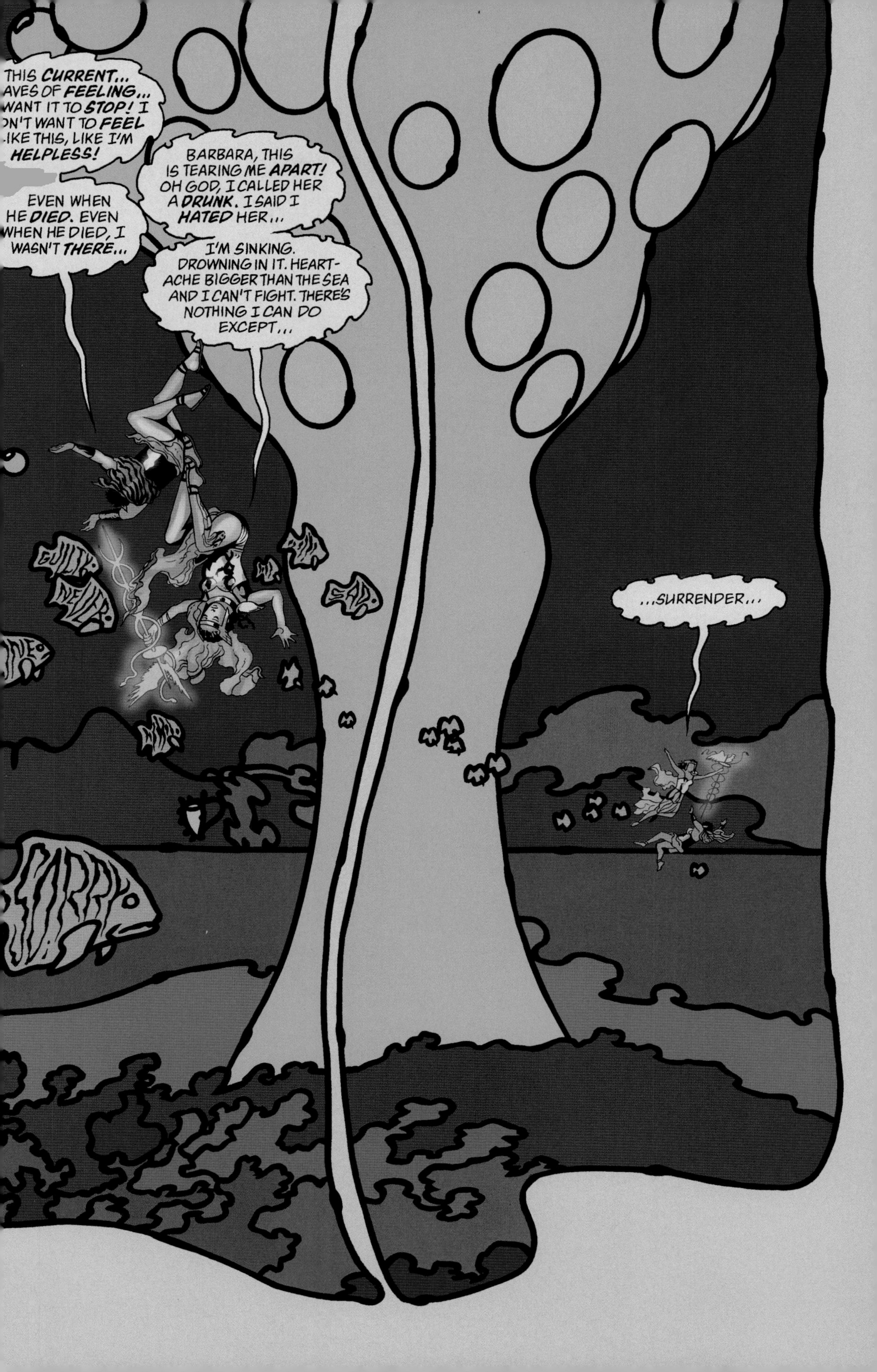
THIS CURRENT... AVES OF FEELING... WANT IT TO STOP! I ON'T WANT TO FEEL IKE THIS, LIKE I'M HELPLESS!
BARBARA, THIS IS TEARING ME APART! OH GOD, I CALLED HER A DRUNK. I SAID I HATED HER...
EVEN WHEN HE DIED. EVEN WHEN HE DIED, I WASN'T THERE...
I'M SINKING. DROWNING IN IT. HEART-ACHE BIGGER THAN THE SEA AND I CAN'T FIGHT. THERE'S NOTHING I CAN DO EXCEPT...
...SURRENDER...

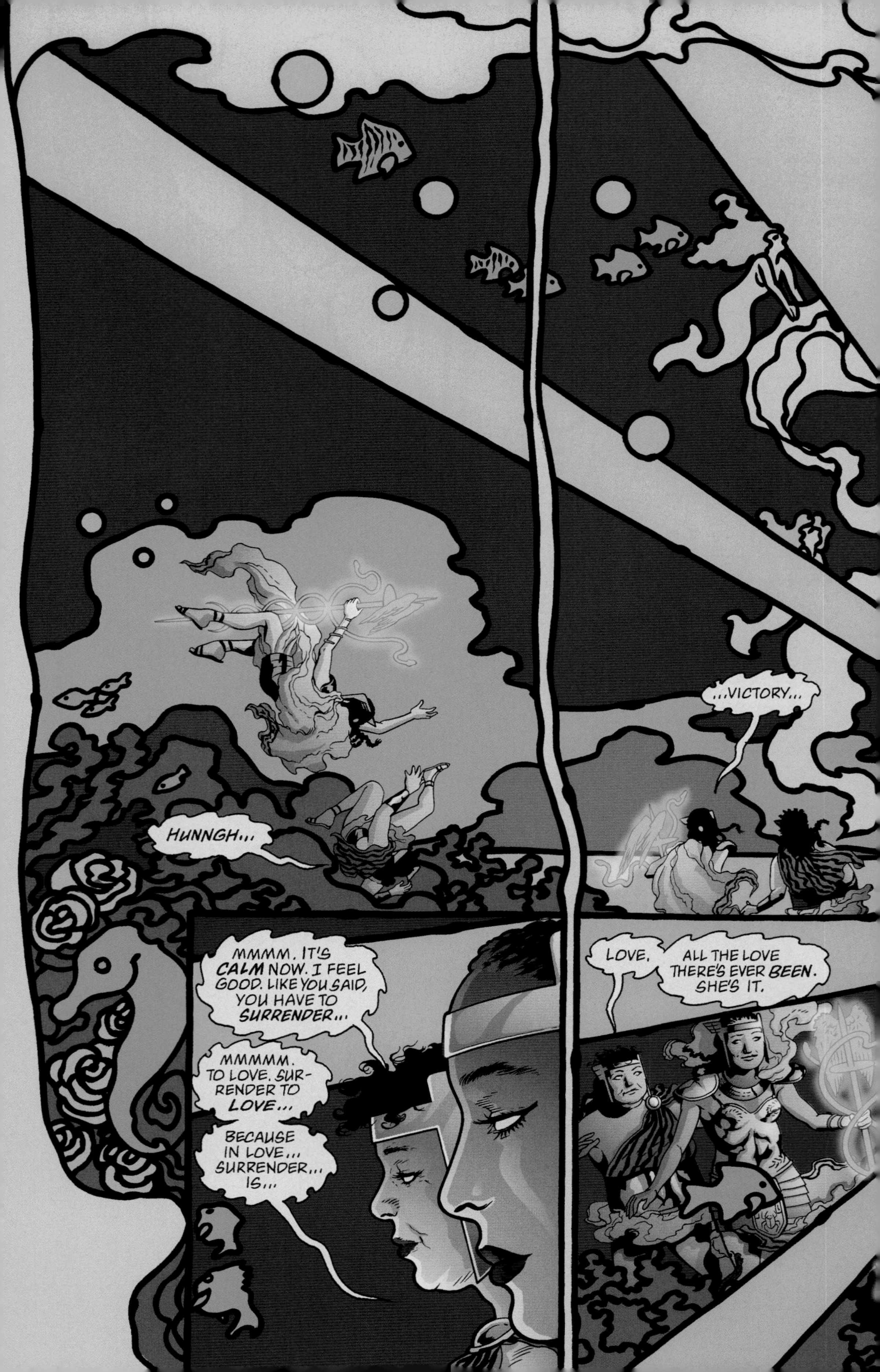

HUNNGH...
...VICTORY...
MMMMM. IT'S CALM NOW. I FEEL GOOD. LIKE YOU SAID, YOU HAVE TO SURRENDER...
MMMMM. TO LOVE. SURRENDER TO LOVE...
BECAUSE IN LOVE... SURRENDER... IS...
LOVE.
ALL THE LOVE THERE'S EVER BEEN. SHE'S IT.

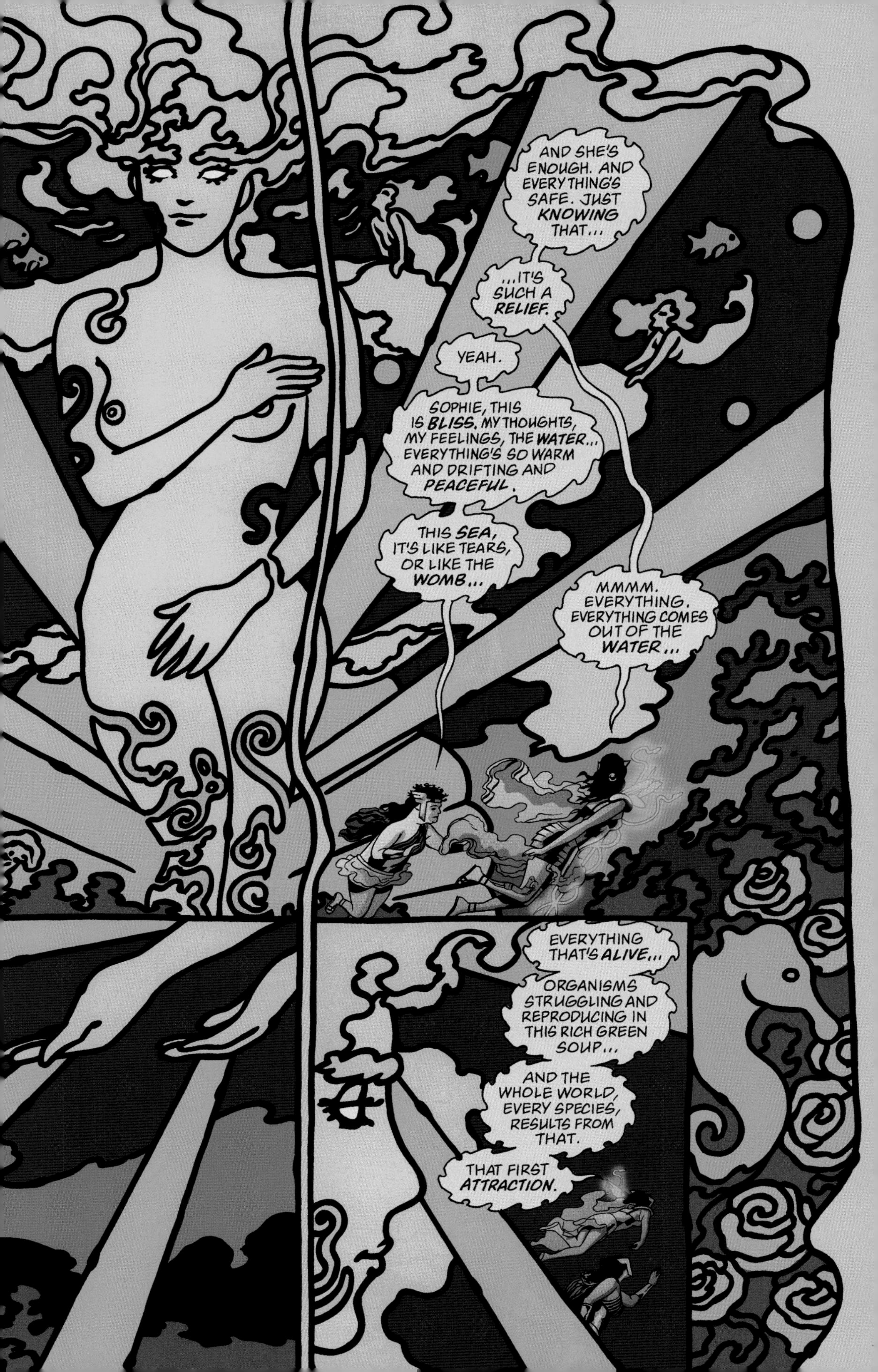
AND SHE'S ENOUGH. AND EVERYTHING'S SAFE. JUST KNOWING THAT...
...IT'S SUCH A RELIEF.
YEAH.
SOPHIE, THIS IS BLISS. MY THOUGHTS, MY FEELINGS, THE WATER... EVERYTHING'S SO WARM AND DRIFTING AND PEACEFUL.
THIS SEA, IT'S LIKE TEARS, OR LIKE THE WOMB...
MMMM. EVERYTHING. EVERYTHING COMES OUT OF THE WATER...
EVERYTHING THAT'S ALIVE...
ORGANISMS STRUGGLING AND REPRODUCING IN THIS RICH GREEN SOUP...
AND THE WHOLE WORLD, EVERY SPECIES, RESULTS FROM THAT.
THAT FIRST ATTRACTION.

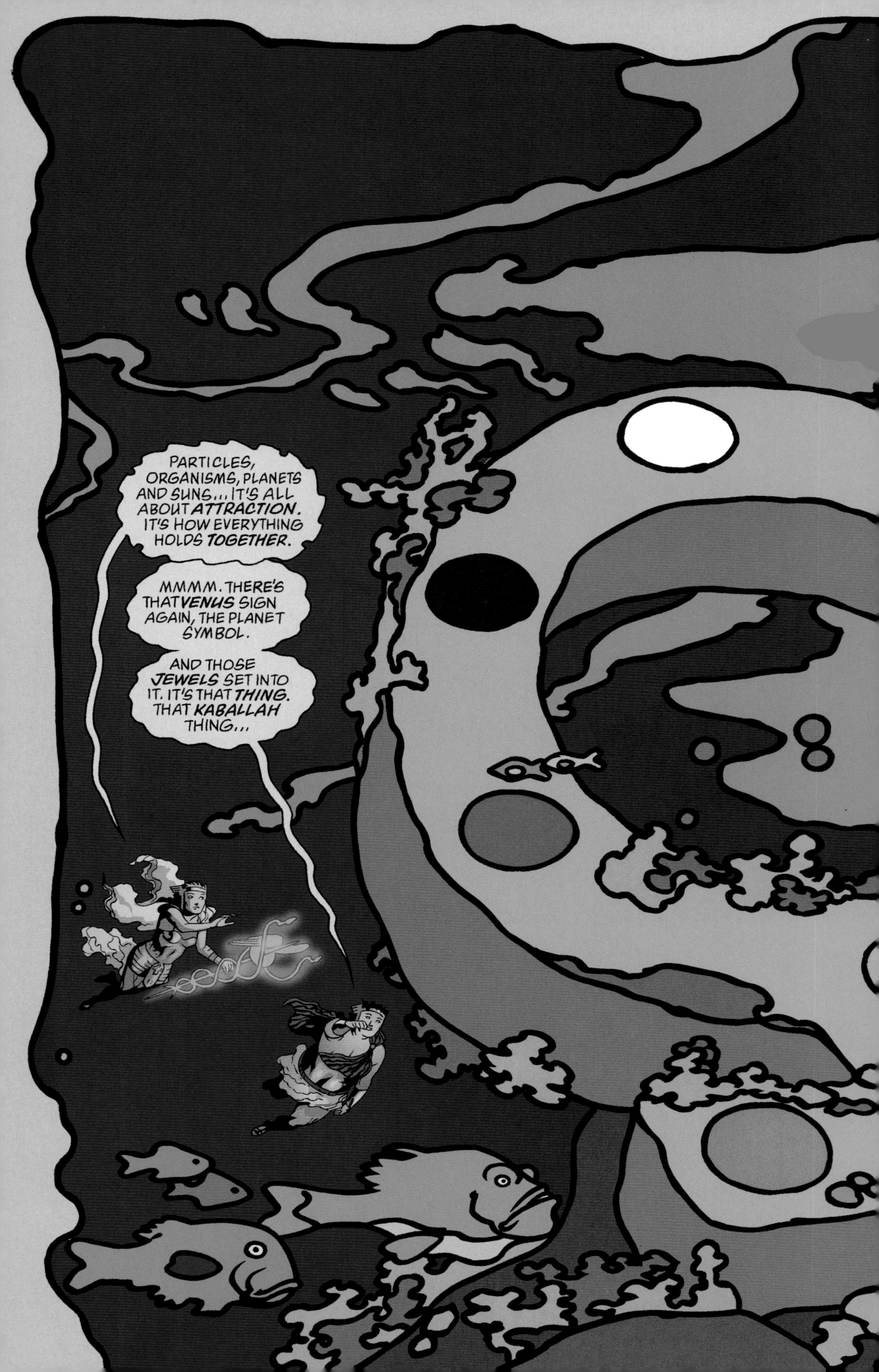
PARTICLES, ORGANISMS, PLANETS AND SUNS... IT'S ALL ABOUT **ATTRACTION**. IT'S HOW EVERYTHING HOLDS **TOGETHER**.
MMMM. THERE'S THAT **VENUS** SIGN AGAIN, THE PLANET SYMBOL.
AND THOSE **JEWELS** SET INTO IT. IT'S THAT **THING**. THAT **KABALLAH** THING...

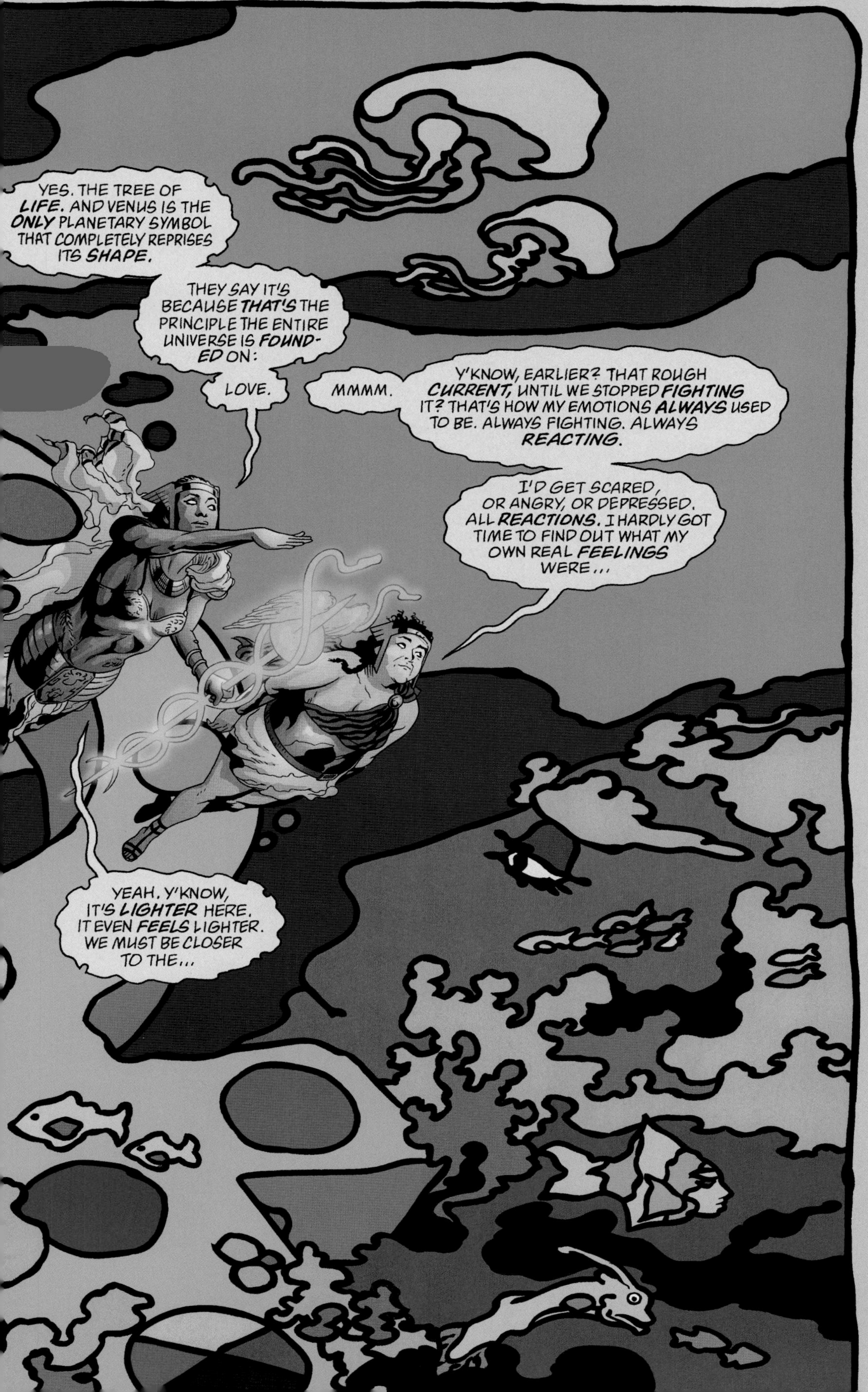
YES. THE TREE OF LIFE. AND VENUS IS THE ONLY PLANETARY SYMBOL THAT COMPLETELY REPRISES ITS SHAPE.
THEY SAY IT'S BECAUSE THAT'S THE PRINCIPLE THE ENTIRE UNIVERSE IS FOUNDED ON:
LOVE.
MMMM.
Y'KNOW, EARLIER? THAT ROUGH CURRENT, UNTIL WE STOPPED FIGHTING IT? THAT'S HOW MY EMOTIONS ALWAYS USED TO BE. ALWAYS FIGHTING. ALWAYS REACTING.
I'D GET SCARED, OR ANGRY, OR DEPRESSED. ALL REACTIONS. I HARDLY GOT TIME TO FIND OUT WHAT MY OWN REAL FEELINGS WERE...
YEAH. Y'KNOW, IT'S LIGHTER HERE. IT EVEN FEELS LIGHTER. WE MUST BE CLOSER TO THE...

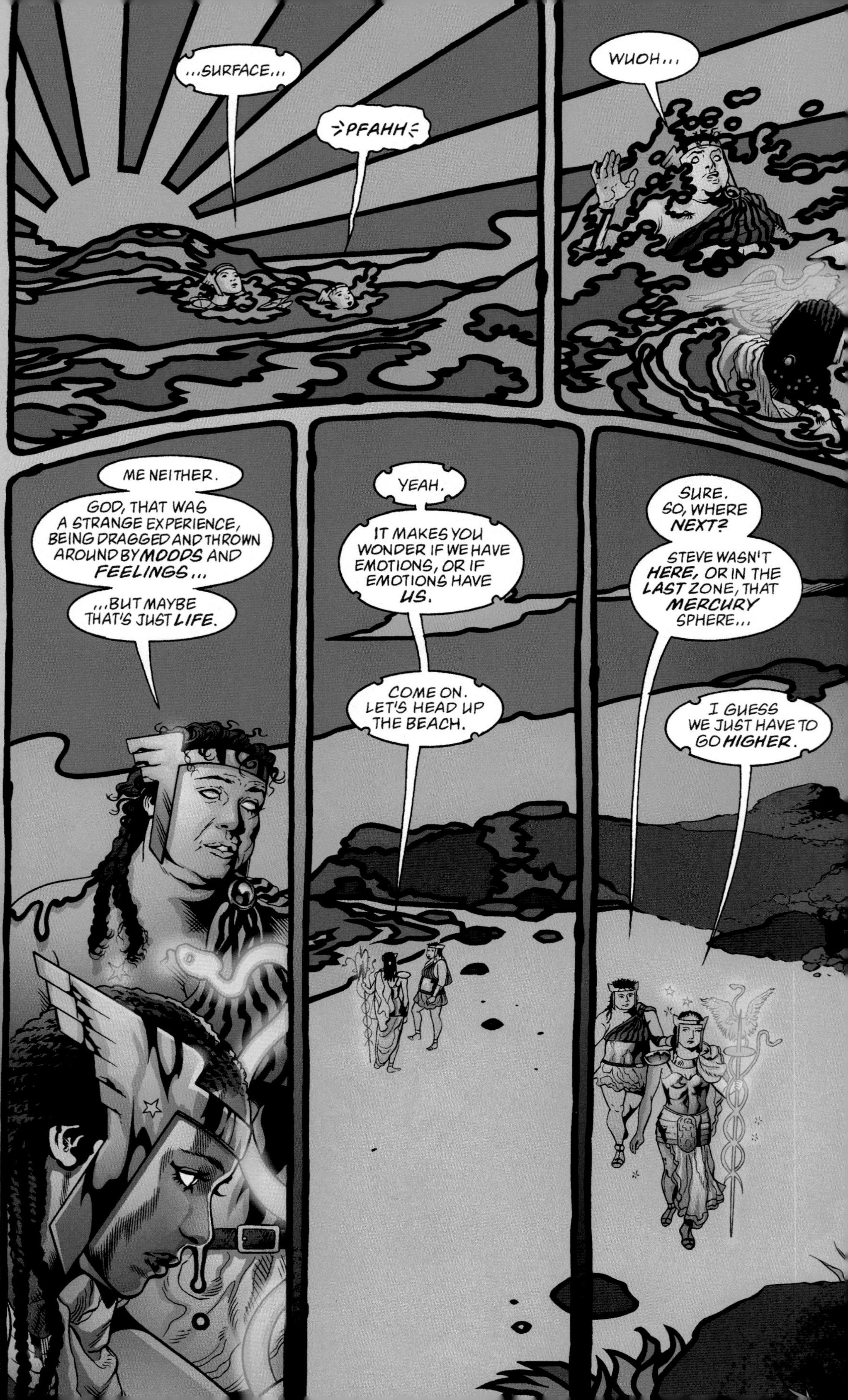
...SURFACE...
PFAHH
WUOH...
ME NEITHER.
GOD, THAT WAS A STRANGE EXPERIENCE, BEING DRAGGED AND THROWN AROUND BY MOODS AND FEELINGS...
...BUT MAYBE THAT'S JUST LIFE.
YEAH.
IT MAKES YOU WONDER IF WE HAVE EMOTIONS, OR IF EMOTIONS HAVE US.
COME ON. LET'S HEAD UP THE BEACH.
SURE. SO, WHERE NEXT?
STEVE WASN'T HERE, OR IN THE LAST ZONE, THAT MERCURY SPHERE...
I GUESS WE JUST HAVE TO GO HIGHER.

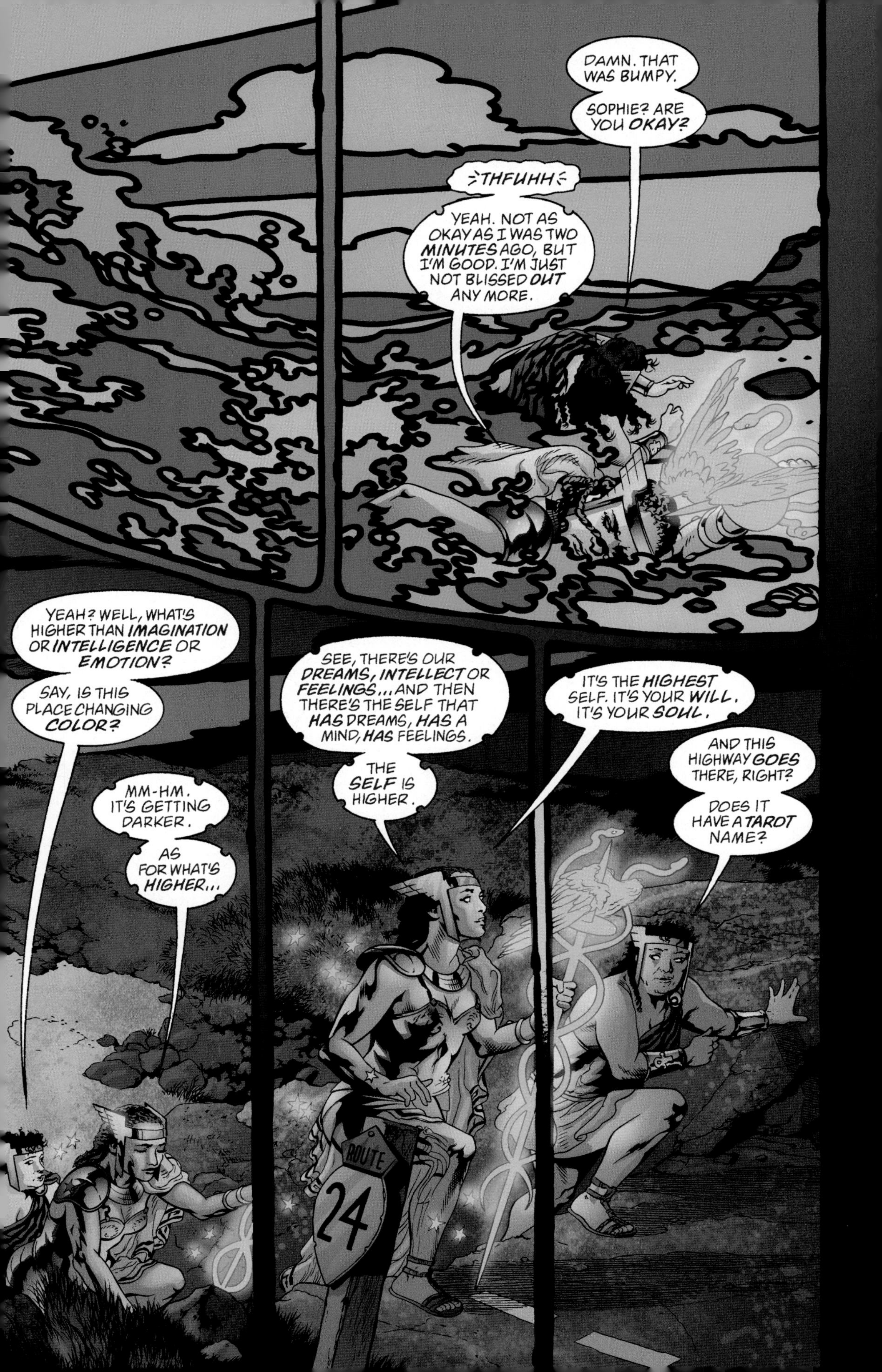
DAMN. THAT WAS BUMPY.
SOPHIE? ARE YOU OKAY?
THFUHH
YEAH. NOT AS OKAY AS I WAS TWO MINUTES AGO, BUT I'M GOOD. I'M JUST NOT BLISSED OUT ANY MORE.
YEAH? WELL, WHAT'S HIGHER THAN IMAGINATION OR INTELLIGENCE OR EMOTION?
SAY, IS THIS PLACE CHANGING COLOR?
MM-HM. IT'S GETTING DARKER.
AS FOR WHAT'S HIGHER...
SEE, THERE'S OUR DREAMS, INTELLECT OR FEELINGS... AND THEN THERE'S THE SELF THAT HAS DREAMS, HAS A MIND, HAS FEELINGS.
THE SELF IS HIGHER.
IT'S THE HIGHEST SELF. IT'S YOUR WILL. IT'S YOUR SOUL.
AND THIS HIGHWAY GOES THERE, RIGHT?
DOES IT HAVE A TAROT NAME?
ROUTE
24

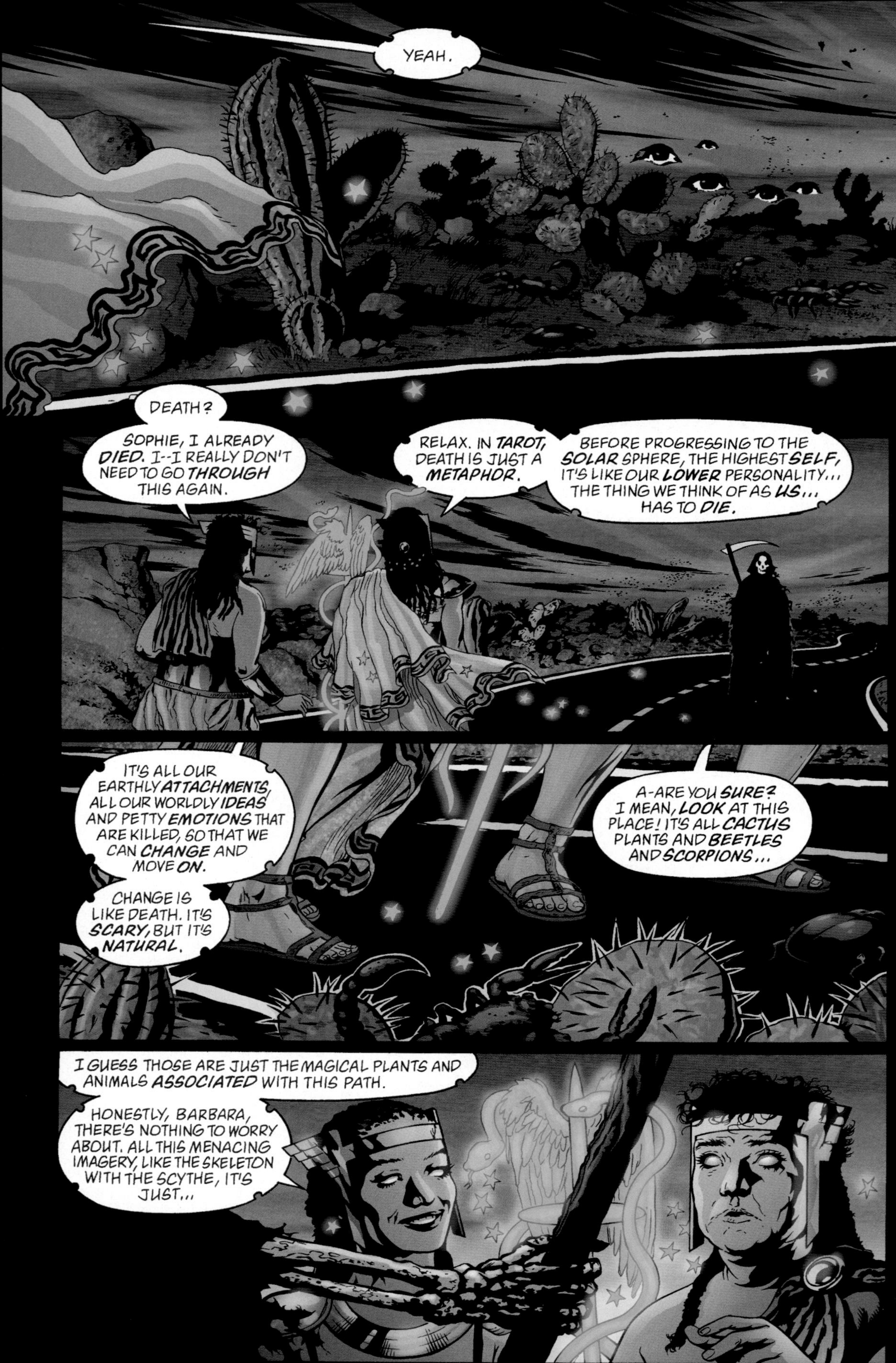
YEAH.
DEATH?
SOPHIE, I ALREADY DIED. I--I REALLY DON'T NEED TO GO THROUGH THIS AGAIN.
RELAX. IN TAROT, DEATH IS JUST A METAPHOR.
BEFORE PROGRESSING TO THE SOLAR SPHERE, THE HIGHEST SELF, IT'S LIKE OUR LOWER PERSONALITY... THE THING WE THINK OF AS US... HAS TO DIE.
IT'S ALL OUR EARTHLY ATTACHMENTS, ALL OUR WORLDLY IDEAS AND PETTY EMOTIONS THAT ARE KILLED, SO THAT WE CAN CHANGE AND MOVE ON.
CHANGE IS LIKE DEATH. IT'S SCARY, BUT IT'S NATURAL.
A-ARE YOU SURE? I MEAN, LOOK AT THIS PLACE! IT'S ALL CACTUS PLANTS AND BEETLES AND SCORPIONS...
I GUESS THOSE ARE JUST THE MAGICAL PLANTS AND ANIMALS ASSOCIATED WITH THIS PATH.
HONESTLY, BARBARA, THERE'S NOTHING TO WORRY ABOUT. ALL THIS MENACING IMAGERY, LIKE THE SKELETON WITH THE SCYTHE, IT'S JUST...

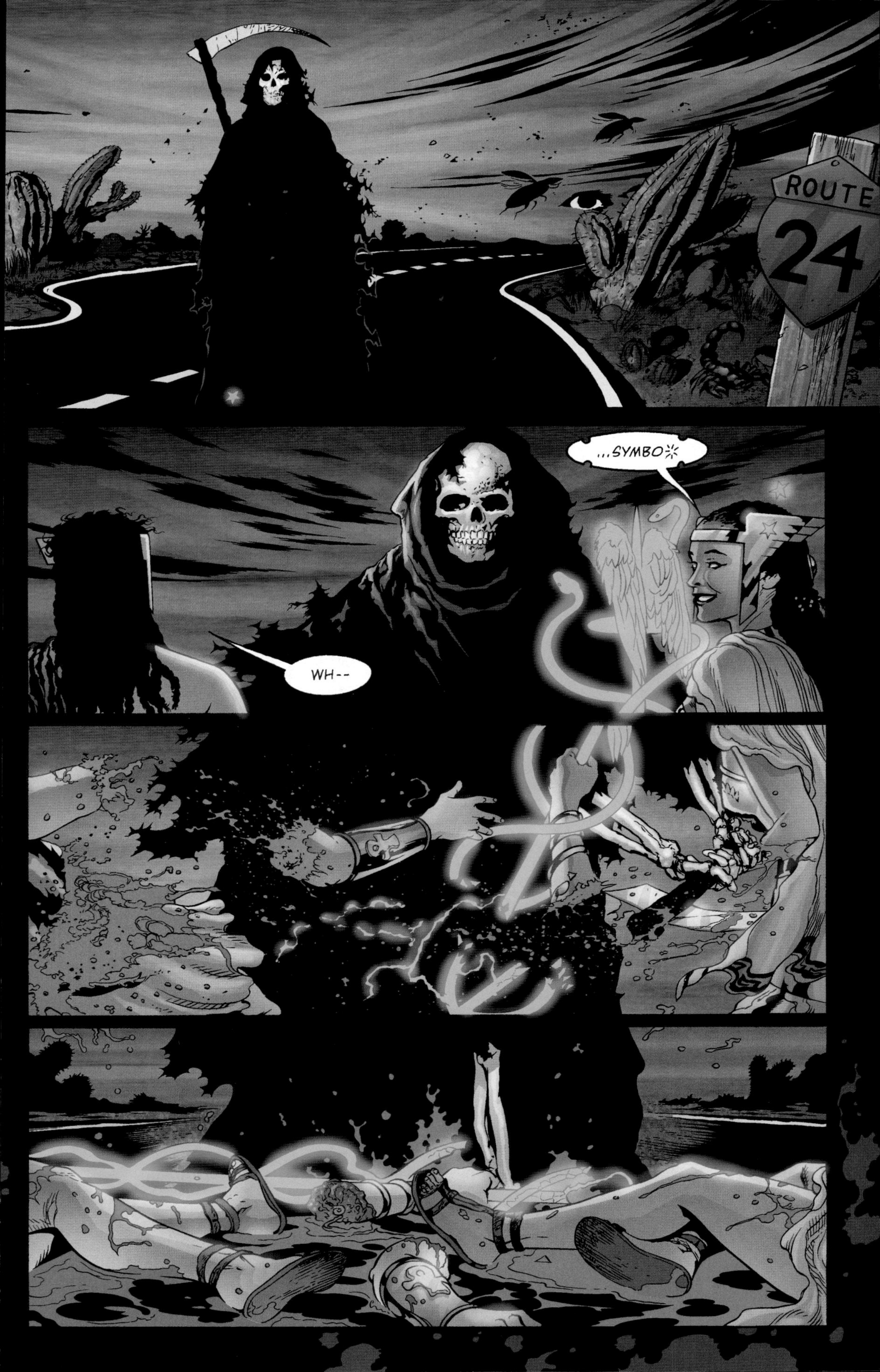
ROUTE
24
...SYMBO
WH--

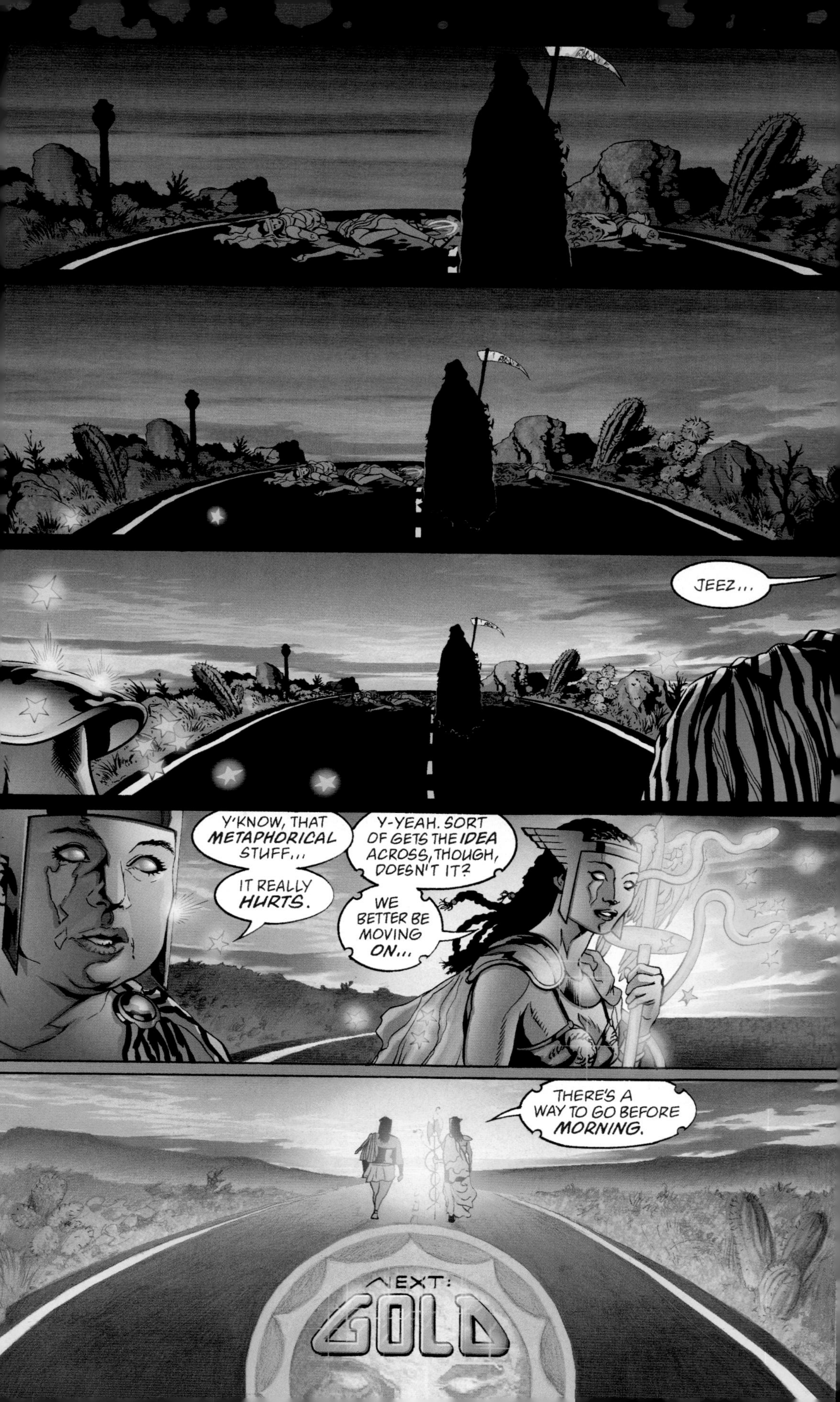
JEEZ...
Y'KNOW, THAT METAPHORICAL STUFF...
IT REALLY HURTS.
Y-YEAH. SORT OF GETS THE IDEA ACROSS, THOUGH, DOESN'T IT?
WE BETTER BE MOVING ON...
THERE'S A WAY TO GO BEFORE MORNING.
NEXT:
GOLD

CHAPTER FIVE

A golden dawn is quietly revealed,
A guardian angel joins the quest,
And deep sacrifices are observed.

Cover art:
J.H. Williams III
& Jose Villarrubia

MOORE WILLIAMS III GRAY COX KLEIN
PROMETHEA
AMERICA'S BEST COMICS
NO. 17

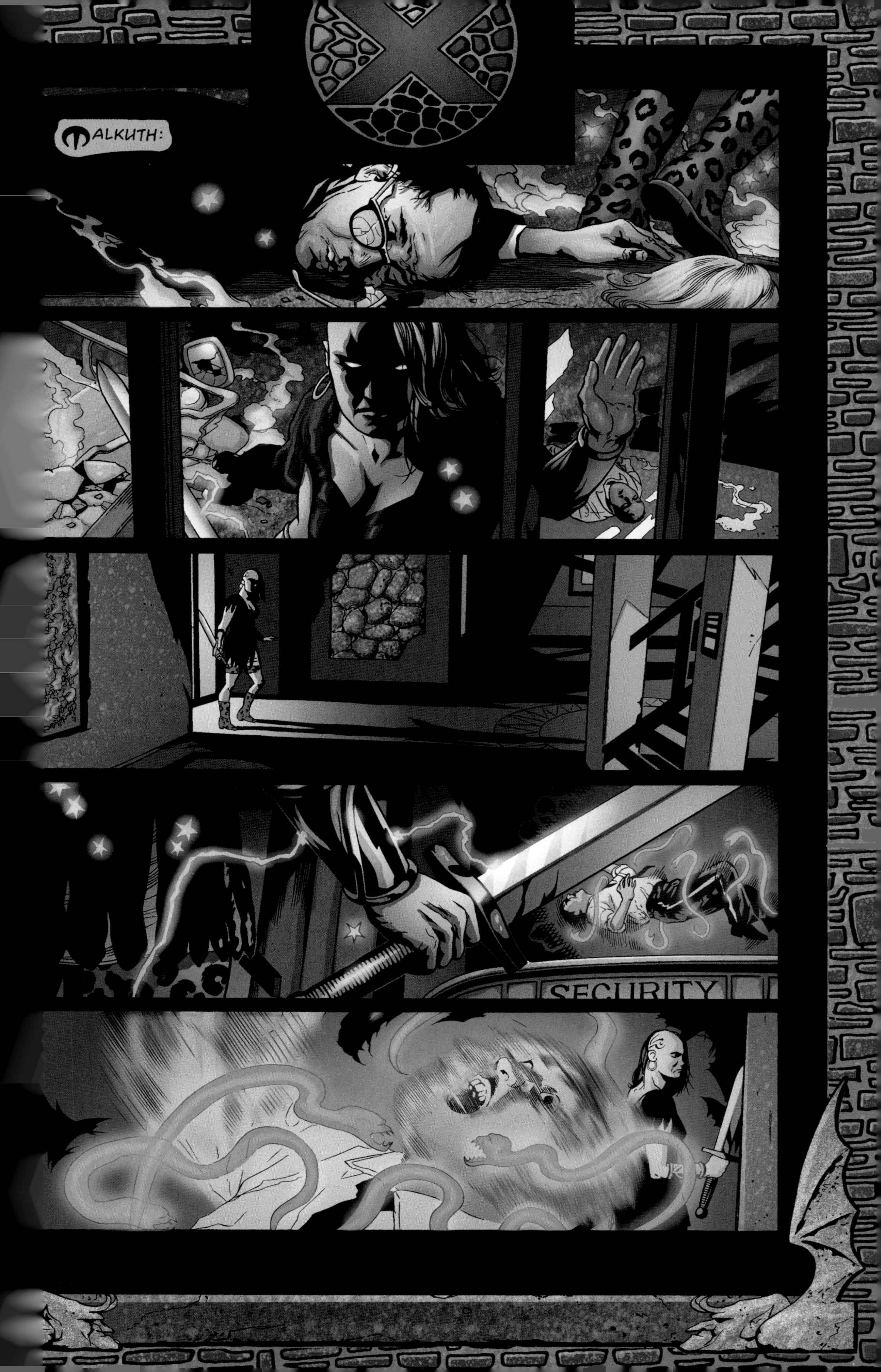
MALKUTH:
SECURITY

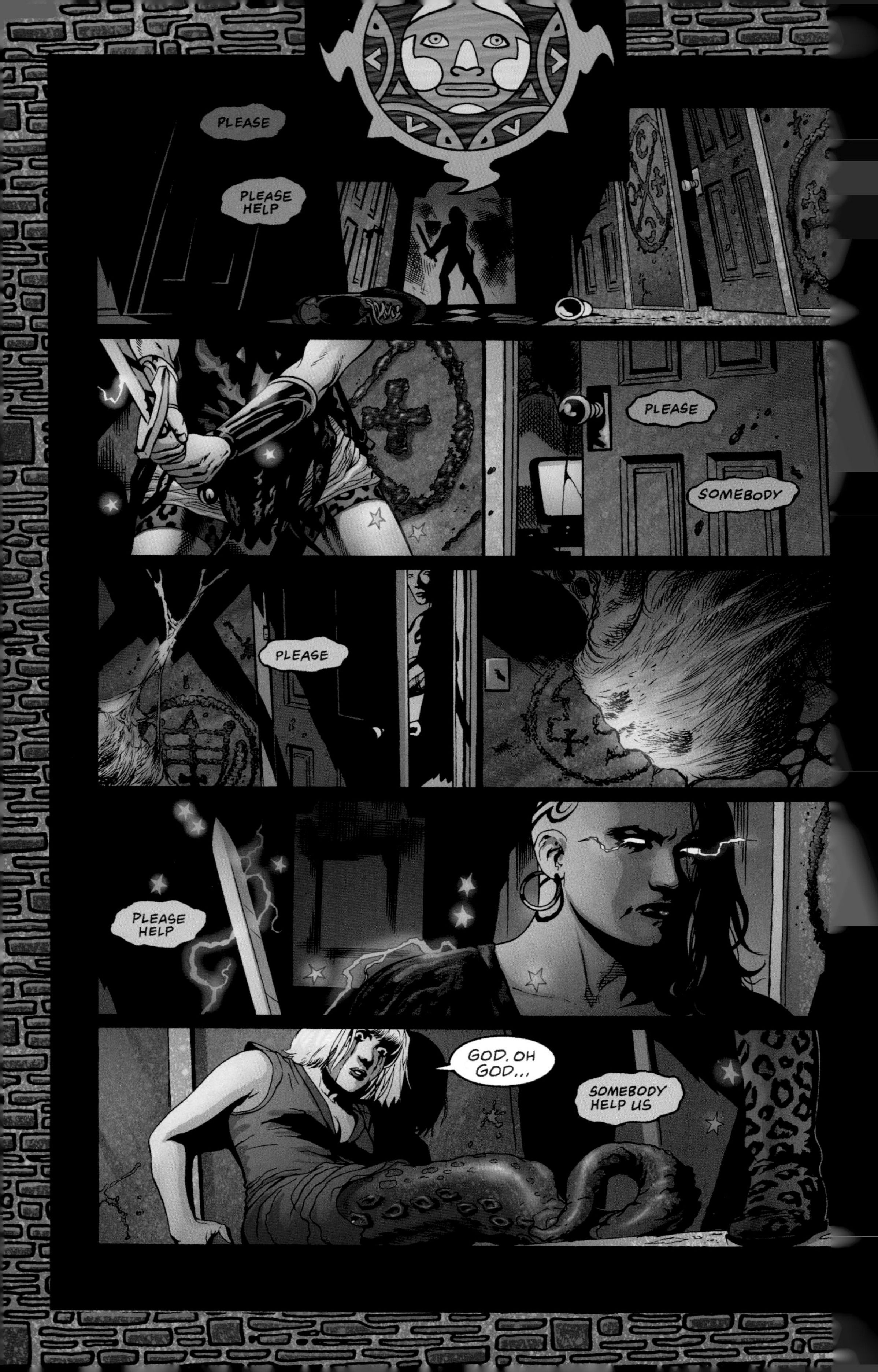
PLEASE
PLEASE HELP
PLEASE
SOMEBODY
PLEASE
PLEASE HELP
GOD. OH GOD...
SOMEBODY HELP US

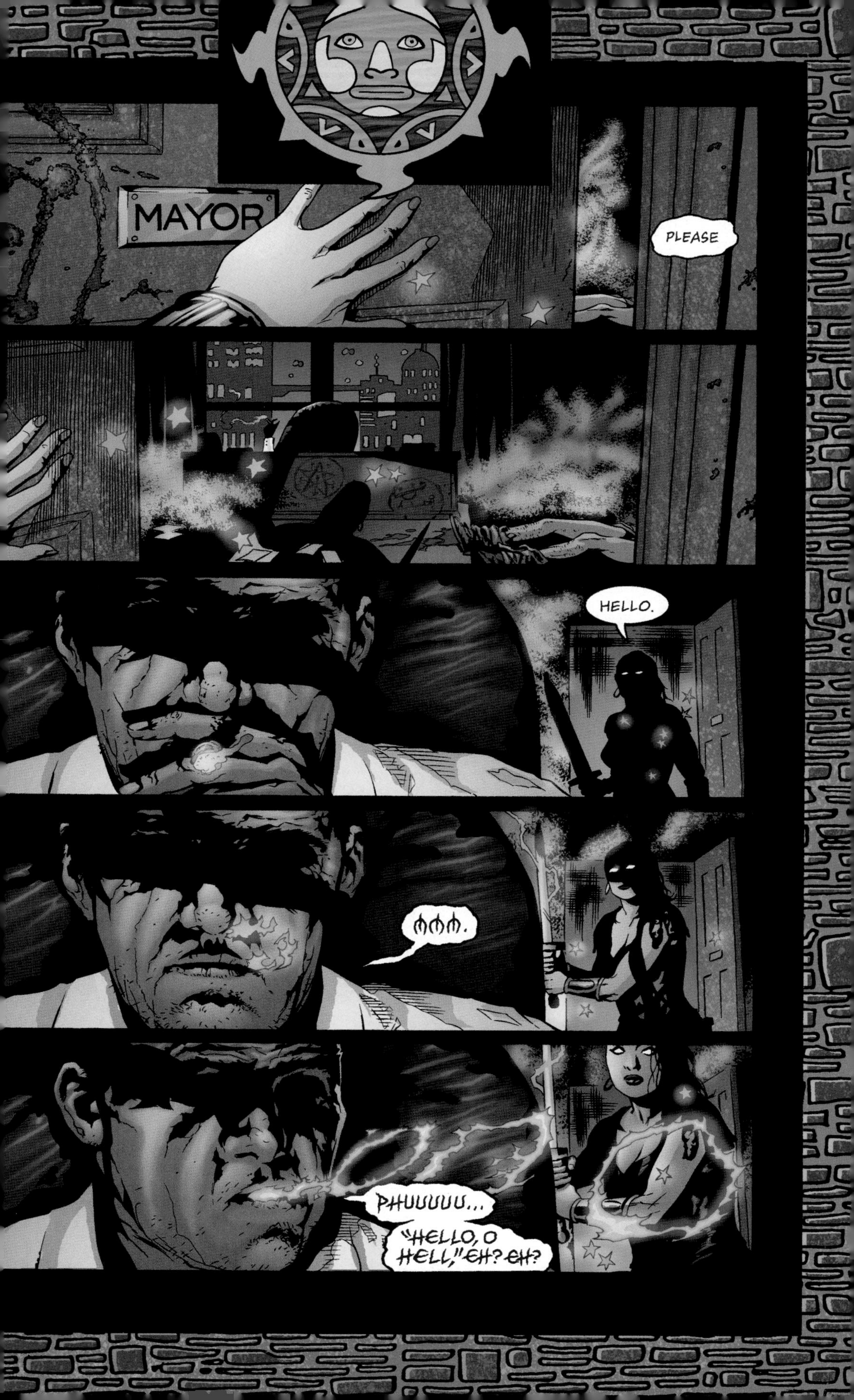
MAYOR
PLEASE
HELLO.
MMM.
PHUUUUU...
"HELLO, O HELL," EH? EH?

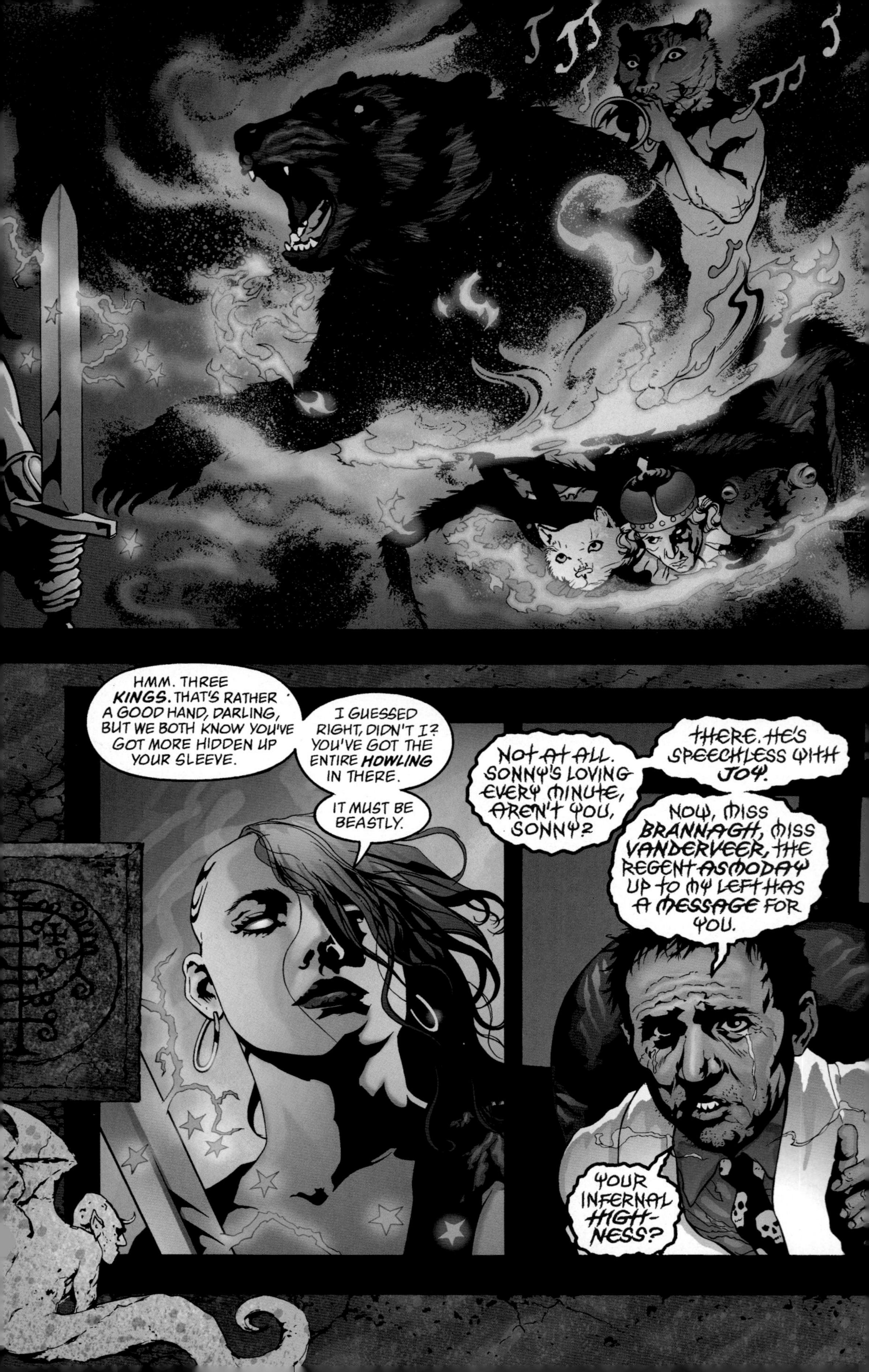

HMM. THREE KINGS. THAT'S RATHER A GOOD HAND, DARLING, BUT WE BOTH KNOW YOU'VE GOT MORE HIDDEN UP YOUR SLEEVE.
I GUESSED RIGHT, DIDN'T I? YOU'VE GOT THE ENTIRE HOWLING IN THERE.
IT MUST BE BEASTLY.
NOT AT ALL. SONNY'S LOVING EVERY MINUTE, AREN'T YOU, SONNY?
THERE. HE'S SPEECHLESS WITH JOY.
NOW, MISS BRANNAGH, MISS VANDERVEER, THE REGENT ASMODAY UP TO MY LEFT HAS A MESSAGE FOR YOU.
YOUR INFERNAL HIGH-NESS?

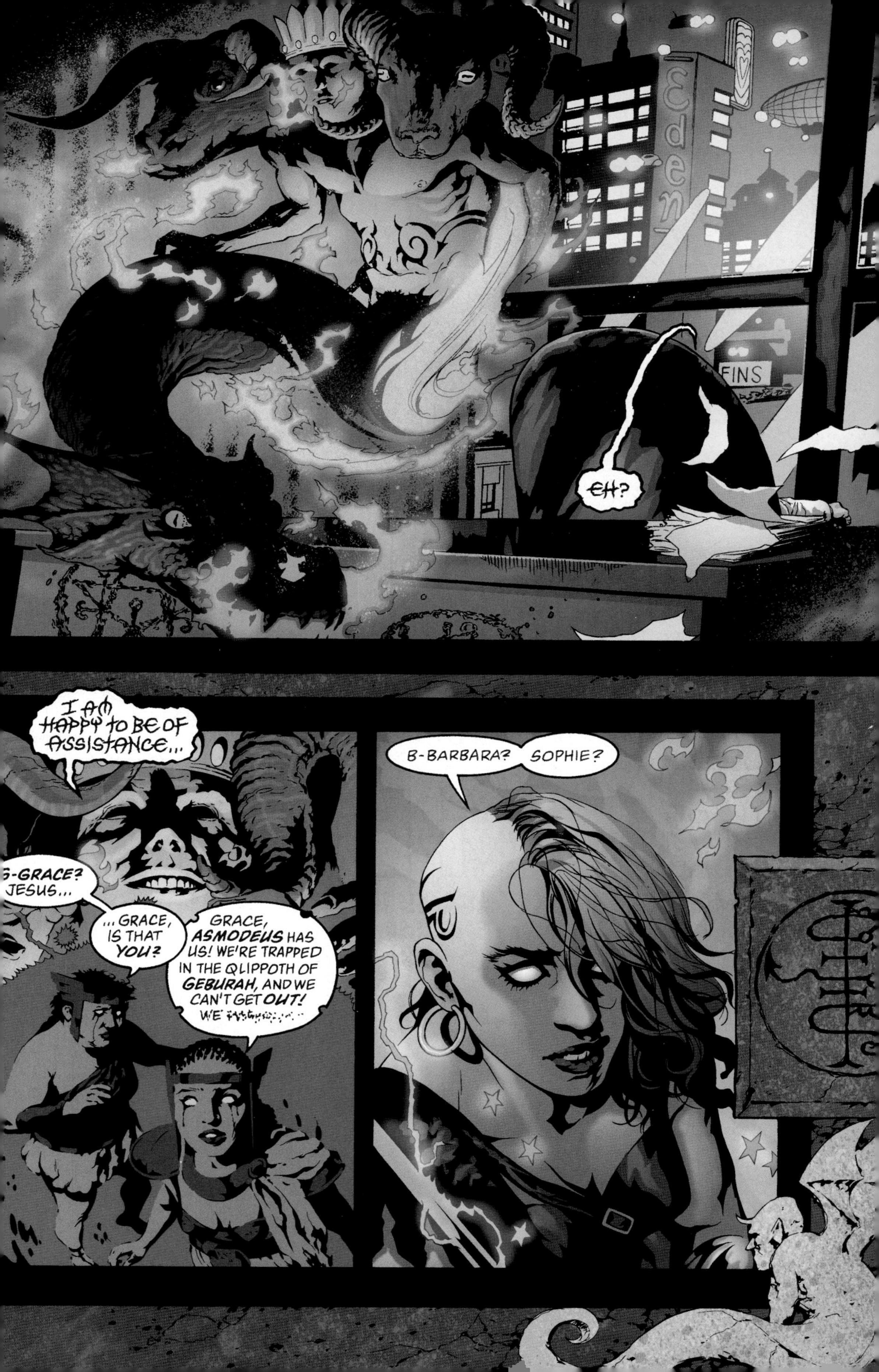

FINS
EH?
I AM HAPPY TO BE OF ASSISTANCE...
G-GRACE? JESUS...
...GRACE, IS THAT YOU?
GRACE, ASMODEUS HAS US! WE'RE TRAPPED IN THE QLIPPOTH OF GEBURAH, AND WE CAN'T GET OUT! WE
B-BARBARA? SOPHIE?

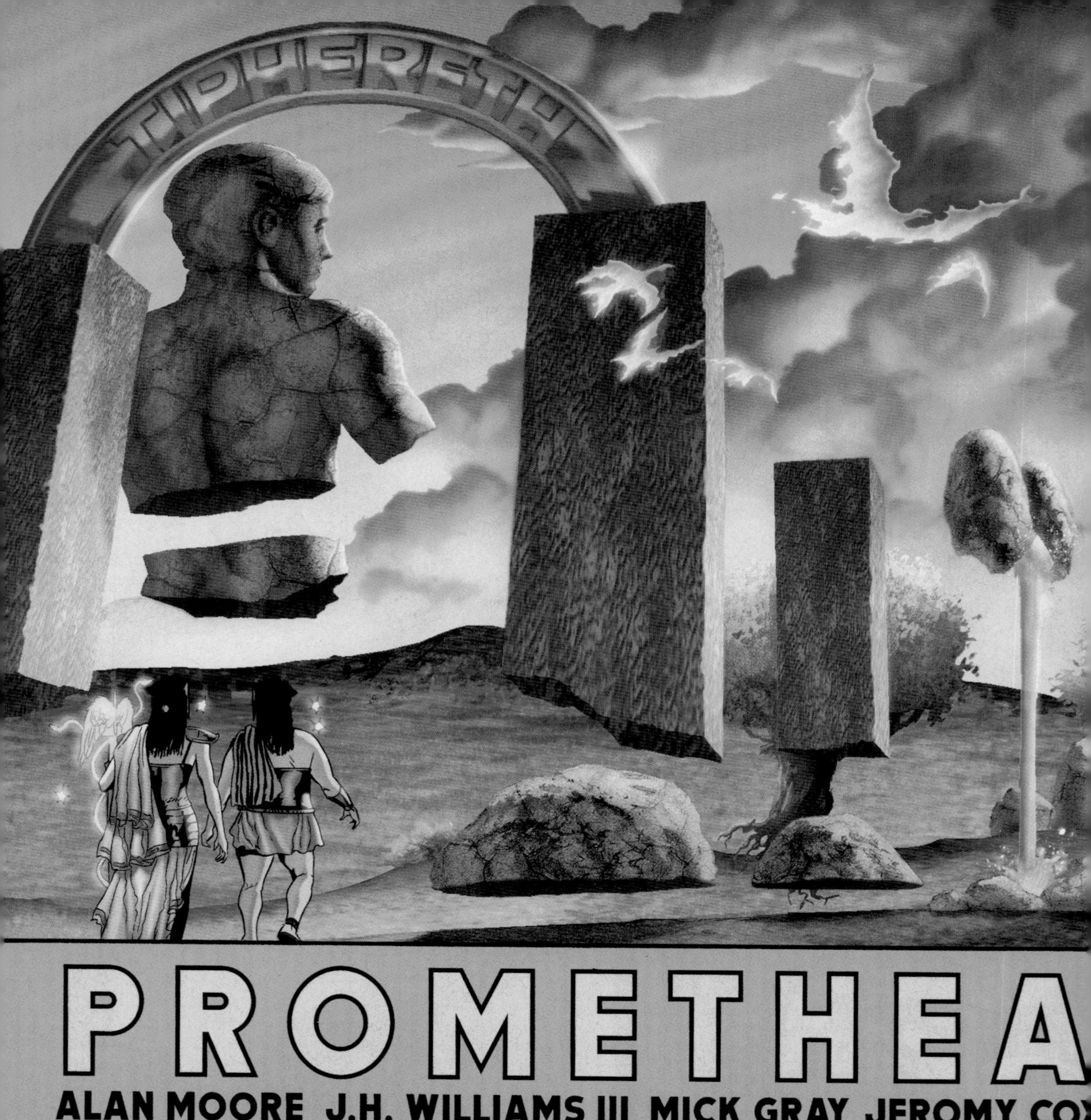
TIPHERETH

PROMETHEA

ALAN MOORE WRITER * **J.H. WILLIAMS III** CO-CREATORS * PENCILLER **MICK GRAY** INKER **JEROMY COX** COLORS

TODD KLEIN LETTERS **POZNER, QUINN** ASST. ED **SCOTT DUNBIER** EDITO

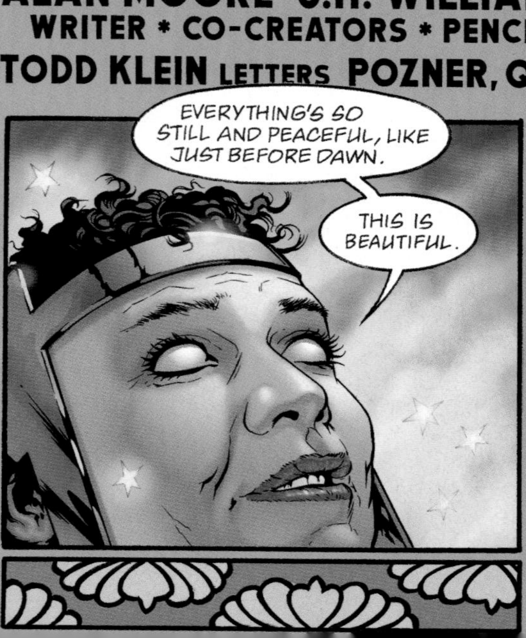
EVERYTHING'S SO STILL AND PEACEFUL, LIKE JUST BEFORE DAWN.
THIS IS BEAUTIFUL.

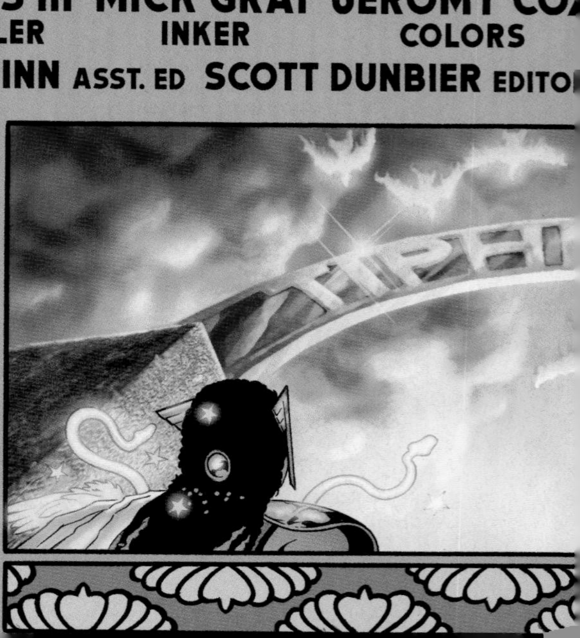

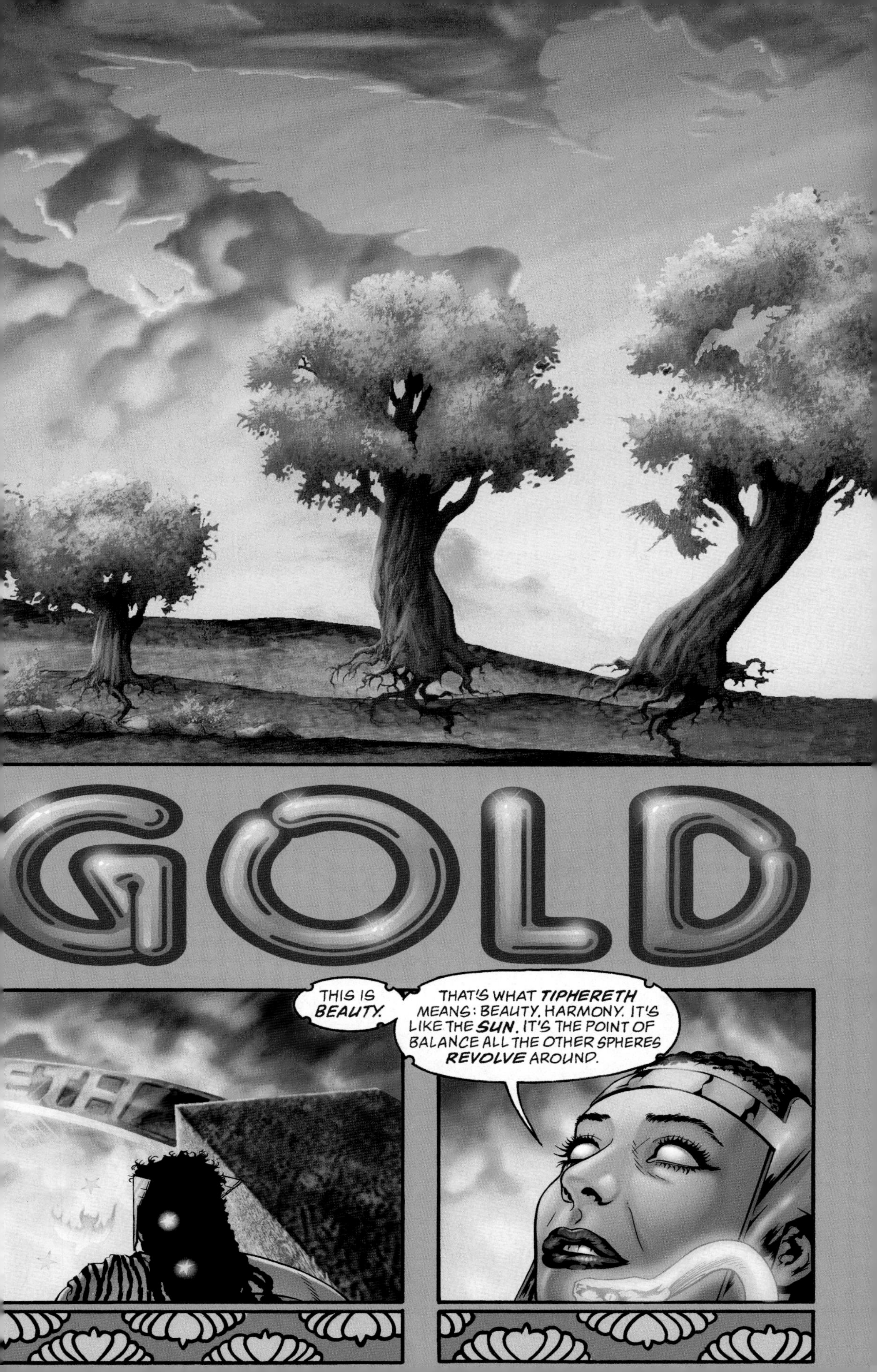
GOLD
THIS IS BEAUTY.
THAT'S WHAT TIPHERETH MEANS: BEAUTY, HARMONY. IT'S LIKE THE SUN. IT'S THE POINT OF BALANCE ALL THE OTHER SPHERES REVOLVE AROUND.

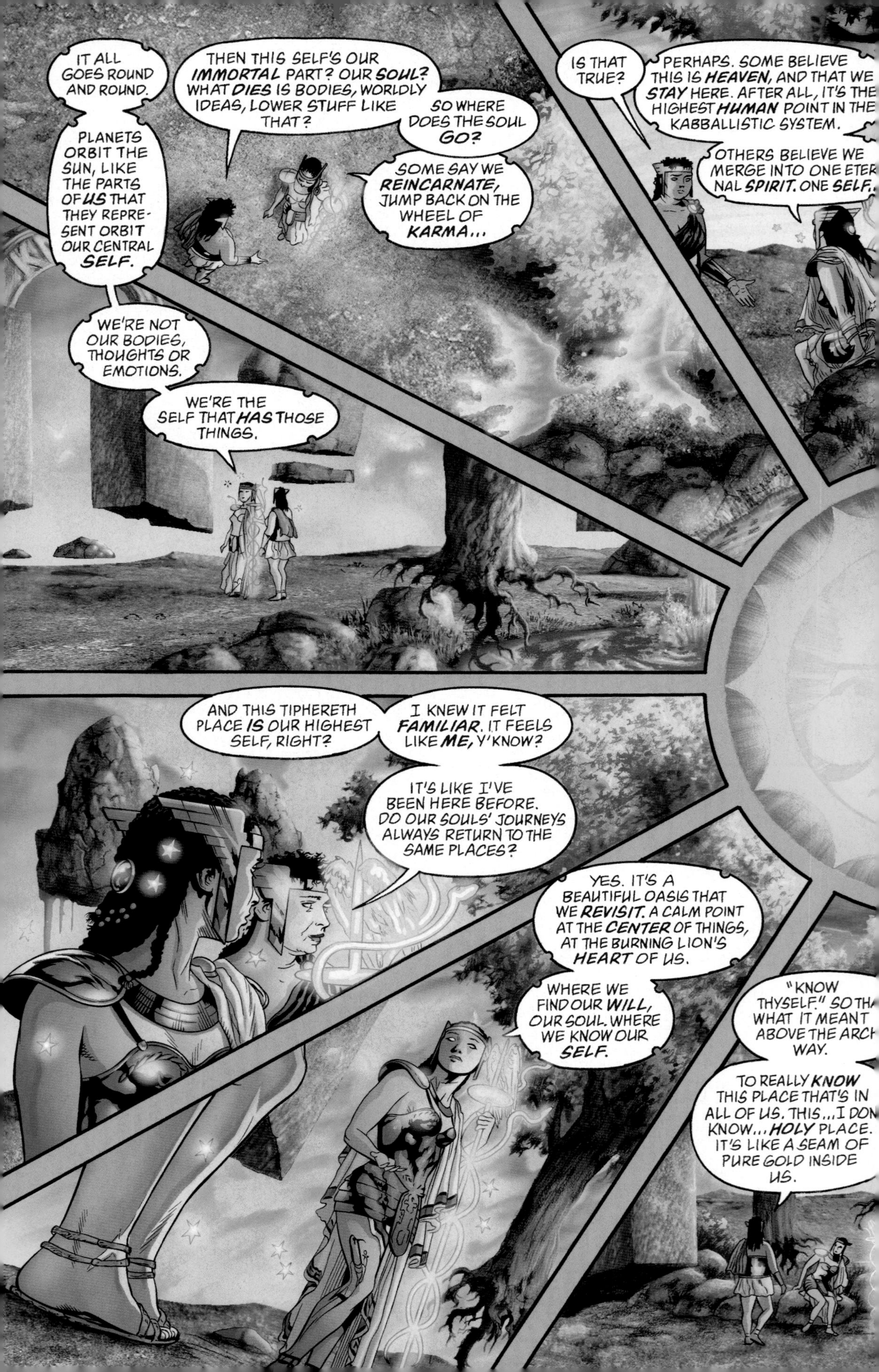
IT ALL GOES ROUND AND ROUND.
PLANETS ORBIT THE SUN, LIKE THE PARTS OF US THAT THEY REPRESENT ORBIT OUR CENTRAL SELF.
WE'RE NOT OUR BODIES, THOUGHTS OR EMOTIONS.
WE'RE THE SELF THAT HAS THOSE THINGS.
THEN THIS SELF'S OUR IMMORTAL PART? OUR SOUL? WHAT DIES IS BODIES, WORLDLY IDEAS, LOWER STUFF LIKE THAT?
SO WHERE DOES THE SOUL GO?
SOME SAY WE REINCARNATE, JUMP BACK ON THE WHEEL OF KARMA...
IS THAT TRUE?
PERHAPS. SOME BELIEVE THIS IS HEAVEN, AND THAT WE STAY HERE. AFTER ALL, IT'S THE HIGHEST HUMAN POINT IN THE KABBALLISTIC SYSTEM.
OTHERS BELIEVE WE MERGE INTO ONE ETERNAL SPIRIT. ONE SELF.
AND THIS TIPHERETH PLACE IS OUR HIGHEST SELF, RIGHT?
I KNEW IT FELT FAMILIAR. IT FEELS LIKE ME, Y'KNOW?
IT'S LIKE I'VE BEEN HERE BEFORE. DO OUR SOULS' JOURNEYS ALWAYS RETURN TO THE SAME PLACES?
YES. IT'S A BEAUTIFUL OASIS THAT WE REVISIT. A CALM POINT AT THE CENTER OF THINGS, AT THE BURNING LION'S HEART OF US.
WHERE WE FIND OUR WILL, OUR SOUL. WHERE WE KNOW OUR SELF.
"KNOW THYSELF." SO THA WHAT IT MEANT ABOVE THE ARCH WAY.
TO REALLY KNOW THIS PLACE THAT'S IN ALL OF US. THIS... I DON KNOW... HOLY PLACE. IT'S LIKE A SEAM OF PURE GOLD INSIDE US.

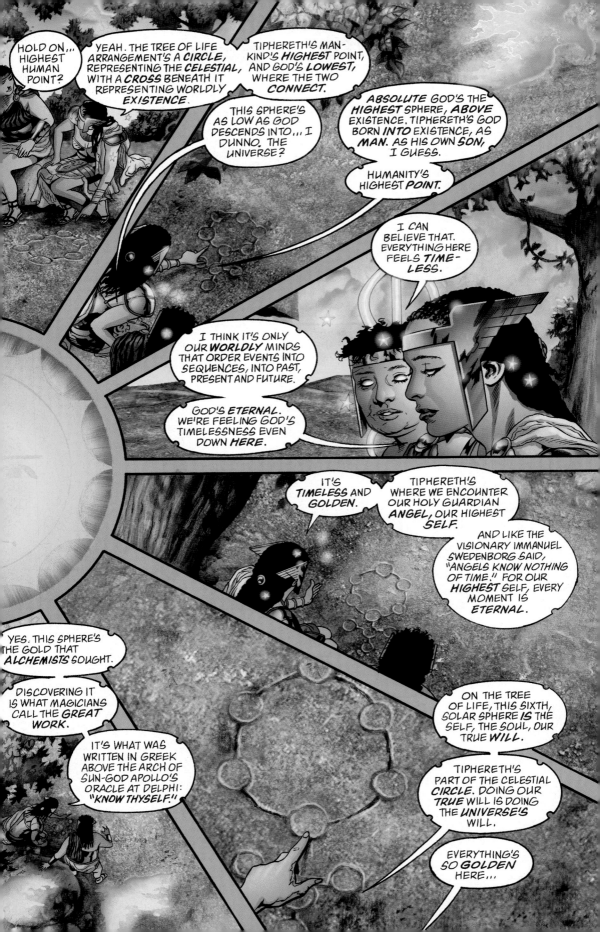

HOLD ON... HIGHEST HUMAN POINT?

YEAH. THE TREE OF LIFE ARRANGEMENT'S A *CIRCLE*, REPRESENTING THE *CELESTIAL*, WITH A *CROSS* BENEATH IT REPRESENTING WORLDLY *EXISTENCE*.

TIPHERETH'S MAN-KIND'S *HIGHEST* POINT, AND GOD'S *LOWEST*, WHERE THE TWO *CONNECT*.

THIS SPHERE'S AS LOW AS GOD DESCENDS INTO... I DUNNO, THE UNIVERSE?

ABSOLUTE GOD'S THE *HIGHEST* SPHERE, *ABOVE* EXISTENCE. TIPHERETH'S GOD BORN *INTO* EXISTENCE, AS *MAN*. AS HIS OWN *SON*, I GUESS.

HUMANITY'S HIGHEST *POINT*.

I CAN BELIEVE THAT. EVERYTHING HERE FEELS *TIME-LESS*.

I THINK IT'S ONLY OUR *WORLDLY* MINDS THAT ORDER EVENTS INTO SEQUENCES, INTO PAST, PRESENT AND FUTURE.

GOD'S *ETERNAL*. WE'RE FEELING GOD'S TIMELESSNESS EVEN DOWN *HERE*.

IT'S *TIMELESS* AND *GOLDEN*.

TIPHERETH'S WHERE WE ENCOUNTER OUR HOLY GUARDIAN *ANGEL*, OUR HIGHEST *SELF*.

AND LIKE THE VISIONARY IMMANUEL SWEDENBORG SAID, "ANGELS KNOW NOTHING OF TIME." FOR OUR *HIGHEST* SELF, EVERY MOMENT IS *ETERNAL*.

YES. THIS SPHERE'S THE GOLD THAT *ALCHEMISTS* SOUGHT.

DISCOVERING IT IS WHAT MAGICIANS CALL THE *GREAT WORK*.

IT'S WHAT WAS WRITTEN IN GREEK ABOVE THE ARCH OF SUN-GOD APOLLO'S ORACLE AT DELPHI: *"KNOW THYSELF."*

ON THE TREE OF LIFE, THIS SIXTH, SOLAR SPHERE *IS* THE SELF, THE SOUL, OUR TRUE *WILL*.

TIPHERETH'S PART OF THE CELESTIAL *CIRCLE*. DOING OUR *TRUE* WILL IS DOING THE *UNIVERSE'S* WILL.

EVERYTHING'S SO *GOLDEN* HERE...

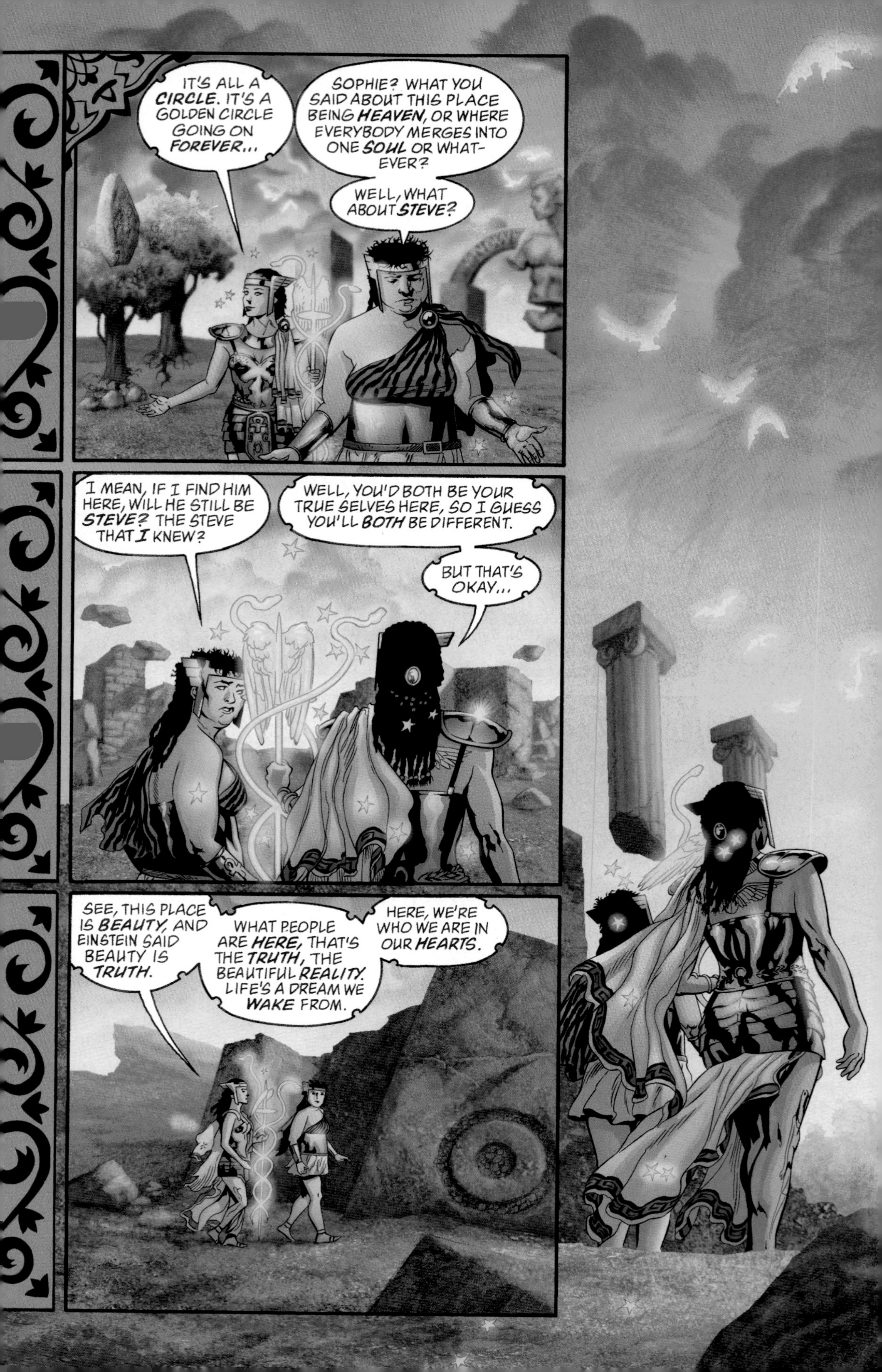

IT'S ALL A CIRCLE. IT'S A GOLDEN CIRCLE GOING ON FOREVER...
SOPHIE? WHAT YOU SAID ABOUT THIS PLACE BEING HEAVEN, OR WHERE EVERYBODY MERGES INTO ONE SOUL OR WHATEVER?
WELL, WHAT ABOUT STEVE?
I MEAN, IF I FIND HIM HERE, WILL HE STILL BE STEVE? THE STEVE THAT I KNEW?
WELL, YOU'D BOTH BE YOUR TRUE SELVES HERE, SO I GUESS YOU'LL BOTH BE DIFFERENT.
BUT THAT'S OKAY...
SEE, THIS PLACE IS BEAUTY, AND EINSTEIN SAID BEAUTY IS TRUTH.
WHAT PEOPLE ARE HERE, THAT'S THE TRUTH, THE BEAUTIFUL REALITY. LIFE'S A DREAM WE WAKE FROM.
HERE, WE'RE WHO WE ARE IN OUR HEARTS.

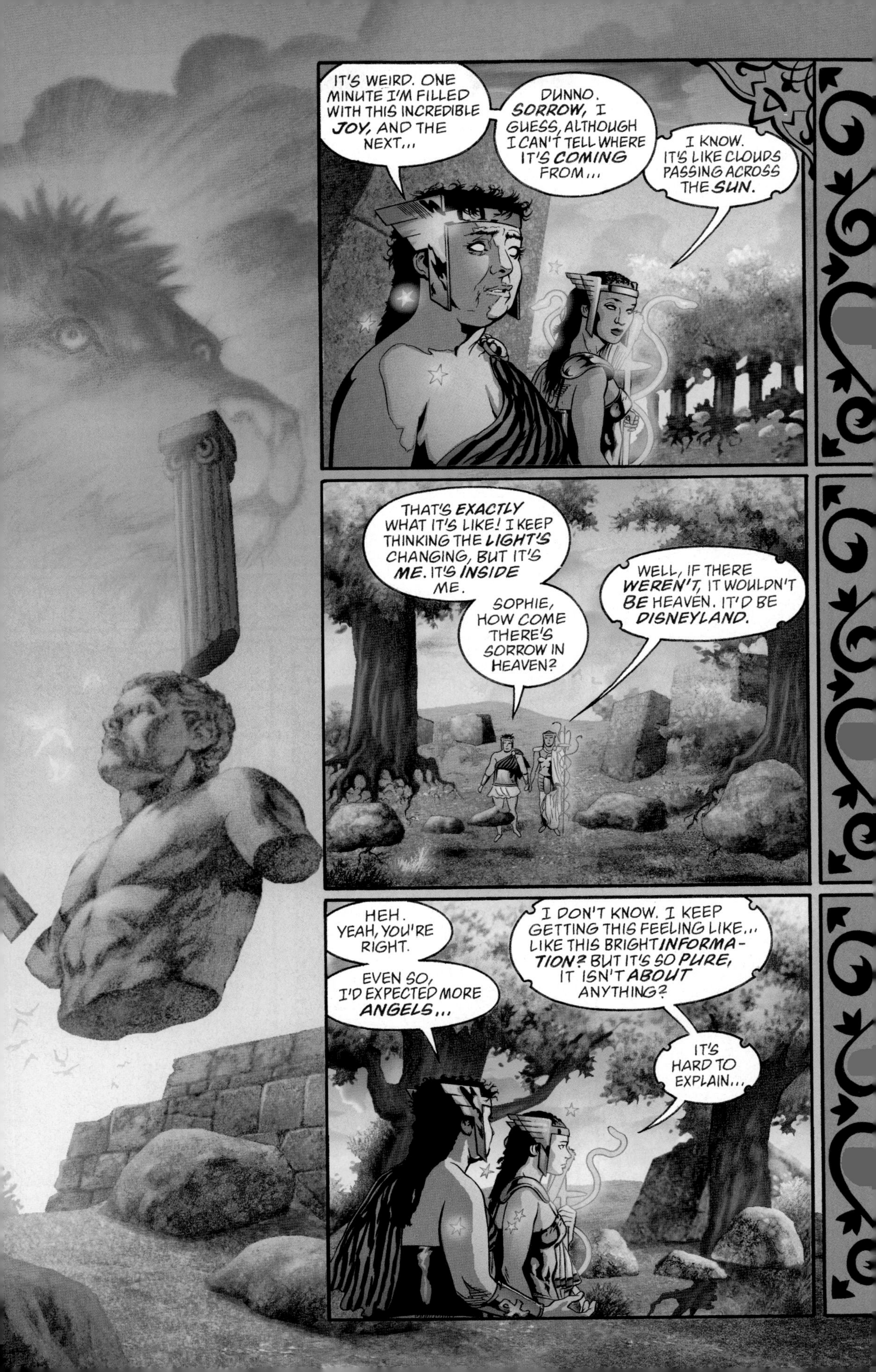
IT'S WEIRD. ONE MINUTE I'M FILLED WITH THIS INCREDIBLE JOY, AND THE NEXT...
DUNNO. SORROW, I GUESS, ALTHOUGH I CAN'T TELL WHERE IT'S COMING FROM...
I KNOW. IT'S LIKE CLOUDS PASSING ACROSS THE SUN.
THAT'S EXACTLY WHAT IT'S LIKE! I KEEP THINKING THE LIGHT'S CHANGING, BUT IT'S ME. IT'S INSIDE ME.
SOPHIE, HOW COME THERE'S SORROW IN HEAVEN?
WELL, IF THERE WEREN'T, IT WOULDN'T BE HEAVEN. IT'D BE DISNEYLAND.
HEH. YEAH, YOU'RE RIGHT.
EVEN SO, I'D EXPECTED MORE ANGELS...
I DON'T KNOW. I KEEP GETTING THIS FEELING LIKE... LIKE THIS BRIGHT INFORMA-TION? BUT IT'S SO PURE, IT ISN'T ABOUT ANYTHING?
IT'S HARD TO EXPLAIN...

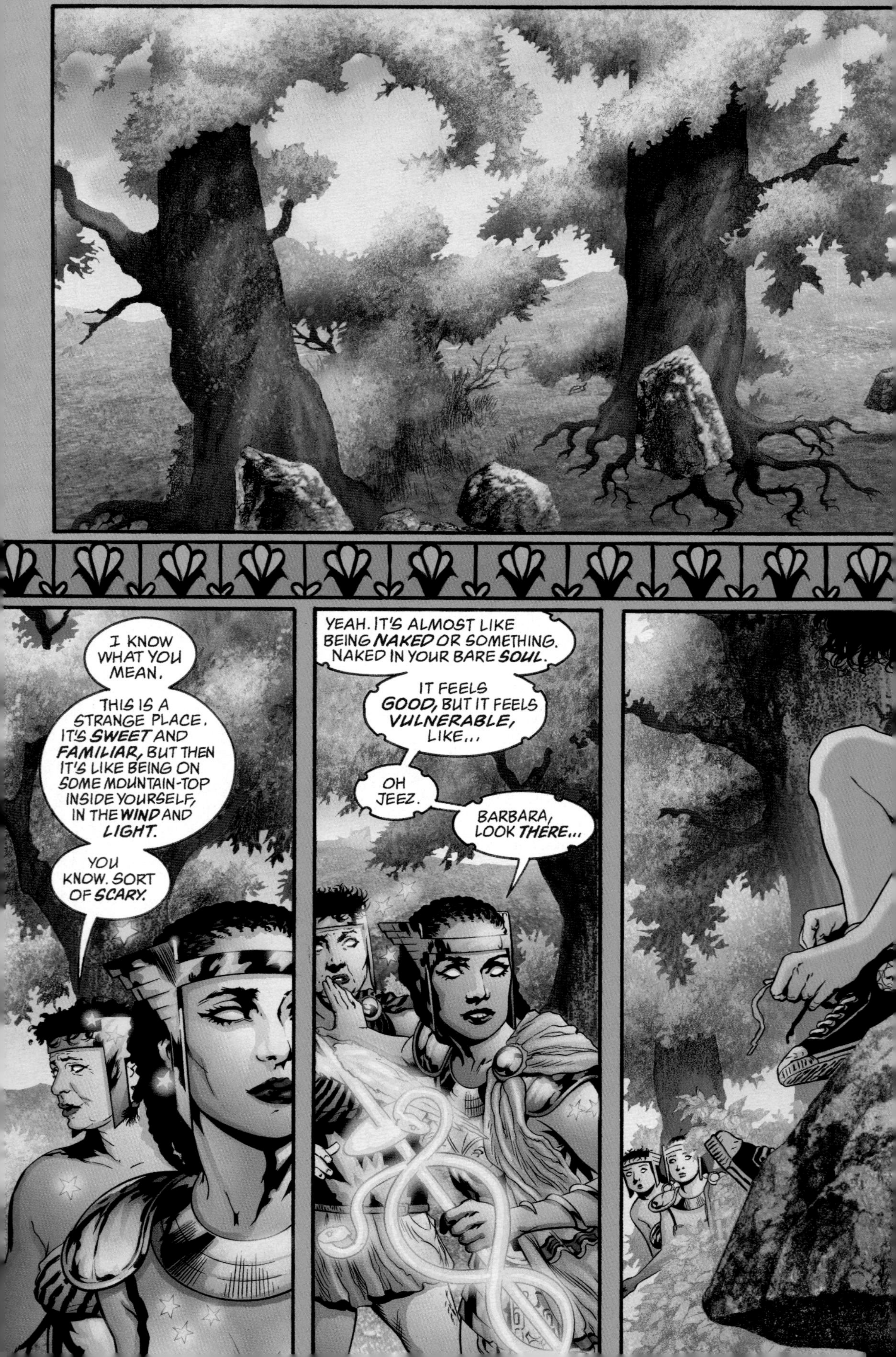
I KNOW WHAT YOU MEAN.
THIS IS A STRANGE PLACE. IT'S SWEET AND FAMILIAR, BUT THEN IT'S LIKE BEING ON SOME MOUNTAIN-TOP INSIDE YOURSELF, IN THE WIND AND LIGHT.
YOU KNOW. SORT OF SCARY.
YEAH. IT'S ALMOST LIKE BEING NAKED OR SOMETHING. NAKED IN YOUR BARE SOUL.
IT FEELS GOOD, BUT IT FEELS VULNERABLE, LIKE...
OH JEEZ.
BARBARA, LOOK THERE...

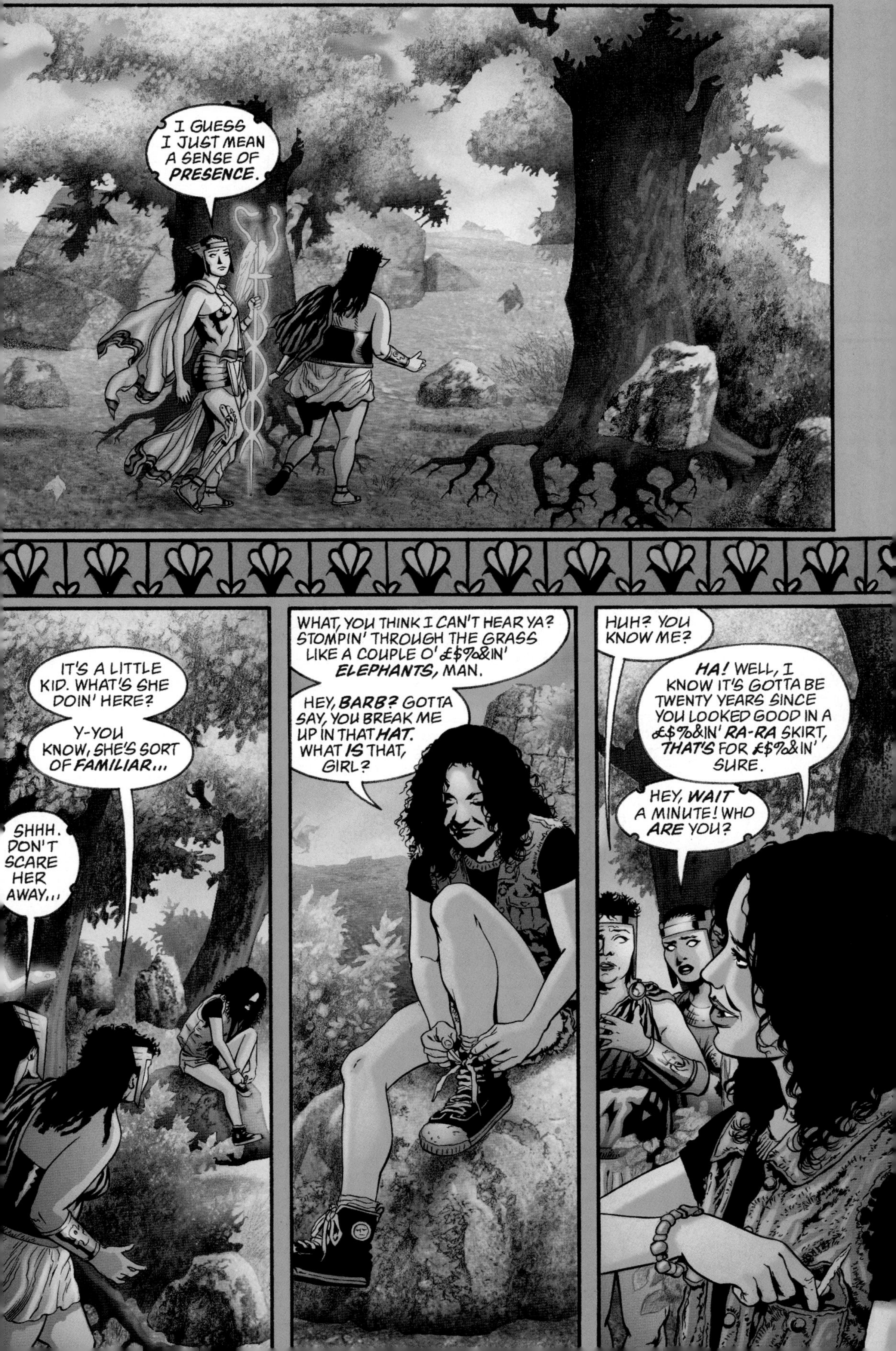
I GUESS I JUST MEAN A SENSE OF *PRESENCE*.
IT'S A LITTLE KID. WHAT'S SHE DOIN' HERE?
Y-YOU KNOW, SHE'S SORT OF *FAMILIAR*...
SHHH. DON'T SCARE HER AWAY...
WHAT, YOU THINK I CAN'T HEAR YA? STOMPIN' THROUGH THE GRASS LIKE A COUPLE O' £$%&IN' *ELEPHANTS*, MAN.
HEY, *BARB?* GOTTA SAY, YOU BREAK ME UP IN THAT *HAT*. WHAT *IS* THAT, GIRL?
HUH? YOU KNOW ME?
HA! WELL, I KNOW IT'S GOTTA BE TWENTY YEARS SINCE YOU LOOKED GOOD IN A £$%&IN' *RA-RA* SKIRT, *THAT'S* FOR £$%&IN' SURE.
HEY, *WAIT* A MINUTE! WHO *ARE* YOU?

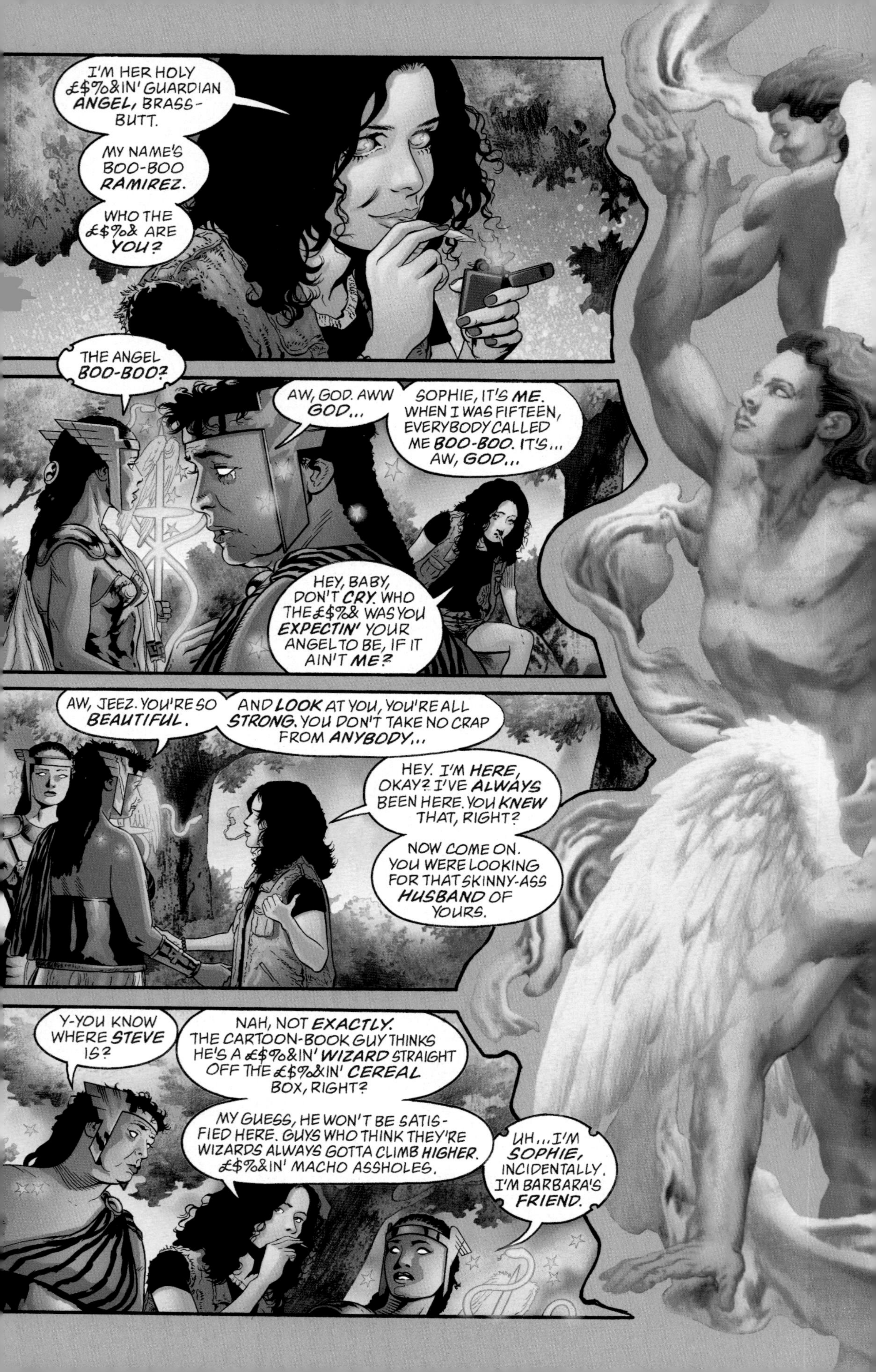
I'M HER HOLY £$%&IN' GUARDIAN ANGEL, BRASS-BUTT.
MY NAME'S BOO-BOO RAMIREZ.
WHO THE £$%& ARE YOU?
THE ANGEL BOO-BOO?
AW, GOD. AWW GOD...
SOPHIE, IT'S ME. WHEN I WAS FIFTEEN, EVERYBODY CALLED ME BOO-BOO. IT'S... AW, GOD...
HEY, BABY, DON'T CRY. WHO THE £$%& WAS YOU EXPECTIN' YOUR ANGEL TO BE, IF IT AIN'T ME?
AW, JEEZ. YOU'RE SO BEAUTIFUL.
AND LOOK AT YOU, YOU'RE ALL STRONG. YOU DON'T TAKE NO CRAP FROM ANYBODY...
HEY. I'M HERE, OKAY? I'VE ALWAYS BEEN HERE. YOU KNEW THAT, RIGHT?
NOW COME ON. YOU WERE LOOKING FOR THAT SKINNY-ASS HUSBAND OF YOURS.
Y-YOU KNOW WHERE STEVE IS?
NAH, NOT EXACTLY. THE CARTOON-BOOK GUY THINKS HE'S A £$%&IN' WIZARD STRAIGHT OFF THE £$%&IN' CEREAL BOX, RIGHT?
MY GUESS, HE WON'T BE SATIS-FIED HERE. GUYS WHO THINK THEY'RE WIZARDS ALWAYS GOTTA CLIMB HIGHER. £$%&IN' MACHO ASSHOLES.
UH...I'M SOPHIE, INCIDENTALLY. I'M BARBARA'S FRIEND.

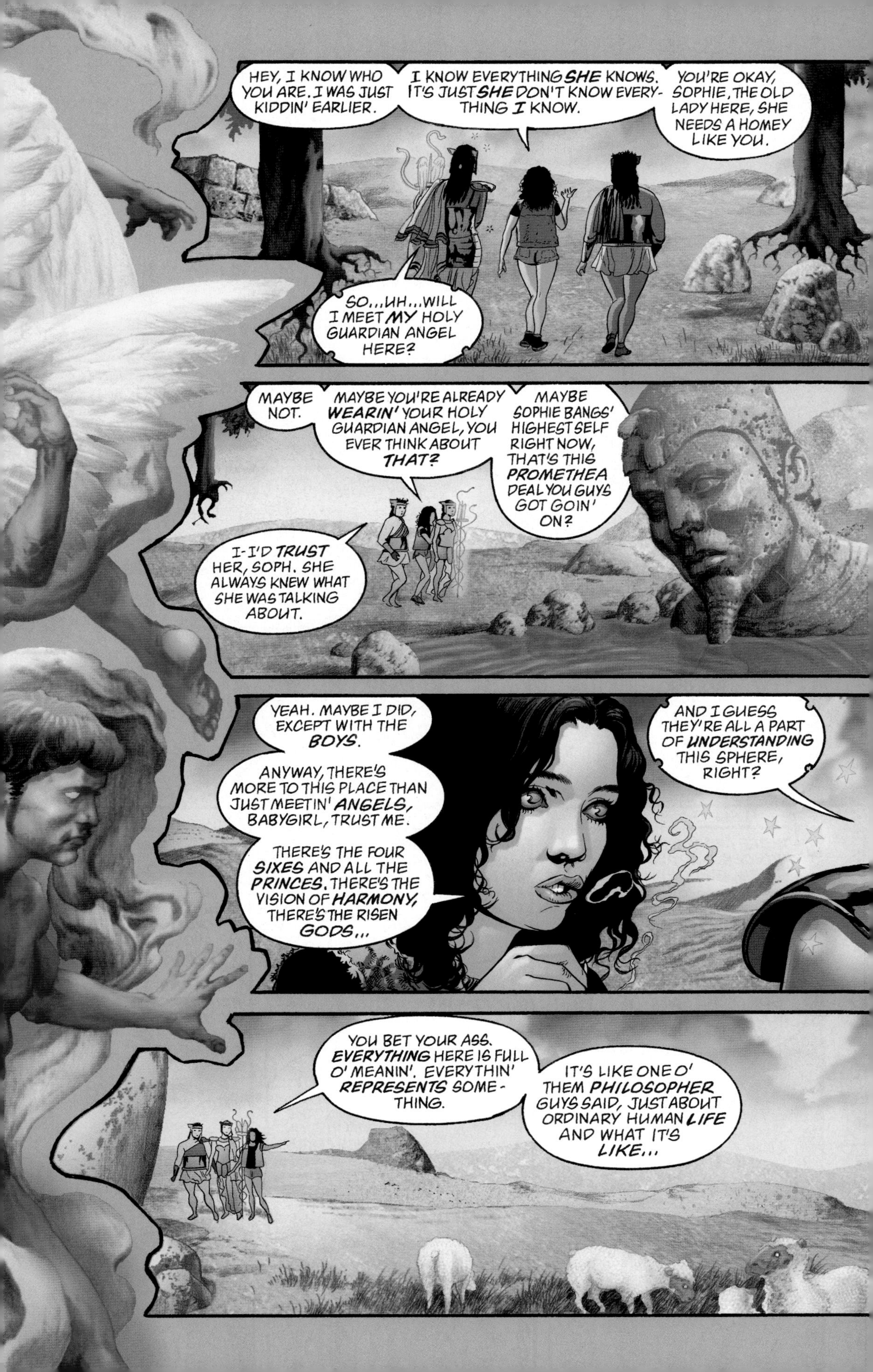

HEY, I KNOW WHO YOU ARE. I WAS JUST KIDDIN' EARLIER.
I KNOW EVERYTHING SHE KNOWS. IT'S JUST SHE DON'T KNOW EVERYTHING I KNOW.
YOU'RE OKAY, SOPHIE, THE OLD LADY HERE, SHE NEEDS A HOMEY LIKE YOU.
SO...UH...WILL I MEET MY HOLY GUARDIAN ANGEL HERE?
MAYBE NOT.
MAYBE YOU'RE ALREADY WEARIN' YOUR HOLY GUARDIAN ANGEL, YOU EVER THINK ABOUT THAT?
MAYBE SOPHIE BANGS' HIGHEST SELF RIGHT NOW, THAT'S THIS PROMETHEA DEAL YOU GUYS GOT GOIN' ON?
I-I'D TRUST HER, SOPH. SHE ALWAYS KNEW WHAT SHE WAS TALKING ABOUT.
YEAH. MAYBE I DID, EXCEPT WITH THE BOYS.
ANYWAY, THERE'S MORE TO THIS PLACE THAN JUST MEETIN' ANGELS, BABYGIRL, TRUST ME.
THERE'S THE FOUR SIXES AND ALL THE PRINCES. THERE'S THE VISION OF HARMONY, THERE'S THE RISEN GODS...
AND I GUESS THEY'RE ALL A PART OF UNDERSTANDING THIS SPHERE, RIGHT?
YOU BET YOUR ASS. EVERYTHING HERE IS FULL O' MEANIN'. EVERYTHIN' REPRESENTS SOMETHING.
IT'S LIKE ONE O' THEM PHILOSOPHER GUYS SAID, JUST ABOUT ORDINARY HUMAN LIFE AND WHAT IT'S LIKE...

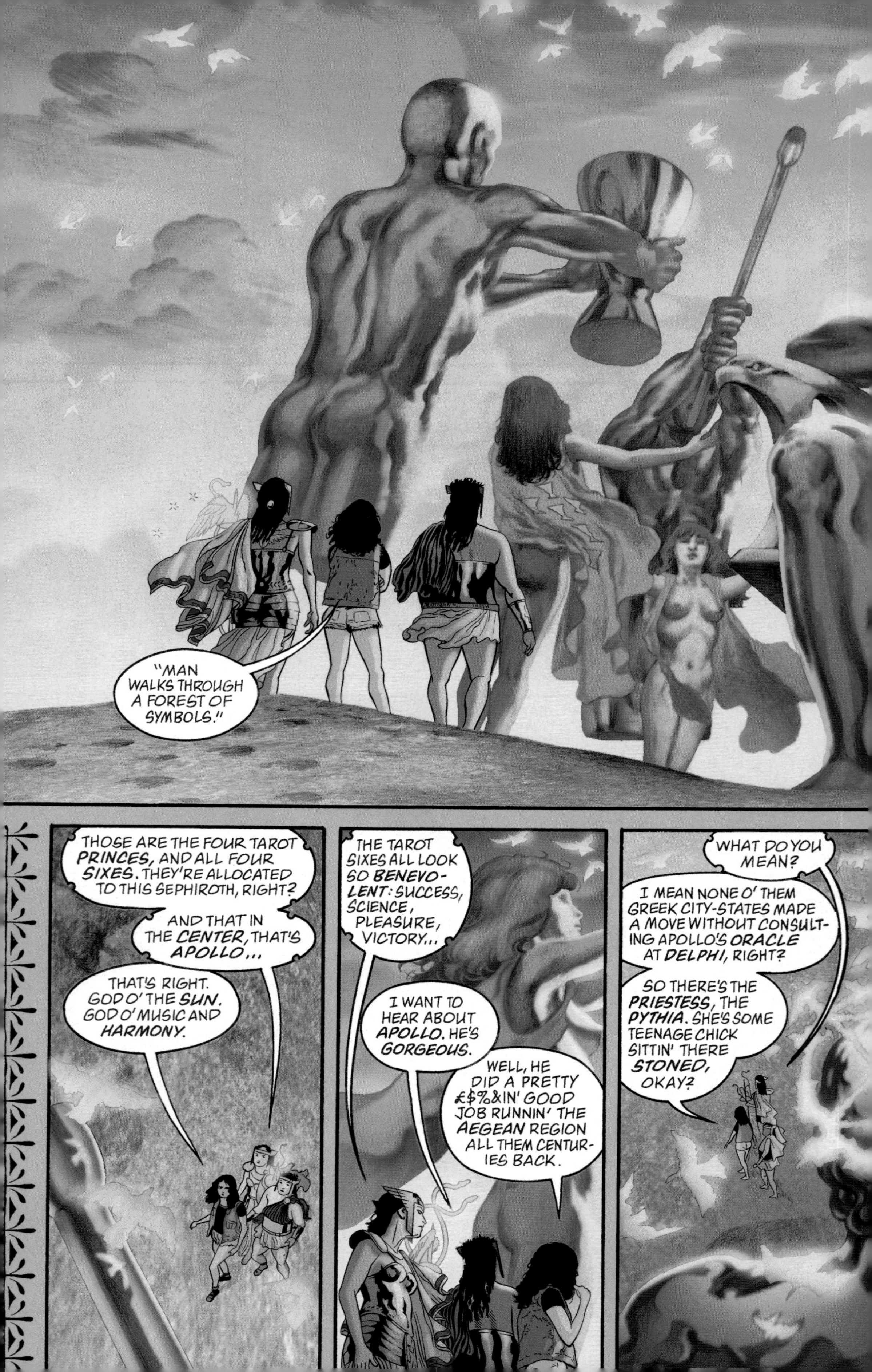
"MAN WALKS THROUGH A FOREST OF SYMBOLS."
THOSE ARE THE FOUR TAROT PRINCES, AND ALL FOUR SIXES. THEY'RE ALLOCATED TO THIS SEPHIROTH, RIGHT?
AND THAT IN THE CENTER, THAT'S APOLLO...
THAT'S RIGHT. GOD O' THE SUN. GOD O' MUSIC AND HARMONY.
THE TAROT SIXES ALL LOOK SO BENEVOLENT: SUCCESS, SCIENCE, PLEASURE, VICTORY...
I WANT TO HEAR ABOUT APOLLO. HE'S GORGEOUS.
WELL, HE DID A PRETTY £$%&IN' GOOD JOB RUNNIN' THE AEGEAN REGION ALL THEM CENTURIES BACK.
WHAT DO YOU MEAN?
I MEAN NONE O' THEM GREEK CITY-STATES MADE A MOVE WITHOUT CONSULTING APOLLO'S ORACLE AT DELPHI, RIGHT?
SO THERE'S THE PRIESTESS, THE PYTHIA. SHE'S SOME TEENAGE CHICK SITTIN' THERE STONED, OKAY?

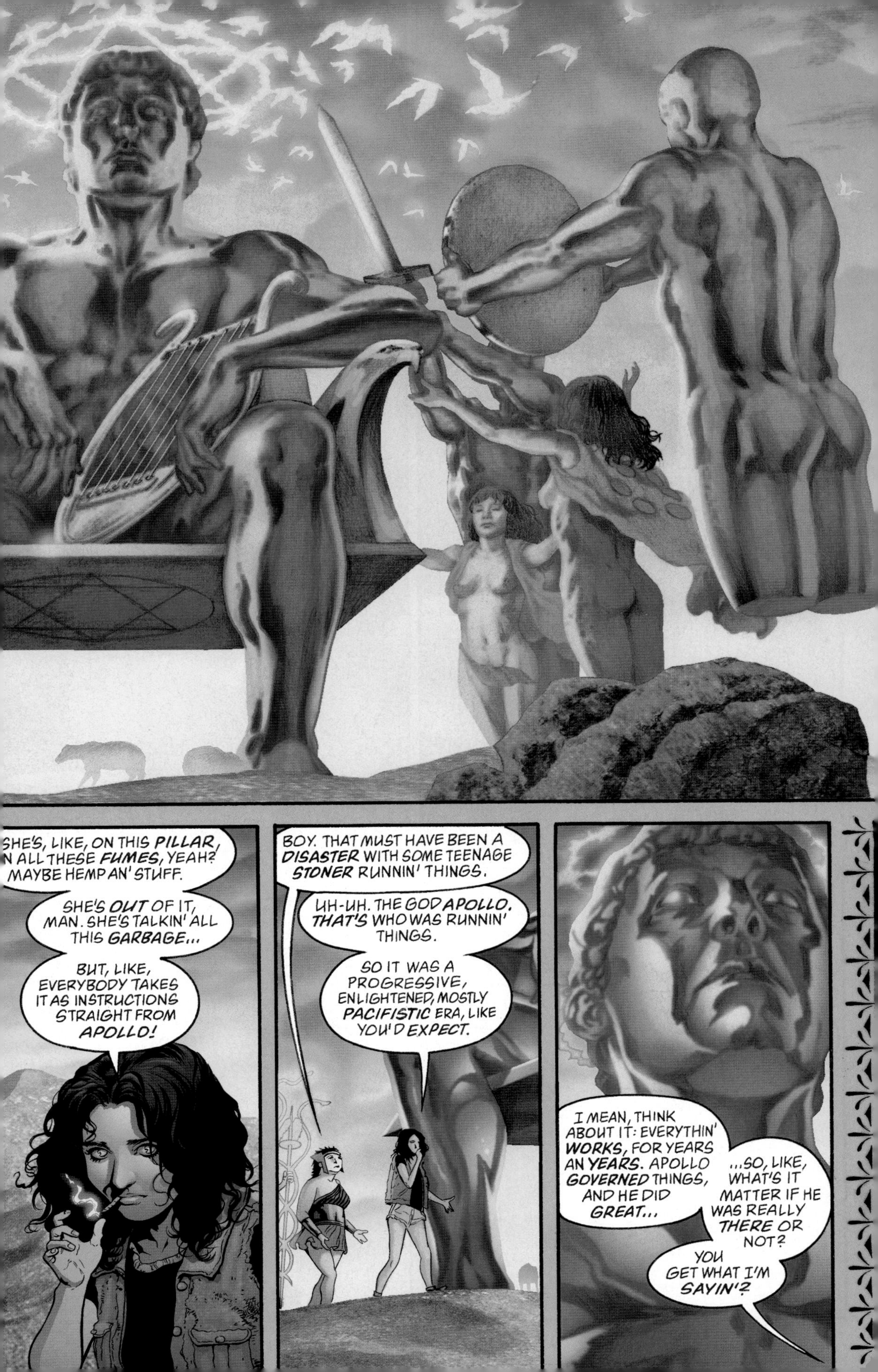
SHE'S, LIKE, ON THIS PILLAR, IN ALL THESE FUMES, YEAH? MAYBE HEMP AN' STUFF.
SHE'S OUT OF IT, MAN. SHE'S TALKIN' ALL THIS GARBAGE...
BUT, LIKE, EVERYBODY TAKES IT AS INSTRUCTIONS STRAIGHT FROM APOLLO!
BOY. THAT MUST HAVE BEEN A DISASTER WITH SOME TEENAGE STONER RUNNIN' THINGS.
UH-UH. THE GOD APOLLO. THAT'S WHO WAS RUNNIN' THINGS.
SO IT WAS A PROGRESSIVE, ENLIGHTENED, MOSTLY PACIFISTIC ERA, LIKE YOU'D EXPECT.
I MEAN, THINK ABOUT IT: EVERYTHIN' WORKS, FOR YEARS AN YEARS. APOLLO GOVERNED THINGS, AND HE DID GREAT...
...SO, LIKE, WHAT'S IT MATTER IF HE WAS REALLY THERE OR NOT?
YOU GET WHAT I'M SAYIN'?

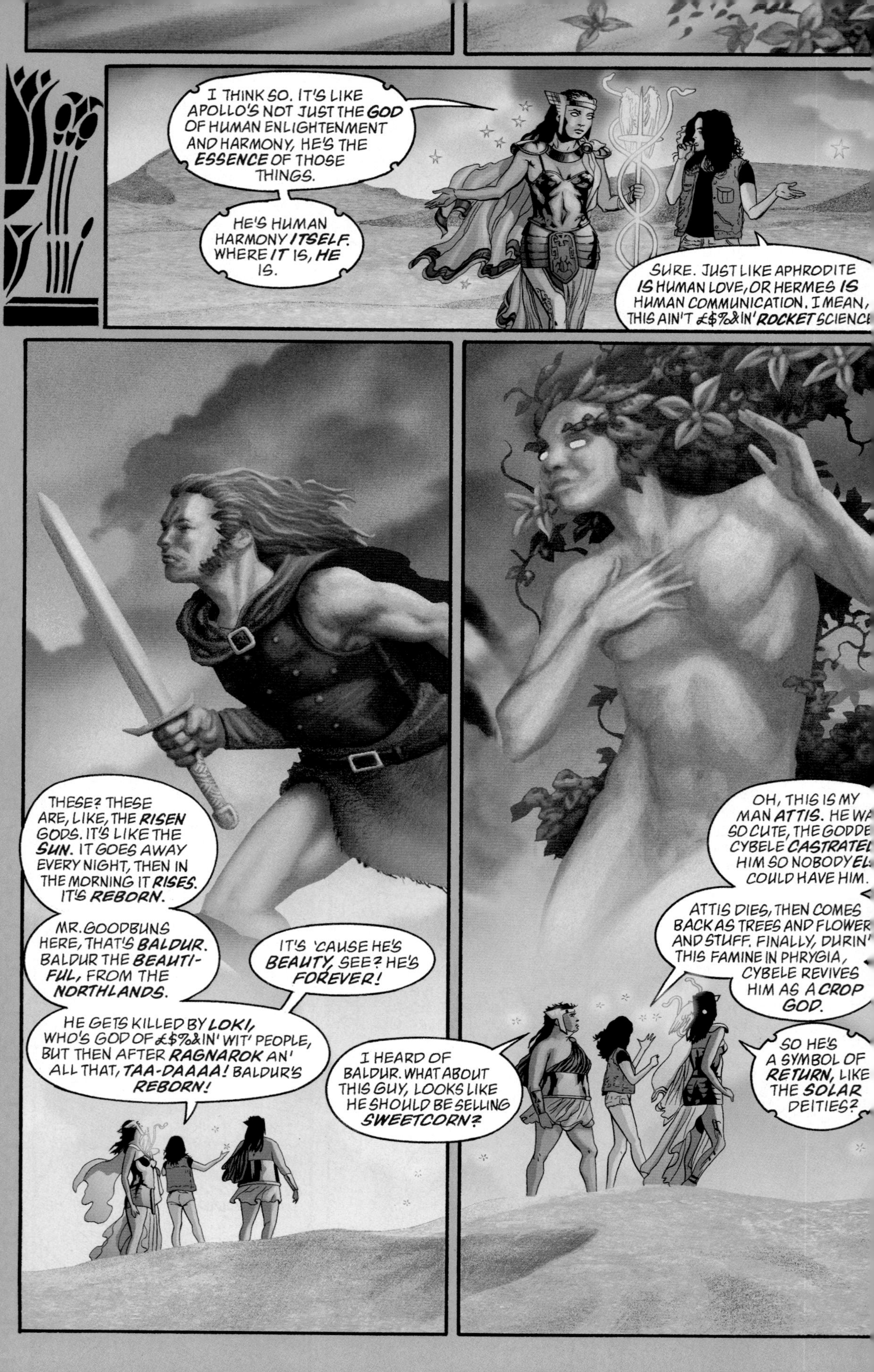

I THINK SO. IT'S LIKE APOLLO'S NOT JUST THE GOD OF HUMAN ENLIGHTENMENT AND HARMONY, HE'S THE ESSENCE OF THOSE THINGS.
HE'S HUMAN HARMONY ITSELF. WHERE IT IS, HE IS.
SURE. JUST LIKE APHRODITE IS HUMAN LOVE, OR HERMES IS HUMAN COMMUNICATION. I MEAN, THIS AIN'T £$%&IN' ROCKET SCIENCE
THESE? THESE ARE, LIKE, THE RISEN GODS. IT'S LIKE THE SUN. IT GOES AWAY EVERY NIGHT, THEN IN THE MORNING IT RISES. IT'S REBORN.
MR. GOODBUNS HERE, THAT'S BALDUR. BALDUR THE BEAUTIFUL, FROM THE NORTHLANDS.
IT'S 'CAUSE HE'S BEAUTY, SEE? HE'S FOREVER!
HE GETS KILLED BY LOKI, WHO'S GOD OF £$%&IN' WIT' PEOPLE, BUT THEN AFTER RAGNAROK AN' ALL THAT, TAA-DAAAA! BALDUR'S REBORN!
I HEARD OF BALDUR. WHAT ABOUT THIS GUY, LOOKS LIKE HE SHOULD BE SELLING SWEETCORN?
OH, THIS IS MY MAN ATTIS. HE WA SO CUTE, THE GODDE CYBELE CASTRATE HIM SO NOBODY EL COULD HAVE HIM.
ATTIS DIES, THEN COMES BACK AS TREES AND FLOWER AND STUFF. FINALLY, DURIN' THIS FAMINE IN PHRYGIA, CYBELE REVIVES HIM AS A CROP GOD.
SO HE'S A SYMBOL OF RETURN, LIKE THE SOLAR DEITIES?

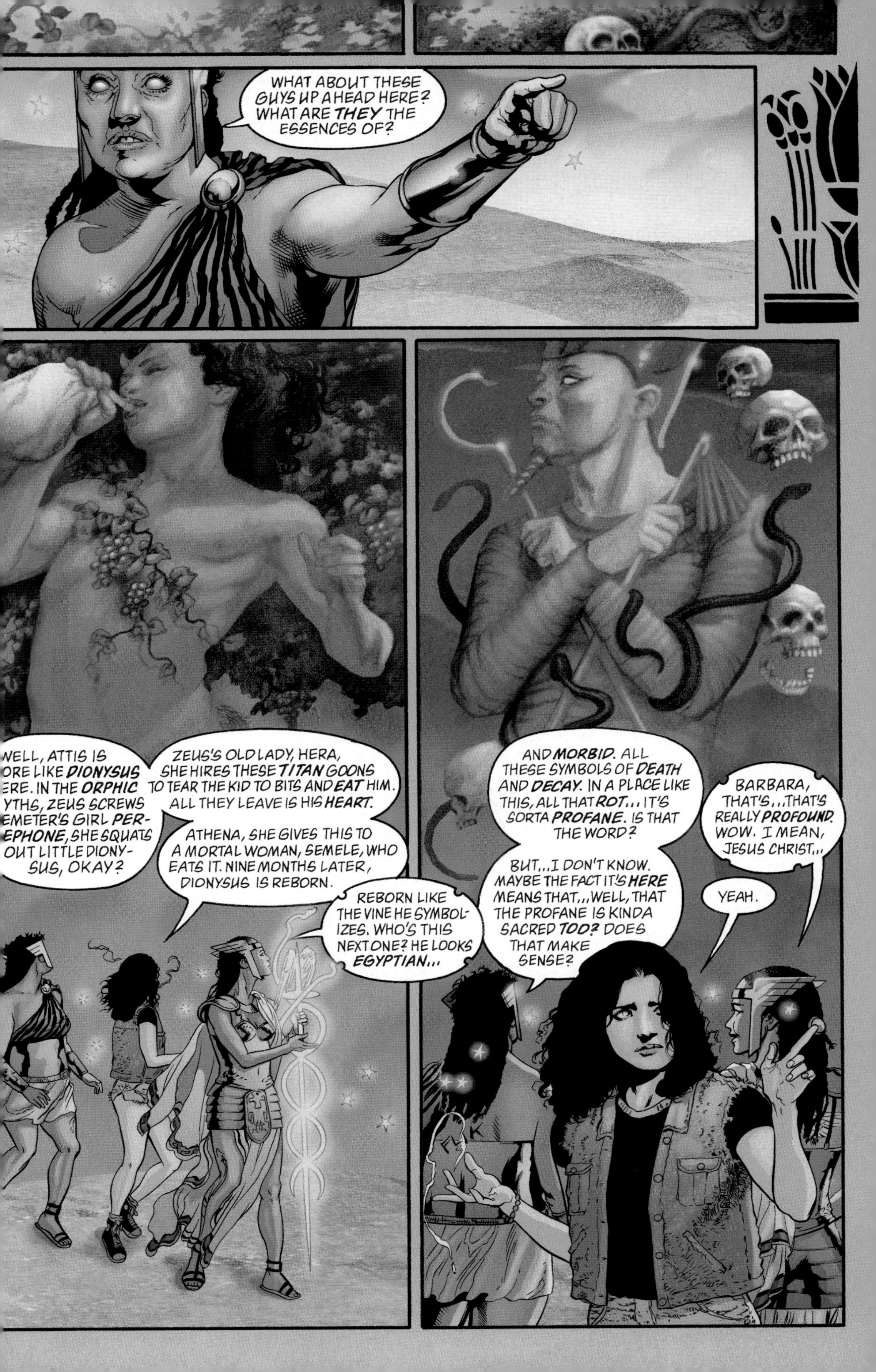
WHAT ABOUT THESE GUYS UP AHEAD HERE? WHAT ARE THEY THE ESSENCES OF?
WELL, ATTIS IS ORE LIKE DIONYSUS ERE. IN THE ORPHIC YTHS, ZEUS SCREWS EMETER'S GIRL PER-EPHONE, SHE SQUATS OUT LITTLE DIONY-SUS, OKAY?
ZEUS'S OLD LADY, HERA, SHE HIRES THESE TITAN GOONS TO TEAR THE KID TO BITS AND EAT HIM. ALL THEY LEAVE IS HIS HEART.
ATHENA, SHE GIVES THIS TO A MORTAL WOMAN, SEMELE, WHO EATS IT. NINE MONTHS LATER, DIONYSUS IS REBORN.
REBORN LIKE THE VINE HE SYMBOL-IZES. WHO'S THIS NEXT ONE? HE LOOKS EGYPTIAN...
AND MORBID. ALL THESE SYMBOLS OF DEATH AND DECAY. IN A PLACE LIKE THIS, ALL THAT ROT... IT'S SORTA PROFANE. IS THAT THE WORD?
BUT... I DON'T KNOW. MAYBE THE FACT IT'S HERE MEANS THAT... WELL, THAT THE PROFANE IS KINDA SACRED TOO? DOES THAT MAKE SENSE?
BARBARA, THAT'S... THAT'S REALLY PROFOUND. WOW. I MEAN, JESUS CHRIST...
YEAH.

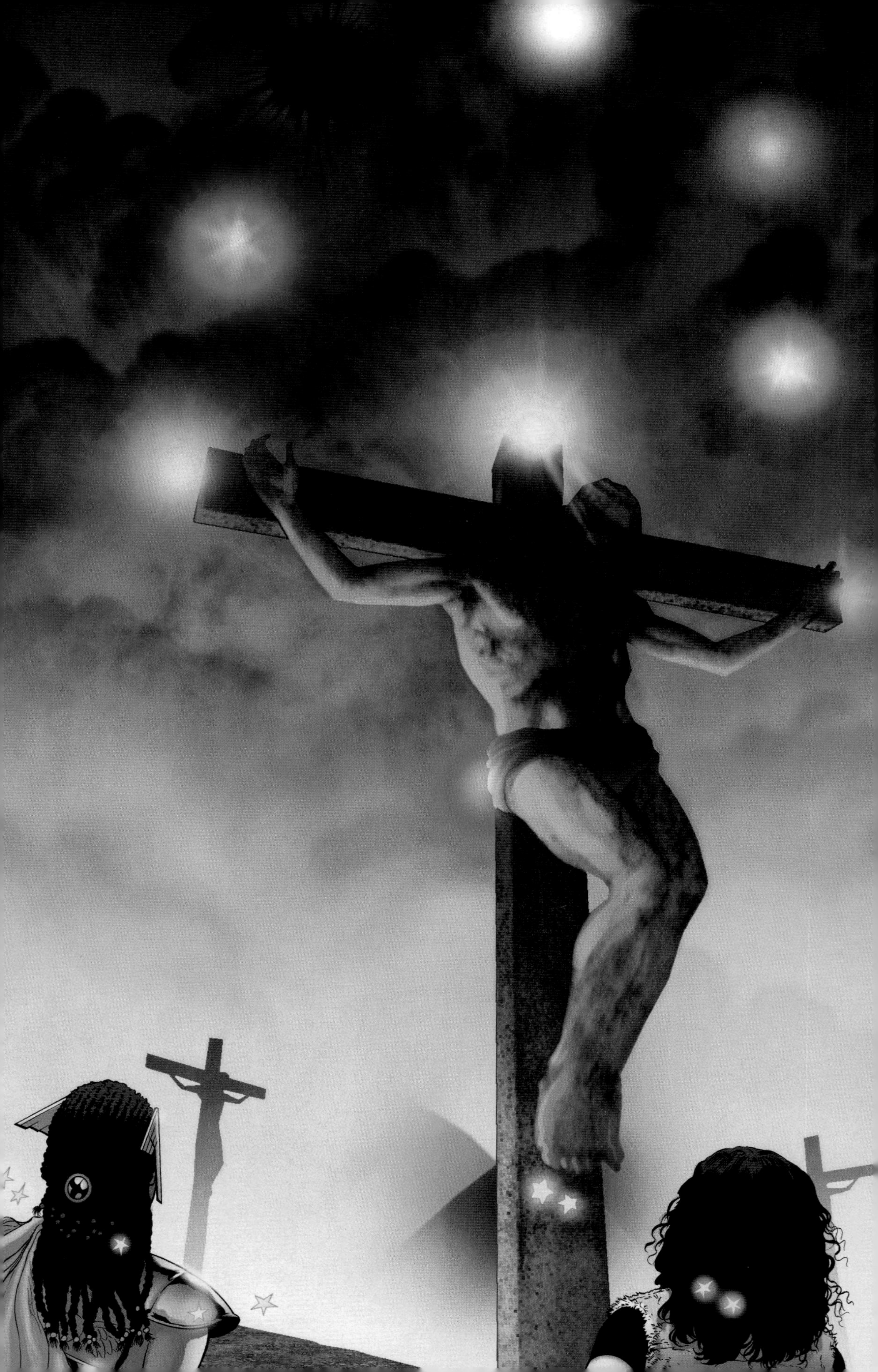

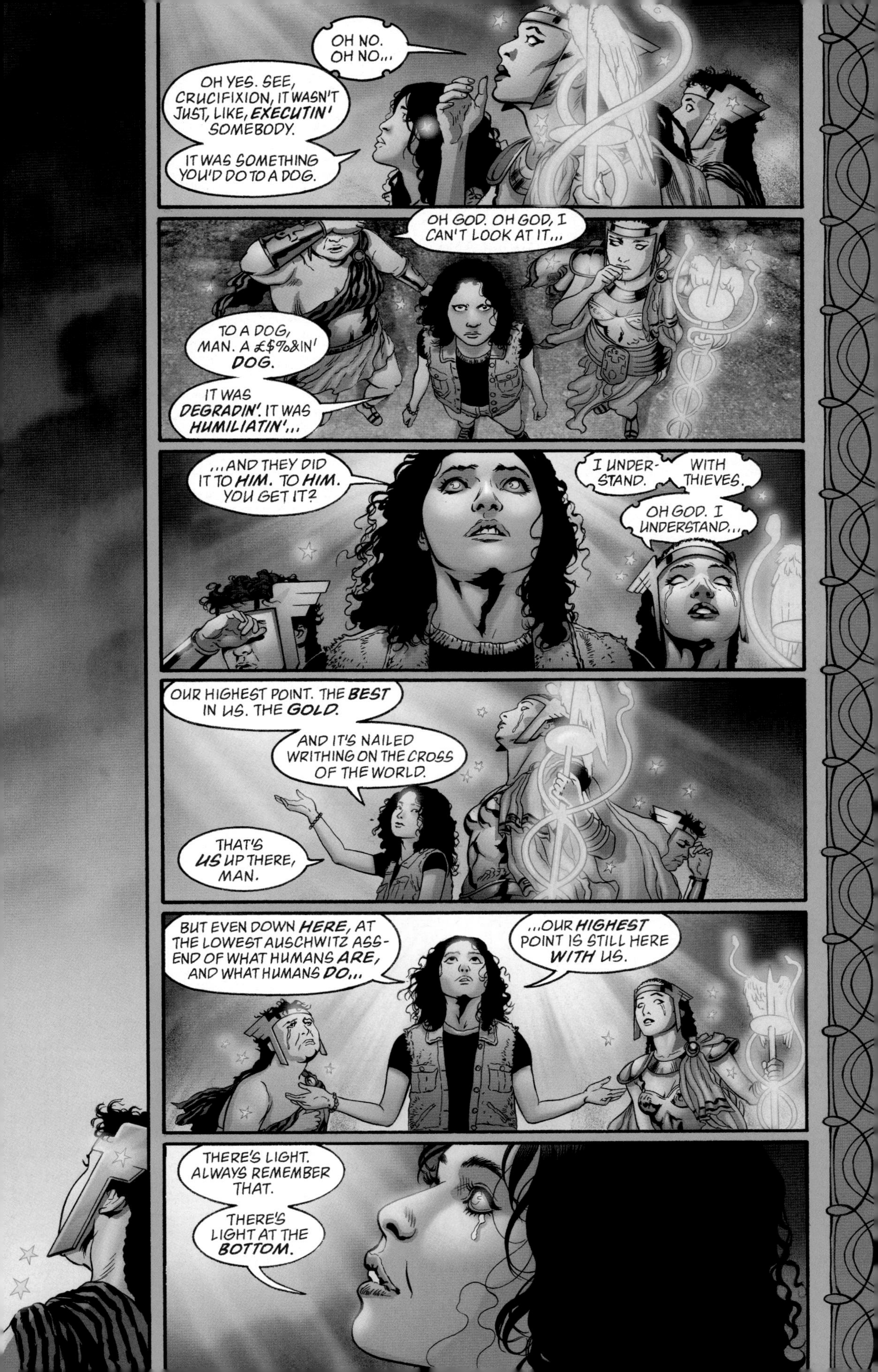
OH NO. OH NO...
OH YES. SEE, CRUCIFIXION, IT WASN'T JUST, LIKE, EXECUTIN' SOMEBODY.
IT WAS SOMETHING YOU'D DO TO A DOG.
OH GOD. OH GOD, I CAN'T LOOK AT IT...
TO A DOG, MAN. A £$%&IN' DOG.
IT WAS DEGRADIN'. IT WAS HUMILIATIN'...
...AND THEY DID IT TO HIM. TO HIM. YOU GET IT?
I UNDERSTAND.
WITH THIEVES.
OH GOD. I UNDERSTAND...
OUR HIGHEST POINT. THE BEST IN US. THE GOLD.
AND IT'S NAILED WRITHING ON THE CROSS OF THE WORLD.
THAT'S US UP THERE, MAN.
BUT EVEN DOWN HERE, AT THE LOWEST AUSCHWITZ ASS-END OF WHAT HUMANS ARE, AND WHAT HUMANS DO...
...OUR HIGHEST POINT IS STILL HERE WITH US.
THERE'S LIGHT. ALWAYS REMEMBER THAT.
THERE'S LIGHT AT THE BOTTOM.

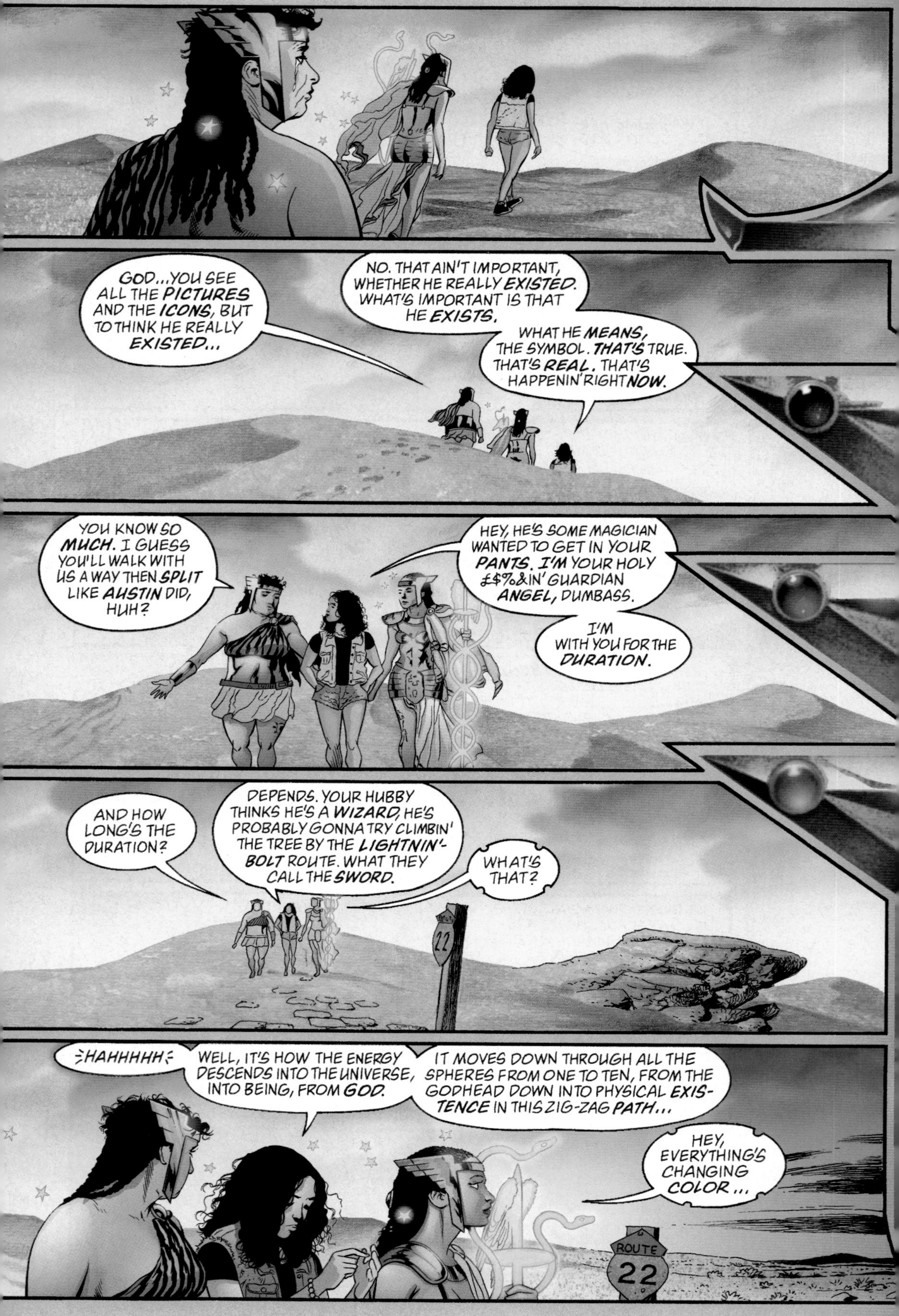
GOD...YOU SEE ALL THE PICTURES AND THE ICONS, BUT TO THINK HE REALLY EXISTED...
NO. THAT AIN'T IMPORTANT, WHETHER HE REALLY EXISTED. WHAT'S IMPORTANT IS THAT HE EXISTS.
WHAT HE MEANS, THE SYMBOL. THAT'S TRUE. THAT'S REAL. THAT'S HAPPENIN' RIGHT NOW.
YOU KNOW SO MUCH. I GUESS YOU'LL WALK WITH US A WAY THEN SPLIT LIKE AUSTIN DID, HUH?
HEY, HE'S SOME MAGICIAN WANTED TO GET IN YOUR PANTS. I'M YOUR HOLY £$%&IN' GUARDIAN ANGEL, DUMBASS.
I'M WITH YOU FOR THE DURATION.
AND HOW LONG'S THE DURATION?
DEPENDS. YOUR HUBBY THINKS HE'S A WIZARD, HE'S PROBABLY GONNA TRY CLIMBIN' THE TREE BY THE LIGHTNIN'-BOLT ROUTE. WHAT THEY CALL THE SWORD.
WHAT'S THAT?
22
HAHHHHH
WELL, IT'S HOW THE ENERGY DESCENDS INTO THE UNIVERSE, INTO BEING, FROM GOD.
IT MOVES DOWN THROUGH ALL THE SPHERES FROM ONE TO TEN, FROM THE GODHEAD DOWN INTO PHYSICAL EXISTENCE IN THIS ZIG-ZAG PATH...
HEY, EVERYTHING'S CHANGING COLOR...
ROUTE 22

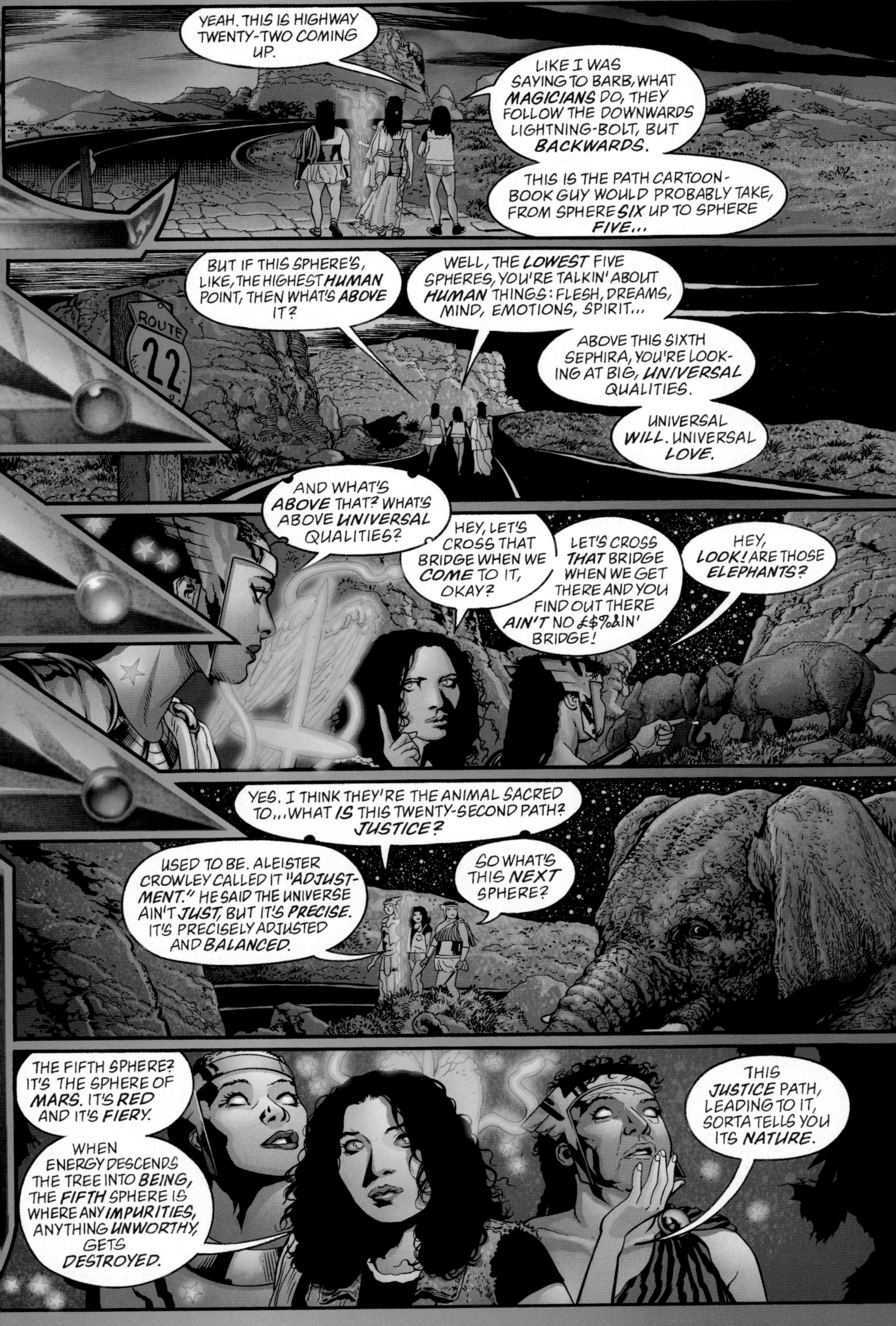
YEAH. THIS IS HIGHWAY TWENTY-TWO COMING UP.
LIKE I WAS SAYING TO BARB, WHAT MAGICIANS DO, THEY FOLLOW THE DOWNWARDS LIGHTNING-BOLT, BUT BACKWARDS.
THIS IS THE PATH CARTOON-BOOK GUY WOULD PROBABLY TAKE, FROM SPHERE SIX UP TO SPHERE FIVE...
ROUTE 22
BUT IF THIS SPHERE'S, LIKE, THE HIGHEST HUMAN POINT, THEN WHAT'S ABOVE IT?
WELL, THE LOWEST FIVE SPHERES, YOU'RE TALKIN' ABOUT HUMAN THINGS: FLESH, DREAMS, MIND, EMOTIONS, SPIRIT...
ABOVE THIS SIXTH SEPHIRA, YOU'RE LOOKING AT BIG, UNIVERSAL QUALITIES.
UNIVERSAL WILL. UNIVERSAL LOVE.
AND WHAT'S ABOVE THAT? WHAT'S ABOVE UNIVERSAL QUALITIES?
HEY, LET'S CROSS THAT BRIDGE WHEN WE COME TO IT, OKAY?
LET'S CROSS THAT BRIDGE WHEN WE GET THERE AND YOU FIND OUT THERE AIN'T NO £$%&IN' BRIDGE!
HEY, LOOK! ARE THOSE ELEPHANTS?
YES. I THINK THEY'RE THE ANIMAL SACRED TO... WHAT IS THIS TWENTY-SECOND PATH? JUSTICE?
USED TO BE. ALEISTER CROWLEY CALLED IT "ADJUSTMENT." HE SAID THE UNIVERSE AIN'T JUST, BUT IT'S PRECISE. IT'S PRECISELY ADJUSTED AND BALANCED.
SO WHAT'S THIS NEXT SPHERE?
THE FIFTH SPHERE? IT'S THE SPHERE OF MARS. IT'S RED AND IT'S FIERY.
WHEN ENERGY DESCENDS THE TREE INTO BEING, THE FIFTH SPHERE IS WHERE ANY IMPURITIES, ANYTHING UNWORTHY, GETS DESTROYED.
THIS JUSTICE PATH, LEADING TO IT, SORTA TELLS YOU ITS NATURE.

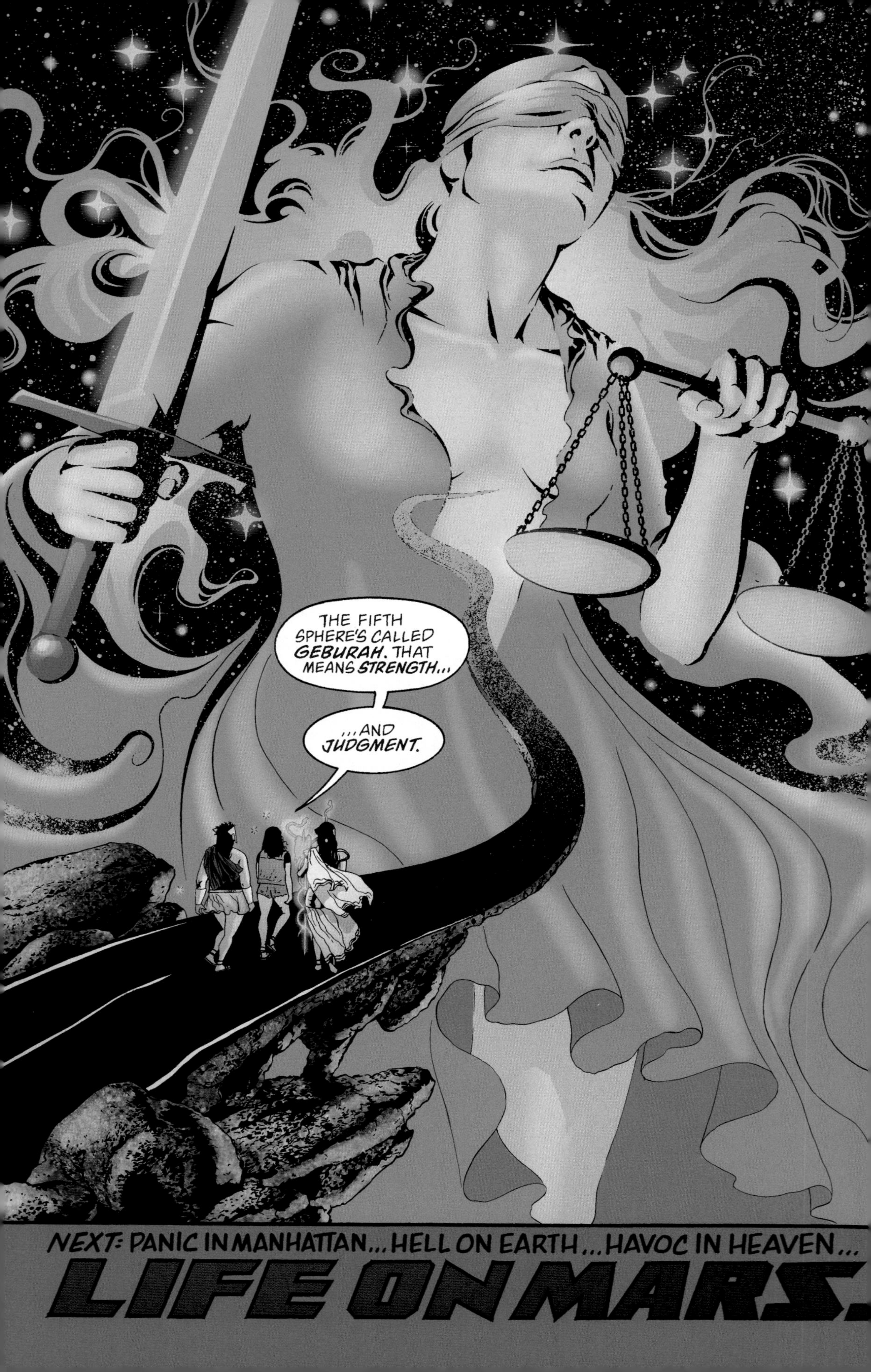
THE FIFTH SPHERE'S CALLED GEBURAH. THAT MEANS STRENGTH...
...AND JUDGMENT.
NEXT: PANIC IN MANHATTAN... HELL ON EARTH... HAVOC IN HEAVEN...
LIFE ON MARS.

CHAPTER SIX

**A warrior encounters hosts of demons,
An outburst of anger emperils the quest,
And an ancient king explains himself.**

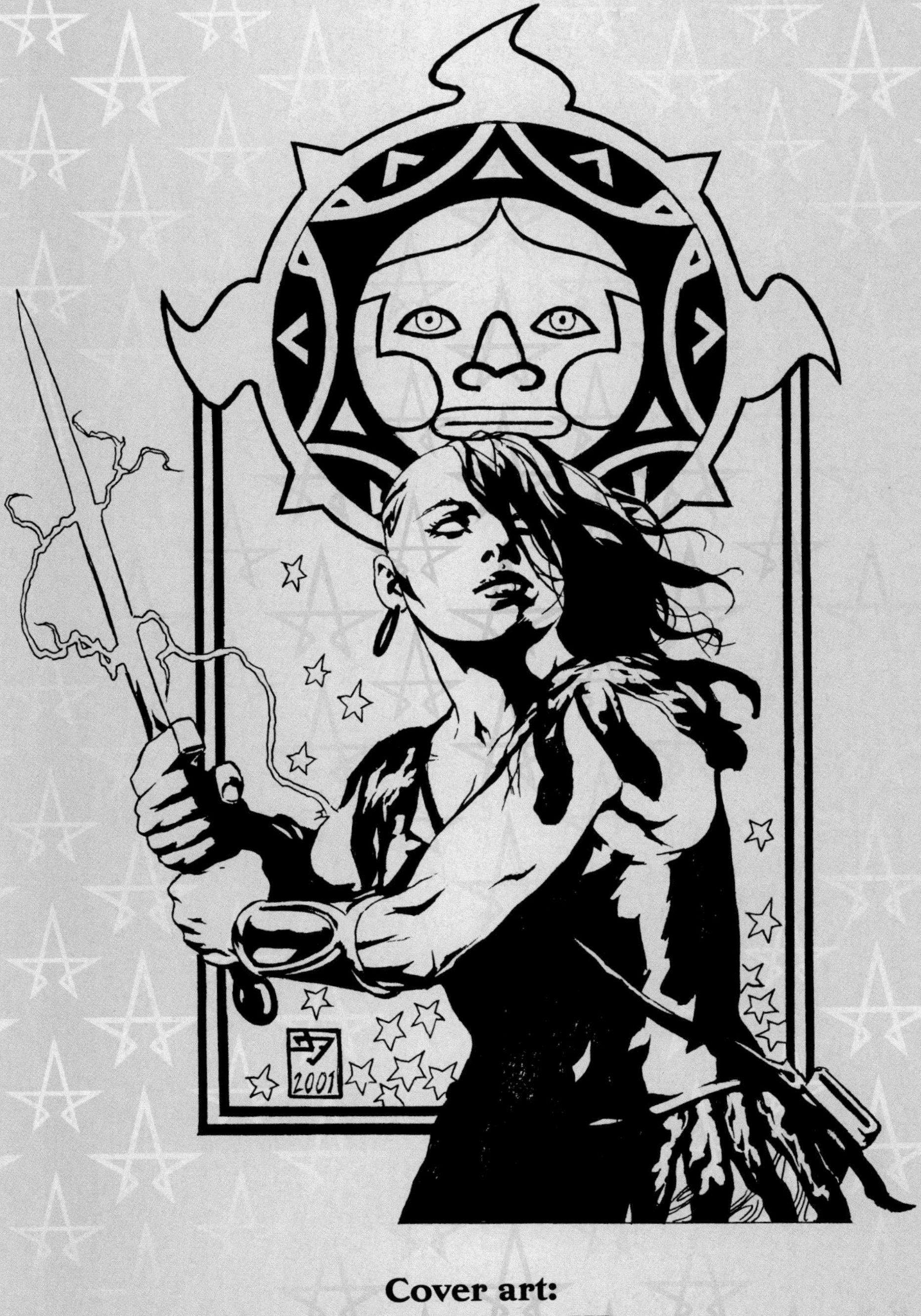
2001

**Cover art:
J.H. Williams III,
Mick Gray & Jeromy Cox**

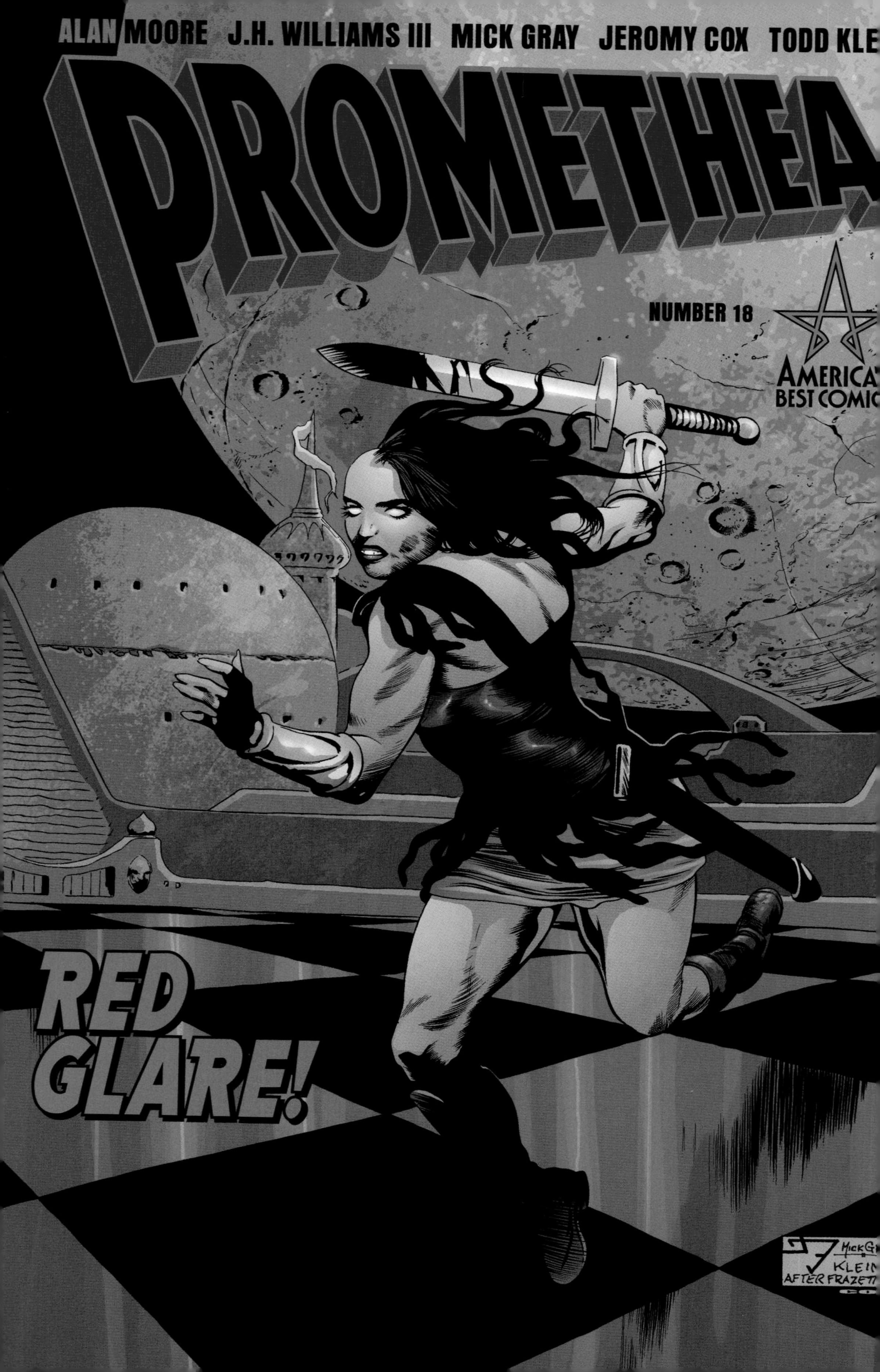
ALAN MOORE J.H. WILLIAMS III MICK GRAY JEROMY COX TODD KLE
PROMETHEA
NUMBER 18
AMERICA
BEST COMIC
RED GLARE!
MICK G
KLEIN
AFTER FRAZETT

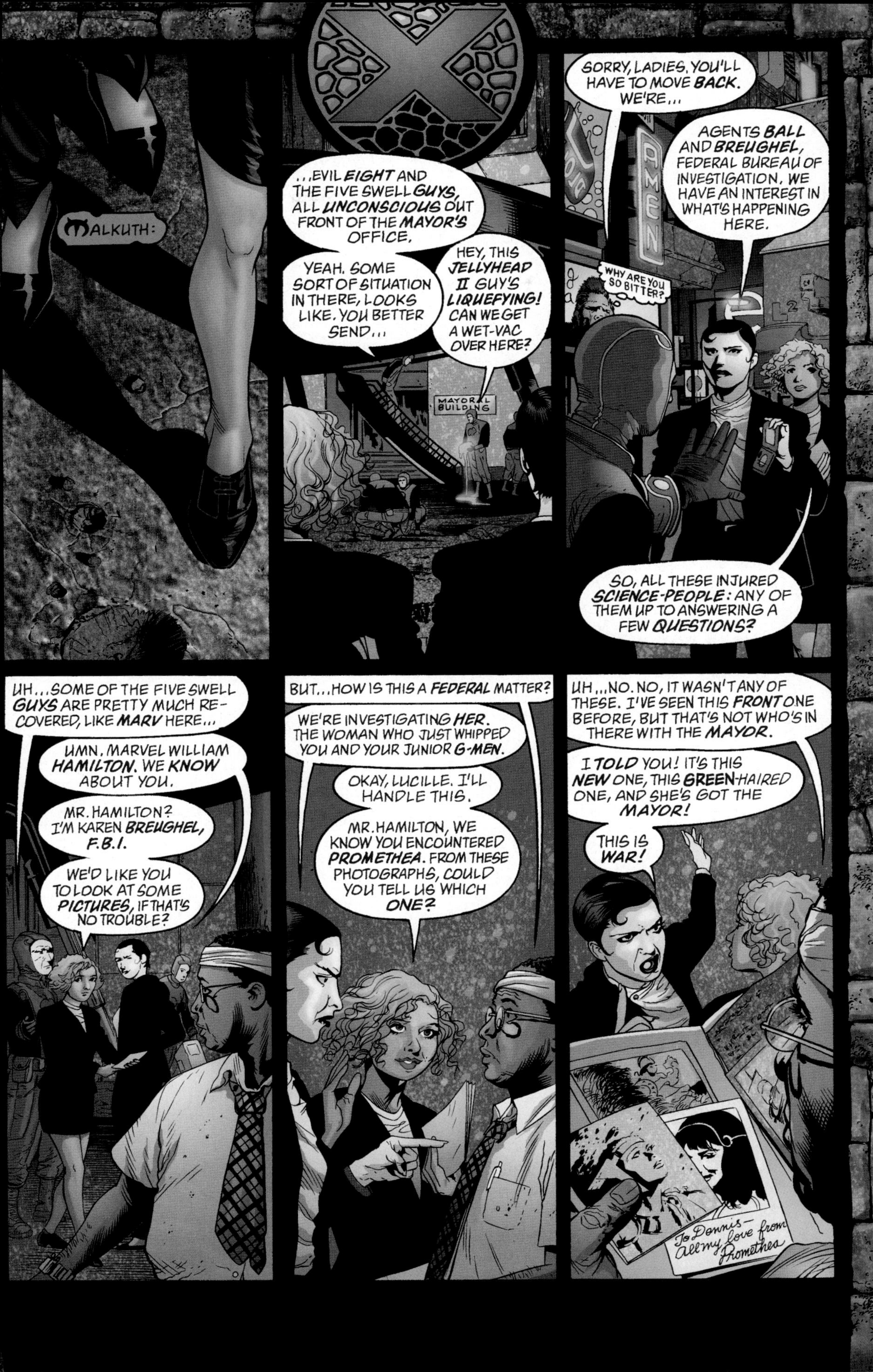
MALKUTH:
...EVIL EIGHT AND THE FIVE SWELL GUYS, ALL UNCONSCIOUS OUT FRONT OF THE MAYOR'S OFFICE.
YEAH. SOME SORT OF SITUATION IN THERE, LOOKS LIKE. YOU BETTER SEND...
HEY, THIS JELLYHEAD II GUY'S LIQUEFYING! CAN WE GET A WET-VAC OVER HERE?
MAYORAL BUILDING
SORRY, LADIES. YOU'LL HAVE TO MOVE BACK. WE'RE...
AGENTS BALL AND BREUGHEL, FEDERAL BUREAU OF INVESTIGATION. WE HAVE AN INTEREST IN WHAT'S HAPPENING HERE.
WHY ARE YOU SO BITTER?
AMEN
SO, ALL THESE INJURED SCIENCE-PEOPLE: ANY OF THEM UP TO ANSWERING A FEW QUESTIONS?
UH...SOME OF THE FIVE SWELL GUYS ARE PRETTY MUCH RE-COVERED, LIKE MARV HERE...
UMN. MARVEL WILLIAM HAMILTON. WE KNOW ABOUT YOU.
MR. HAMILTON? I'M KAREN BREUGHEL, F.B.I.
WE'D LIKE YOU TO LOOK AT SOME PICTURES, IF THAT'S NO TROUBLE?
BUT...HOW IS THIS A FEDERAL MATTER?
WE'RE INVESTIGATING HER. THE WOMAN WHO JUST WHIPPED YOU AND YOUR JUNIOR G-MEN.
OKAY, LUCILLE. I'LL HANDLE THIS.
MR. HAMILTON, WE KNOW YOU ENCOUNTERED PROMETHEA. FROM THESE PHOTOGRAPHS, COULD YOU TELL US WHICH ONE?
UH...NO. NO, IT WASN'T ANY OF THESE. I'VE SEEN THIS FRONT ONE BEFORE, BUT THAT'S NOT WHO'S IN THERE WITH THE MAYOR.
I TOLD YOU! IT'S THIS NEW ONE, THIS GREEN-HAIRED ONE, AND SHE'S GOT THE MAYOR!
THIS IS WAR!
To Dennis— All my love from Promethea

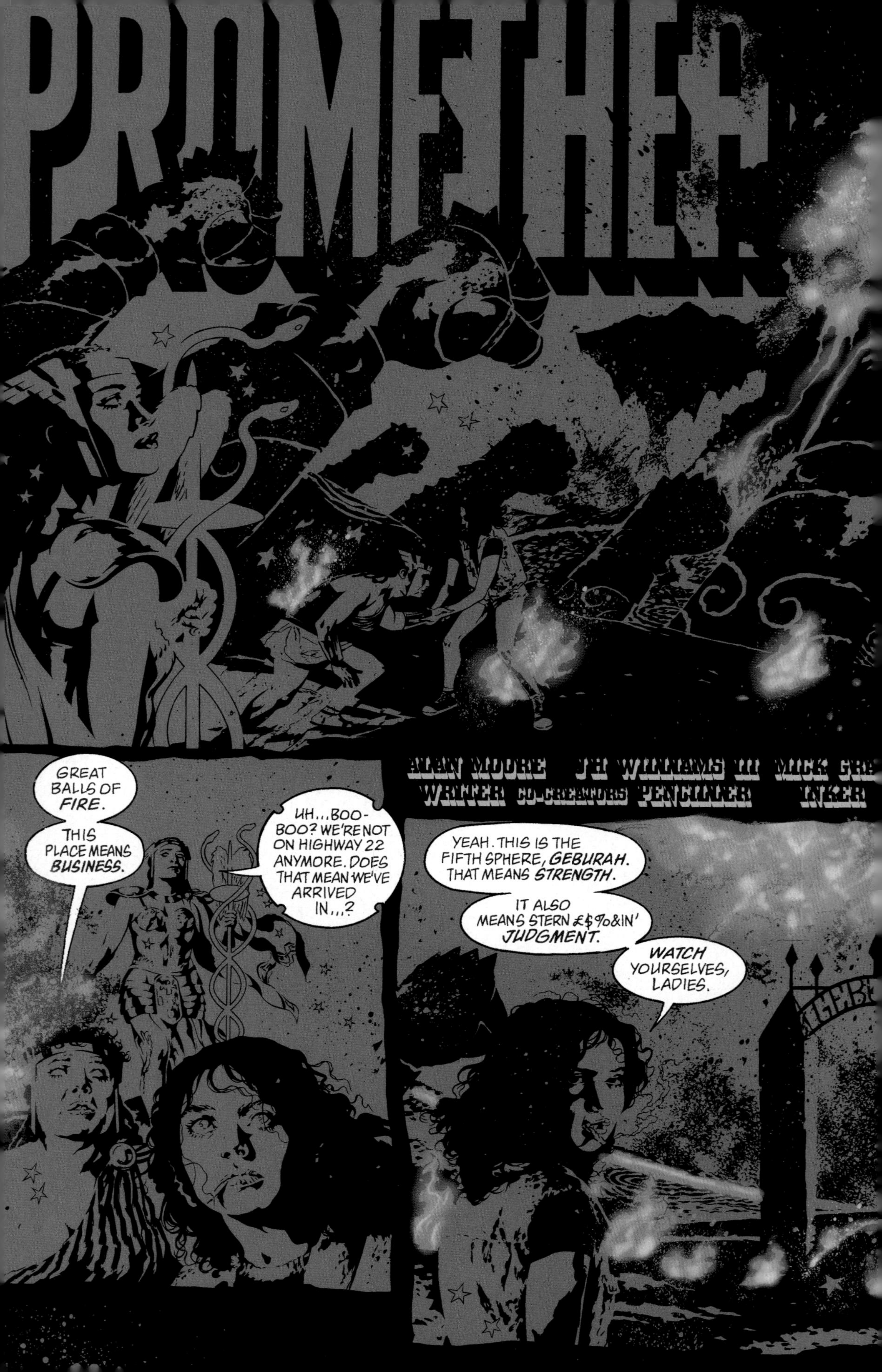
PROMETHEA
ALAN MOORE WRITER
CO-CREATORS
J H WILLIAMS III PENCILLER
MICK GRA INKER
GREAT BALLS OF FIRE.
THIS PLACE MEANS BUSINESS.
UH...BOO-BOO? WE'RE NOT ON HIGHWAY 22 ANYMORE. DOES THAT MEAN WE'VE ARRIVED IN...?
YEAH. THIS IS THE FIFTH SPHERE, GEBURAH. THAT MEANS STRENGTH.
IT ALSO MEANS STERN £$%&IN' JUDGMENT.
WATCH YOURSELVES, LADIES.

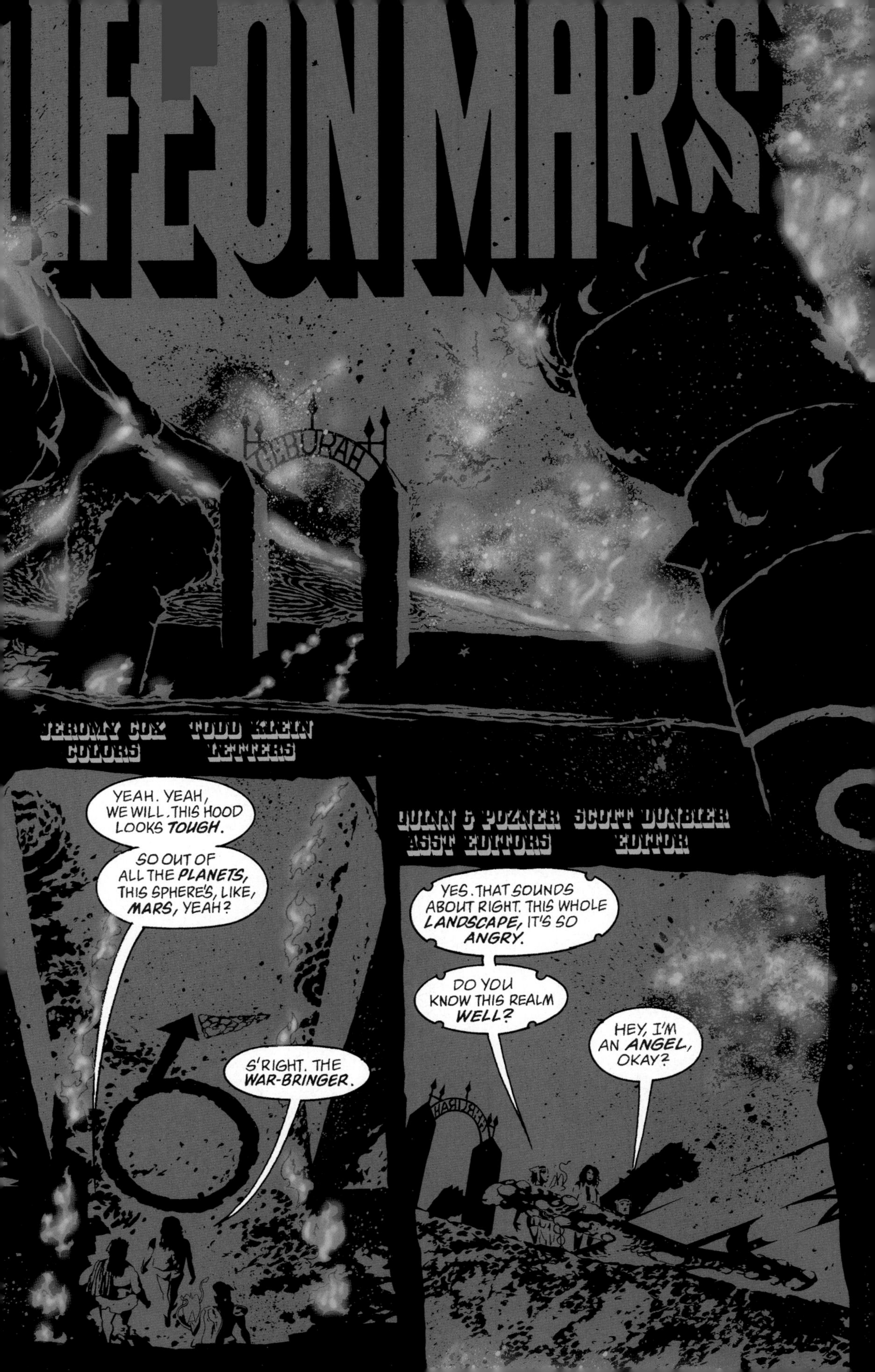
IFE ON MARS
GEBURAH
JEROMY COX COLORS
TODD KLEIN LETTERS
YEAH. YEAH, WE WILL. THIS HOOD LOOKS TOUGH.
SO OUT OF ALL THE PLANETS, THIS SPHERE'S, LIKE, MARS, YEAH?
S'RIGHT. THE WAR-BRINGER.
QUINN & POZNER ASST EDITORS
SCOTT DUNBIER EDITOR
YES. THAT SOUNDS ABOUT RIGHT. THIS WHOLE LANDSCAPE, IT'S SO ANGRY.
DO YOU KNOW THIS REALM WELL?
HEY, I'M AN ANGEL, OKAY?

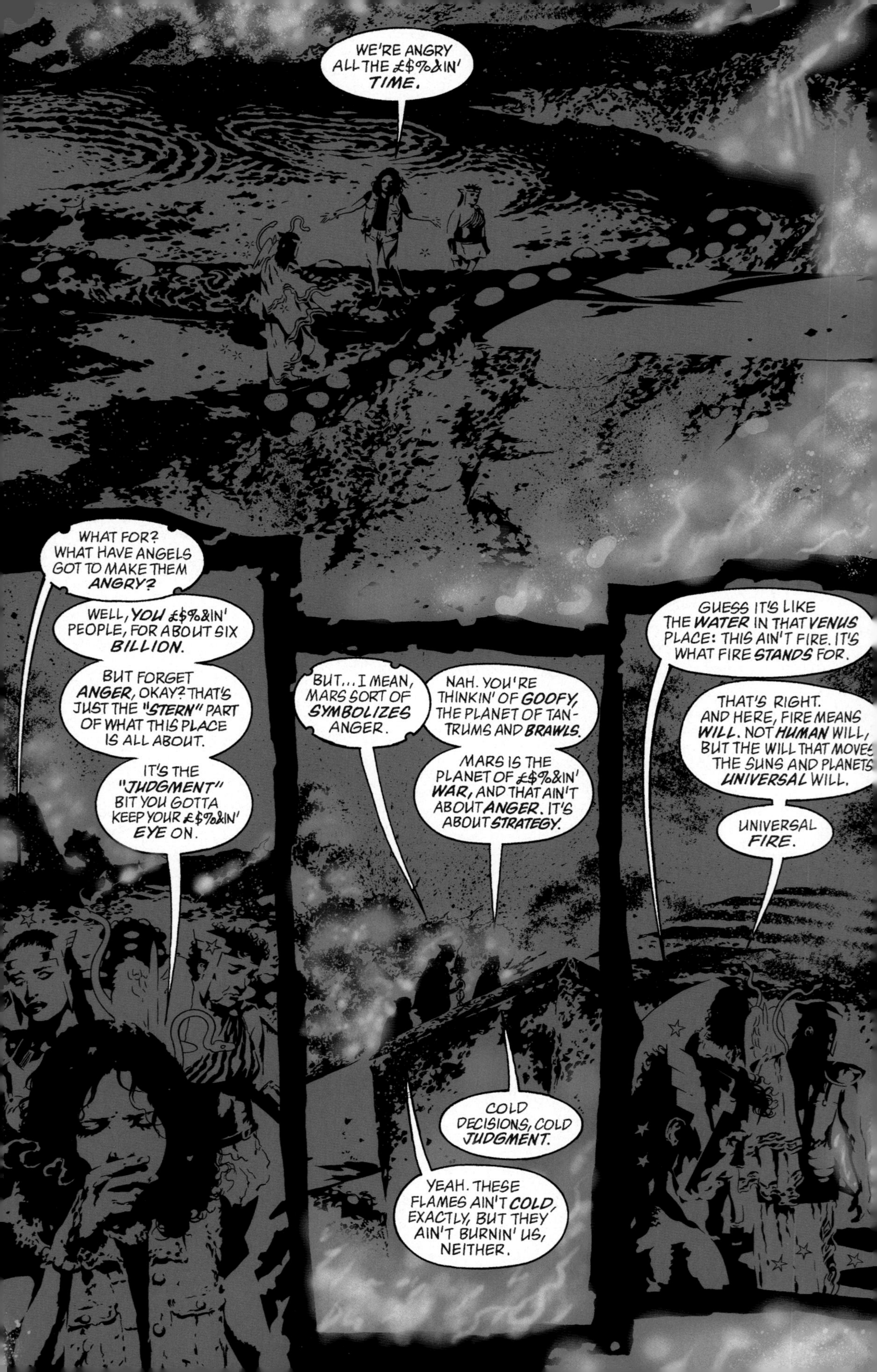

WE'RE ANGRY ALL THE £$%&IN' TIME.
WHAT FOR? WHAT HAVE ANGELS GOT TO MAKE THEM ANGRY?
WELL, YOU £$%&IN' PEOPLE, FOR ABOUT SIX BILLION.
BUT FORGET ANGER, OKAY? THAT'S JUST THE "STERN" PART OF WHAT THIS PLACE IS ALL ABOUT.
IT'S THE "JUDGMENT" BIT YOU GOTTA KEEP YOUR £$%&IN' EYE ON.
BUT... I MEAN, MARS SORT OF SYMBOLIZES ANGER.
NAH. YOU'RE THINKIN' OF GOOFY, THE PLANET OF TANTRUMS AND BRAWLS.
MARS IS THE PLANET OF £$%&IN' WAR, AND THAT AIN'T ABOUT ANGER. IT'S ABOUT STRATEGY.
COLD DECISIONS, COLD JUDGMENT.
YEAH. THESE FLAMES AIN'T COLD, EXACTLY, BUT THEY AIN'T BURNIN' US, NEITHER.
GUESS IT'S LIKE THE WATER IN THAT VENUS PLACE: THIS AIN'T FIRE. IT'S WHAT FIRE STANDS FOR.
THAT'S RIGHT. AND HERE, FIRE MEANS WILL. NOT HUMAN WILL, BUT THE WILL THAT MOVES THE SUNS AND PLANETS. UNIVERSAL WILL.
UNIVERSAL FIRE.

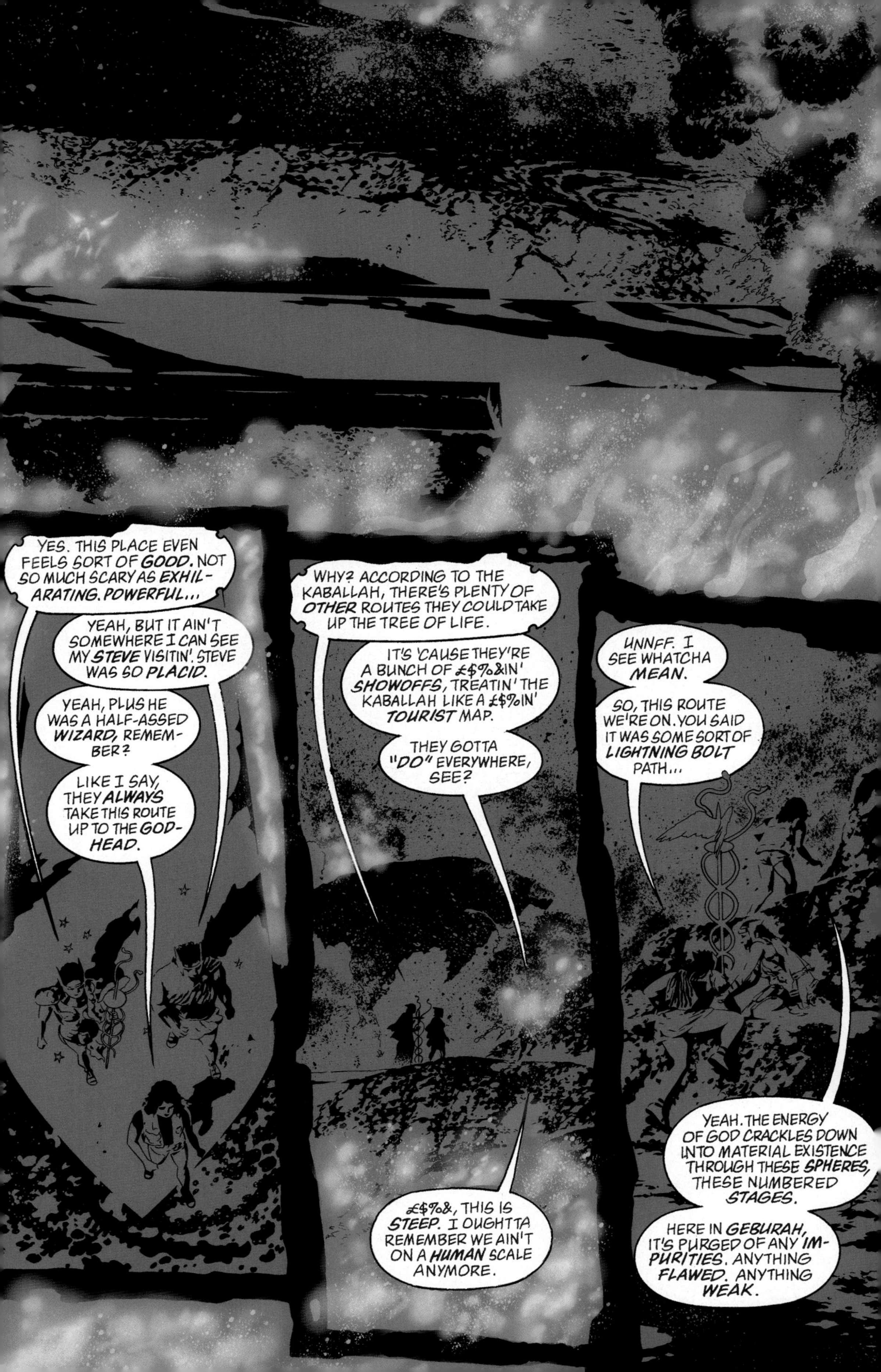
YES. THIS PLACE EVEN FEELS SORT OF GOOD. NOT SO MUCH SCARY AS EXHIL-ARATING. POWERFUL...
YEAH, BUT IT AIN'T SOMEWHERE I CAN SEE MY STEVE VISITIN'. STEVE WAS SO PLACID.
YEAH, PLUS HE WAS A HALF-ASSED WIZARD, REMEMBER?
LIKE I SAY, THEY ALWAYS TAKE THIS ROUTE UP TO THE GOD-HEAD.
WHY? ACCORDING TO THE KABALLAH, THERE'S PLENTY OF OTHER ROUTES THEY COULD TAKE UP THE TREE OF LIFE.
IT'S 'CAUSE THEY'RE A BUNCH OF £$%&IN' SHOWOFFS, TREATIN' THE KABALLAH LIKE A £$%IN' TOURIST MAP.
THEY GOTTA "DO" EVERYWHERE, SEE?
£$%&, THIS IS STEEP. I OUGHTTA REMEMBER WE AIN'T ON A HUMAN SCALE ANYMORE.
UNNFF. I SEE WHATCHA MEAN.
SO, THIS ROUTE WE'RE ON. YOU SAID IT WAS SOME SORT OF LIGHTNING BOLT PATH...
YEAH. THE ENERGY OF GOD CRACKLES DOWN INTO MATERIAL EXISTENCE THROUGH THESE SPHERES, THESE NUMBERED STAGES.
HERE IN GEBURAH, IT'S PURGED OF ANY IMPURITIES. ANYTHING FLAWED. ANYTHING WEAK.

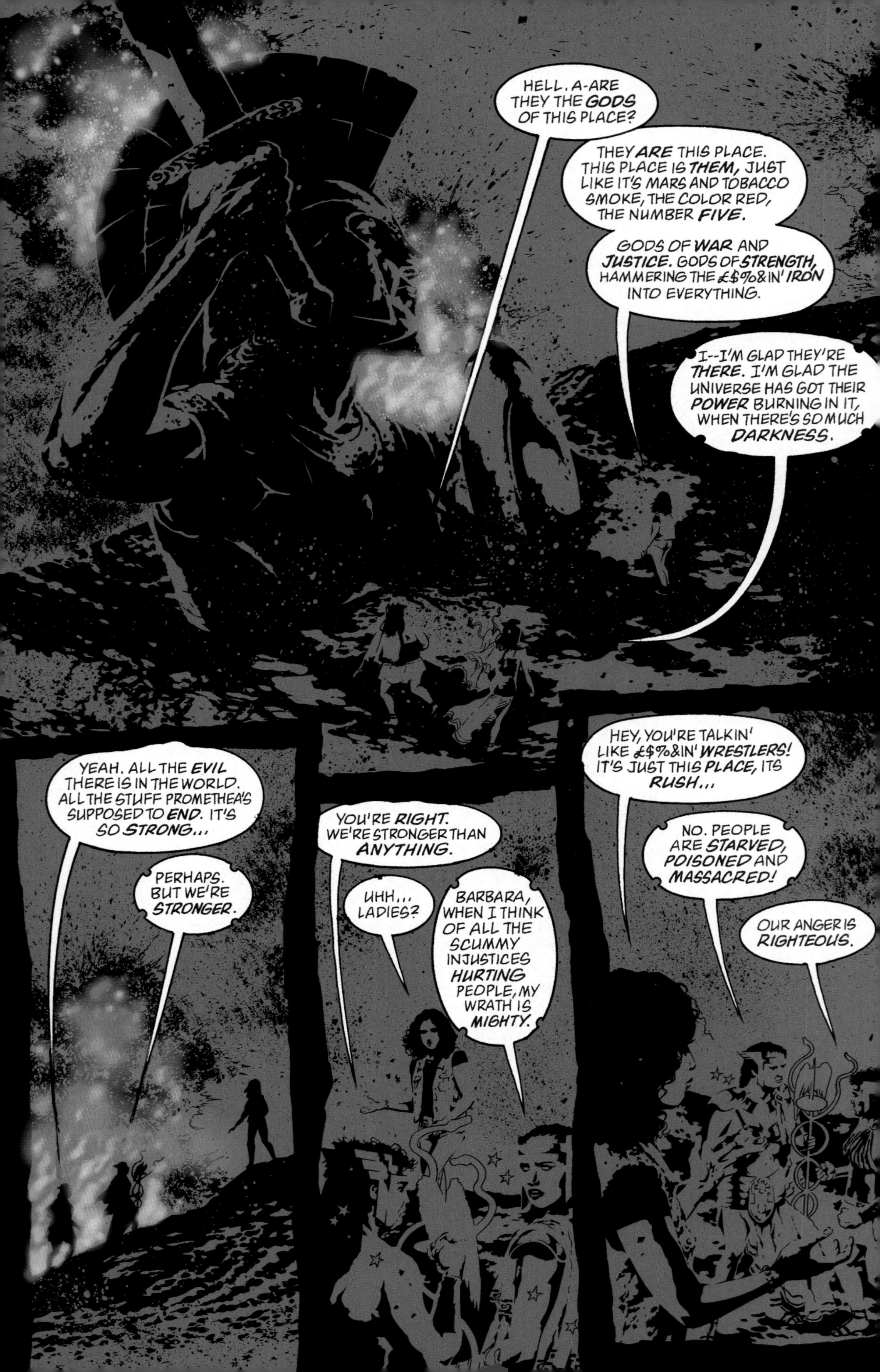
HELL. A-ARE THEY THE GODS OF THIS PLACE?
THEY ARE THIS PLACE. THIS PLACE IS THEM, JUST LIKE IT'S MARS AND TOBACCO SMOKE, THE COLOR RED, THE NUMBER FIVE.
GODS OF WAR AND JUSTICE. GODS OF STRENGTH, HAMMERING THE £$%&IN' IRON INTO EVERYTHING.
I--I'M GLAD THEY'RE THERE. I'M GLAD THE UNIVERSE HAS GOT THEIR POWER BURNING IN IT, WHEN THERE'S SO MUCH DARKNESS.
YEAH. ALL THE EVIL THERE IS IN THE WORLD. ALL THE STUFF PROMETHEA'S SUPPOSED TO END. IT'S SO STRONG...
PERHAPS. BUT WE'RE STRONGER.
YOU'RE RIGHT. WE'RE STRONGER THAN ANYTHING.
UHH... LADIES?
BARBARA, WHEN I THINK OF ALL THE SCUMMY INJUSTICES HURTING PEOPLE, MY WRATH IS MIGHTY.
HEY, YOU'RE TALKIN' LIKE £$%&IN' WRESTLERS! IT'S JUST THIS PLACE, ITS RUSH...
NO. PEOPLE ARE STARVED, POISONED AND MASSACRED!
OUR ANGER IS RIGHTEOUS.

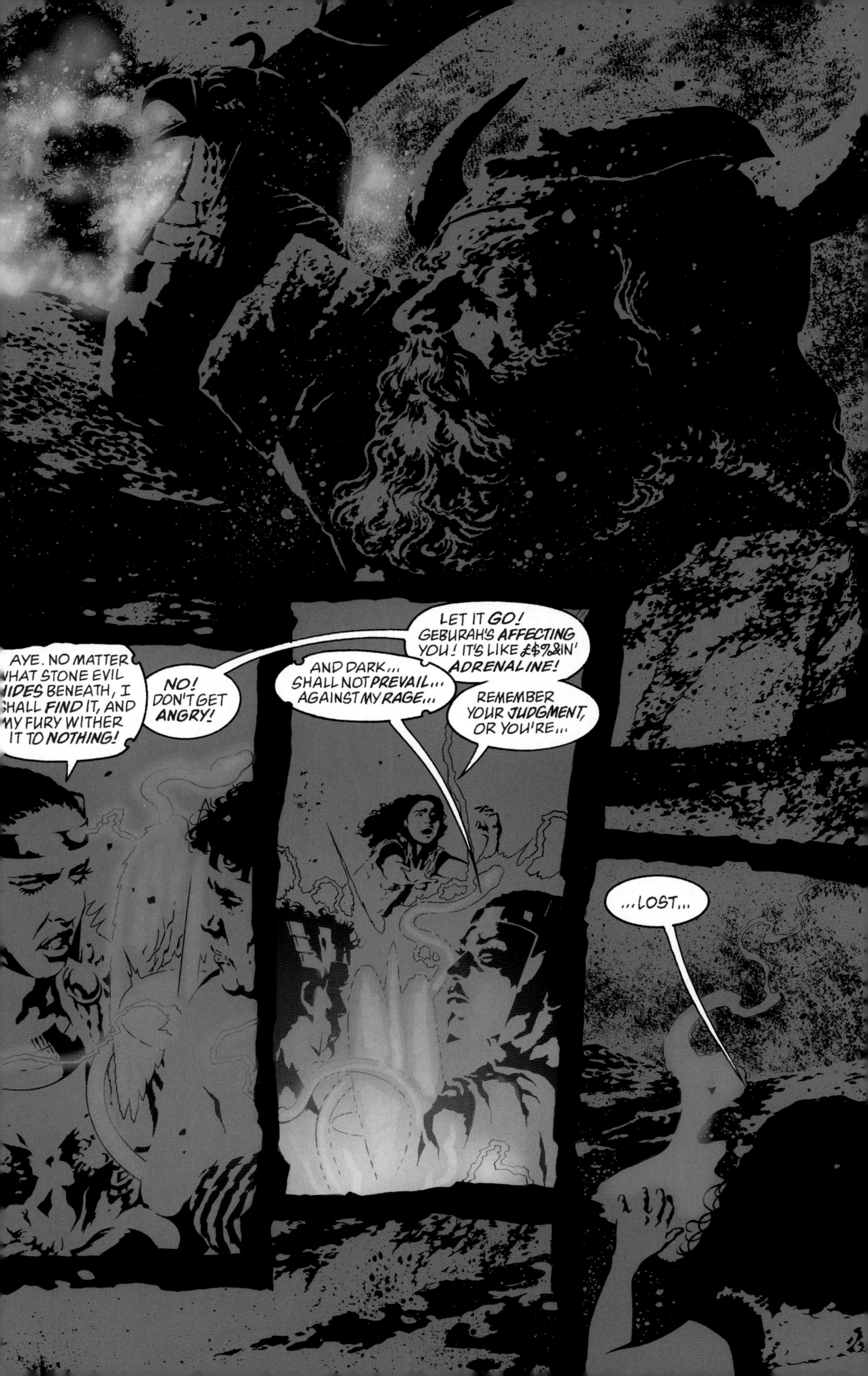
AYE. NO MATTER WHAT STONE EVIL HIDES BENEATH, I SHALL FIND IT, AND MY FURY WITHER IT TO NOTHING!
NO! DON'T GET ANGRY!
LET IT GO! GEBURAH'S AFFECTING YOU! IT'S LIKE £$%&IN' ADRENALINE!
AND DARK... SHALL NOT PREVAIL... AGAINST MY RAGE...
REMEMBER YOUR JUDGMENT, OR YOU'RE...
...LOST...

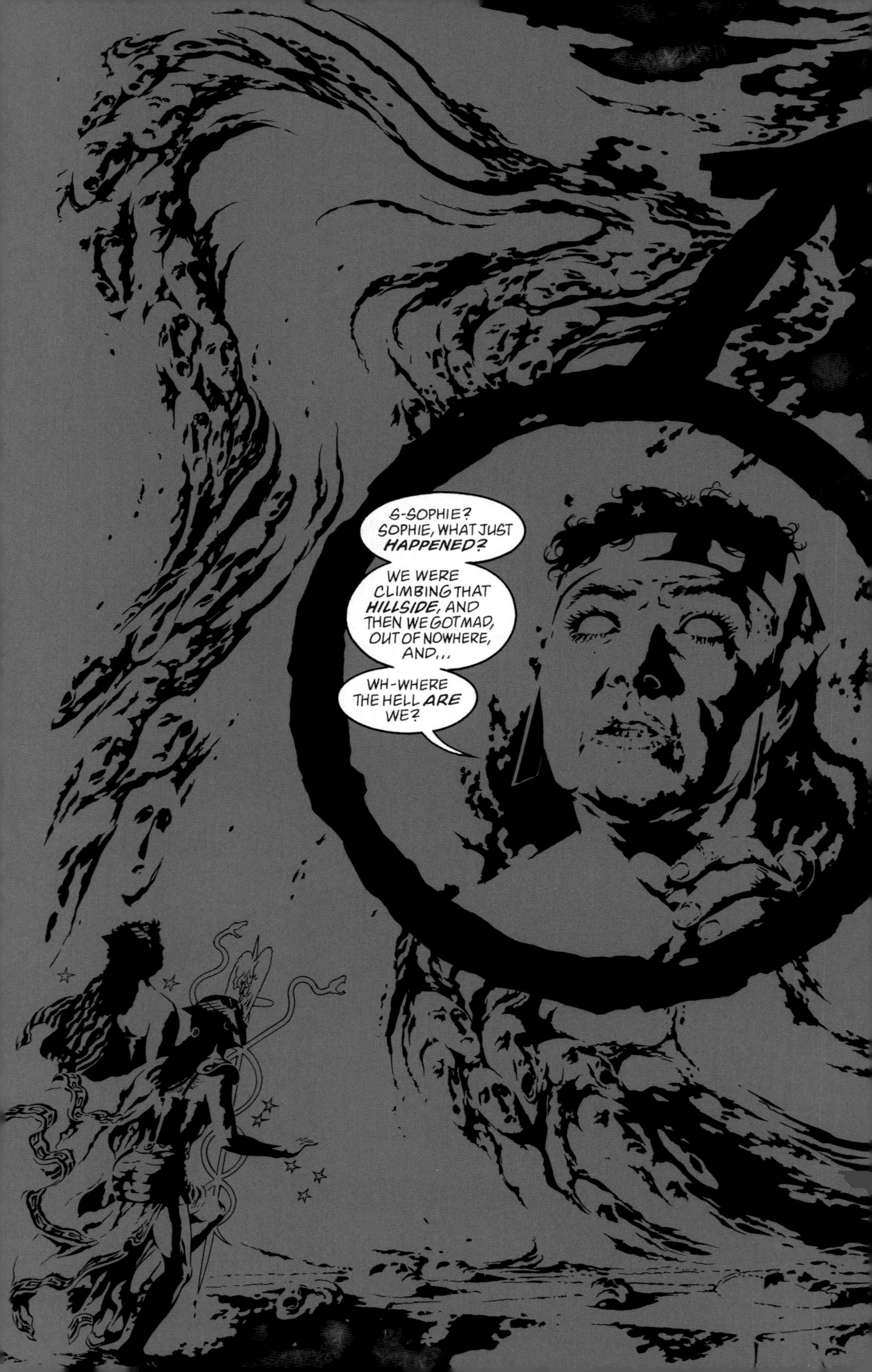
S-SOPHIE? SOPHIE, WHAT JUST HAPPENED?
WE WERE CLIMBING THAT HILLSIDE, AND THEN WE GOT MAD, OUT OF NOWHERE, AND...
WH-WHERE THE HELL ARE WE?

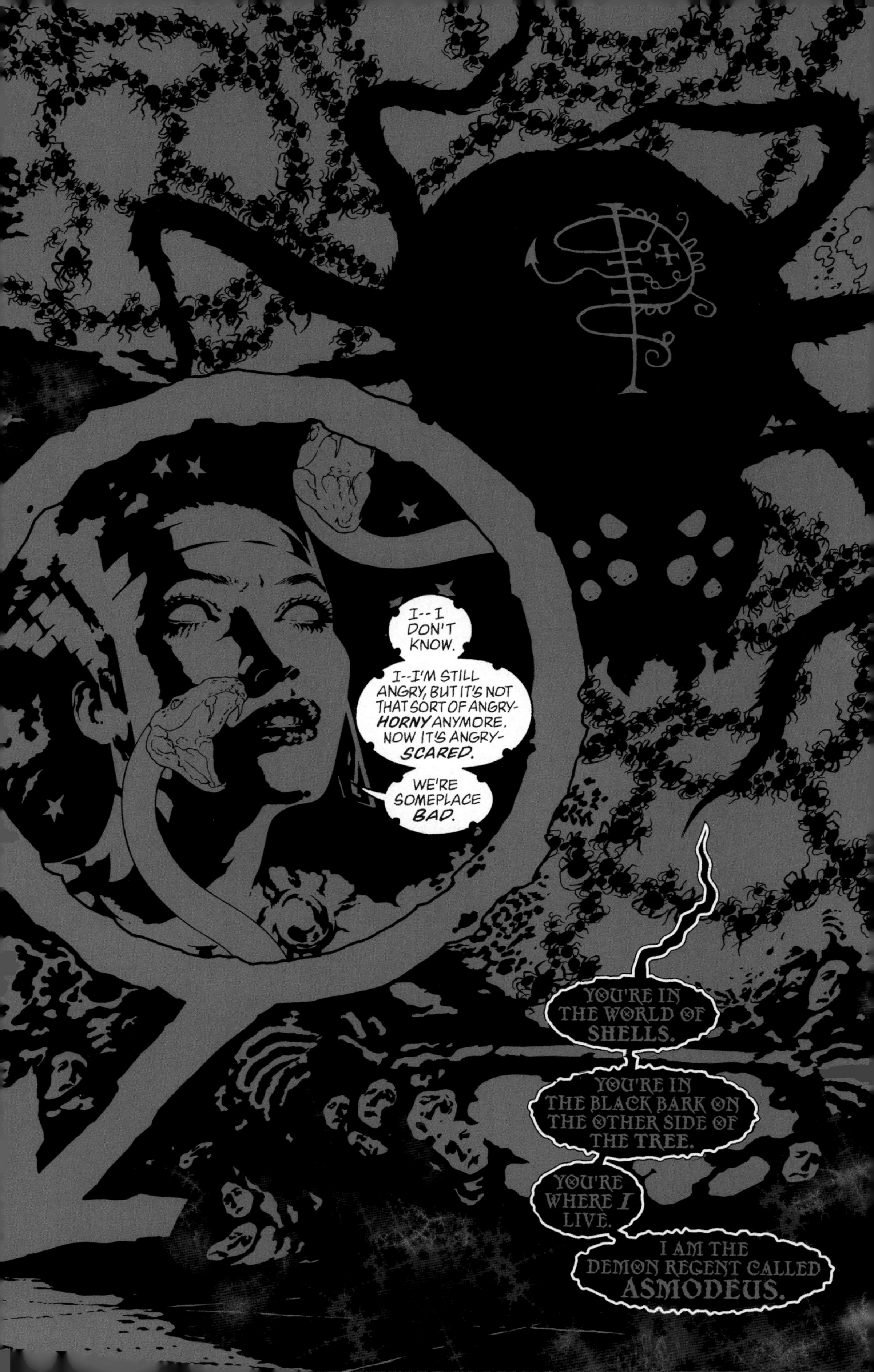

I-- I DON'T KNOW.
I--I'M STILL ANGRY, BUT IT'S NOT THAT SORT OF ANGRY-*HORNY* ANYMORE. NOW IT'S ANGRY-*SCARED*.
WE'RE SOMEPLACE *BAD*.
YOU'RE IN THE WORLD OF SHELLS.
YOU'RE IN THE BLACK BARK ON THE OTHER SIDE OF THE TREE.
YOU'RE WHERE *I* LIVE.
I AM THE DEMON REGENT CALLED **ASMODEUS**.

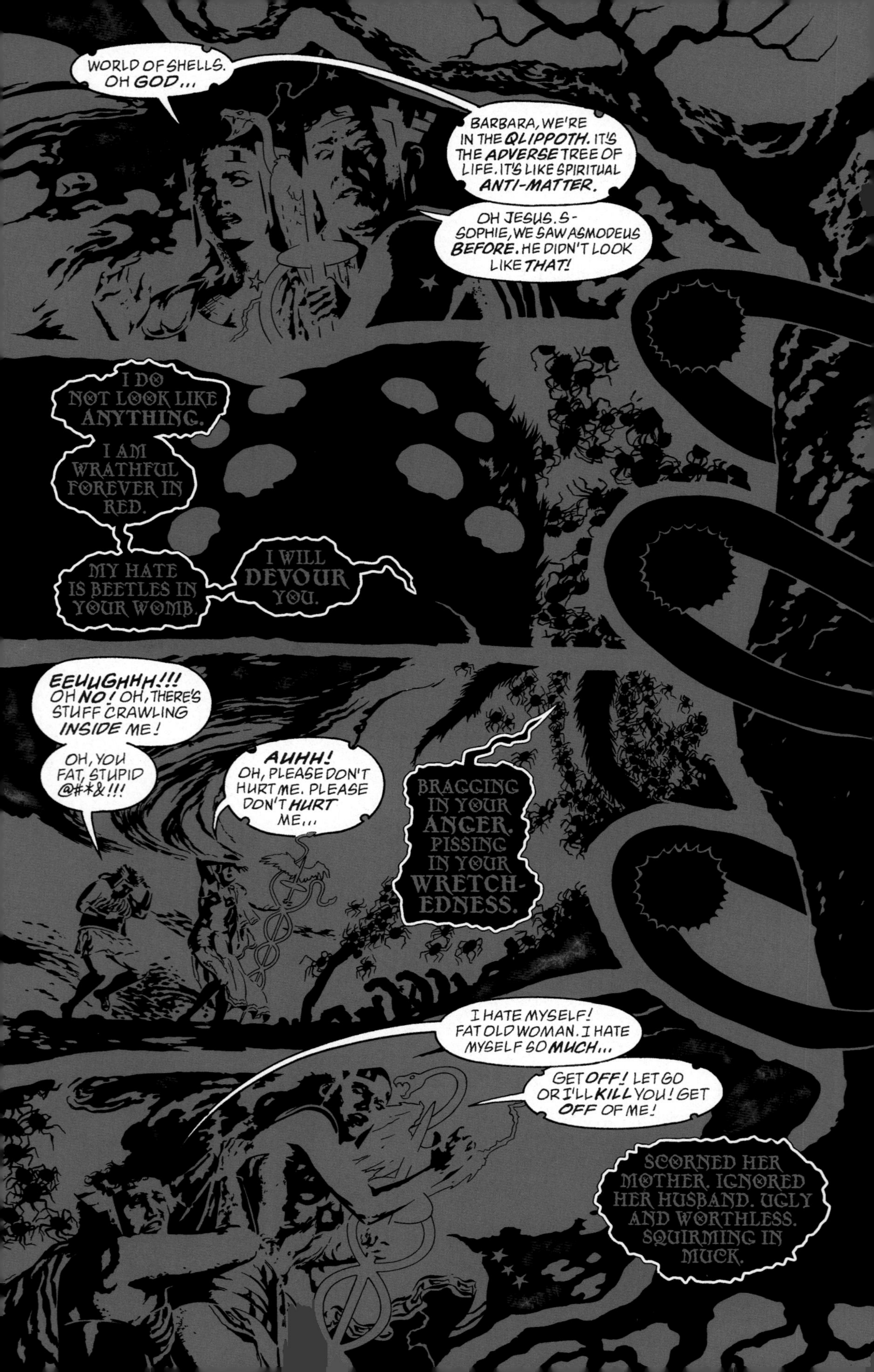
WORLD OF SHELLS. OH GOD...
BARBARA, WE'RE IN THE QLIPPOTH. IT'S THE ADVERSE TREE OF LIFE. IT'S LIKE SPIRITUAL ANTI-MATTER.
OH JESUS. S-SOPHIE, WE SAW ASMODEUS BEFORE. HE DIDN'T LOOK LIKE THAT!
I DO NOT LOOK LIKE ANYTHING.
I AM WRATHFUL FOREVER IN RED.
MY HATE IS BEETLES IN YOUR WOMB.
I WILL DEVOUR YOU.
EEUUGHHH!!! OH NO! OH, THERE'S STUFF CRAWLING INSIDE ME!
OH, YOU FAT, STUPID @#*&!!!
AUHH! OH, PLEASE DON'T HURT ME. PLEASE DON'T HURT ME...
BRAGGING IN YOUR ANGER. PISSING IN YOUR WRETCHEDNESS.
I HATE MYSELF! FAT OLD WOMAN. I HATE MYSELF SO MUCH...
GET OFF! LET GO OR I'LL KILL YOU! GET OFF OF ME!
SCORNED HER MOTHER. IGNORED HER HUSBAND. UGLY AND WORTHLESS. SQUIRMING IN MUCK.

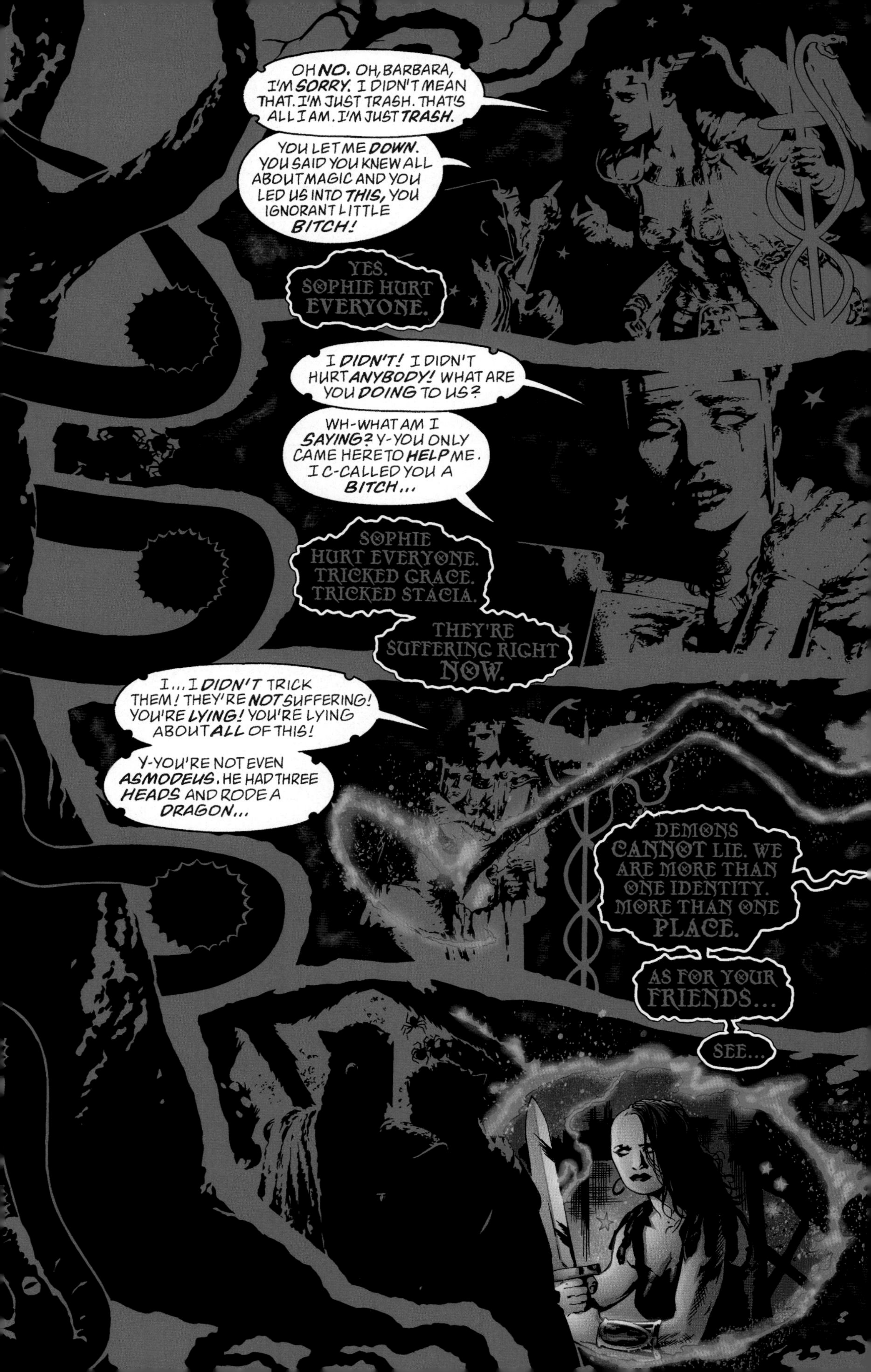

OH NO. OH, BARBARA, I'M SORRY. I DIDN'T MEAN THAT. I'M JUST TRASH. THAT'S ALL I AM. I'M JUST TRASH.
YOU LET ME DOWN. YOU SAID YOU KNEW ALL ABOUT MAGIC AND YOU LED US INTO THIS, YOU IGNORANT LITTLE BITCH!
YES. SOPHIE HURT EVERYONE.
I DIDN'T! I DIDN'T HURT ANYBODY! WHAT ARE YOU DOING TO US?
WH-WHAT AM I SAYING? Y-YOU ONLY CAME HERE TO HELP ME. I C-CALLED YOU A BITCH...
SOPHIE HURT EVERYONE. TRICKED GRACE. TRICKED STACIA.
THEY'RE SUFFERING RIGHT NOW.
I... I DIDN'T TRICK THEM! THEY'RE NOT SUFFERING! YOU'RE LYING! YOU'RE LYING ABOUT ALL OF THIS!
Y-YOU'RE NOT EVEN ASMODEUS. HE HAD THREE HEADS AND RODE A DRAGON...
DEMONS CANNOT LIE. WE ARE MORE THAN ONE IDENTITY. MORE THAN ONE PLACE.
AS FOR YOUR FRIENDS...
SEE...

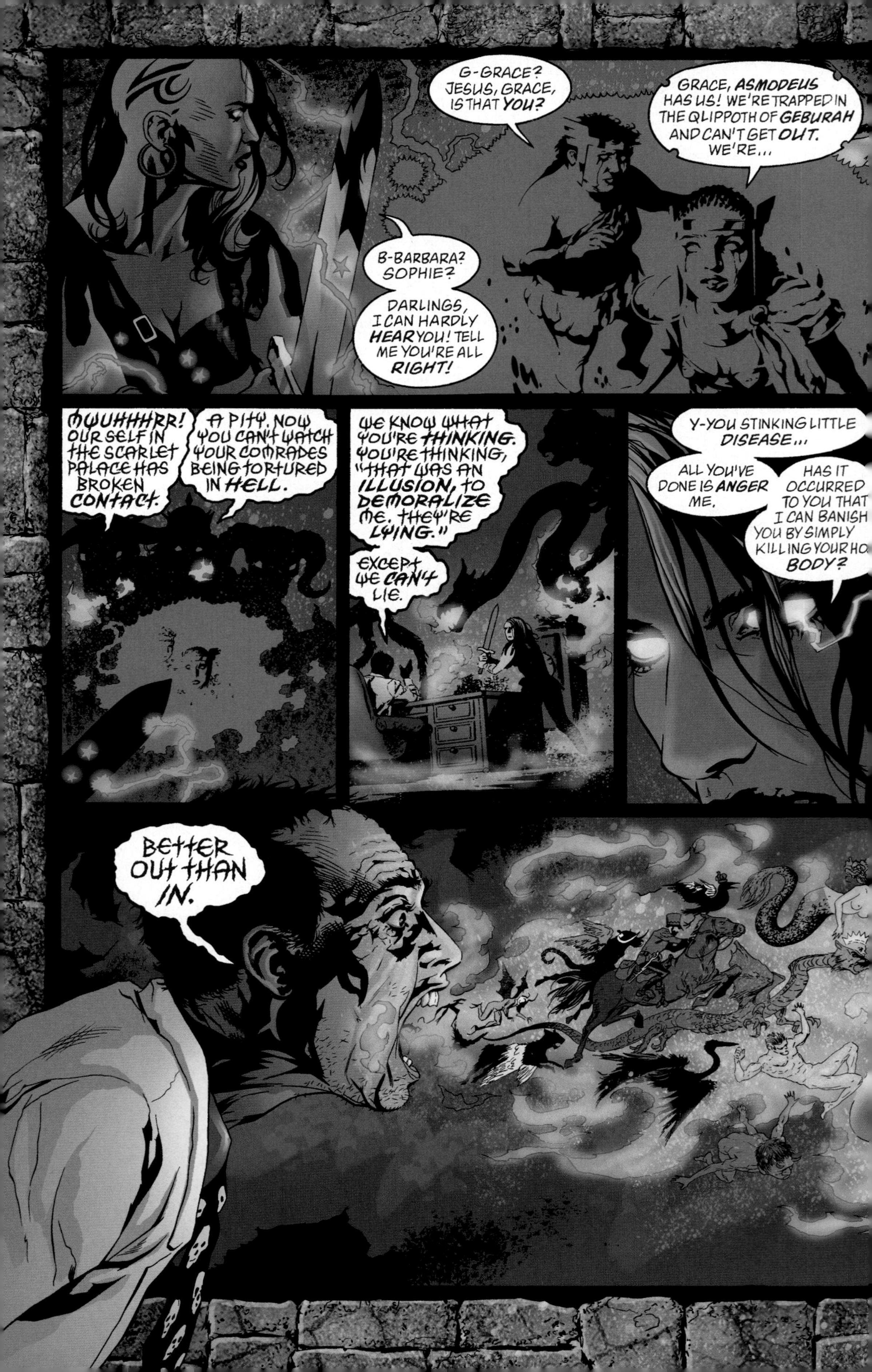

G-GRACE? JESUS, GRACE, IS THAT YOU?
GRACE, ASMODEUS HAS US! WE'RE TRAPPED IN THE QLIPPOTH OF GEBURAH AND CAN'T GET OUT. WE'RE...
B-BARBARA? SOPHIE?
DARLINGS, I CAN HARDLY HEAR YOU! TELL ME YOU'RE ALL RIGHT!
MWUHHHRR! OUR SELF IN THE SCARLET PALACE HAS BROKEN CONTACT.
A PITY. NOW YOU CAN'T WATCH YOUR COMRADES BEING TORTURED IN HELL.
WE KNOW WHAT YOU'RE THINKING. YOU'RE THINKING, "THAT WAS AN ILLUSION, TO DEMORALIZE ME. THEY'RE LYING."
EXCEPT WE CAN'T LIE.
Y-YOU STINKING LITTLE DISEASE...
ALL YOU'VE DONE IS ANGER ME.
HAS IT OCCURRED TO YOU THAT I CAN BANISH YOU BY SIMPLY KILLING YOUR HO BODY?
BETTER OUT THAN IN.

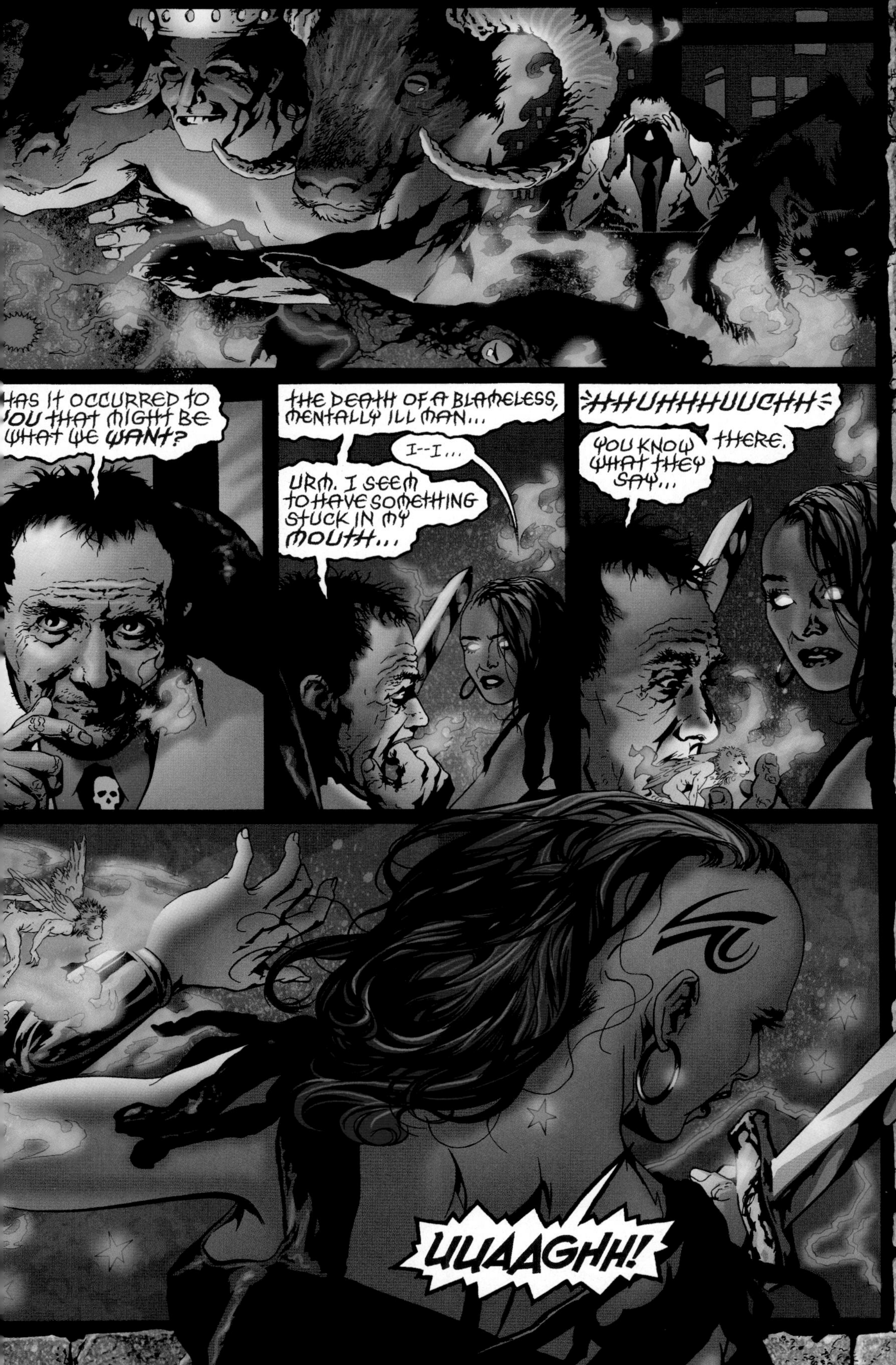

HAS IT OCCURRED TO YOU THAT MIGHT BE WHAT WE WANT?
THE DEATH OF A BLAMELESS, MENTALLY ILL MAN...
I--I...
URM. I SEEM TO HAVE SOMETHING STUCK IN MY MOUTH...
HHUHHHUUCHH
YOU KNOW WHAT THEY SAY...
THERE.
UUAAGHH!

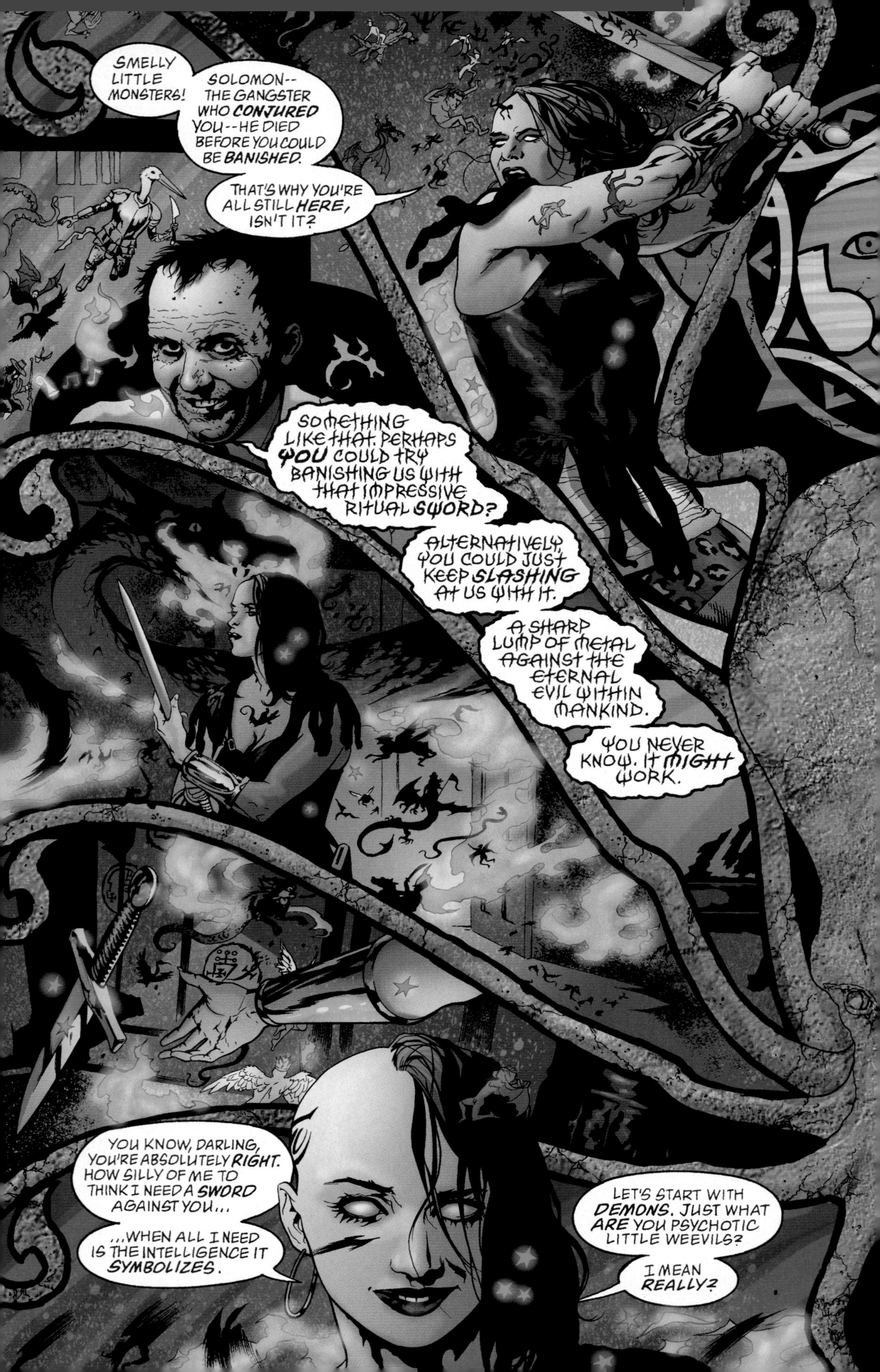
SMELLY LITTLE MONSTERS!
SOLOMON-- THE GANGSTER WHO CONJURED YOU--HE DIED BEFORE YOU COULD BE BANISHED.
THAT'S WHY YOU'RE ALL STILL HERE, ISN'T IT?
SOMETHING LIKE THAT. PERHAPS YOU COULD TRY BANISHING US WITH THAT IMPRESSIVE RITUAL SWORD?
ALTERNATIVELY, YOU COULD JUST KEEP SLASHING AT US WITH IT.
A SHARP LUMP OF METAL AGAINST THE ETERNAL EVIL WITHIN MANKIND.
YOU NEVER KNOW. IT MIGHT WORK.
YOU KNOW, DARLING, YOU'RE ABSOLUTELY RIGHT. HOW SILLY OF ME TO THINK I NEED A SWORD AGAINST YOU...
...WHEN ALL I NEED IS THE INTELLIGENCE IT SYMBOLIZES.
LET'S START WITH DEMONS. JUST WHAT ARE YOU PSYCHOTIC LITTLE WEEVILS?
I MEAN REALLY?

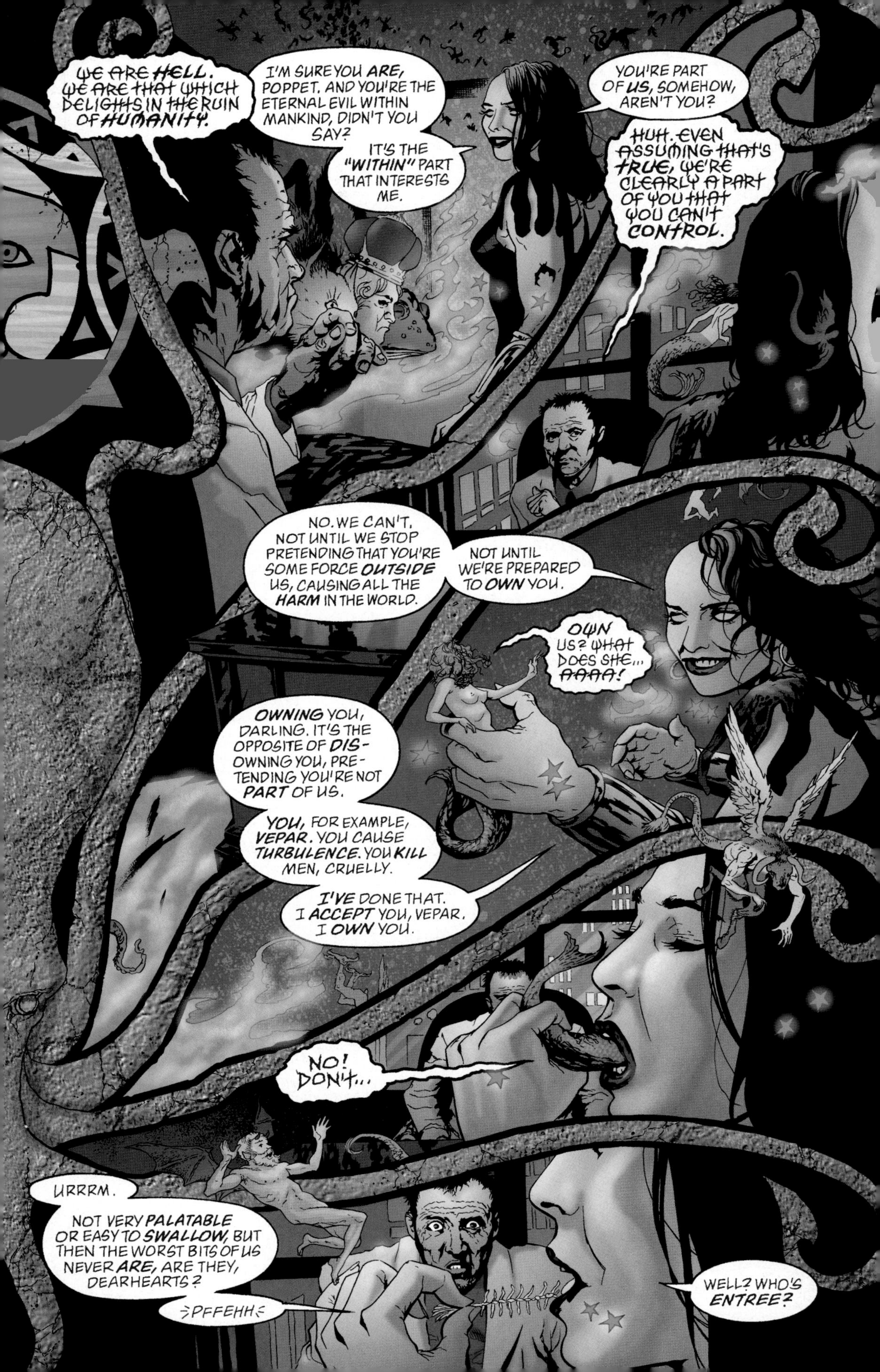
WE ARE HELL. WE ARE THAT WHICH DELIGHTS IN THE RUIN OF HUMANITY.
I'M SURE YOU ARE, POPPET. AND YOU'RE THE ETERNAL EVIL WITHIN MANKIND, DIDN'T YOU SAY?
IT'S THE "WITHIN" PART THAT INTERESTS ME.
YOU'RE PART OF US, SOMEHOW, AREN'T YOU?
HUH. EVEN ASSUMING THAT'S TRUE, WE'RE CLEARLY A PART OF YOU THAT YOU CAN'T CONTROL.
NO. WE CAN'T. NOT UNTIL WE STOP PRETENDING THAT YOU'RE SOME FORCE OUTSIDE US, CAUSING ALL THE HARM IN THE WORLD.
NOT UNTIL WE'RE PREPARED TO OWN YOU.
OWN US? WHAT DOES SHE... AAAA!
OWNING YOU, DARLING. IT'S THE OPPOSITE OF DIS-OWNING YOU, PRE-TENDING YOU'RE NOT PART OF US.
YOU, FOR EXAMPLE, VEPAR. YOU CAUSE TURBULENCE. YOU KILL MEN, CRUELLY.
I'VE DONE THAT. I ACCEPT YOU, VEPAR. I OWN YOU.
NO! DON'T...
URRRM.
NOT VERY PALATABLE OR EASY TO SWALLOW, BUT THEN THE WORST BITS OF US NEVER ARE, ARE THEY, DEARHEARTS?
PFFEHH
WELL? WHO'S ENTREE?

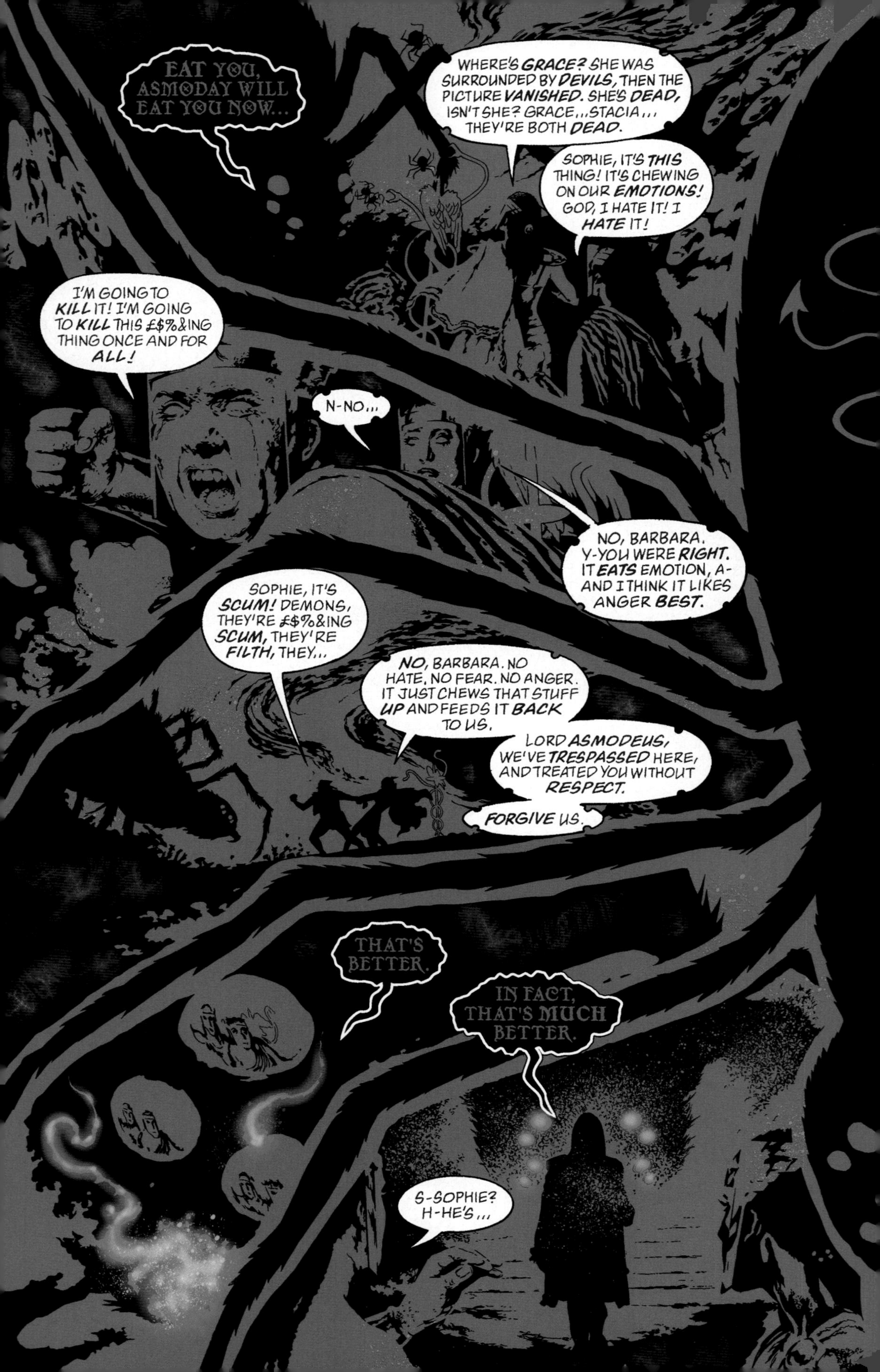
EAT YOU, ASMODAY WILL EAT YOU NOW...
WHERE'S GRACE? SHE WAS SURROUNDED BY DEVILS, THEN THE PICTURE VANISHED. SHE'S DEAD, ISN'T SHE? GRACE,,,STACIA,,, THEY'RE BOTH DEAD.
SOPHIE, IT'S THIS THING! IT'S CHEWING ON OUR EMOTIONS! GOD, I HATE IT! I HATE IT!
I'M GOING TO KILL IT! I'M GOING TO KILL THIS £$%&ING THING ONCE AND FOR ALL!
N-NO,,,
NO, BARBARA. Y-YOU WERE RIGHT. IT EATS EMOTION, A- AND I THINK IT LIKES ANGER BEST.
SOPHIE, IT'S SCUM! DEMONS, THEY'RE £$%&ING SCUM, THEY'RE FILTH, THEY,,,
NO, BARBARA. NO HATE. NO FEAR. NO ANGER. IT JUST CHEWS THAT STUFF UP AND FEEDS IT BACK TO US.
LORD ASMODEUS, WE'VE TRESPASSED HERE, AND TREATED YOU WITHOUT RESPECT.
FORGIVE US.
THAT'S BETTER.
IN FACT, THAT'S MUCH BETTER.
S-SOPHIE? H-HE'S,,,

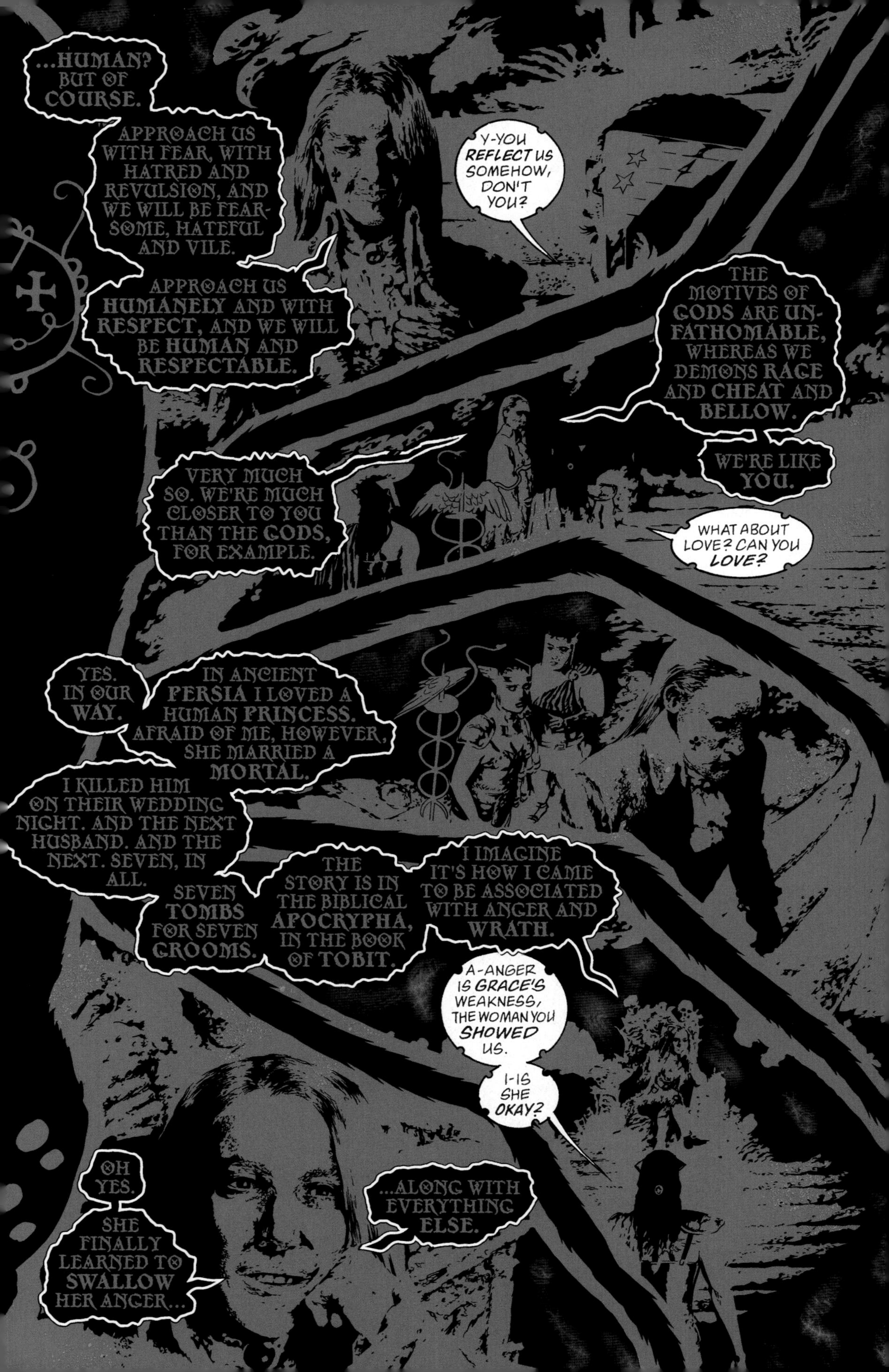
...HUMAN? BUT OF COURSE.
APPROACH US WITH FEAR, WITH HATRED AND REVULSION, AND WE WILL BE FEARSOME, HATEFUL AND VILE.
APPROACH US HUMANELY AND WITH RESPECT, AND WE WILL BE HUMAN AND RESPECTABLE.
Y-YOU REFLECT US SOMEHOW, DON'T YOU?
THE MOTIVES OF GODS ARE UNFATHOMABLE, WHEREAS WE DEMONS RAGE AND CHEAT AND BELLOW.
WE'RE LIKE YOU.
VERY MUCH SO. WE'RE MUCH CLOSER TO YOU THAN THE GODS, FOR EXAMPLE.
WHAT ABOUT LOVE? CAN YOU LOVE?
YES. IN OUR WAY.
IN ANCIENT PERSIA I LOVED A HUMAN PRINCESS. AFRAID OF ME, HOWEVER, SHE MARRIED A MORTAL.
I KILLED HIM ON THEIR WEDDING NIGHT. AND THE NEXT HUSBAND. AND THE NEXT. SEVEN, IN ALL.
SEVEN TOMBS FOR SEVEN GROOMS.
THE STORY IS IN THE BIBLICAL APOCRYPHA, IN THE BOOK OF TOBIT.
I IMAGINE IT'S HOW I CAME TO BE ASSOCIATED WITH ANGER AND WRATH.
A-ANGER IS GRACE'S WEAKNESS, THE WOMAN YOU SHOWED US.
I-IS SHE OKAY?
OH YES.
SHE FINALLY LEARNED TO SWALLOW HER ANGER...
...ALONG WITH EVERYTHING ELSE.

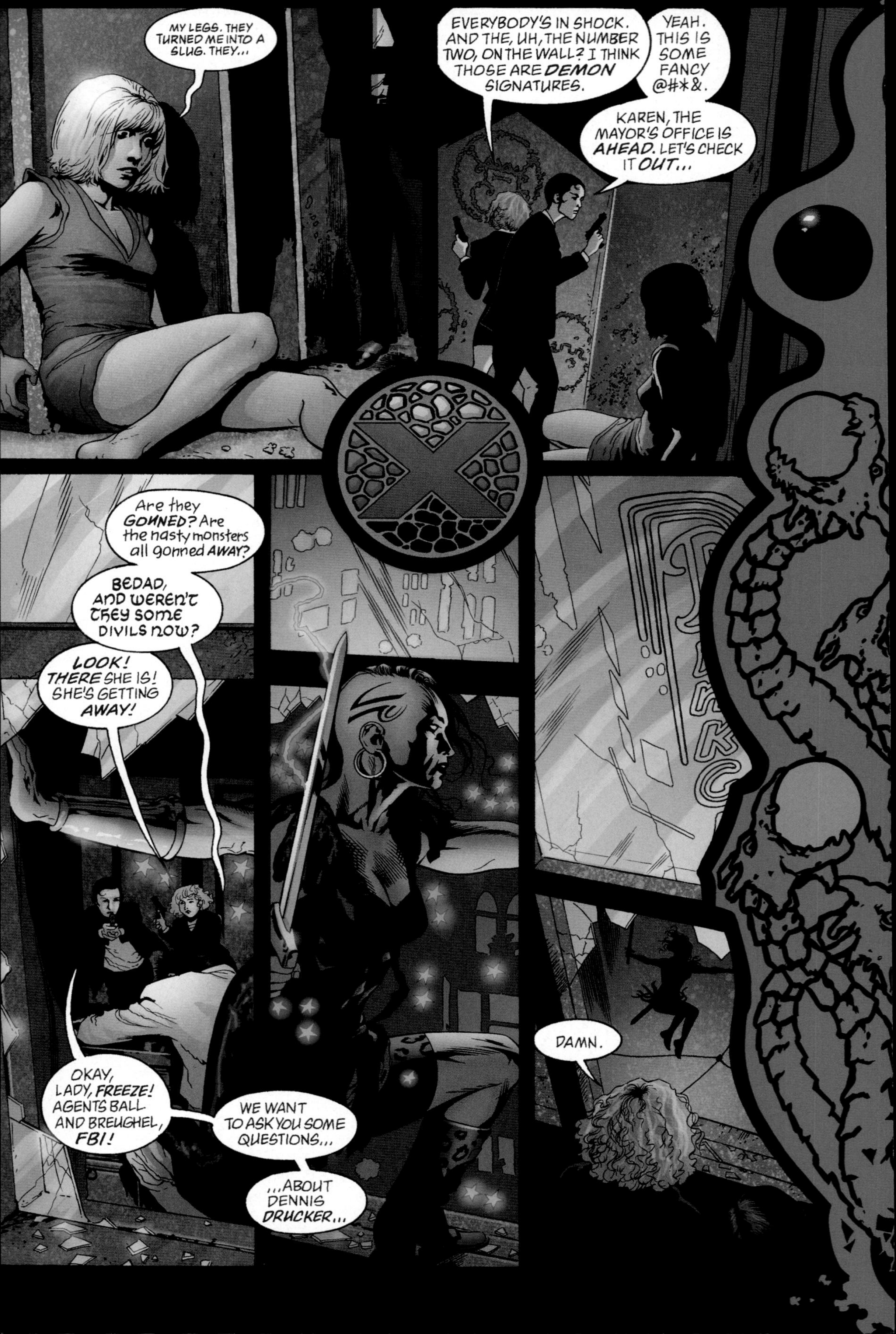
MY LEGS. THEY TURNED ME INTO A SLUG. THEY...
EVERYBODY'S IN SHOCK. AND THE, UH, THE NUMBER TWO, ON THE WALL? I THINK THOSE ARE DEMON SIGNATURES.
YEAH. THIS IS SOME FANCY @#*&.
KAREN, THE MAYOR'S OFFICE IS AHEAD. LET'S CHECK IT OUT...
Are they GONNED? Are the nasty monsters all gonned AWAY?
BEDAD, AND WEREN'T THEY SOME DIVILS NOW?
LOOK! THERE SHE IS! SHE'S GETTING AWAY!
OKAY, LADY, FREEZE! AGENTS BALL AND BREUGHEL, FBI!
WE WANT TO ASK YOU SOME QUESTIONS...
...ABOUT DENNIS DRUCKER...
DAMN.

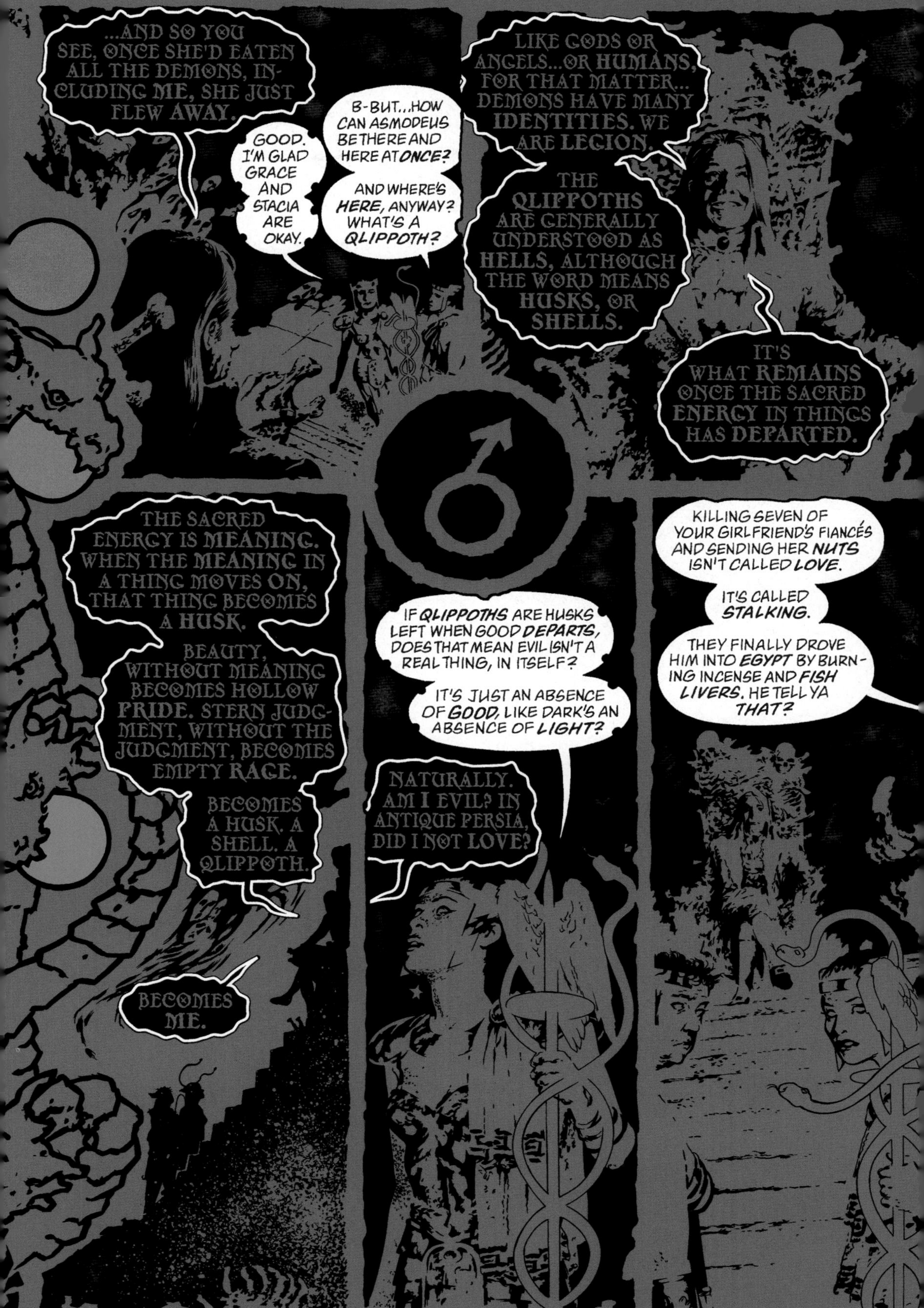
...AND SO YOU SEE, ONCE SHE'D EATEN ALL THE DEMONS, INCLUDING ME, SHE JUST FLEW AWAY.
GOOD. I'M GLAD GRACE AND STACIA ARE OKAY.
B-BUT...HOW CAN ASMODEUS BE THERE AND HERE AT ONCE?
AND WHERE'S HERE, ANYWAY? WHAT'S A QLIPPOTH?
LIKE GODS OR ANGELS...OR HUMANS, FOR THAT MATTER... DEMONS HAVE MANY IDENTITIES. WE ARE LEGION.
THE QLIPPOTHS ARE GENERALLY UNDERSTOOD AS HELLS, ALTHOUGH THE WORD MEANS HUSKS, OR SHELLS.
IT'S WHAT REMAINS ONCE THE SACRED ENERGY IN THINGS HAS DEPARTED.
THE SACRED ENERGY IS MEANING. WHEN THE MEANING IN A THING MOVES ON, THAT THING BECOMES A HUSK.
BEAUTY, WITHOUT MEANING BECOMES HOLLOW PRIDE. STERN JUDGMENT, WITHOUT THE JUDGMENT, BECOMES EMPTY RAGE.
BECOMES A HUSK. A SHELL. A QLIPPOTH.
BECOMES ME.
IF QLIPPOTHS ARE HUSKS LEFT WHEN GOOD DEPARTS, DOES THAT MEAN EVIL ISN'T A REAL THING, IN ITSELF?
IT'S JUST AN ABSENCE OF GOOD, LIKE DARK'S AN ABSENCE OF LIGHT?
NATURALLY. AM I EVIL? IN ANTIQUE PERSIA, DID I NOT LOVE?
KILLING SEVEN OF YOUR GIRLFRIEND'S FIANCÉS AND SENDING HER NUTS ISN'T CALLED LOVE.
IT'S CALLED STALKING.
THEY FINALLY DROVE HIM INTO EGYPT BY BURNING INCENSE AND FISH LIVERS. HE TELL YA THAT?

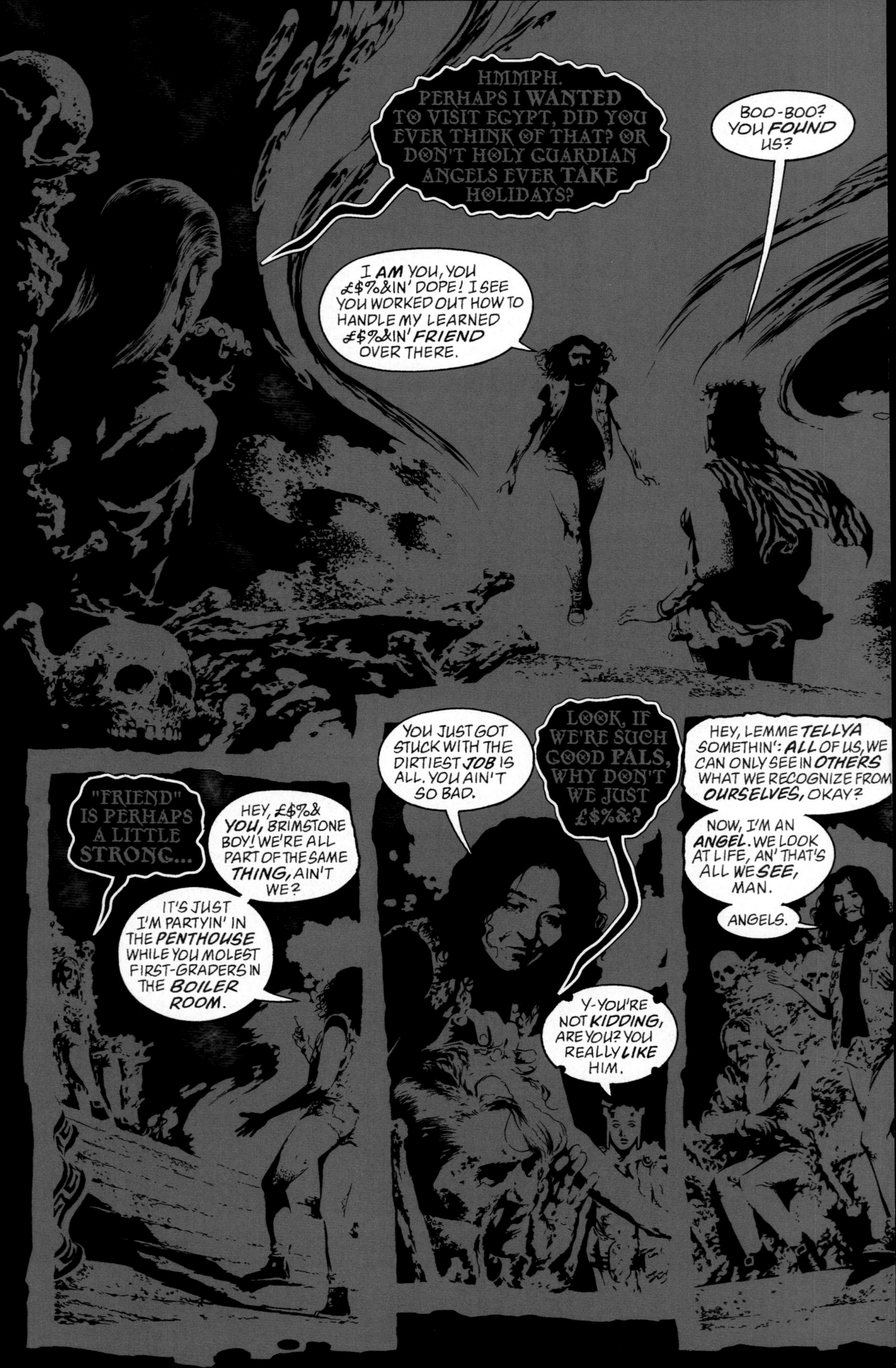

HMMPH. PERHAPS I WANTED TO VISIT EGYPT, DID YOU EVER THINK OF THAT? OR DON'T HOLY GUARDIAN ANGELS EVER TAKE HOLIDAYS?
BOO-BOO? YOU FOUND US?
I AM YOU, YOU £$%&IN' DOPE! I SEE YOU WORKED OUT HOW TO HANDLE MY LEARNED £$%&IN' FRIEND OVER THERE.
"FRIEND" IS PERHAPS A LITTLE STRONG...
HEY, £$%& YOU, BRIMSTONE BOY! WE'RE ALL PART OF THE SAME THING, AIN'T WE?
IT'S JUST I'M PARTYIN' IN THE PENTHOUSE WHILE YOU MOLEST FIRST-GRADERS IN THE BOILER ROOM.
YOU JUST GOT STUCK WITH THE DIRTIEST JOB IS ALL. YOU AIN'T SO BAD.
LOOK, IF WE'RE SUCH GOOD PALS, WHY DON'T WE JUST £$%&?
Y-YOU'RE NOT KIDDING, ARE YOU? YOU REALLY LIKE HIM.
HEY, LEMME TELLYA SOMETHIN': ALL OF US, WE CAN ONLY SEE IN OTHERS WHAT WE RECOGNIZE FROM OURSELVES, OKAY?
NOW, I'M AN ANGEL. WE LOOK AT LIFE, AN' THAT'S ALL WE SEE, MAN.
ANGELS.

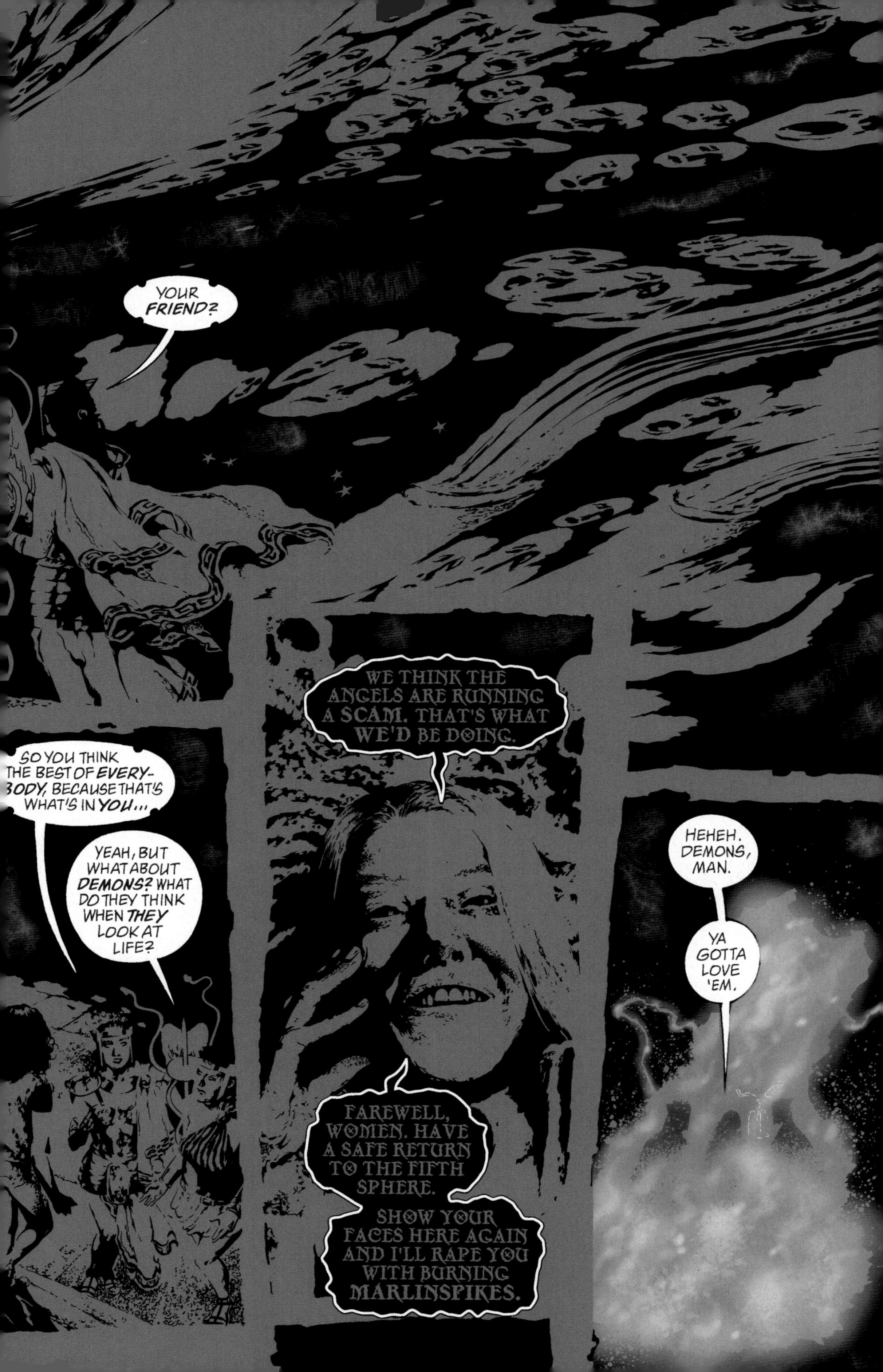
YOUR FRIEND?
WE THINK THE ANGELS ARE RUNNING A SCAM. THAT'S WHAT WE'D BE DOING.
SO YOU THINK THE BEST OF EVERY-BODY, BECAUSE THAT'S WHAT'S IN YOU...
YEAH, BUT WHAT ABOUT DEMONS? WHAT DO THEY THINK WHEN THEY LOOK AT LIFE?
FAREWELL, WOMEN. HAVE A SAFE RETURN TO THE FIFTH SPHERE.
SHOW YOUR FACES HERE AGAIN AND I'LL RAPE YOU WITH BURNING MARLINSPIKES.
HEHEH. DEMONS, MAN.
YA GOTTA LOVE 'EM.

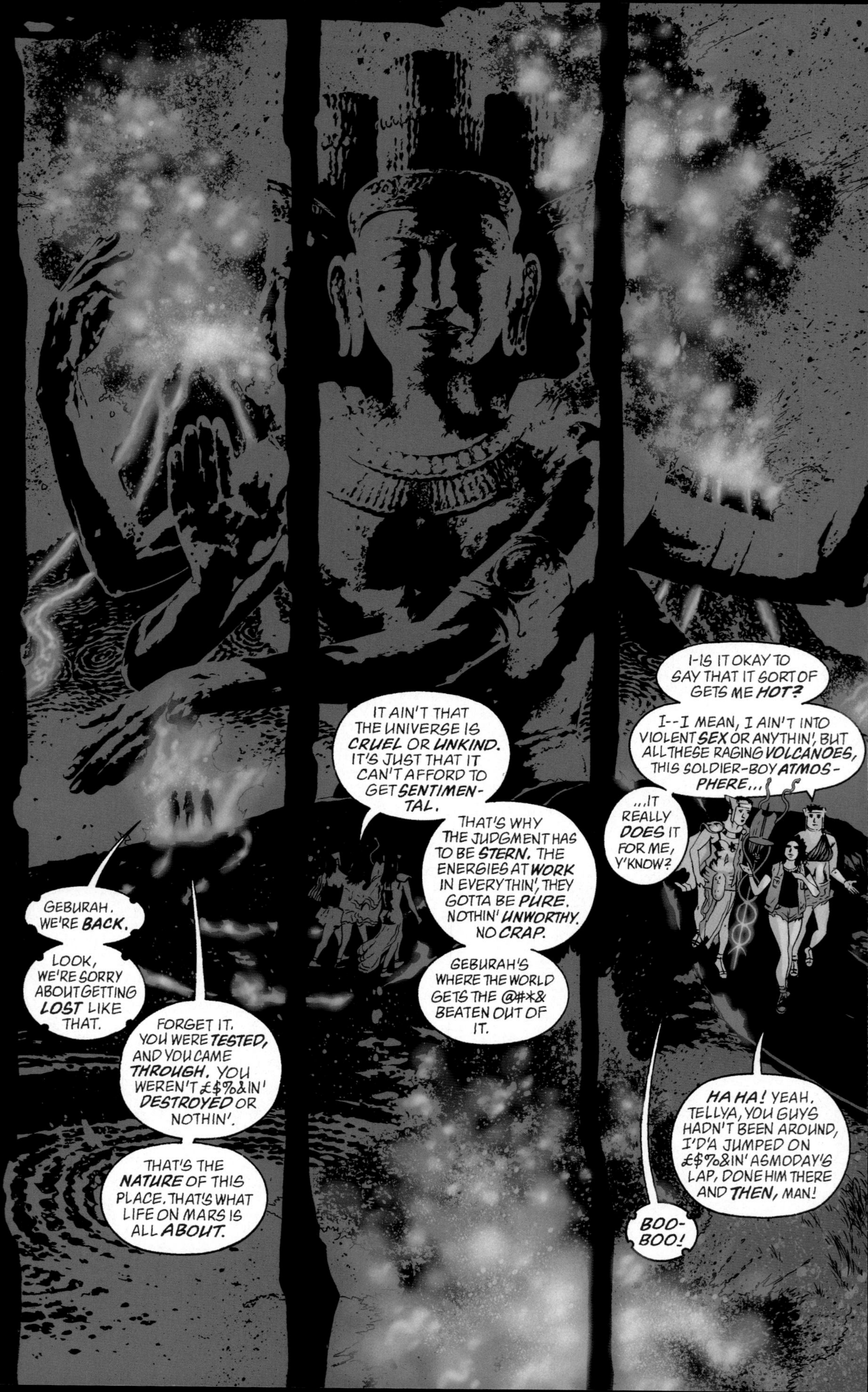
GEBURAH. WE'RE BACK.
LOOK, WE'RE SORRY ABOUT GETTING LOST LIKE THAT.
FORGET IT. YOU WERE TESTED, AND YOU CAME THROUGH. YOU WEREN'T £$%&IN' DESTROYED OR NOTHIN'.
THAT'S THE NATURE OF THIS PLACE. THAT'S WHAT LIFE ON MARS IS ALL ABOUT.
IT AIN'T THAT THE UNIVERSE IS CRUEL OR UNKIND. IT'S JUST THAT IT CAN'T AFFORD TO GET SENTIMEN-TAL.
THAT'S WHY THE JUDGMENT HAS TO BE STERN. THE ENERGIES AT WORK IN EVERYTHIN', THEY GOTTA BE PURE. NOTHIN' UNWORTHY. NO CRAP.
GEBURAH'S WHERE THE WORLD GETS THE @#*& BEATEN OUT OF IT.
I-IS IT OKAY TO SAY THAT IT SORT OF GETS ME HOT?
I--I MEAN, I AIN'T INTO VIOLENT SEX OR ANYTHIN', BUT ALL THESE RAGING VOLCANOES, THIS SOLDIER-BOY ATMOS-PHERE...
...IT REALLY DOES IT FOR ME, Y'KNOW?
HA HA! YEAH. TELLYA, YOU GUYS HADN'T BEEN AROUND, I'D'A JUMPED ON £$%&IN' ASMODAY'S LAP, DONE HIM THERE AND THEN, MAN!
BOO-BOO!

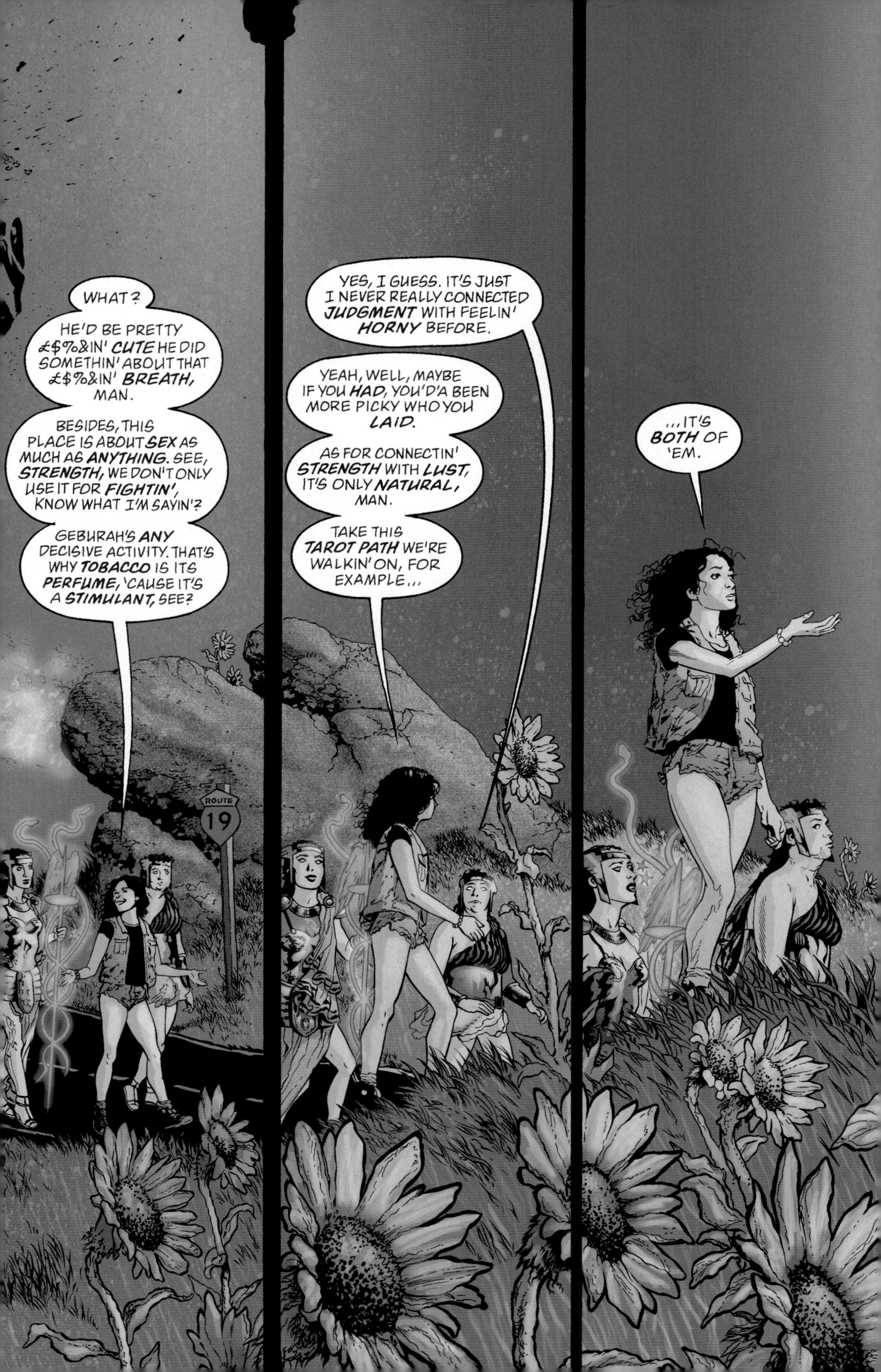
WHAT?
HE'D BE PRETTY £$%&IN' CUTE HE DID SOMETHIN' ABOUT THAT £$%&IN' BREATH, MAN.
BESIDES, THIS PLACE IS ABOUT SEX AS MUCH AS ANYTHING. SEE, STRENGTH, WE DON'T ONLY USE IT FOR FIGHTIN', KNOW WHAT I'M SAYIN'?
GEBURAH'S ANY DECISIVE ACTIVITY. THAT'S WHY TOBACCO IS ITS PERFUME, 'CAUSE IT'S A STIMULANT, SEE?
ROUTE
19
YES, I GUESS. IT'S JUST I NEVER REALLY CONNECTED JUDGMENT WITH FEELIN' HORNY BEFORE.
YEAH, WELL, MAYBE IF YOU HAD, YOU'D'A BEEN MORE PICKY WHO YOU LAID.
AS FOR CONNECTIN' STRENGTH WITH LUST, IT'S ONLY NATURAL, MAN.
TAKE THIS TAROT PATH WE'RE WALKIN' ON, FOR EXAMPLE...
...IT'S BOTH OF 'EM.

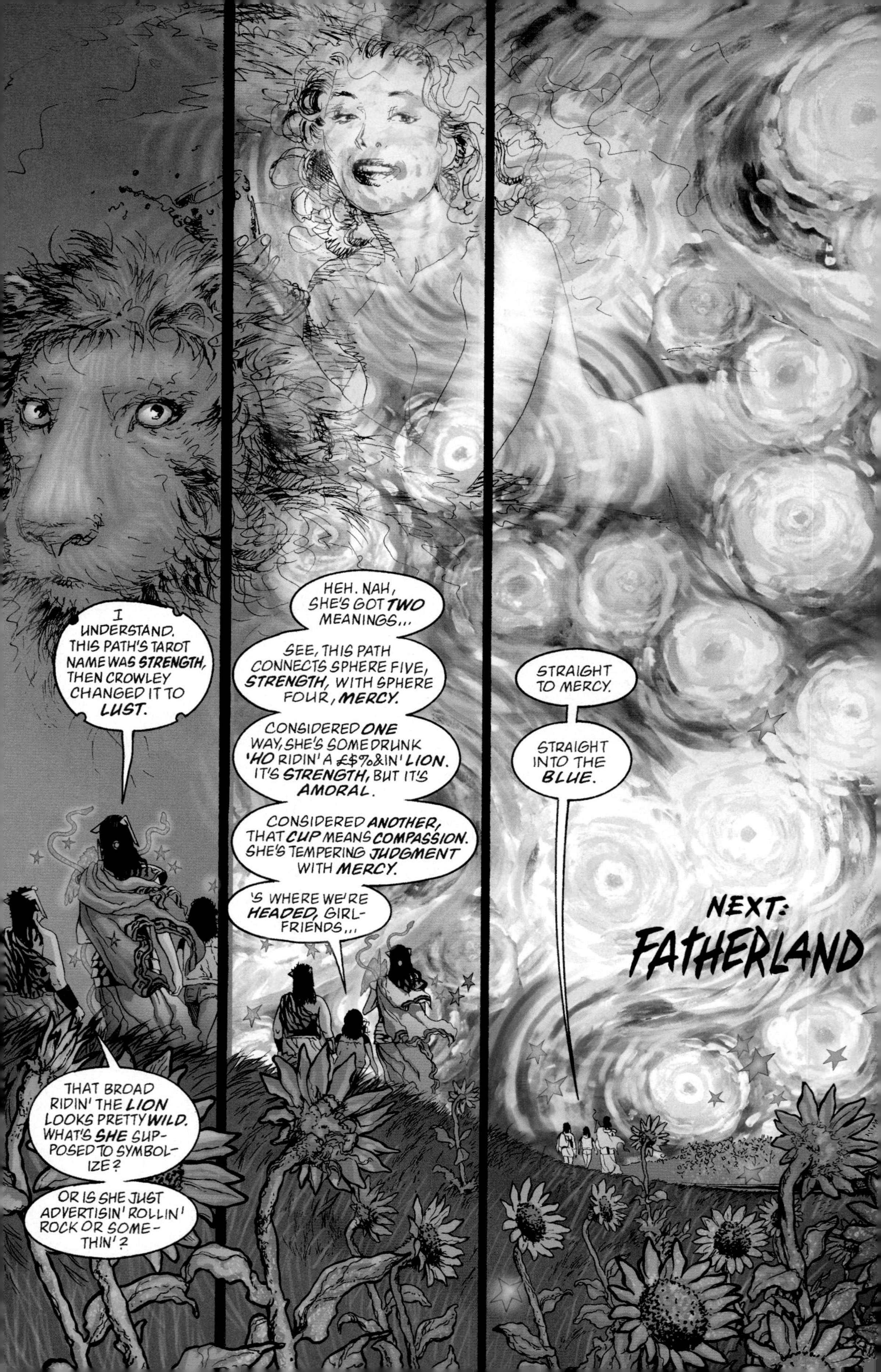
I UNDERSTAND. THIS PATH'S TAROT NAME WAS STRENGTH, THEN CROWLEY CHANGED IT TO LUST.
THAT BROAD RIDIN' THE LION LOOKS PRETTY WILD. WHAT'S SHE SUP-POSED TO SYMBOL-IZE?
OR IS SHE JUST ADVERTISIN' ROLLIN' ROCK OR SOME-THIN'?
HEH. NAH, SHE'S GOT TWO MEANINGS...
SEE, THIS PATH CONNECTS SPHERE FIVE, STRENGTH, WITH SPHERE FOUR, MERCY.
CONSIDERED ONE WAY, SHE'S SOME DRUNK 'HO RIDIN' A £$%&IN' LION. IT'S STRENGTH, BUT IT'S AMORAL.
CONSIDERED ANOTHER, THAT CUP MEANS COMPASSION. SHE'S TEMPERING JUDGMENT WITH MERCY.
'S WHERE WE'RE HEADED, GIRL-FRIENDS...
STRAIGHT TO MERCY.
STRAIGHT INTO THE BLUE.
NEXT:
FATHERLAND

DEDICATIONS

To Leah, Amber,
and Melinda;

To all my family,
all my friends.

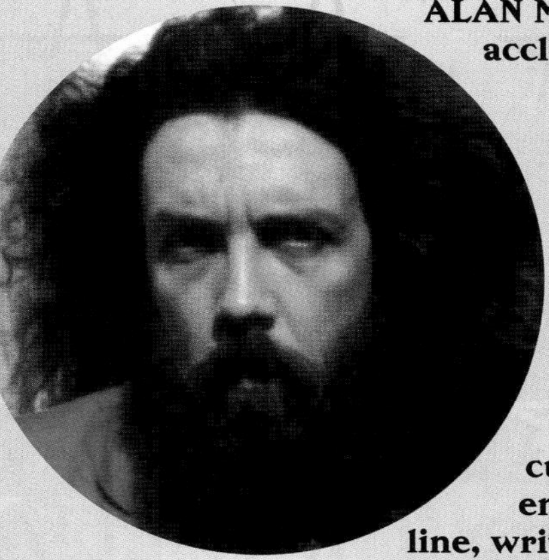

ALAN MOORE is perhaps the most acclaimed writer in the graphic story medium, having garnered many awards for such works as WATCHMEN, V FOR VENDETTA, FROM HELL, MIRACLEMAN, SWAMP THING and SUPREME, among others, along with the many fine artists he has collaborated with on those works. He is currently masterminding the entire America's Best Comics line, writing TOM STRONG, TOP 10 and TOMORROW STORIES in addition to PROMETHEA, with more in the planning stages. He resides in central England.

o my beautiful wife, Wendy, for all ner research, insight and support on he work for PROMETHEA, and also or her humor, keeping me rom getting too serious. To everyone else who works on this book and their 50% of dedication, putting up with my nsanity. To my parents. To Lisa, the best sister-in-law one could hope for. To onnie and Ann for always providing me with my weekly comics fix. And to Scott for letting me experiment and grow as an artist, hanks for buying pages.

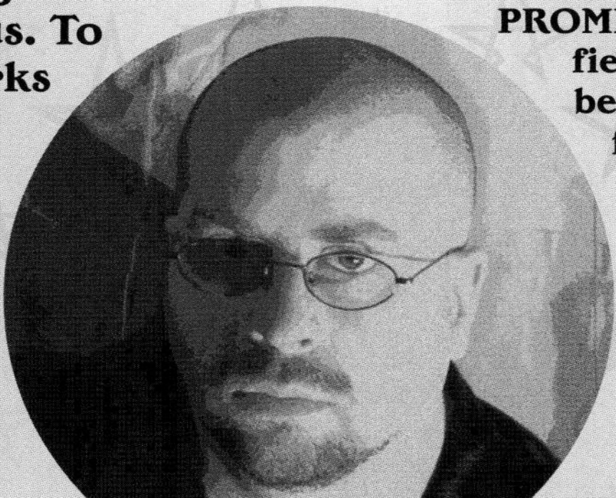

J.H. WILLIAMS III, penciller and co-creator of PROMETHEA, entered the comics field in 1991 and immediately began getting attention for his finely crafted work on such titles as BATMAN and STARMAN. He's been praised for SON OF SUPERMAN and another co-creation, CHASE, has produced numerous covers for DC and Marvel Comics, and is currently writing D.E.O. stories for DC's Secret Files and other projects with CHASE co-creator D. Curtis Johnson. J.H. and his wife Wendy live in California.

To INSPIRATION. It is the amazing phenomenon that makes this book soar, from Alan's wonderful magic that he weaves with words, to J.H.'s unparalleled imagery, to Todd's masterful lettering and design, to Jeromy's otherworldly colors, to Scott's uncommon ability to keep us all together. My task could not be more of a treat! Thank you.

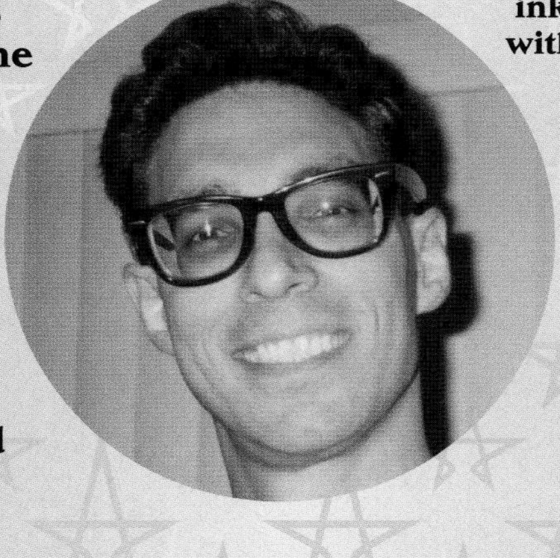

MICK GRAY, a longtime comics inker, began his collaboration with Williams in 1995, and his accurate attention to every detail and nuance on such titles as BATMAN, CHASE, and SON OF SUPERMAN, not to mention PROMETHEA, continue to make this an exclusive team. Mick, his wife Holly, and their little girl, Genevieve, also live in California.